Reinhold Niebuhr
and
John Dewey

Reinhold Niebuhr
and
John Dewey

An American Odyssey

DANIEL F. RICE

STATE UNIVERSITY OF NEW YORK PRESS • ALBANY

The following publisher has generously given permission to use extended quotations from copyrighted works. Reprinted with the permission of Charles Scribner's Sons; an imprint of Macmillan Publishing Company from *Moral Man and Immoral Society*, by Reinhold Niebuhr. Copyright 1932 Charles Scribner's Sons; copyright renewed © 1960 Reinhold Niebuhr. Reprinted with the permission of Charles Scribner's Sons; an imprint of Macmillan Publishing Company from *The Children of Light and the Children of Darkness* by Reinhold Niebuhr. Copyright 1944 Charles Scribner's Sons; copyright renewed © 1972 Ursula Niebuhr. Reprinted with the permission of Charles Scribner's Sons; an imprint of Macmillan Publishing Company from *Faith and History*, by Reinhold Niebuhr. Copyright 1949 Charles Scribner's Sons; copyright renewed © 1977 Ursula Niebuhr. Reprinted with the permission of Charles Scribner's Sons; an imprint of Macmillan Publishing Company from *Beyond Tragedy*, by Reinhold Niebuhr. Copyright 1937 Charles Scribner's Sons; copyright renewed © 1965 Reinhold Niebuhr. Reprinted with the permission of Charles Scribner's Sons; an imprint of Macmillan Publishing Company from *The Irony of American History*, by Reinhold Niebuhr. Copyright 1952 Charles Scribner's Sons; copyright renewed © 1980 Ursula Niebuhr. Reprinted with the permission of Charles Scribner's Sons; an imprint of Macmillan Publishing Company from *The Structure of Nature and Empires*, by Reinhold Niebuhr. Copyright 1959 Reinhold Niebuhr.

Photo credits: plates 2, 4, 6, 7—Courtesy of The Morris Library, Southern Illinois University at Carbondale; 1, 9—Courtesy of the Prints and Photographs Division, Library of Congress; 3, 5, 8—Courtesy of The Union Theological Seminary, The Burke Library, New York.

Published by
State University of New York Press, Albany

© 1993 State University of New York

For information, address State University of New York Press, State University Plaza, Albany, N.Y., 12246

Production by Cathleen Collins
Marketing by Dana Yanulavich

Library of Congress Cataloging in Publication Data

Rice, Daniel F., 1935–
    Reinhold Niebuhr and John Dewey : an American odyssey / Daniel F. Rice
        p.   cm.
    Includes bibliographical references and index.
    ISBN 0–7914–1345–4 — ISBN 0–7914–1346–2 (pbk.)
    1. Niebuhr, Reinhold, 1892–1971.   2. Dewey, John, 1859–1952.
    I. Title.
    BX4827.N5R53   1993   92–4270
    191—dc20   CIP

    10 9 8 7 6 5 4 3 2 1

To Judy—for so very much
and
to Cheryl, Nancy, Jeannine and John
as life's most precious gifts

Contents

Illustrations

Following page 82

1 From the John Dewey Papers.

Following page 90

1 Reinhold Niebuhr at Union Theological Seminary in New York
in the early 1930s near the time of the appearance
of *Moral Man and Immoral Society.*

2 John Dewey in his early seventies in the early part of the 1930s.

3 Reinhold Niebuhr in the early to mid-1930s.

4 John Dewey surrounded by his children and his second wife,
Roberta, on October 20, 1949, at his 90th birthday celebration
at the Waldorf Astoria Hotel, New York.

5 Reinhold Niebuhr at Union Theological Seminary at the zenith
of his career in the late 1940s.

6 John Dewey in 1943 at the time the second volume of
Niebuhr's Gifford Lectures, *The Nature and Destiny of Man*,
had been published.

7 John Dewey at 90 relaxing at Maple Lodge in 1949.

8 Reinhold Niebuhr and friends sometime between
1953 and 1960 after Niebuhr's stroke.

9 Reinhold Niebuhr at the time of his retirement in 1960.

Foreword

Reinhold Niebuhr and John Dewey cast lengthy shadows across the American landscape during the twentieth century. Both men, native to the American scene, achieved the very pinnacles in their respective fields, and up until 1939, were two of only five Americans invited to deliver the prestigious Gifford Lectures in Edinburgh.[1] Niebuhr and Dewey shared a rather unusual distinction in having had a marked influence upon vast numbers of individuals in areas of endeavor outside their own specializations. The result was that both men made significant and unique impacts on a wide variety of fields of interest extending across the intellectual spectrum of American life. A careful look at the relationship between John Dewey and Reinhold Niebuhr is of particular importance because these two men, although sharing much in the way of pragmatic orientation, engaged in sharp but sporadic conflict with one another over a period of twenty years. Niebuhr and Dewey differed over issues relating to the character and credibility of religious faith, the limits of naturalism, scientific method and the "human studies" (Dilthey's *Geisteswissenschaften*), the liberal tradition, and the nature and prospect of democracy. The issues over which they diverged resonated with much of the inner turmoil at the heart of so much of America's intellectual life. Moreover, the precise manner in which Dewey and Niebuhr formulated such issues stood at the very center of, and often led the way for, the course taken by the cultural dialogue of their day.

Their contact with one another started shortly after Niebuhr's arrival at Union Theologial Seminary in 1928 and continued on and off until Dewey's death in 1952. The lives of Niebuhr and Dewey intersected at several points—geographical, political and literary—although their personal contacts were both minimal and primarily official.

After completing his graduate work at Johns Hopkins, Dewey took teaching jobs at the universities of Michigan and Chicago. Subsequent to his epoch-making decade in both education and philosophy at the University of Chicago, Dewey joined the faculty at Columbia University in New York City in 1904. On the other hand, Niebuhr, with only a Yale masters degree, was summoned by Henry Sloane Coffin to Union

Theological Seminary from a parish in Detroit. The invitation came
after a close vote among the Union faculty, some of whom were troubled
by "Niebuhr's lack of an earned doctorate and his polemical style."[2]
Nonetheless, as Robert Handy has noted, his "brilliance and virtuosity
as a teacher, preacher, and writer quickly flowered as he became a con-
spicuous world leader of Christian thought and life."[3] In fact, Niebuhr's
star would rise so rapidly that he not only was invited to deliver the Gifford Lectures in 1939, but also received tempting invitations from both
Yale (1929) and Harvard (1942) as well as being offered a residence at the
Princeton Institute for Advanced Studies in 1958.

It is important to remember that John Dewey, who was thirty-two
years Niebuhr's senior, belonged to a different generation than Niebuhr.
Born in 1859, the year Darwin's *Origin of Species* appeared, Dewey was
shaped by influences quite different from those that would, a generation
later, galvanize the young Niebuhr. Dewey, along with his fellow pragmatists William James (1842–1910) and George Herbert Mead (1863–
1931), lived in

> an environment marked by Hegel's struggle to concretize uni-
> versals in an effort to preserve rational certainty on the one
> hand and underscore novelty and change on the other. It is an
> environment in which the empiricist, J. S. Mill, must try to jus-
> tify the cogency of abstract mathematical reasoning without
> the aid of the propositional interpretation of the synthetic/
> analytic distinction. It is an environment in which August
> Comte presents a hierarchy of the sciences with Sociology
> (viewed as the most complex science) at the very top. It is [above
> all] an environment in which Darwin grapples with nature in
> an effort to wrench biology out of the grasp of the Aristotelian
> taxonomical categories, as Newton had done with macro-
> physics a century and a half earlier.[4]

These influences were fundamental to several of Dewey's central
emphases: his dynamic and organistic naturalism, his sociocultural understanding of human nature, and the missionary zeal with which he
strove to extend the sway of scientific method over the domain of the
human studies. By the time Niebuhr was coming to intellectual maturity in the 1920s and 1930s, many of the positions Dewey had taken would
themselves become grist for Niebuhr's own grinding attack. Indeed,
major points of controversy between Niebuhr and Dewey centered on
some of the themes which had so enamored Dewey in his formative years.
The fact that existentialism and the historicism of Dilthey, and most
especially Troeltsch, were important in shaping Niebuhr's thinking is

every bit as significant a reason for their disagreement as Niebuhr's theological orientation, per se.

Dewey's generation at Columbia included, among others, the famed American naturalist Frederick J. Woodbridge, Felix Adler, Wendell T. Bush, John Cross, and William Pepperell Montague. A certain number of students who studied with Dewey and the others during the early part of the twentieth century eventually came back to teach at Columbia. They constituted a generation of Columbia philosophers who came to know Niebuhr in the decades after Dewey's retirement in 1929. Their numbers included James Gutmann, John Herman Randall, Jr., Herbert W. Schneider, and Horace L. Friess.

Schneider, while remaining in the Department of Philosophy, was assigned a "new Professorship in Religion . . . in 1928"—the year Niebuhr came to Union—and proceeded to build on the nascent program in the study of religion.[5] After 1943 Columbia had instituted a graduate program in the field of religion leading to the Ph.D. degree. A program was established under an interfaculty committee (including Schneider, its first executive secretary, Friess, members from other departments at Columbia, and individuals "from the Faculty at Union Theological Seminary") with subfields in "(1) History of Religion, (2) Literature of Religion (mainly, Bible), (3) Philosophy of Religion and Ethics, (4) Religion and Society."[6] It was in connection with the latter field that "Reinhold Niebuhr and John Bennett at the Seminary, Salo W. Baron, Herbert Schneider, and others at the university" were involved.[7] Niebuhr, according to Roger L. Shinn, "chaired the 'Religion and Society' section for years. Later Salo Baron succeeded him in that role."[8]

Many of the Columbia philosophers who knew both Niebuhr and Dewey provided worthwhile recollections of them. Schneider who said Woodbridge's stimulating eloquence "had an enormous impact on all of us [speaking of Schneider's student years], more so than Dewey did personally," nonetheless acknowledged that "Dewey's work influenced us more than Woodbridge's work."[9] Schneider said that he became

> personally attached to Dewey, but [that Dewey] wasn't personally so imposing as Woodbridge was. He was impressive enough intellectually—he was a good friend and all that—but he didn't try to be eloquent and so on. He tried to say what he had to say, and what he had to say turned out to be very important. We were very fond of Dewey and close to him, but in his classes Dewey didn't pay much attention to the class at all—he talked to himself or out of the window. He would come to the room with some problem that really bothered him. . . . He wasn't prepared to lecture, and he didn't believe in lecturing.[10]

James Gutmann corroborated this impression of Dewey as a teacher but put it in different terms: "The feeling of Dewey was what Emerson called 'man thinking.' He was not regarded as a particularly good teacher, in the conventional sense of the term. . . . In a lecture, he would often seem to be wandering from his theme. . . . But one had the feeling of a man really hammering out his thought."[11]

Niebuhr's oratorical talents, on the other hand, both in and out of the classroom were legendary. He was, in brief, the quintessential "preacher-teacher." James Gutmann recalled with a note of serious humor: "I have often said that Niebuhr put more energy into brushing his teeth in the morning than I would have for an entire day's work."[12] According to an example offered by June Bingham, "listening to [Niebuhr and Will Herberg] talk is like watching a tennis match played at triple speed; the observer's head nearly comes off from the strain of having to move it back and forth so fast."[13] In an article published the year prior to the appearance of his biography on Niebuhr, Richard W. Fox remarked that

> Those who knew Niebuhr are unanimous about one thing: None of them ever knew another person remotely like him. Words such as "charismatic," "intense," and "energetic" fall repeatedly from their lips. "Reinie," they say, immediately dominated any group, large or small. Legendary fast-talkers such as Felix Frankfurter and Isaiah Berlin were captivated because they had met their match. Niebuhr outtalked, outdebted, and outquipped the quickest tongues in the English-speaking world.[14]

Perhaps Horace M. Kallen's comparison of Dewey with William James applies equally well to the contrast between Dewey and Niebuhr. Kallen noted: "Dewey, always shy, deliberate, hesitant in speech and not often graceful in expression; James, outgoing, swift, vivid, with sudden insights and light-creating phrases."[15] Certainly all evidence points to the fact that those who knew and worked with Niebuhr—as well as many who opposed him—were of one mind with respect to the power of Niebuhr as a personal presence.[16] Fox returned to the subject in his biography when he wrote of Niebuhr:

> His admirers and opponents alike understood they were confronted by a man of uncommon gifts. Many sober-minded observers, not just among his friends, insisted on calling him a prophet—a label that always embarrassed him. . . .
> He already had the prophet's intensity and single-minded-

ness. He spoke as one possessed, driven—not just in church, but with friends, in meetings, in the classroom. His charisma was no pulpit act; his gift was far less manageable than that. He was strikingly unselfconscious in public, unconcerned with social form. He was totally without ostentation, constitutionally unable to condescend.[17]

Both Dewey and Niebuhr had reputations for being open and available to endless demands on their time. In the case of both men, friends often wondered how they found the time to write as much as they did and expressed a desire to find a way of protecting them against themselves. In spite of extensive speaking engagements that took him far and wide across the country, Niebuhr was open and available to friends and students alike.[18] Dewey and Niebuhr both answered virtually every letter they received, however trivial or from whatever source. Niebuhr was in the habit of lunching with students in the refectory at Union Seminary, and once a week his wife Ursula Niebuhr, who taught at Barnard College across the street from Union Seminary, would join him. Moreover, the Niebuhrs had weekly Thursday night open house at their apartment for students and other guests—a time that was considered sacrosanct. Dewey, it was said, preferred to lunch at Columbia with the social scientists. Herbert Schneider once remarked in this regard:

> Well, what of course stimulated most of us was that Dewey was more outside the department. . . . For instance, when he ate lunch, he was always with the social scientists rather than with fellow philosophers. Most of his conversation and personal doings were with social scientists . . . people like Beard and Shotwell and James Harvey Robinson and . . . Wesley Mitchell, the economist . . . and the sociologist, MacIver . . . and some of the Law School staff. He had such an interdepartmental mind . . .[19]

Niebuhr and Dewey were also both noted polemicists. According to Schneider, "Dewey was so different in his personal context than in his writings. His writings were polemic and you were bound to argue with him there. . . . But in his personal contacts he wouldn't take the initiative. . . . He was excessively sociable and willing to see the other fellow's point of view."[20] Nonetheless, in his writing, as Schneider said in another interview, Dewey "enjoyed that polemic." Even in many of his more technical writings where he engaged the Idealists and Realists, for example, one finds Dewey engaging in polemics. Most certainly "his political articles, too, are quite polemical"—so much so "that most people thought he was a fighting kind of person . . . and he never was a

fighter personality at all; but his articles really carry this fighting tone.
. . . The articles in the *New Republic* and in the *Journal of Philosophy* are
fighting propaganda."[21] During "an informal evening of reminiscences
and personal impressions of John Dewey" at the home of Corliss Lamont
in 1958, the following dialogue took place between the author James T.
Farrell and Columbia University philosopher James Gutmann:

Farrell: Of course Dewey was a very good polemicist. Some of his best
          writing was polemical.
Gutmann: Didn't that sometimes get in the way of his historical presen-
          tation? . . . [especially] in his treatment of classical
          philosophers sometimes . . .
Farrell: He was concerned with advancing the view that was non-
          traditional. He was concerned not so much with history; he
          was concerned in the present with what he considered a new
          view that was more or less all-embracing. I mean that's why
          there was so much polemics on his part.[22]

What is so important about this brief exchange is that what is said
about Dewey's so-called political distortion of history is equally applicable to Niebuhr. Indeed, both men have been charged at various times
with being highly selective and even unfair in their representation of
particular thinkers. Referring specifically to Dewey's approach to religion, John Herman Randall, Jr., found Dewey selecting "what will fit into
his distinctions and interests and rejecting the greater part of what he
finds."[23] Niebuhr is certainly open to comparable charges which apply to
his appropriation and criticism of Dewey, as we shall have occasion to
note in due course.

Both as an apologist for his understanding of Christian faith as well
as in his political writings, Niebuhr was a polemicist to a fault. He, in
contrast to Dewey, could be, on occasion, as polemical in his spoken word
as he often was in his written words. John Dillenberger is reported by
June Bingham to have gone up to Niebuhr at one point in the late 1940s
as a representative of a group of worried students and said: "Look, Reinie
. . . you're running like mad. It's no good. On the public platform you've
become merciless; you lambaste everyone. Only in class do you take time
to be fair. We want you to slow down a bit and make like a theologian."[24]
Niebuhr knew that all polemics—not the least of all, his own—were not
always fair. In a letter written to Morton White in 1956, Niebuhr remarked: "If you have not always been fair as you desire, you have been
much fairer than most polemical arguments turn out to be, including my
own."[25] In a published interview ten years later Niebuhr made a qual-

ified apology for the extreme polemics of his earlier years. Responding to a question, Niebuhr remarked:

> There is no need for polemics today and there was no need for them when I wrote. My polemics were of an impatient young man who had certain things to say, and wanted to get them said clearly and forcefully. However, I learned a few things as I got older. My latest book (I hope it will not be my last one), *Man's Nature and His Communities* [Scribner's 1965] included the revisions, Augustine would call them recantations, of all my previous remarks on that subject. I said there that I have become less polemical, and that I regret my polemical attitude toward Catholicism. I was also polemical against orthodox Reformation Protestantism because of its rather fantastic and excessive devotion to secular authority. I agree with the Catholics and liberal Protestants who say that the Reformation was a catastrophe for what one might call a responsible ethic of justice. I don't reject the previous positions which I took on these questions, but I do reject my polemical attitude of the past. Yet there is always a place for honest speaking, and I hope that I have tried to be as honest as possible even in my polemical days.[26]

During that same period Niebuhr admitted that he had been too severe in his criticism of John Dewey suggesting, moreover, that they shared more common ground than Niebuhr had been aware. Professor James A. Martin, Jr., who was present at the time, reflected on the circumstances of this incident:

> It is my recollection that, on an evening some time in the early sixties, a few of us gathered in the apartment of Roger Shinn for some informal conversation with Reinhold Niebuhr. It is also my recollection that, in the course of the conversation, some of us remarked on what we perceived to be similarities between some positions that Niebuhr had taken on public issues, and the process through which he arrived at those positions, and positions taken by John Dewey on those and similar issues. In response Niebuhr remarked, as I recall, that perhaps his criticisms of Dewey at an earlier time were too harsh—that perhaps they had more in common on many matters than he had realized at the time.
>
> This would certainly have coincided with the view that some of us who had worked at both Union and Columbia in the early forties had come to hold.[27]

Niebuhr and Dewey both had reputations for being considerate men and neither, at minimum, intended anything ad hominem in their polemical writings. This was even the case where Niebuhr and Dewey had sharp disagreement. James Gutmann, for example, thought that although "Niebuhr was polemical" toward Dewey, it was not out of maliciousness, but "because of the abundance of his energy."[28] Moreover, the attitude of the Columbia philosophers toward Niebuhr, most of whom were both former students and friends of Dewey's, was one of "personal liking" and "admiration." Overall, according to Gutmann, it was believed that Dewey took Niebuhr's criticism of him "lightly."[29] John Bennett was also of the opinion "that Niebuhr had no personal ill feelings toward Dewey. I have often said that while Niebuhr was using Dewey as a target in some of his writings, he would be on a committee with him engaged in founding a new political party or trying to get some poor fellow out of jail."[30] Sidney Hook, who knew both Dewey and Niebuhr very well, had an interesting reflection on the matter of Dewey's feelings toward Niebuhr. Hook wrote that

> my impression is quite strong that Dewey did not feel that N[iebuhr] was like B[ertrand] Russell who during most of his life was hostile. After all, Dewey knew that Randall, Fries [sic], Schneider, and possibly at long remove, Gutmann, his colleagues for whom D[ewey]'s views were gospel, admired N[iebuhr] and were always building bridges to Dewey. . . .
>
> Also possibly altho D[ewey] was a very modest man he may *unconsciously* have been annoyed that a relative newcomer to the philosophical community in N.Y.(if N[iebuhr] was not on the scene until the late '20s) should command such admiration and sympathy among a group which regarded Dewey and Woodbridge as the twin peaks of modern American philosophy.[31]

Dewey was a philosopher of first rank—a proverbial titan among his peers both in America and abroad. His role was not that of the pure scholar, any more than Niebuhr's was, although both men had a wide-ranging knowledge of the history of thought. Dewey's strength as a philosopher was in his ground-breaking originality. He had a unique and brilliant mind that appropriated scholarship for his own purposes.

Niebuhr was actually insecure at times about his lack of a Ph.D. as well as about his deviation from a strict scholarly form of writing. It seems as if one of Niebuhr's later books, *The Structure of Nations and Empires* (1959), written while he was in residence at the Princeton Institute for Advanced Studies, was undertaken, in part, as an effort to demonstrate to himself and perhaps others that he could do a work of a more traditional scholarly type. When asked about this matter, Niebuhr's longtime friend and colleague John C. Bennett wrote: "Yes he was often very much aware of this. I do have a letter which says that he had been living on the edge of scholarship all his life but that he was not really a scholar." These sensitivities, however, were misplaced if not unfortunate in the sense that they detract from Niebuhr's real powers. Bennett pinpointed Niebuhr's strength when he went on to say:

> He would say things like that to me and I would answer that *he had given the scholars a great deal to write about.* When he was holding forth in the territory of more specialized scholars he was not at the time intimidated or lacking in confidence. . . . This was true of his "Irony of American History." That was true of his work on foreign policy . . . *One had to be a generalist to do what Niebuhr did* (Emphases mine)[32]

Niebuhr's forte was that he possessed a remarkable, even astounding, capacity for intellectual synthesis and could go to the heart of an issue as well as see wide patterns of relationships. He had both a sweeping and penetrating intellect that was, as Bennett notes, the mark of a generalist. Niebuhr's friend and sometime adversary Sidney Hook once noted affectionately that "to hold [Niebuhr] to rigorous analytic discourse would be like imposing a proper logical syntax upon a poem."[33] Being the type of thinker he was, Niebuhr turned much soil for others to cultivate.

Dewey and Niebuhr had little personal contact outside of a common involvement with various political activities during the late 1920s and 1930s. They shared political causes and occasional forums with Norman Thomas and were actively involved in support of Thomas's presidential bid in 1932—at the same time Niebuhr himself was running for Congress from his own home district in New York.[34] Both men held membership in diverse organizations including the League for Industrial Democracy (both served as president), Paul Douglas's League for Independent Political Action[35] (for which Dewey served as chairman for five years), and New York's Liberal Party (where Dewey was honorary chairman), among others. Even down into the early 1950s Sidney Hook managed to get Dewey and Niebuhr to join his Congress for Cultural Freedom, where both served as honorary chairmen in succession, although Dewey could not have been very active. This group gained the reputation of being composed of "cold war liberals" by many of its detractors.[36]

Although Dewey and Niebuhr were members of the famed New York Philosophy Club,[37] there is no evidence they ever attended at the same time.[38] Founded in 1902 by Adler and Woodbridge, Dewey was an early member and was quite active prior to his retirement in 1930. Dewey had asked President Butler to relieve him of his teaching duties at Columbia at the end of the 1929–30 academic year so that he might go into retirement. The first half of Dewey's request was granted, but Butler convinced Dewey, in the president's own words, to "keep your stated office on Morningside Heights, offer occasional lectures, meet graduate students for conferences and direction, and do all the other things which are appropriate and interesting in themselves to a life-long university scholar."[39] Dewey was appointed Professor Emeritus of Philosophy in Residence, effective on June 30, 1930, and continued his presence at Columbia for almost another decade. At his own request Dewey had his status at the university changed "from professor emeritus of philosophy in residence to professor emeritus of philosophy as of June 1939."[40] George Dykhuizen claims that

> During his years as professor emeritus, Dewey went regularly to his office in Philosophy Hall, continuing his personal contacts with members of the department. Woodbridge, Montague, Bush, Schneider, Randall, Edman, Friess, Gutmann, and Nagel, who had offices in the same building, saw him frequently. When spending the day on the campus, Dewey usually had luncheon at the Faculty Club where he met other close friends and associates in the university. He also maintained his long-time membership in the Philosophic Club [and] whenever possible, he attended its monthly meeting.[41]

In spite of Dewey's continuing membership in the Philosophy Club, however, by the time Niebuhr arrived on the scene, Dewey was not as active as Dykhuizen's account might suggest. According to the recollections of Hook and Gutmann, Dewey rarely came to meetings during the 1940s when Niebuhr and Paul Tillich were invited into membership and would have been most likely to attend.[42]

John Dewey was one of the most revered philosphers of the age and was regarded as the elder statesman within America's liberal intellectual circles at the very time Niebuhr was only beginning to gain his identity at Union. As the American historian Henry Steele Commager once put it,

> So faithfully did Dewey live up to his own philosophical creed that he became the guide, the mentor, and the conscience of the American people: it is scarcely an exaggeration to say that for a generation no major issue was clarified until Dewey had spoken. Pioneer in educational reform, organizer of political par-

ties, counselor to statesmen, champion of labor, of women's rights, of peace, of civil liberties, interpreter of America abroad and of Russia, Japan, China, and Germany to the American people, he was the spearhead of a dozen movements, the leader of a score of crusades, the advocate of a hundred reforms. He illustrated in his own career how effective philosophy could be in that reconstruction of society which was his preoccupation and its responsibility.[43]

The crucial period in the emerging conflict between Niebuhr and Dewey was between the publication of *Moral Man and Immoral Society* in 1932 and the period of hysteria over the alleged "new failure of nerve" in the early 1940s. Until the publication of *Moral Man*, Niebuhr was virtually unknown to Dewey except as a compatriate in various political activities. *Moral Man*, however, opened with a broadside against Dewey. In the wake of this assault on Dewey in 1932, Niebuhr must have appeared, at best, as a relatively youthful and stridently energetic upstart (forty years old as compared to Dewey's seventy-three) who, in Dewey's eyes appeared rather abrasive. Moreover, the middle-aged Niebuhr persisted in confessional and institutional identification with the religious tradition that Dewey's brand of humanism sought to lay to rest.

From Niebuhr's perspective, on the other hand, the situation must have appeared quite different in those early years. Dewey was a venerated and formidable figure in American intellectual life. Indeed, Niebuhr early on respected Dewey as a practical philosopher turned social reformer. Correctly perceiving Dewey to be the most prestigious voice on the American intellectual scene, and—in Niebuhr's judgment—the major figure through which an ineffectual liberalism continued to endure as an obstacle to much needed intellectual and political reorientation, Niebuhr assumed the role of a David with John Dewey as his contemporary Goliath. In effect, Niebuhr targeted Dewey in *Moral Man* as the symbol and symptom of all that was wrong in the liberal tradition. It was only after the publication of *Moral Man*, therefore, that Dewey had any reason to take Niebuhr at all seriously. It also was not very long, as Paul Merkley observed, that Niebuhr was "to be among the most prized exhibits between the covers of the liberal journals, ranking with such idols of the liberal left as Charles Beard, John Dewey, and R. H. Tawney."[44]

A word is now in order concerning both the scope of this present work and my own orientation in writing it. This work seeks to illuminate the points of engagement and areas of conflict between Reinhold Niebuhr and John Dewey. It does so, first, by tracing their engagements in their chronological setting in Part One. Part Two selects major themes at issue between them that deserve separate extended treatment. Moreover, both the conception and scope of this work, based as they are upon the specific encounters between Niebuhr and Dewey, preclude any attempt to undertake a systematic analysis of either Dewey's or Niebuhr's thought as a whole.

My own predilections in the venture are also of some importance to the reader. I came to this project out of an interest in and deep appreciation for the contributions of Reinhold Niebuhr to American life and thought. This means that I approach the relationship between these two individuals with an eye to the background, development and character of Niebuhr's thought. It does not mean, however, that a slavish and uncritical loyalty will be at work here. In fact, as this investigation progressed I gained a tremendous respect for John Dewey, both as a human being and as a major force in American intellectual history. Richard Rorty's recent neo-pragmatic attempt to situate Dewey at the end of the road toward which much more contemporary thought has been moving—however valid on its own merits—was also instrumental in my newly gained appreciation of John Dewey. It is certainly my aim to represent Dewey's case as fairly as possible.

In addition to an appreciation of the pragmatic wisdom of both Niebuhr and Dewey, this study has given me an ever-increasing awareness of the pragmatism of Niebuhr. Niebuhr, of course, has always been recognized (and sometimes maligned) for his political pragmatism. I mean something quite different, however. I am convinced that Niebuhr was also a theological pragmatist in the sense that a pragmatic perspective was central to his conception of both theology and theological relevance. Although the pragmatic aspects in Niebuhr are recognized at various points throughout the book and his *theological* pragmatism is touched upon in the Afterword, any sustained and comprehensive attempt to make a case for Niebuhr's fundamental pragmatism goes far beyond the boundaries of this work. I would hope to address this most crucial matter at a different time and place. Nonetheless, the view that whereas Dewey was one of the architects of American pragmatism, Niebuhr should, in part, be seen as a second-generation pragmatist who, having learned well from both James and Dewey, was in the process of forging his own unique species of theological pragmatism, has a certain import for this present study. Viewing Niebuhr as a pragmatist involves a couple of risks. First, it is to risk encouraging the ever-present wrath of those who are incapable of seeing pragmatism in any way other than as kin to the work of some devil or other. Because I do not see pragmatism in that light, but view it rather as a positive and moderating approach to the intellectual life, I feel no apology is in order. A second risk is somewhat amusing. Dewey loyalists who disassociate themselves from

Niebuhr for both his religious orientation and what they deem to be his unjust attacks on Dewey, might be quite reluctant to consider seriously that Niebuhr, being the pragmatist that he was, must be regarded, in the final analysis, as one of their own.

These considerations, of course, raise another problem compounding the already delicate task of achieving reasonable fairness to both Dewey and Niebuhr. An effort such as this is a risky business on the simple ground that whatever is said about their relationship is likely to antagonize, prima facie, many Niebuhrians and Deweyites alike. As much of the relationship between Niebuhr and Dewey was adversarial, there was, at the time of their engagement, a sharp division of loyalists forming behind each man. One can hopefully and even rightfully expect that the distance of a generation has ameliorated that problem.

Antagonisms at the time Dewey and Niebuhr were alive, interestingly enough, were sufficiently intense to have largely obscured both the breadth and the depth of the common ground they shared. Although this study touches on that common ground, it deals primarily with the issues that sharply divided Niebuhr from Dewey since those issues were, in fact, the substance of their engagement. Ideally, too, it will be recognized that this labor is being carried out with a pronounced sympathy and high degree of respect for both Niebuhr and Dewey as individuals and for the work each strove to bring to fruition.

Acknowledgments

This book owes a variety of things to very many people and one special place. There are, of course, the principals, Reinhold Niebuhr and John Dewey, whose lives and labors the work owes everything. In this regard a special debt is owed to my former professor and lifelong friend Edmund Perry, who, in what now seems like another world ago, introduced me to Reinhold Niebuhr in an undergraduate seminar at Northwestern University. A great debt is also owed to both Gordon Harland and Will Herberg, who, in subsequent years, supplied me with various opportunities of being drawn into the orbit of Niebuhr's thought and influence. My debt to Will Herberg includes having been offered the opportunity of taking a course with Niebuhr at Union Theological Seminary during one of the last years he taught at that institution. To Gordon Harland belongs not only the debt of learning something valuable about Niebuhr's thought, but also the pleasure of a family friendship for which the term *debt* is totally inappropriate.

Although my familiarity with and interest in Niebuhr go back to the beginning, it was not until quite recently that I was made earnestly aware of John Dewey. This came in part through the pleasure of the company of a special colleague, Bruce Jannusch. It also came by way of the renewed interest in Dewey and pragmatism occasioned by the significant labors of Richard Rorty. Because Niebuhr's rather sharp controversies with Dewey were the immediate focus of my attention, I am also obligated to Niebuhr for taking Dewey seriously. It must be said, however, that I came to appreciate and admire Dewey in a way that transcended the limited critical attention Niebuhr had given him. This increased respect and appreciation came quite readily in the process of turning to Dewey's writings and gaining a familiarity with a coterie of his disciples. It should be noted that this newfound attitude toward Dewey did not diminish either my appreciation of or admiration for Niebuhr. Because they were at loggerheads over so many issues, this improbability can be rendered somewhat probable by pointing out two things. First of all, there were others besides myself, who, though having special loyalties towards either Niebuhr or Dewey, maintained a friendship and respect for both men. This was especially true of Sidney Hook, who, among others, had firsthand knowledge of each man's powerful talents. Second, beyond this, there is a very personal matter to consider. In my own case there is the fact that Niebuhr and Dewey represented two quite divergent yet respectable ways of looking at a variety of issues. In this regard their divergent dialogue has an autobiographical dimension to it. As an "interior event" I find that the oppositions have been an intimate part of my own life and are more to be suffered than resolved.

In the actual writing of this book a unique gratitude is owed to Sidney Hook who gave extensively and intensively, *always intensively,* of himself to me by way of a telephone interview and lengthy correspondence in response to additional questions that invariably arose. In the same vein I am indebted to Professor James Gutmann, who, a few months prior to his death, granted me an interview at his home in New York City. A word of thanks also goes to Professor Ursula Niebuhr, wife of Reinhold Niebuhr, and to Christopher Niebuhr, their son, both of whom patiently answered my correspondence over the past few years.

I must at this point express a special thanks to Gordon Harland, my colleague Bruce Jannusch, and Roger Shinn for having taken the time and effort to read the entire manuscipt prior to submission for publication. Knowing Professor Jannusch's considered devotion to Dewey I most appreciated the fairness with which he approached this task. I had never met Professor Shinn, president emeritus of Union Theological Seminary, until I walked in on him uninvited while I was in New York doing research for this book. Not only was Professor Shinn kind enough to spend time with me in his office that cold January day, but he later responded willingly and enthusiastically to my request that he read the manuscript. A very deep appreciation goes to Karl Andresen, a former colleague now retired from my own institution's Political Science Department. In reading portions of the manuscript for which he has particular expertise, Professor Andresen gave unselfishly of both his time and his critical insights.

I wish also to thank the staffs of the Manuscript Division of the Library of Congress and the Columbia University Library who were so helpful to me in my research. Of particular note is the debt of gratitude I owe to the kindness and expertise of several individuals at the Morris Library, Southern Illinois University at Carbondale. In particular I wish to thank David V. Koch, curator of special collections and university archivist; Karen D. Dickamer, curator of manuscipts; and Shelley Cox, rare books librarian.

I also owe my own institution, the University of Wisconsin at Eau Claire, thanks for travel grants and a sabbatical leave that afforded me the opportunity of helping to complete this project. In this regard the attentive help provided by the graduate dean and director of research,

Ronald Satz, proved most beneficial. Kay Henning and Richard Bell— interlibrary loan and reference librarians, respectively—provided generous assistance in obtaining needed materials. Of course, my appreciation goes to State University of New York Press which gave literary incarnation to this project. Here I wish to extend my special thanks to Priscilla C. Ross and Cathleen Collins for their kindness and professionalism during this entire process.

Above all, this book owes the very most in the way of a personal nature to my wife, Judy. Her patience and support were of inestimable value. On a very practical level her prior experience in editing at Silver Burdett and Scott Foresman, and her generosity in offering me that unique talent, has made this project so much more bearable.

Finally, I must also, in all candor, pay homage to a very special place as well. For it was at our cottage on a vast and island-studded lake near Sioux Narrows, Ontario, that some portions of this book were written and most all of it was reworked and brought to completion. This most delicate and beautiful setting, a lake that the Indians had called *Lac Aux Isles* and the French mistranslated the "Lake of the Woods," offered the peace, the privacy and the restful solitude so essential to a project of this sort.

Part One

Conflict Through Time

1

The Early Years

When Niebuhr was called upon to write a brief review of Dewey's occasional papers—*Characters and Events* (1929)—for Norman Thomas's *The World Tomorrow*, Dewey had just celebrated his seventieth birthday. Moreover, Dewey's book *The Quest for Certainty*, based on the prestigious Gifford Lectures he had delivered in the spring of 1929, had recently been published. Niebuhr, at this time, was a mere thirty-eight years of age, and having only recently arrived at Union Theological Seminary in New York, he was still three years away from the publication of *Moral Man* in which he both launched his own career and targeted Dewey for special criticism. In his 1929 review, however, Niebuhr lauded Dewey for being among that rare breed of philosophers willing to "descend from their ant-hill of scholastic hairsplitting to help the world of men regulate its common life and discipline its ambitions and ideals."[1] Having just recently acknowledged in his book *Does Civilization Need Religion?* that whatever relevance religion might possess in the modern world depended partly on *pragmatic*-consequential criteria, Niebuhr praised Dewey as "a statesman for the reason that, though he has not had actual political responsibility, he has helped to form political thought and guide political conduct."[2] He noted also that Dewey's recent seventieth birthday celebration "gave his friends an opportunity to rejoice in the triumphs of his spirit and purpose in philosophy, in education and in social reform."[3]

No matter how sharp or severe their controversy became in later years, Niebuhr and Dewey made common cause in many social and political ventures from their socialist activism in the late 1920s to their participation in Sidney Hook's Congress of Cultural Freedom in the early 1950s. For all Niebuhr's subsequent criticism of Dewey, his willingness to situate Dewey among the "socially minded educators" was an expression of open admiration. In his remarks of 1929 there is not the slightest hint of vehement criticism of Dewey that lay immediately ahead.

Niebuhr simply saw *Characters and Events* as "an excellent survey" of
Dewey's thought. Indeed, at this juncture Niebuhr chose to include the
American John Dewey, along with England's Bertrand Russell, in a
select party of two, whose "extraordinary contemporary influence" in
the task of "molding the political and social thought of their people"
this particular generation is quite fortunate to possess.[4]

Niebuhr was barely established at Union Seminary in 1929. Arthur
Schlesinger, Jr., noted that he "came to intellectual maturity under the
influence of the Social Gospel and of pragmatism" and was thus "a child
of the pragmatic revolt."[5] In this context it is somewhat curious that
John Dewey's name was never mentioned in his initial book, *Does Civilization Need Religion?* published in 1927. Although Niebuhr's work shared
much with Dewey's social and ethical thinking, both his common ground
with Dewey and signs of the sharp and pointed attack he would make on
him in 1932 were nowhere apparent.

In part, this was simply the result of the broad territory occupied by
all pragmatic liberals of that day. It is also true that Niebuhr appealed to
philosophers like Alfred North Whitehead, whose rendition of the prevailing moral language of the day was more congruent with Niebuhr's
own religious vision. This religious vision embraced "a protected sphere
of spirit" (to borrow a phrase from Niebuhr's biographer Richard Fox). It
also emphasized a sense of divine transcendence that traded off of
nineteenth century idealism and thus stood in radical opposition to
Dewey's "naturalism." Niebuhr did employ language similar to that of
Dewey when he contended that "the religious interpretation of the world
is essentially an insistence that the ideal is the real and that the real can
be understood only in the light of the ideal."[6] But in so doing he shared
Whitehead's metaphysical viewpoint that the ideal is never simply
rooted in the realm of the real; that is, in nature as the ground and limit
of the possibility of the ideal. In 1927, at least, Niebuhr took his
metaphysical comforts where he could find them in a world otherwise
overwhelmed by what he saw as insidious forms of naturalism.

In 1927 Niebuhr believed religion to be the last "champion of personality in a seemingly impersonal world." Religion, he insisted, was our
one and only source for believing that we inhabit "a universe in which
the human spirit is guaranteed security against the forces of nature
which always seem to reduce it to a mere effervescence unable to outlast
the collocation of forces which produced it."[7] Religion alone could provide "reasons" for avoiding moral enervation. He insisted that

> A purely naturalistic ethics will not only be overcome by a sense
> of frustration and sink into despair, but it will lack the force to

restrain the self-will and self-interest of men and of nations. If life cannot be centered in something beyond nature, it will not be possible to lift men above the brute struggle for survival.[8]

This type of concern and the apologia based upon it were in essential agreement with Niebuhr's youthful Yale B.D. thesis of 1914 (entitled "The Validity and Certainty of Religious Knowledge"). In an altered and more sophisticated form this orientation remained with him throughout his theological career.

In this early period Niebuhr hoped that there could be developed, as Chapter 8 of his book puts it, "A Philosophy for an Ethical Religion." He thought that personality, with its accompanying traits of "freedom" and "moral responsibility," could only be safeguarded on a traditional religious basis. Yet what must be avoided at all costs, however consistent they might appear on purely logical grounds, were monistic and pantheistic metaphysics. In Niebuhr's account both monism and pantheism ended in a denial of the very freedom and responsibility essential to personal life. Niebuhr advocated *some* form of dualism as necessary for the plausibility of religious conviction. The tensions and contradictions in the actual world could be maintained and appreciated only on such a basis. What is significant is that even in these early years Niebuhr's rationale was a pragmatic one. He insisted that

> What is needed is a philosophy and a religion which will do justice both to the purpose and to the frustration which purpose meets in the inertia of the concrete world, both to the ideal which fashions the real and to the real which defeats the ideal, both to the essential harmony and to the inevitable conflict in the cosmos and in the soul. In a sense there is not a single dualism in life; rather there are many of them. In his own life man may experience a conflict between his moral will and the anarchic desires with which nature has endowed him; or he may experience a conflict between his cherished values and the caprices of nature which know nothing of the economy of values in human life. In the cosmic order the conflict is between creativity and the resistance which frustrates creative purpose. Whether the dualism is defined as one of mind and matter, or thought and extension, or force and enertia, or God and the devil, it approximates the real facts of life. It may be impossible to do full justice to the two types of facts by any set of symbols or definitions; but life gives the lie to any attempt by which one is explained completely in terms of the other.[9]

Whereas the youthful Niebuhr felt that metaphysics could provide a way to lend rational support to religious claims, the focus was on what he deemed to be vitally at stake in such claims. Niebuhr was a consequentialist, even in his early choice and defense of metaphysical grounding. And although in 1927 he held that such grounding was important, he was prepared to grant that metaphysical grounding was far less important than ethical considerations. The oppositions that propelled Niebuhr to adopt a dualism were oppositions or tensions that he discerned *in experience.* He was prompted to embrace, with qualifications, a tenuous metaphysical position fraught with inconsistencies. At the same time, Niebuhr definitely subordinated the rational defense of religion to its compelling ethical urgency. In effect, Niebuhr's defense of dualism as a way of making sense out of the facts was based on pragmatic considerations. This pragmatic bent of mind also led him to doubt the possibility of any type of metaphysical grounding which would be rationally compelling. It should be noted that Niebuhr's sense of the "oppositions" or "tensions" eventually evolved into the "paradoxes" of a later day which required of him a more dialectical reading of experience without metaphysical defense. These tensions were increasingly argued to be features of experience most adequately expressed within the language of a religious tradition that modern thought prematurely dismissed.

In 1927 the ethical dimension of religion took precedence over all other considerations, for Niebuhr. By this he meant that religion must provide guidance for life and could justify itself to civilization as a viable enterprise only insofar as it succeeded in doing so. This was proximate to Dewey's understanding of philosophy. In this Niebuhr and Dewey shared a pragmatic-consequentialist view of the ideals of life. This emphasis, albeit in different form and with far more theological sophistication, remained central to Niebuhr's thought up until the period when he vehemently opposed the Barthian tendency to deny theological grounds for making discriminate moral judgments.

In the early period Niebuhr contended that it was far "better for religion to forego perfect metaphysical consistency," both for the sake of the facts, and also "for the sake of moral potency." Throughout *Does Civilization Need Religion?* Niebuhr's theme was that religion's failure in the modern age did not reside primarily at the level of metaphysical deficiency. The vast majority who were then irreligious were irreligious precisely "because religion has failed to make civilization ethical (rather) than because it has failed to maintain its intellectual respectability."[10] Niebuhr's doubts about metaphysical grounding never tempted him to embrace Barthian positivism because a debilitating social irrelevance was the end product of the one as much as of the other. Of course, Niebuhr soon abandoned his hope that religion (much less anything else) could "make civilization ethical." The task of making the "ethical and social resources available for the solution of the moral problems of modern civilization"[11] took priority then as always, with Niebuhr, although later on he would speak *only* of "proximate" solutions. Indeed, the task of finding a way to achieve social and political relevance set Niebuhr's lifelong agenda as a theological ethicist.

Richard Fox notes that Niebuhr's book, published in 1927, was "written in short spurts beginning in 1923" and was essentially a reworking of material which had appeared in the *Christian Century* "between 1923 and 1926." The book, according to Fox,

> displayed no signs whatsoever of the major developments in his thinking since the summer of 1926: the critique of the AFL, of Ford, and of unethical power and privilege; the "despair" over the racial issue; the stress on workers' autonomy; the hesitant movement leftward to the ideological outskirts of socialism. It was a polishing of his earlier thoughts. It made no effort to incorporate his most recent insights.[12]

It is quite true that Niebuhr's efforts here constituted "a general moral stance" and "a proclamation of radical intent" rather than a progression beyond the "political content" of the previous year as Fox suggests.[13] What Fox overlooks, however, is that the programmatic title *Does Civilization Need Religion?* sharply raised pragmatic considerations and contexts that increasingly governed Niebuhr's understanding of theological relevance. This book proved to be a convenient resting point, transitional in nature, reflecting the important shifts in Niebuhr's thinking between the time he was at Yale in 1914 and his iconoclastic bombshell of 1932 published under the title *Moral Man and Immoral Society*. The transition was from the youthful yearnings of a religious idealist to the maturing insights of a strident realist in which the force of transition was an increasingly pragmatic reading initially of politics and at a later time of theology.

Although Niebuhr's understanding of religion remained deeply connected to the ethical concerns common to both "religious" and "secular" liberalism, he moved rather decisively away from his earlier focus on personal morality to an ethic oriented toward social realities. He increasingly emphasized the fact that "life had moved on and the practical needs of modern society demand an ethic which is not individualistic and a religion which is not unqualifiedly optimistic."[14] "Modern" liberal religious thought, in his estimation, was hardly modern enough—reflecting as it did the outdated individualism of the nineteenth century. It is surely true that Niebuhr reflected Schlesinger's "Social-Gospel–

Dewey amalgam" when he claimed that "it is the quest for what is not real but is always becoming real, for what is not true but is always becoming true, that makes man incurably religious."[15] Niebuhr's language, as well as his moral conception, was virtually interchangeable with that of Dewey; the difference being simply that which divided the *religious* liberal from the liberalism of religiously inclined *humanistic-naturalist* of that day. But at this point Niebuhr was still a long way from any substantive turn toward those insights based on theological tradition with which he would effectively critique the entire liberal culture.

As comfortably liberal as Niebuhr's religious and political ideas remained in 1927, a few notes were sounded that would gain volume and achieve clarity in subsequent years. He began to identify a "moral simplicity in Protestantism which is closely related to its individualism,"[16] and he anticipated *the* major theme of *Moral Man* in his recognition that "all human groups tend to be more predatory than the individuals which compose them."[17] He recognized the sentimentality that had corrupted both moral and religious idealism and rendered such idealism largely oblivious to the harsh, even brutal, conflict of modern economic life. Nonetheless, in *Does Civilization Need Religion?* Niebuhr still glorified an abstract "social intelligence" that could produce "a finer fruit than the type of prudence which characterizes the international policy of modern states."[18] He had yet to become highly suspicious of "social intelligence" or sufficiently appreciative of the serpentine wisdom required by effective statecraft.

To put the matter differently, in 1927 Niebuhr had yet to see the liberal concept of "social intelligence" as itself a piece of exaggerated idealism and excessive optimism. At this point he was reticent about "social intelligence" mostly because he believed that it was kin to the kind of "cynicism which discounts all moral and personal factors in social reconstruction and places its hope entirely in a new social strategy."[19] This is crucial enough to give us pause, not only because it pointed to a region of serious conflict with Dewey, but also because it reflected extremely early sentiments that persisted in Niebuhr's thought.

In his earliest days Niebuhr defended "supernaturalism" against "naturalism" because he believed that supernaturalism alone could safeguard both the "person" and those values such as freedom and responsibility which were thought essential to personal life. Mere "social intelligence"—indeed the life of reason as such—was prone to a cynical despair productive of a debilitation of the will. In one form or another Niebuhr would sound this note over and over again throughout the years. However sophisticated his theological vision became, some measure of this viewpoint remained in his polemic against "naturalistic rationalism." Yet in fairness to Niebuhr, his criticisms of "social intelligence," "reason," and "naturalism" became much more telling as they deepened and shifted to different grounds. It was not just a religious versus a nonreligious anthropology that would eventually govern the course of his criticism. The point where his attack upon Dewey's favorite shibboleths became interesting was where Niebuhr moved to an analysis of power, conflict, and a wholesale reassessment of liberal culture. This, too, of course, would propel him toward a deeper level of theological reflection. It reintroduced a richer and far more complex anthropology than was present in these early years. The direction of Niebuhr's maturing thought was only hinted at in 1927, when he suggested that intelligence alone could not achieve conciliation because "even at best human nature is so imperfect"[20] that much more than rational intelligence was required.

Niebuhr did introduce a definition of the religious life that stayed with him. He defended transcendence as a resource for "a sense of both humility and security before the holiness which is at once the source and the goal of his virtue" and which "saves him at the same time from premature complacency and ultimate despair."[21] He argued that a religious idealism should issue in "humility which becomes the basis of self-respect," whereas an irreligious idealism tends toward pride. It was thus that social intelligence based on an irreligious idealism, although it "may be a partner in the process of conciliation" so essential to resolving group conflicts, "cannot bear the burden alone when a disposition to humility and a capacity for mercy is lacking."[22] Such attributes, Niebuhr thought, arose solely out of a religious spirit, authentically understood. He declared that

> The task of making complex group relations ethical belongs primarily to religion and education because statecraft cannot rise above the universal limitations of human imagination and intelligence. A robust ethical idealism, an extraordinary spiritual insight and a high degree of intelligence are equally necessary for such a social task. The difficulties of the problem are enhanced by the fact that the religious imagination and astute intelligence which are equally necessary for its solution are incompatible with each other. Religion is naturally jealous of any partner in a redemptive enterprise; and the same intelligence which is needed to guide moral purpose in a complex situation easily lames the moral will and dulls the spiritual insight.[23]

John Dewey, of course, did not see things this way at all. Niebuhr was inclined to join the chorus of those theologians who claimed that those who did not praise God invariably praise man. There are indeed many instances of this to draw upon, but as Niebuhr well knew, there were those among the pious who in praising God were praising themselves. Be that as it may, there were also those among the naturalists—Dewey being the prime example—who neither praised God nor saw reason to praise man too highly. Certainly, Dewey saw hope for humankind in its natural setting in spite of life's finality. He saw social intelligence neither in cynical terms nor as cut off from the values of personal and moral life. He developed his own theory of "religious" values within a particular version of naturalism decidedly antithetical to Niebuhr's own theism. Although he gave his undivided attention to religion only in his seventh decade, he did formulate his ideas on the subject in 1934 in his book *A Common Faith*.

2

Queries: Pragmatic and Social

By 1930 many of Niebuhr's concerns resurfaced and were focused specifically, though somewhat indirectly, on Dewey himself. Niebuhr referred to Dewey in an address he was invited to give at the sixty-eighth annual meeting of the National Education Association. The meeting was held at Columbia University between June 28 and July 4, 1930.[1] Speaking on the issue of education to an NEA audience on Dewey's own turf at Columbia in the year of his retirement was, in itself, an adventurous undertaking. Niebuhr had a point to make, and it was rooted in his basic Jamesean pragmatic conviction that life's primary motivations were supplied by commitments and that such commitments inevitably defied the canons of abstract rational detachment.

Niebuhr spoke of the "spirit of life" as consisting of energy (vitality), reason, and "something which is neither energy nor reason, but related to both, out of which springs poetry, man's imaginative life and religion."[2] He suggested that we call it *imagination.* Playing on the word *intelligence,* Niebuhr showed how the very problem-solving calculations of reason frequently, and sometimes quite tragically, generated more problems than reason itself could resolve. Such a situation resulted in the fact that "our intelligence has first of all created a world too large for our imagination and for our social sympathy."[3] Under the overarching and overwhelming impact of our vast technological achievements we fantasize a unity and purpose to life that would flow automatically in the wake of the expanding horizons of intelligence itself. Instead we have a time of universal conflict and the threat of moral enervation. "We are living in a world," Niebuhr argued, "in which a higher degree of technological achievement, and to a certain degree, a higher intelligence, brings us in closer and closer contact with all the world, but we haven't the intelligence by which we may make our common life sufferable."[4]

Niebuhr, in effect, argued for the kind of "intelligence" that transcended mere "rational" intelligence as a way to restore the imaginative-spiritual dimension of life. He was pleading for a wisdom beyond the kind of technocratic intelligence wedded to the mechanistic naturalisms so widespread in that age of science. There was nothing much new in this, of course. It was the cry of both idealism and romanticism against one type of empirical naturalism connected with scientific history. Niebuhr stressed that it was only by means of an educational enhancement of introspective imagination that "this confused and perplexed modern man" might "find some new unity to life, to achieve some great passion or conviction, or some loyalty to a great tradition, or to give himself to a vocational task and program, or so to analyze himself that he can bring the various multifarious forces of his life under the domain of a central passsion."[5] Rationalism in its variant forms had tragically vitiated the very energy out of which the raison d'être of life itself arose and was sustained. With a measure of "irony," Niebuhr wrote

> These same rational forces which bring infrarational forces under control seem also to destroy the ultra-rational forces of life, man's imagination, his poetry, the dreams that he has of a better world, the energy by which he gives himself to this better world, the irrational and ultrarational dynamic which is the basis of his life. It is so necessary to bring man's prejudices, bigotries, and impulses under the control of reason, and there are so many people who suffer from the miseries created by unreason that there are not very many people who are willing to admit that anything evil can come out of the cultivation of intelligence or the rational approach to life.[6]

In lamenting the erosion of those ultrarational dimensions of life that Niebuhr believed alone gave rise to values, projects, and goals, he seemed to hold out hope that mere exhortation, or perhaps a capacity to will the world back to what it once was, would suffice. Of course, he knew better. The "will to believe," as James understood it, might well lack force for lacking any believable object. Niebuhr, however, was not quite prepared to give the field over to the Joseph Wood Krutches of the world!

Niebuhr pointed out that John Dewey's faith in democracy "which moves the great rational people is [itself] an irrational faith. That is their religion, at least a part of their religion, and as long as they can hold to it, they can be effective people." However, "if they reason too much about it, perhaps then that last remnant of their religion will be gone."[7] With a prescience greater than he knew, Niebuhr was identifying one aspect of Dewey's "common faith" and revealed it to be beyond the boundaries of reason within which Dewey sought so ardently to confine it. Niebuhr was suggesting something here that he would stress over and over again in the course of his debate with Dewey; namely, that the ultimate grounds of a person's commitments are incapable of rational demonstration. It has been charged that Dewey's overarching set of values presupposed and reflected the antecendent values of the American liberal-democratic culture from which he came. Yet it must be said that both Dewey and Niebuhr held to a far more complex view of the cultural locus of values than is evident in such a judgment.

Niebuhr first of all was insisting that both the fact and the persistence of the transrational aspects of life pointed to the need for exhortation and sheer exercise of will. Moreover, he was attempting to disclose the nonrational presuppositions in back of positions parading behind the cloak of pure rationality. Niebuhr's second point was more plausible and therefore more interesting. With an obvious, yet indirect, reference to Dewey, Niebuhr insisted

> Here is a man, for instance, who believes that all education ought to be for the purpose of cultivating a more democratic way of life. I wouldn't know myself how to put it better than to say that all education ought to individualize people on the one hand, socialize them on the other, and make it possible for them to have mutual relationships for their fellowmen. But the idea that democracy is a rational goal of life is itself an irrational prejudice.[8]

Niebuhr's choice of the term *irrational* was clearly an unfortunate one. He was not, however, denying that reasons can be given or justifications provided on behalf of this or that set of value commitments. He was making the point that, at bottom, one's most cherished commitments were themselves "ultrarational" in his sense of that term. As Niebuhr elsewhere stated, a "religious element" is always present "in the hope of a just society." Indeed, "without the ultrarational hopes and passions of religion no society will ever have the courage to conquer despair and attempt the impossible; for the vision of a just society is an impossible one, which can be approximated only by those who do not regard it as impossible."[9]

Niebuhr appealed to the kind of education that would generate contions by which men and women could lead lives of purpose and direction. In short, he wanted to see education aim "to discipline life without destroying its energies, to refine the impulses of life without enervating them, to create the union between life's highest rational and its highest ultrarational forces." Niebuhr saw this to be the "most challenging of all the problems which face those of us who are guiding each new generation."[10]

Later that same year Niebuhr, in an essay on "Mechanical Men in a Mechanical Age," made his case in a slightly different context. Under the impact of the modern age, he contended, human beings in the Western world had lost their sense of organic unity with the natural universe and any sense of community within the context of societal relations. Although Niebuhr held that science should assist "in the development of the kind of social intelligence necessary for the ordering of our common lives," he judged it utterly incapable of reviving or sustaining "the social passions by which we will that our common life be ordered." An allegedly pure rationality could not solve our social problems. The issues here involved a more complex anthropology than was to be found in the assumptions of the prevailing dogmas of the age. The central problem, he wrote, was that

> Neither our ultimate faith by which we adjust ourselves to the universe, nor our moral will through which we find ourselves in our society can be expressed in terms of pure reason. The energies of life are not rational. Reason may guide them but it cannot create them. . . . Man comes to terms with his universe only by heroic and poetic insights, and he is nerved to undertake them only as he gains sufficient self-respect in his moral relationships to his fellowmen to feel that the human spirit must be taken into account when the effort is made to penetrate the ultimate mysteries.[11]

In the years immediately preceding the appearance of *Moral Man and Immoral Society* Niebuhr and Dewey had some occasional associations relating to the political activities of the day. Both men were members of the League for Independent Political Action in company with University of Chicago economist, and later United States senator from Illinois, Paul H. Douglas. They were both among those members of that organization who seriously considered third-party alternatives. However, according to Richard Fox, "after a meeting on November 24 with John Dewey, Oswald Garrison Villard (editor of the *Nation*), and other fellow members of the LIPA's executive committee, he [Niebuhr] realized that a new party was out of the question," if for no other reason than that their impotency being a predominantly academic-oriented group was made painfully clear to them.[12] Such individuals were estranged from the major political parties and disillusioned with the failure of socialist Norman Thomas to show respectably even in the supposed area of his strength (the race of borough president of Manhattan in the autumn election of 1931).

In the context of these political activities a fissure between Niebuhr and Dewey was about to open up and would inaugurate a protracted controversy into which all parties would be drawn. According to Fox, Dewey was blissfully ignorant of Niebuhr's impending assault upon him. He writes that "at a banquet in [Niebuhr's] honor on October 2, [1932], John Dewey, Haywood Broun and Morris Hillquit all spoke. The irony of Dewey's appearance," Fox points out, "was known only to Niebuhr, since only he knew that the manuscript of *Moral Man* singled Dewey out as an impotent liberal unacquainted with power and struggle."[13]

Aside from common political and organizational ventures, Dewey and Niebuhr both contributed to socialist Norman Thomas's journal *The World Tomorrow* in the late 1920s and early 1930s. Indeed, Niebuhr had been brought to New York by Sherwood Eddy to work on the editorial staff of this journal as well as to teach at Union Theological Seminary. Dewey no doubt saw an occasional article of Niebuhr's such as his "Why We Need a New Economic Order," which appeared in the same October 1928 issue of *The World Tomorrow* as Dewey's own "Critique of American Civilization." Niebuhr at this time, however, would have written very little to command Dewey's attention. Generally speaking, aside from their common political association, there was no reason for Dewey to take special note of Reinhold Niebuhr in any other context than his presence as a kindred spirit in the arena of social action.

Dewey was aware of Niebuhr's presence at Union Seminary, of course, and in a letter written to John Herman Randall, Jr's wife Mercedes (in subsequent years the Randalls were to become friends of the Niebuhrs as well as of the Deweys) corrected a previous error on his part regarding Niebuhr's alleged departure from that institution. Dewey wrote that "I was wrong about Mr. Niebuhr having resigned [from Union]. I was misled by a statement in one of the letters that the writer in common with Mr. N was resigning. But he had evidently no authority for the statement."[14]

During the five-year period between the publication of *Does Civilization Need Religion?* in 1927 and *Moral Man and Immoral Society* in December 1932, Niebuhr's thought was undergoing a significant transition. He was moving toward both an expanded social understanding of the human situation and a more radical conception of the kind of social action necessary for the reconstruction of society. The confusions and contradictions surrounding prohibition and Alfred E. Smith's 1928 presidential candidacy aided in this shift. Niebuhr increasingly broke with the individualistic and moralistic liberalism that still colored his thinking in spite of the social tone of *Does Civilization Need Religion?* The transition came into sharp focus in 1929 when Niebuhr emphasized the need for a "new economic order" prior to either any expected reformation of society or a perfection of personality. Now the pressing question became one of

whether society can gain sufficient social intelligence to modify
the present system step by step as the need arises and as traditional methods become unworkable or whether through the
stubbornness and blindness of the holders of power and
privilege and through the ignorance of the masses the system
will be permitted to disintegrate until change can come only
through revolution and social convulsion.[15]

By this time Niebuhr's views on the role of social intelligence were
quite ambivalent. Although qualifiedly praising the role of "social intelligence," he indicted the "assumptions of good people in the world of education and religion who imagine they are creating a new and better
world through intellectual and religious inspiration."[16] Niebuhr was
willing to go even further: "it is the chronic weakness of our conventional
'idealism' that it fails to deal realistically with basic prejudices and
assumptions. If this weakness cannot be cured," he warned, then "the future of modern society will be determined by conflict and not by adjustment."[17]

The paralysis of liberalism and an increasing appreciation of the
element of conflict in the resolution of social problems surfaced in the
same month that his *Moral Man* was reaching completion. In September
1932 Niebuhr posed the question in *The World Tomorrow* by the very title of
his essay: "Is Peace or Justice the Goal?" He gave some credence to the
wisdom of the "secular radical" of the day — "in contemporary terms, the
real Marxian" who is "contemptuous of the social resources of religion."
Such contempt, Niebuhr pointed out, was a proper reaction against the
sentimental dreams of a just society which would ideally emerge if only
people could be taught "to love each other, or if only all men will become
more intelligent and socially minded."[18] A line was now crossed and the
substantive issue joined. Reflecting on the character of his own liberal
religious tradition, Niebuhr remarked that "once the religious idealist
has arrived at the conclusion that justice cannot be established by education alone, he is of course forced to condone the use of social coersion and
resistance for the attainment of social justice. In some sense or other he
is forced to accept the idea of the class struggle."[19] Then he turned his attention to the secular liberal community so congenial to John Dewey
and suggested that "if anything, the modern educator is being more
romantic than the liberal Christian." The Christian, after all, "has
something in his tradition about all men being sinners, which prevents
him from being as completely romantic as the educator [which should be
sufficient to save that tradition] from complete capitulation to the illusions of liberalism."[20]

3

The Opening Attack on Liberalism

As is well-known, the fundamental shift in Niebuhr's thought surfaced in his book *Moral Man and Immoral Society*. This volume entered the 1932 landscape with explosive force and sent a series of shockwaves through America's liberal Protestant community. He specifically attacked John Dewey, whose prestige acted as a lightning rod for Niebuhr's broadside against the entire bastion of liberal idealism, both secular and religious. Inasmuch as Niebuhr acknowledged a "polemical interest," it was aimed squarely at "the moralists, both religious and secular, who imagine that the egoism of individuals is being progressively checked by the development of rationality or the growth of a religiously inspired goodwill and that nothing but the continuance of this process is necessary to establish social harmony between all the human societies and collectives."[1]

It is in *Moral Man* that the adversarial relationship between Niebuhr and Dewey was ignited. Repudiating the love-perfectionism of the religious liberals and the rational-perfectionism of the secular liberals, *Moral Man*, as Arthur Schlesinger, Jr., succinctly put it, "was a somber and powerful rejection of the Social–Gospel–Dewey amalgam, with it politics of love and reason."[2] Richard Fox contends that Niebuhr "sneered at liberal heroes like John Dewey" and went about the business of "constructing an ideal-type opponent who was easy to take down."[3] Given his respect for Dewey as a human being and as a socially committed philosopher, however much Niebuhr would assail what he held to be Dewey's liberal illusions, it is highly unlikely he ever "sneered" at Dewey. The issue Fox raises is a legitimate one, but his treatment of it is somewhat facile and given to hyperbole. His "strawman" formulation of the problem is, at best, oversimplified. The charge that Niebuhr was prone to engage in selectivity, oversimplification, and stereotyping in representing the position of others was made by a few of Niebuhr's critics. At the pinnacle of Niebuhr's career, Robert L. Calhoun at Yale and Daniel Day Williams, then at Chicago, were forceful in making this

point. Williams put it most charitably when, in 1956, he pointed out that
Niebuhr employed a typological "method of characterizing broad cultural movements and theological positions" which must be acknowledged to see clearly both Niebuhr's genius and limitations. As Williams
noted, Niebuhr

> views the history of thought as exhibiting a series of "types" of
> outlooks [and] arranges these according to certain key concepts
> and problems in which he is interested. . . . Thus Niebuhr is not
> so much concerned to trace nuances of meaning in different
> philosophies, or to work out the complex lines of historical de-
> velopment. He is rather an apologist and critic who tries to get
> directly at the basic principles by which various faiths grasp
> the meaning of life.
>   This "typology" method seems to me one of the major
> reasons that Niebuhr's cultural criticism has been so effective.
> His great genius in using the method permits him to go swiftly
> to the heart of a vast and complex cultural movement, to lift out
> the central idea which gives it its drive, and which also betrays
> in many cases its weaknesses. Though the method produces a
> considerable oversimplification, it permits the discovery and
> concise statement of fundamental issues. Its disadvantage is
> that it permits Niebuhr to deal with the point of view he is
> criticizing by using its most exaggerated, and sometimes even
> its most fatuous, expressions to represent the entire position.[4]

Niebuhr's lifelong engagement with Dewey's thought indeed reflected the issues and insights presented by Williams. His *Moral Man and
Immoral Society* was polemically apologetic. Its tone was strident, and this
tone, as Fox points out, "was an integral part of its message" which
moved along on both "cerebral and pugnacious" levels.[5] It is true that
Niebuhr failed to deal with Dewey, either in depth or in terms of the
whole cloth. He certainly overlooked the core of Dewey's philosophical
position. Whatever the case may be on this score, it is quite true that
Niebuhr selectively highlighted certain aspects or tendencies of Dewey's
thought for special emphasis. And a reasonable case can be made that
Niebuhr overexaggerated Dewey's position on certain issues. Dewey, of
course, engaged in some of the same sins according to his friend and colleague, John Herman Randall, Jr.
    At the same time another side to this coin needs to be mentioned. As
Williams noted, both the apologetic force of Niebuhr's critical analysis
and his capacity to capture the core of a position or movement were the

sources of his strength as well as of his rather remarkable genius. We are better instructed, therefore, to see Niebuhr's ongoing treatment of Dewey on both sides at once. Although we had best never lose sight of his partial and sometimes fatuous treatment of Dewey, we ought to recognize that Niebuhr was extremely adept at isolating and identifying flaws which could not be masked by ineffective qualification. The manner in which Niebuhr represented Dewey to us moved between these two extremes and makes the task of fairly assessing his perspective on Dewey most difficult. That Dewey was singled out by Niebuhr should come as no surprise. Dewey, after all, was American social liberalism personified. He was the exemplary model for that tradition.

Niebuhr's rather selective use of Dewey's thought certainly misrepresented him, as friends of both Niebuhr and Dewey have noted. The fury heaped upon Niebuhr by some Dewey loyalists cannot be fully accounted for simply for those reasons alone, however. Neither can the measure of anger be explained solely on the basis of the pretentions of a relatively younger man of forty unleashing an attack upon a seventy-three-year-old living legend. The point is that Niebuhr had struck so forcefully at the very heart of social liberalism that its erstwhile defenders, who were legion in both secular and religious circles, were quite shocked and soon went on the offensive. Moreover, the wolf who was now inside the door of the liberal establishment was indisputably one of its own. This made the shock and anger more intense than ever. There is also irony in all of this, for so potent was the force of Niebuhr's attack on Dewey, that its impact on liberal circles virtually obscured down to the present day the degree of affinity Niebuhr had with both Dewey and the pragmatic movement in American intellectual history.

Niebuhr's thesis in *Moral Man and Immoral Society* was that there exists a substantive distinction between the moral behavior of individuals and that of collectives. Overlooking or underestimating that distinction spells disaster for any serious effort of achieving a realistic understanding of political life. Human communities, he contended, have far "less reason to guide and check impulse, less capacity for self-transcendence, less ability to comprehend the need of others and therefore more unrestrained egoism than the individuals who compose the group reveal in their personal relationships."[6] Tragically, both educators and moralists alike "underestimate the conflict of interest in political and economic relations, and attribute to disinterested ignorance what ought usually to be attributed to interested intelligence."[7] Although Niebuhr would later rue the day he chose the precise title of his book, he did not at all construe the distinction to mean that individuals are moral whereas groups are not.[8] Yet he did hold that *by comparison*

Individual men may be moral in the sense that they are able to consider interests other than their own in determining problems of conduct, and are capable, on occasion, of preferring the advantages of others to their own. They are endowed by nature with a measure of sympathy and consideration for their kind, the breadth of which may be extended by an astute social pedagogy. Their rational faculty prompts them to a sense of justice which educational discipline may refine and purge of egoistic elements until they are able to view a social situation, in which their own interests are involved, with a fair measure of objectivity.[9]

Considering the relationship between moral and coercive politics, many of the "socially minded educators" of the early 1930s sought to salvage society by using the school system as an agency for extending the social and political intelligence of the general community. This tendency, of course, was to be credited to the tremendous impact of John Dewey and his influence on his liberal scions. According to Niebuhr,

While this hope of the educators, which in America finds its most telling presentation in the educational philosophy of Professor John Dewey, has some justification, political redemption through education is not as easily achieved as the educators assume. The very terms in which they state the problem proves that they are themselves bound by middle-class perspectives, which will naturally increase in force and narrowness in proportion to the distance from the ideal of the educator.[10]

Niebuhr rejected what he held to be the false hope that educators in a society such as ours can achieve and promulgate "a significant critical detachment from a contemporary culture and its official propagation in the public schools."[11] Moreover, the belief that the abolition of the rights of property based in the "socially minded educators'" view of a planned society would occur once the wisdom was achieved and educationally conveyed struck Niebuhr as utterly incredulous:

The fact is the interests of the powerful and dominant groups, who profit from the present system of society, are the real hindrance to the establishment of a rational and just society. It would be pleasant to believe that the intelligence of the general community could be raised to such a height that the irrational injustices of society would be eliminated. But unfortunately there is no such general community. There are many classes, all of them partially deriving their perspectives from, or suffering them to be limited by, their economic interest. The failure of modern socially minded educators to realise this fact proves that their very educational theory, which partly transcends the impulses of the dominant groups by force of sheer intellectual honesty and penetration, is also partly bound and limited by the environment of their own class, the middle class. For this class, living in comfort and security, is unable to recognise the urgency of the social problem; and, living in a world of individual relationships, is unable to appreciate the consistency with which economic groups express themselves in terms of pure selfishness.[12]

These reflections followed upon an assessment of educational theorist Harold Ruggs, whom Niebuhr regarded as "one of the most prominent and most imaginative" of that group. Niebuhr saw Ruggs's book *Culture and Education in America* as embodying the very worst of the liberal illusions. Ruggs argued on behalf of a high school curriculum which would openly and courageously inform young people of the class interest in American economic life and thus release their imaginations for the creative task of preparing for a planned society. He recommended that a nationwide regime of expert planners be established whose task would involve facilitating the redirection of society along more inclusive an more equitable lines.

The final absurdity Niebuhr saw in all of this rested with a thoroughly naive reliance upon expertise which seems to color the "socially minded educator's" excessively rationalistic schemes of planning. He remarked (in specific relation to Ruggs) that the very suggestion "that what society needs, and if intelligent enough, will be able to secure, is 'trained and experienced specialists' to perform the 'expert functions' of government" is quite ludicrous. Moreover, "it betrays an additional class prejudice, the prejudice of the intellectual, who is so much the rationalist, that he imagines the evils of government can be eliminated by the expert knowledge of specialists." With penetrating realism Niebuhr saw the element of transparency in the "expert" occasioned by the relativity of cultural perspectives. The expert could easily function under any type of regime. Niebuhr observed that "the inclination of the human mind for beginning with assumptions which have been determined by other than rational considerations, and building a superstructure of rationally acceptable judgments upon them," leads one to conclude that "the expert is quite capable of giving any previously determined tendency both rational justification and efficient detailed application."[13]

Dewey came in for singularly sharp criticism inasmuch as Niebuhr

pegged him as the quintessential representative of those educators and
social analysts whose theories "lead to a very considerable moral and
political confusion in our day."[14] More than this, however, Niebuhr identified John Dewey as a living paradigm for all that was bankrupt in the
liberal tradition, secular or religious. There was a rather definite shift
between 1929 when Niebuhr praised Dewey for "molding . . . political
and social thought" in order "to help the world of men regulate its common life" and 1932 when his introduction to *Moral Man* indicted Dewey
for betraying "the confusion of an analyst who has no clear counsels
about the way to overcome social inertia."[15]

Niebuhr had not only arrived at the point of severely restricting the
capacity of both the moral conscience and the rational faculty in resolving social conflict, he now openly acknowledged that the tendencies of
class domination and imperial impulse could be prevented from exploit-
ing weakness only if "power is raised against it."[16] Liberal moral
idealism was consistently embarrassed by the existence of power in social relationships, and its inability to take this factor into the center of
its thinking rendered its social policy recommendations dangerous and
misleading. Conscience and reason, according to Niebuhr, could only
ameliorate but never abolish the conflicting struggle between social
groups. Even then such a qualification was marginally possible only
under highly stable and homogeneous cultural contexts.

In Niebuhr's view, Dewey had fallen victim to the most persistent
and misguided error of interpreting social conflict in accordance with
the folly of the "cultural lag" theory. According to that theory, current
"social differences" were held to be "due to the failure to the social sciences to keep pace with the physical sciences which have created our
technological civilization."[17] Accordingly, solutions to any social problem await only the time that it would require to bring the social sciences
into line with the sophisticated developments of the natural sciences. In
essence the solution to social problems awaited only an advance of
human intelligence in the social arena patterned after the kind of experimental intelligence evident in the physical sciences. Niebuhr
quoted Dewey's *Philosophy and Civilization* at some length at the very beginning of *Moral Man*

> "It is," declares Professor John Dewey, "our human intelligence
> and our human courage which is on trial; it is incredible that
> men who have brought the technique of physical discovery, in-
> vention and use to such a pitch of perfection will abdicate in the
> face of the infinitely more important human problem. What
> stands in the way (of a planned economy) is a lot of outworn
> traditions, moth-eaten slogans and catchwords that do substi-

tute duty for thought, as well as our entrenched predatory self-interest. We shall only make a real beginning in intelligent thought when we cease mouthing platitudes.... Just as soon as we began to use the knowledge and skills we have to control social consequences in the interest of a shared, abundant and secured life, we shall cease to complain of the backwardness of our social knowledge.... We shall then take the road which leads to the assured building up of social science just as men built up physical science when they actively used techniques and tools and numbers in physical experimentation."[18]

Niebuhr agreed that the "human problem" was indeed "infinitely more important," as Dewey suggested. But he also contended that it was infinitely more complex, largely because of forces and factors that defied the rational expectations of an idealized "scientific intelligence." The nature and extent of the fundamental human problem was precisely what was at issue. And the prevailing mode of understanding, as Niebuhr perceived it, was both simplistic and dangerously self-deceiving. Acknowledging "Professor Dewey's great interest in and understanding of the modern social problem," Niebuhr saw little wisdom or clarity in Dewey's remarks. Although possessing an apparent recognition of the source of the problem, Dewey studiously ignored it when it came to his social analysis. Niebuhr claimed that "the real cause of social inertia, 'our predatory self-interest' is mentioned only in passing without influencing his [Dewey's] reasoning, and with no indication that he understands how much social conservatism is due to the economic interest of the owning classes."[19] The kind of ignorance that Dewey viewed as the basic cause of humankind's collective social ills betrayed the "natural bias of the educator" whose cultural influences stressed an abstract and excessive rationalism. Moreover, "the suggestion that we will only make a beginning in intelligent thought when we 'cease mouthing platitudes,'" Niebuhr argued, "is itself so platitudinous that it rather betrays the confusion of an analyst who has no clear counsels about the way to overcome social inertia."[20]

The abstract and sterile rationalism of such an approach to social conflict (irrespective of whether it accurately represented Dewey's thought) led Niebuhr to an indictment of the social engineering model of political life with its tendency to reduce the self's historical character to the dimensions of a technomechanical model of nature. In this connection Niebuhr saw Dewey, as Arthur Schlesinger, Jr., aptly put it, "as a symbol of a kind of social-planning rationalism that Niebuhr felt overlooked the intractability of man."[21] It is worth noting here that the excessive rationalism of liberal moral idealism operated as a basic source for

both Niebuhr's criticism of naturalism and his later rationale for insisting on an ever-increasing distinction between "history" and "nature." At
this time, however, he was basically content to stress the "difference between the very character of [the] social and physical sciences." In the
early 1930s this came down to the fact that "since reason is always, to
some degree, the servant of interest in a social situation, social injustice
cannot be resolved by moral and rational persuasion alone, as the
educator and social scientist usually believes. Conflict is inevitable,"
Niebuhr reiterated "and in this conflict power must be challenged by
power."[22] Those who hold that ignorance rather than self-interest is the
cause of social conflict will continue to miss the mark and give us false
counsel in the domain of political wisdom. They will persist in the view
that conflict is easily and perhaps always rationally manageable.

For Niebuhr the social wisdom stemming from the liberal era was
plagued by an inordinate, if not almost exclusive, emphasis upon either
"higher intelligence" or "sincere morality." Reason and love were offered
as panaceas for resolving social conflict—conflict begrudgingly acknowledged as an "expedient of the moment" at the very most. Niebuhr's criticisms were essentially directed at secular liberal idealism because, in
his estimation, "modern religious idealists usually follow in the wake of
social scientists in advocating compromise and accommodation as the
way to social justice."[23] The problem is that American culture "is still
pretty firmly enmeshed in the illusions and sentimentalities of the Age
of Reason."[24] Niebuhr saw Dewey as the representative voice and embodiment of this tradition. Across the board, according to Niebuhr,

> What is lacking among all these moralists, whether religi-
> ous or rational, is an understanding of the brutal character of
> the behavior of all human collectives, and the power of self-in-
> terest and collective egoism in all inter-group relations. . . .
> They regard social conflict either as an impossible method of
> achieving morally approved ends or as a momentary expedient
> which a more perfect education or a purer religion will make
> unnecessary. They do not see that the limitations of the human
> imagination, the easy subservience of reason to prejudice and
> passion, and the consequent persistence of irrational egoism,
> particularly in group behavior, make social conflict an inevita-
> bility in human history, probably to its very end.[25]

Even in his most polemical moments, however, Niebuhr never rejected the role of reason in the attainment of justice. What he found deplorable was the degree to which advocates of reason were themselves

sentimental and naively optimistic about their notion of reason. In a letter written in 1956 to one of Dewey's ardent defenders, Morton White, Niebuhr recalled that

> I have been called an "irrationalist" for holding to this conviction [of holding that a major error of the modern age has been "the failure to recognize the intimate relation between reason and interest and passion in all historical judgments"], though I would not think it irrational to call attention to empirical evidence of the taint of interest upon the purity of reason. I know of no political scientist or historian, many of whom share my convictions, who are accused of irrationalism.[26]

Approximately seven weeks later in another letter Niebuhr lamented that "If one has empirical objections to this kind of faith in reason, one is called an 'irrationalist.' I find this mode of reasoning almost as obscurantist as reason subject to religious dogma." He went on to suggest that for him "The real issue is whether it is necessary to have absolute faith in the purity of reason in all situations to be admitted into the camp of the 'rational' men, who may be very unreasonable in defending their own faith."[27] Perhaps Waldo Frank best captured Niebuhr's spirit when, in recalling a meeting they both attended he remarked, "Reinhold Niebuhr was there, with his head of an eagle and his eloquent warm words assuring himself that he was a rational student of the world's irrationalities."[28]

Political justice, Niebuhr insisted, demanded setting power over against power precisely because the entrenched self-interest of privileged and powerful groups would not yield to rational persuasion. Those possessing power, wealth, or prestige seldom relinquish their advantage through an appeal to reason or conscience. Thus there is an entire strata of collective reality accompanying social conflict that an overly simplistic confidence in reason overlooks at great peril. In 1932 Niebuhr gave fairly wide latitude to the role of reason. He agreed that

> A growing rationality in society destroys the uncritical acceptance of injustice. It may destroy the morale of dominant groups by making them more conscious of the hollowness of their pretensions, so that they will be unable to assert their interests and protect their special privileges with the same degree of self-deception. It may furthermore destroy their social prestige in the community of revealing the relation between their special privileges and the misery of the underprivileged. It may make

those who suffer from injustice more conscious of their rights in society and persuade them to assert their rights more energetically.[29]

Niebuhr here paid homage to the rational aspect involved in a community's search for justice and continued to do so throughout his life, albeit within the context and limitations of a more highly developed theological interpretation of self-love. In the interests of social harmony, reason places restraints on inordinate claims of the self. Social intelligence, therefore, in a restricted and thereby realistic sense, is of perennial importance to the life of any viable community. But in the present context Niebuhr saw justice as essentially a *political* problem rather than a purely rational one. By this he meant that justice "is established by the assertion of power against power as well as by the rational comprehension of, and arbitration between, conflicting rights."[30] There is also no doubt that the measure of justice thus obtained would fail to attain the level of moral purity demanded by the individual's sense of "morally created social values." But this was precisely Niebuhr's point in *Moral Man.* Such value perspectives, however marginally applicable to individual life, had virtually no bearing on the complex issues and moral possibilities of collective life.

As Niebuhr saw it, "nature has not established the same degree of order in the human as in the lower creatures." The preestablished harmony that seems to relate impulses in the animal life is lacking in humans. Because "instincts are not as fully formed in human life . . . natural impulses may therefore be so enlarged and extended that the satisfaction of one impulse interferes with the satisfaction of another."[31] The lack of harmony and the existence of cross-purpose in human life led Niebuhr to another specific criticism of Dewey. Niebuhr knew that reason was able to project "goals more inclusive, and socially more acceptable, than those which natural impulse prompts."[32] In response to the question that arises here—"how an adequate dynamic toward the more inclusive objective is gained"—the social philosophers of Deweyite persuasion, according to Niebuhr, were wholly inadequate. He claimed

> In the theory of social philosophers, for whom Professor Dewey may be regarded as a typical and convenient example, the dynamic is simply the total impulsive character of life. Life according to this school is energy; and its dynamic character provides that it will move forward. If reason cuts straight and broad channels for the stream of life, it will flow in them. Without reason life spends itself in the narrow and tortuous beds,

which have been cut by ages of pre-rational impulse, seeking immediate outlets for its energy.[33]

This interpretation failed to do justice to the actual complexities of human behavior, in Niebuhr's view. Part of these complexities for Niebuhr involved "the inevitable conflicts between the objectives determined by reason and those of the total body of impulse rationally unified but bent upon more immediate goals than those which man's highest reason envisages."[34] The self may indeed "achieve a rational unity of impulse around the organizing centre of the possessive instinct or the will-to-power," Niebuhr thought, and yet still have "a faint sense of obligation to achieve social objectives, which transcend or are in conflict with, their will-to-power."[35] Niebuhr will return to the relationship between reason and impulse in his Gifford Lectures at the end of the decade where the issue received a more mature treatment reflecting his subsequent theological development. What was finally at stake for him in his conflict with Dewey in 1932 was a sharply diverging interpretation of what Niebuhr here termed *the limitations of human nature*.

4

The Dialogue Begins in Earnest

By 1933 Dewey chose to openly respond to Niebuhr in print. The occasion was a series of articles for *The World Tomorrow* in which Niebuhr, who was on the editorial staff, might well have had a hand in organizing. The journal asked that contributors write an assessment of the American scene. In March of that year Niebuhr inaugurated the series with his "After Capitalism—What?" and Dewey's essay "Unity and Progress" followed one week later.

At this time Niebuhr was entering his most radical phase. Striking an apocalyptic pose, Niebuhr proclaimed "liberalism in philosophy" to be "a spent force." He also sounded the death knell of capitalism, which he now viewed as totally incapable of internal reform. Niebuhr made the point that his essay "is written on the assumption that capitalism is dying and with the conviction that it ought to die."[1] In its unwillingness to share its wealth with those who participated in the productive process, capitalism's demise was deemed both inevitable and well-deserved. The only debatable issue here for Niebuhr was whether capitalism, in its "inevitable" drift towards fascism, would collapse of its own weight or by means of violent revolution.

It was in the context of *The World Tomorrow* series that Dewey elected to reply to Niebuhr. And it was certainly of no minor importance that Dewey broke silence in a public forum soon after the publication of Niebuhr's *Moral Man and Immoral Society.* In "Unity and Progress" Dewey rationalized the direct attention he gave to Niebuhr "in the interest of continuity" with respect to the theme of the series itself. Dewey, of course, was responding to much more than Niebuhr's own essay. He had been definitely affected by Niebuhr's attack on him in *Moral Man.* After writing that "my intent, however, is not to write negatively, as would be the case if my article's main purpose was criticism of Dr. Niebuhr's view,"[2] Dewey proceeded to react to Niebuhr by name in all but two paragraphs of the essay.

Ostensibly Dewey's criticism of Niebuhr's article "After Capitalism—What?" was that Niebuhr's preoccupation with "long range
views and predictions" seems to "predicate political policies for the present upon a conception of what the future is practically sure to be." And
he openly chided Niebuhr for having virtually "no doubt as to what the
dominant forces are and what is to be their certain outcome."[3] Dewey accused Niebuhr of "deplorable vagueness about what needs to be done
and how to do it,"[4] particularly in light of Niebuhr's professed call for "an
adequate social and political strategy for the attainment of a just society
or of the attainment of a higher approximation of justice than a decadent
capitalism grants."[5] Niebuhr was also indicted for demanding "a general philosophy of history as a prerequisite of a political analysis which
will direct political action."[6] Dewey dismissed Niebuhr's approach by relegating it to those "Christian theodicies" whose "supernatural interests" have long since ebbed away.

Dewey viewed himself as forming "a conception of what future society might become on the basis of actualities in the present, and then
[striving] to bring this future about." Instead of indulging in "highly
dubious forecasts of a long-term future," he would rather begin by determining "the urgent needs of the present and then try to shape policies to
meet those needs."[7] Although Dewey expressed his agreement with considerable portions of Niebuhr's basic political outlook, he believed that
his own methods would more likely guarantee that "politics would then
be used to help determine the future" in some truly constructive way.

Dewey's attack on Niebuhr's apparent need for a speculative
philosophy of history prior to serious political action was something of a
ruse. He had a different and more legitimate purpose in taking aim at
Niebuhr at this particular time. Niebuhr gained Dewey's attention precisely because of the blistering attack he delivered against the entire
edifice of liberal tradition. And it appears quite evident that barely beneath the surface of "Unity and Progress" lay a sharp repudiation of both
Niebuhr's indictment of liberalism and his identification of Dewey as its
leading proponent. "Unity and Progress" was Dewey's initial, yet circuitous reply to the Niebuhr of *Moral Man and Immoral Society.*

Niebuhr had found Dewey to be "a typical and convenient example" of
what was systemically wrong with social and educational philosophy in
American culture. In "After Capitalism—What?" Niebuhr referred to
"the futility of liberalism." The sentimentality, optimism, and naivete of
the liberal tradition are assumed as background to Niebuhr's charge that

> educational and religious idealists shrink from the conclusions
> to which a realistic analysis of history forces the careful stu
> dent, partly because they live in the false hope that the im-

pulses of nature in man can be sublimated by mind and conscience to a larger degree than is actually possible, and partly
because their own personal idealism shrinks from the "brutalities" of the social struggle which a realistic theory envisages.[8]

Dewey took offense at being included among those who represent
the kind of sentimental liberalism which he himself deplored. His disclaimer was evident in the insistence that his method

> is very different from that which Dr. Niebuhr criticizes under
> the name of "liberalism." It has nothing to do with the sen-
> timentalism to which he gives that name. There has been and
> still is an immense amount of political immaturity and
> economic illiteracy in the American citizenship, and I am not
> questioning either the existence or the futility of what Dr.
> Niebuhr calls liberalism. I am concerned only to point out the
> irrelevancy of his description and condemnation to the kind of
> procedure which I am proposing.[9]

All else paled before the burden of this crucial passage. Dewey sought to
defend *his* liberal methods against Niebuhr's criticisms and to make it
unmistakably evident that these methods were to be radically distinguished from the stereotypical liberal errors by which Niebuhr was
rightly disturbed. Dewey wanted it to be known that, in his estimation,
Niebuhr's polemical salvos in no way applied to John Dewey's particular
species of liberalism or to the methods of social reform derived from it.

As early as 1920 in *Reconstruction in Philosophy*, Dewey severed any
connection between his view of social intelligence and "Reason as
employed by historic rationalism." Historic rationalism "has tended to
carelessness, conceit, irresponsibility, and rigidity—in short absolutism."[10] The scientific rationality that Dewey defended as the appropriate method for moral and social philosophy was not superimposed
on experience from above in a fashion reminiscent of an order of universal, absolute, and transexperimental truth. Rather, "intelligence" was
defined along the following lines:

> Concrete suggestions arising from past experiences, developed
> and matured in the light of the needs and deficiencies of the
> present, employed as aims and methods of specific reconstruc-
> tion, and tested by success or failure in accomplishing the task
> of readjustment, suffice. To such empirical suggestions used in
> constructive fashion for new ends the name intelligence is
> given.[11]

In an introduction written in 1948 for an enlarged edition of *Recon-struction*, Dewey reflected on the quarter century that had passed since the book's original publication. Without mentioning Niebuhr, Dewey recognized and rejected an identifiably Niebuhrian criticism; namely, that "the work and office of philosophy [rest] upon a romantic exaggera-tion of what can be accomplished by 'intelligence.'" With great care Dewey suggested

> If the latter word were used as a synonym for what one impor-
> tant school of past ages called "reason" or "pure intellect," the
> criticism would be more than justified. But the word names
> something very different from what is regarded as the highest
> organ or "faculty" for laying hold of ultimate truths. It is a
> shorthand designation for great and ever-growing methods of
> observation, experiment and reflective reasoning which have in
> a very short time revolutionized the physical and, to a consider-
> able degree, the physiological conditions of life, but which have
> not as yet been worked out for application to what is itself dis-
> tinctively and basically *human*. It is a newcomer even in the
> physical field of inquiry; as yet it hasn't developed in the vari-
> ous aspects of the human scene. The reconstruction to be under-
> taken is ready-made. It is to carry over into any inquiry into
> human and moral subjects the kind of method (the method of
> observation, theory as hypothesis, and experimental test) by
> which understanding of physical nature has been brought to its
> present pitch.[12]

Niebuhr would certainly have agreed that such methods were per-fectly appropriate to an increased understanding of the human world. He would have done so on pragmatic grounds while outrightly rejecting the ideological theory of a "cultural lag" implied in Dewey's position. Cultural lag theories, for Niebuhr, did very little explaining. Instead, they reflected the historic drift of "scientific intelligence" toward the dogmatization of science—a phenomenon Niebuhr labeled *scientism*. Niebuhr would also have agreed that Dewey's view of intelligence was at odds with the conception of "Reason" involved in absolutistic "Rationalism." Yet his point—both at the time of Dewey's "Unity and Progress" and thereafter—was that Dewey's use of intelligence, however modest and pragmatic in appearance, remained deeply embedded in romantically overoptimistic views of both science and society. Thus, Dewey's disclaimer notwithstanding, the actual applications and expec-tations of "experimental intelligence" in Dewey's sociopolitical thought had profound affiliations with broader motifs belonging to liberal culture as a whole.

In "After Capitalism—What?" Niebuhr had argued that "social intelligence can have a part in guiding social impulse only if it does not commit the error of assuming that intelligence has destroyed and sublimated impulse to such a degree that impulse is no longer potent. That, "Niebuhr claimed, "is the real issue between liberalism and political realism."[13] Dewey believed that Niebuhr's viewpoint had hindered the achievement of a unity of thought and action on the radical front—an achievement that Dewey's two conditions were intended to address. Dewey's method would take into consideration both the "urgent needs and ills and measures which will cope with them" and the task "of forming an idea of the kind of society we desire to bring into existence, which will give continuity of direction to political effort."[14]

If these methods were pursued in rigorous experimental fashion, then the conditions of unifying radical thought and action could be accomplished. Dewey felt that his position was exempt from the illusions of a facile liberalism which Niebuhr had otherwise quite rightly identified and targeted. Niebuhr's mistake was that he unjustly associated this position with Dewey himself. Niebuhr, on his part, saw no reason to change his mind about Dewey's place among those whose liberalism was too rationalistic, too optimistic, and too far removed from the kind of realism so desperately needed in the arena of political reconstruction. Niebuhr persisted in this judgment right on through Dewey's most sophisticated statement on these matters (*Liberalism and Social Action* in 1935), as we shall have occasion to note later on. Niebuhr described the liberal as "an idealist who imagines that his particular type of education or his special kind of religious idealism will accomplish what history has never before revealed: the complete sublimation of the natural impulse of a social group."[15] Throughout his career Niebuhr continued to apply this interpretation to Dewey's social thought. In 1933 he was willing to concede that, once the brutalities of social conflict are acknowledged and accepted, then and only then was there "every possibility of introducing very important ethical elements into the struggle."[16] Consequently, Niebuhr could maintain that

> All this does not mean that intellectual and moral idealism are futile. They are needed to bring decency and fairness into any system of society; for no basic reorganization of society will ever guarantee the preservation of humaneness if good men do not preserve it. Furthermore, the intelligence of a dominant group will determine in what measure it will yield in time under pres-

sure or to what degree it will defend its entrenched positions so
uncompromisingly that an orderly retreat becomes impossible
and a disorderly rout envelops the whole of society in chaos.
That ought to be high enough stake for those of us to play for
who are engaged in the task of education and moral suasion
among the privileged. If such conclusions seem unduly cynical
they will seem so only because the moral idealists of the past
century, both religious and rational, have been unduly sentimental in their estimates of human nature.[17]

The degree to which Niebuhr and Dewey actually differed simply in
terms of diverging emphases, rather than because of substantive "estimates of human nature," is a legitimate point of debate—particularly
in the context of the early 1930s. Later on, of course, Niebuhr would
sharpen and deepen his criticism of the effectiveness of "moral idealism"
in bringing "decency and fairness into any system of society." Indeed, his
conception of the relationship between love and justice gained such a
measure of sophistication that his use of the sort of moral language just
employed was totally abandoned. Niebuhr eventually came to recognize
this language as a part of the tradition of liberal idealism that he had yet
to exorcise from his own thought.
    Dewey found the force of Niebuhr's criticism of the liberal view of in-
telligence quite disturbing. He chose to reply openly and directly to
Niebuhr through an article written for the *New Republic* in April 1934.
The controversy that Niebuhr initiated in *Moral Man* had broadened out
since 1932 and captured increasing attention among the liberal intellectual community to which both he and Dewey belonged. Dewey's response
was published on April 25 under the title "Intelligence and Power."
    Dewey acknowledged the relative ease with which critics can make
appear ridiculous "those who contend that intelligence is capable of
exercising a significant role in social affairs" and further advocate that
it have "a much larger part" in such matters.[18] With an indirect reference
to the type of religious orientation Niebuhr represented, Dewey cited
"habit, custom and tradition" as examples of the difficulty intelligence
has making its way in the world. He chided Niebuhr by suggesting that
"at critical times, widespread illusions, generated by intense emotions,
have played a role in comparison with which the influence of intelligence
is negligible."[19] Dewey's program aimed at bringing the critical-experi-
mental intelligence of the natural sciences to bear against those debilitating forces of "habit, custom and tradition" which had reinforced
vested interest and hindered *intelligent* social redirection. According to
Dewey, critics like Niebuhr mistakenly believed that his advocacy of social intelligence was oblivious to the inertial forces of self-interest. This

constituted a prima facie case in opposition to an appeal against intelligence per se. Dewey resented the fact that "Mr. Niebuhr imputes to me middle-class prejudices in ignoring the role of class interest and conflict in social affairs!" Niebuhr, Dewey said, charged me with

> a great exaggeration of the possibilities of education in spite of the fact that I have spent a good deal of energy in urging that no genuine education is possible without active participation in actual conditions, and have pointed out that economic interests are the chief cause why this change in education is retarded and deflected.[20]

Dewey's view was that "intelligence has no power *per se*." To the extent that Niebuhr attacked a type of abstract rationalism he was quite correct. In this regard Dewey concurred with David Hume, who, though overemphasizing the opposite point of view, "was nearer the truth . . . when he said 'reason is and always must be the slave of passion'—or interest." To the extent that a doctrinaire rationalism prevailed which regarded intelligence as "something complete in itself" quite separate from action, then Dewey "should more than agree with the critics who doubt that intelligence has any particular role in bringing about needed social change."[21] Such a view represented the separation of theory and practice so characteristic of past history and so representative of everything against which Dewey relentlessly inveighed.

Dewey acknowledged the "power" of dominant, and often unjust, interest in society and knew that "intelligence becomes a *power* only when it is brought into the operation of other forces than itself."[22] Because in the context of social struggle the dominant force was never the exclusive force, "the real problem," as Dewey described it, "is whether there are strong interests now active which can best succeed by adopting the method of experimental intelligence into their struggles, or whether they too should rely upon the use of methods that may have brought the world to its present estate, only using them the other way around."[23] Just as the natural sciences once had to free themselves from dominant interests rooted in ignorance, so too the methods of rational intelligence represented by the social sciences must overcome contemporary forms of ignorance. Dewey insisted that he knew very well that "interests" and "classes" are inseparable from this struggle. Just as the natural sciences won their way by finding "a lodgment in other social interests than the dominant ones and [were] backed by the constantly growing influence of other interests,"[24] so too the social sciences would succeed to the extent that they achieved similar support.

Dewey was adamant in insisting that intelligence was not a mere reflex divorced from action. However, as reason operated neither independent of, nor prior to, action, he felt it was quite an injustice to represent him as advocating a form of intelligence separate from, or oblivious to, the interplay of interests in the social arena. The issue as Dewey viewed it was only whether or not interests could be sufficiently enlightened so as to come to rely on methods of experimental intelligence, rather than on traditional methods that had brought us to our present sorry state of affairs.

It was precisely here that the issue between Dewey and Niebuhr was joined. Dewey disparaged the older "methods that had brought the world to its present estate" and, from Niebuhr's perspective, romanticized "experimental intelligence" as something to be set over against the "methods" of the past. Niebuhr rejected any such conception of detached intelligence. He also regarded the past as often superior in political wisdom to the kind of nonsense advanced by those who touted "experimental intelligence" as if it were a panacea in human affairs. Moreover, much of what Dewey labeled the *methods of the past* Niebuhr saw as legitimate responses to certain perennial aspects of individual and collective life—methods with which any realistic *political* intelligence must forever contend. Dewey saw the traditional methods in terms of an unfortunate recrudescence of institutional history—of some recurring legacy of the past to be overcome by combatively setting experimental intelligence vis-á-vis the forces of irrationality. In a later context, reflecting an additional fifteen years of reflection on his own part, Niebuhr observed:

> According to Dewey the divisive elements in human culture are vestigial remnants of outmoded religious prejudices which will yield to the universal perspectives which modern education will inculcate. This education will create practical unanimity among men of good will. Modern culture was generating new fierce ideological conflicts, not remotely connected with traditional religious concepts while Professor Dewey was writing this book [*A Common Faith*].[25]

During the period after 1936 Niebuhr steadily developed a theological framework for his earlier understanding of conflict and self-interest. He increasingly saw the forces of conflicting interests to be rooted in the self's inordinate and persistent self-love. In 1944 Niebuhr observed that although secular thought uniformly rejected the doctrine of original sin, this doctrine, understood in terms of self-love,

> makes an important contribution to any adequate social and political theory the lack of which has robbed bourgeois theory of

real wisdom; for it emphasizes a fact which every page of human history attests. Through it one may understand that no matter how wide the perspectives which the human mind may reach, how broad the loyalties which the human imagination may conceive, how universal the community which human statecraft may organize, or how pure the aspirations of the saintliest idealists may be, there is no level of human moral or social achievement in which there is not some corruption of inordinate self-love.[26]

Niebuhr sadly, but surely, acknowledged the perennial effects of self-love across the entire range of existence from the individual to the collective life of human beings. In such a context "experimental intelligence" of the sort Dewey recommended had only marginal application to the domain of politics and history. The reason was that neither experimental intelligence nor its advocates were as exempt from the effects of self-interest as was sometimes imagined. In other words, there was no "freed intelligence" in the sense Dewey used the term. Intelligence, for Niebuhr, was always tainted by self-interest and therefore no "interests" were as rationally enlightened as rationalists proclaimed them to be.

Returning to the controversy of 1934, we see that, while displaying a modicum of displeasure at what he believed to be Niebuhr's misconception of his views of intelligence and education, Dewey claimed that "the question is not a personal one . . . and it is not worth notice on personal grounds." His countercharge was

Just because dominant economic interests are the chief cause for non-use of the method of intelligence to control social change, opponents of the method play into the hands of those interests when they discourage the potentialities of this method. In my judgment they perpetuate the present confusion, and they strengthen the forces that will introduce evil consequences into the result of any change, however revolutionary it may be, brought about by means into which the method of intelligence has not entered. "Education" even in its wildest sense cannot do everything. But what is accomplished without education, again in its broadest sense, will be badly done and much of it will have to be done over.[27]

Dewey felt that his view of intelligence was not a naively romantic one as Niebuhr had charged and that, all things considered, it represented the only viable alternative we possess. He concluded his essay by insisting that "the very fact that intelligence in the past has operated for narrow ends and in behalf of class interests is a reason for putting a high estimate upon its possible role in social control, not a reason for disparaging it."[28] Dewey, as Richard Fox puts it, "has some reason to insist that the radical movement commit itself to a belief in 'intelligence' if it was to build a social order."[29] Yet Niebuhr was not attacking "intelligence." The point he wished to make (as stated in a response to George A. Coe's criticism that Niebuhr simply dismissed the power of rational and moral force in *Moral Man*) was that "I believe that once rational and religious idealists stop fooling themselves and recognize the basic fact of a social struggle in society they will be the more able to direct it morally and rationally."[30] Niebuhr went on to insist that there

> has of course been a cumulation of social experience and intellectual discipline [with respect to human intelligence in history]. I place some hope in that because I think it will teach us how to build an ordered and decent society, *not by vainly hoping that selfish men will become unselfish but by placing every possible social and inner check upon their egoism.* By recognizing that men will remain selfish to the end we will be saved from the errors of both a liberalism which wants to achieve political ends by purely ethical means and a radicalism which hopes to achieve ethical ends by purely political means.[31] (Italics mine.)

Niebuhr's point, perhaps stated most succinctly in 1936 in *Reflections on the End of an Era*, was that the "counsels of the wise man" and the advocates of the "cultural lag" theory were forever attributing "to *disinterested ignorance* what ought be ascribed to *interested intelligence*"[32] (italics mine). History, both now as well as in the past, was infected with the taint of ideology. *All* intelligence is *interested* intelligence and any historical retrospect that sees the past as a matter of *disinterested* ignorance in contrast to an ostensibly enlightened present is patently foolish.

Nonetheless, Dewey's central reaction to Niebuhr focused elsewhere; namely, on Niebuhr's appeal to the function of "illusion" as a transrational spring of motivation. Niebuhr's rhetorical flair and penchant for exaggeration brought Dewey's somewhat snide and biting criticism down on his head. Dewey wrote that although "the net outcome of the domination of the methods of institutional force, custom and illusion does not encourage one to look with great hope upon dependence on new combinations among them for future progress," nonetheless,

> The situation is such that it is calculated to make one look around, even if from sheer desperation, for some other method, however desperate. And under such circumstances, it also

seems as if the effort to stimulate resort to the method of intelligence might present itself as at least one desperate recourse, if not the only one that remains untried. In view of the influence of collective illusion in the past, some case might be made out for the contention that even if it be an illusion, exaltation of intelligence and experimental method is worth a trial. Illusion for illusion, this particular one may be better than those upon which humanity has usually depended.[33]

Quite obviously, Dewey did not seriously regard his version of "intelligence" as an "illusion" in the sense that Niebuhr employed the term—in spite of the quip that "illusion for illusion" the "exaltation of intelligence and experimental method is worth a trial." This particular passage footnoted Niebuhr's observation in *Moral Man* that "the truest visions of religions are illusions which may be partially realized by being resolutely believed. For what religion believes to be true is not wholly true but ought to be true; and may become true if its truth is not doubted."[34] Niebuhr voiced the Jamesean pragmatic perspective that humankind requires supra-rational "hopes" to sustain the earnest sense of a genuine and worthwhile struggle to life. Niebuhr wrote a rather startling closing paragraph to his *Moral Man and Immoral Society* that illustrated Dewey's concern—a paragraph for which Niebuhr would publish a retraction within the year. The paragraph read:

> In the task of that redemption the most effective agents will be men who have substituted some new illusions for the abandoned ones. The most important of these illusions is that the collective life of mankind can achieve perfect justice. It is a very valuable illusion for the moment; for justice cannot be approximated if the hope of its perfect realizaiton does not generate *a sublime madness in the soul. Nothing but such madness will do battle with malignant power and "spiritual weakness in high places."*[35] (Emphasis mine.)

Niebuhr publicly admonished himself for the extreme to which he had gone[36] and eventually added a warning in a later edition of *Moral Man* in which he wrote: "The illusion is dangerous because it encourages terrible fanaticisms. It must therefore be brought under the control of reason. One can only hope that reason will not destroy it before its work is done."[37]

Dewey, later in *A Common Faith*, simply expected that rationally based hopes would do the job. Nonetheless, Dewey's own appeal to the pivotal role of imagination in constituting the "religious" dimension of life rested on "supra-rational" notions of its own.

Niebuhr saw Dewey's vision of experimental intelligence as a kind
of religious vision—quite as much as any other vision that finally came
to rest on "ultrarational hopes and passions." Intelligence, in Dewey's
thought, was surely an "ideal" whose realization might never be fully attainable. The religious quality here was rooted in a set of historical and
cultural conditions which "gave a momentary plausibility to the hope
that human reason could create a universal social harmony in the
world."[38] Since the conception was idealized beyond all connection with
the realities of political existence, it operated, in Niebuhr's judgment, as
Dewey's "illusion." More important, as it was tied to a conception of disinterested science with its alleged capacity to apply an objective set of
standards to historical strife, Dewey's vision struck Niebuhr as "illusory" in the worst sense. It was not only a hope beyond rational limits but
also gave expression to dangerous utopian misconceptions regarding the
political sphere.

Given religion's abysmal historical record, Dewey had a pronounced
confidence in the translation of scientific rationality to the whole of life,
including the domain of social problems. His rhetorical question "What
are the alternatives to experimental intelligence?" was given an equally
rhetorical answer, "dogmatism, reinforced by the weight of unquestioned custom and tradition, the disguised or open play of class interests,
dependence upon brute force and violence." Niebuhr, on the other hand,
regarded such confidence as inordinate and took exception to what he
viewed as the dangerously exaggerated claims of the Western world's
most recent dogma—a dogma, as we have seen, on which he pinned the
name *scientism*. Niebuhr used the term *scientism* to point to all dogmatic
claims made in the name of science that go beyond the strictures of science as such. He often employed the charge in two ways: first, to find a
place for religion by insisting that, at bottom, most pretentious claims
made in the name of science were themselves religious; and second, to
point to dangerously unrealistic utopian claims made on behalf of
human political existence that parade under the guise of "scientific objectivity" or "scientific rationality." Niebuhr moved back and forth between both uses of *scientism* in his critiques of Dewey. On the one hand,
Dewey simply failed to grasp the sad fact that class interest and the presence of force were recurring perennial features of the quest for justice.
In this sense Niebuhr's critical reservations regarding "reason" and
"freed intelligence" reflected a crucial and agonizing debate on the extremely important issue of the limits of *political* rationality. On the other
hand, Niebuhr indicted Dewey for underestimating the degree to which
there was a "religious" dimension underlying all "faiths" by which all
life was actually lived. Such "faiths" involved a very real and dangerous

risk of fanaticism, which was potentially present even under the guise of "reason," as history had shown.

Dewey, as everyone knows, was not prone to the sin of fanaticism. Yet what Niebuhr regarded as a transrational "religiosity"—the mild and moving "dogma" of an inspired humanist—comes through Dewey's rather stirring paragraph at the close of *Reconstruction in Philosophy*:

> Poetry, art, religion are precious things. They cannot be maintained by lingering in the past and futilely wishing to restore what the movement of events in science, industry and politics has destroyed. They are an out-flowering of thought and desires that unconsciously converge into a disposition of imagination as a result of thousands and thousands of daily episodes and contact. They cannot be willed into existence or coerced into being. The wind of the spirit bloweth where it listeth and the kingdom of God in such things does not come with observation. But while it is impossible to retain and recover by deliberate volition old sources of religion and art that have been discredited, it is possible to expedite development of the vital sources of a religion and art that are yet to be. Not indeed by action directly aimed at their production, but by substituting faith in the active tendencies of the day for dread and dislike of them, and by the courage of intelligence to follow whither social and scientific changes direct us. We are weak today in ideal matters because intelligence is divorced from aspiration. The bare force of circumstance compels us onwards in the daily detail of our beliefs and acts, but our deeper thoughts and desires turn backwards. When philosophy shall have co-operated with the course of events and made clear and coherent the meaning of the daily detail, science and emotion will interpenetrate, practice and imagination will embrace. Poetry and religious feeling will be the unforced flowers of life. To further this articulation and revelation of the meanings of the current course of events is the task and problem of philosophy in the days of transition.[39]

5

A "Common Faith"

Dewey's exhortation at the end of *Reconstruction in Philosophy* was both moving and characteristically American, especially in 1920 when the book originally appeared. The religious character of Dewey's humanistic naturalism, however, found its most explicit formulation in three essays which formed the Terry Lectures delivered at Yale University in 1933, a series devoted to the theme of science and religion. These lectures were published as *A Common Faith* in 1934 and have become, as Horace Friess characterized them, the "statement of ideas on religion with which Dewey will be lastingly identified."[1] Dewey's willingness to undertake a sustained treatment of the subject of religion initially bothered many of his philosophical colleagues.[2] After all, Dewey, only four years earlier had confessed that he was not "able to attach much importance to religion as a philosophic problem" largely because "that attachment seems to" require "a subordination of candid philosophic thinking to the alleged but factitious needs of some special set of convictions."[3]

Dewey had delivered an address in 1892 on "Christianity and Democracy" before the University of Michigan Students' Christian Association.[4] And intermittently over the years he had touched on the issue of religion in one form or another. Yet it is the case, as Willard Arnett pointed out, that Dewey, "for the largest part of his long career was blithely unconcerned with religion and religious problems."[5] Once he was prompted to deliver the Terry Lectures, however, Dewey's mature mind focused on the subject of religion in a fashion that allowed him both to assess religion in its traditional sense and to use that assessment as a counterpoint for developing his own interpretation of the religious aspect of experience.

Herbert Schneider and Horace Friess provided some interesting background on what prompted Dewey to write *A Common Faith*. According to an interview with Schneider in 1967, Dewey was pressured into speaking on religion at Columbia "because a few of us were working on religion against odds at the Union Seminary. We thought it would be nice to have Dewey talk about religion just to tease the Union people." Dewey resisted. Nonetheless, it was quietly advertised that Dewey would deliver a lecture at Columbia on the subject. When the word spread to the general public via the Teachers' College people, such an overflowing crowd turned out that the lecture had to be moved across Broadway (to Barnard College, in Friess's account of the incident). According to Schneider "Dewey was so irritated by the whole business that he hardly said a thing and afterwards he said to me, 'I hate to do this sort of thing to satisfy a lot of people that must want to see a monkey hang by his tail.' "[6] Friess's rendition of the story during an interview also given at Southern Illinois University one year earlier essentially corroborates Schneider's account, but adds a unique and illuminating perspective. Friess places the event in or around 1930 and indicates Dewey's embarrassment or annoyance "at the appearance that something sensational was about to happen in that he would now talk to a general audience on religion which he didn't usually do." Afterwards, in Friess's account

> what [Dewey] said was quite interesting. He said that "classically religion is generally praised and appreciated as an approach to the eternal verities and to something above and beyond the changes and the ephemeral circumstances of our every day life." And he added, "You know that in my point of view in philosophy, I've taken occasion to criticize this overemphasis of classic philosophy on the stable, the constant, the permanent, so I want to say now, on behalf of religion that if you don't look at just the theologies, and the dogmas, and the doctrines, but pick up the devotional literature, the hymnology, the prayers, the meditations, you will enter into a very variegated world that often expresses in quite intimate ways the specific circumstances because they are intensely pertinent to somebody in a given situation." He said, "I would rather like to throw my emphasis tonight on that side of the importance of religion as a channel in which that kind of expression can flourish." It was a nice point. I haven't come across any recording of that talk in print or anywhere else; I doubt if you would encounter anyone who would mention it.[7]

Of particular importance in this account is that approximately three to four years prior to his Terry Lectures delivered at Yale in January 1934, Dewey had emphasized the function of religion as a channel through which the highly specific and personal side of the "religious" is able to flourish. Friess wanted to record the fact that Dewey had these things on his mind that night back in approximately 1930, even though a few years later he would "approach the problem of a common faith, a universal faith."[8]

Schneider quoted Dewey as saying that the constructive aspect of *A Common Faith* is "as far as I'm concerned, just a restatement of my earlier faith that I got at the University of Vermont through Marsh and Coleridge.'" Schneider went on to say, "I think if you go back to Coleridge, it's easy enough to see that by *Common Faith* [Dewey] simply meant faith in the most general sense and it's very close to Coleridge in revision of Kant, the continuity of the ideal and the real is what he had in mind."[9] Long after his initial contact with Coleridge, Dewey would also find that position reinforced through Edward Scribner Ames at the University of Chicago.

Dewey's way of conceiving the distinction between "religion" and the "religious" reinforced his longstanding antisupernaturalism. It also provided the basis and the rationale for his defense of what he termed *natural piety,* a sense of the religious that was "both natural and moral."[10] In effect, Dewey aimed at disassociating (and thereby rescuing) the "religious" from "religion" in order to naturalize and, thereby, humanize the religious life. Denying that there was anything denoted by the noun substantive *religion* (other than a mere collective term pointing not to a universal but only to a multitude of religions), he sought to shift the discussion to "the quality of experience that is designated by an adjective," the *religious.*[11] The *religious,* for Dewey, "denotes nothing in the way of a specifiable entity, either institutional or as a system of beliefs" (in contradistintion to the "religions"). Rather it denotes "attitudes that may be taken toward every object and every proposed end or ideal."[12]

Both Friess and Randall have observed that there was something essentially polemical governing the distinction Dewey made between the two terms. Friess claimed,

> To set "religion and religions" as institutional entities over against "the religious" as a quality of life thus meant for Dewey far more than the making of a formal or semantic distinction. As he developed the contrast between "religion" and "the religious," he gathered into it: his reasons for a naturalistic outlook rejecting "supernaturalism"; his case for "co-operative inquiry" and "idealizing imagination" as reliable methods; his envisioning of a greater freedom as dependent not just on "particular resolve," but on knowledge, imagination, and "the organic plentitude of our being"; his lifelong effort for a more thorough common culture expanding the values of natural human relations in democratic society. Dewey thus associated this opposition of

"religion *versus* the religious" with the most pervasive and crucial issues in world-view, in method, in psychological attitude, in society and culture.[13]

John Herman Randall, Jr., put the matter more forcefully still. In an important essay, "The Religion of Shared Experience," written for a commemorative volume celebrating Dewey's eightieth birthday, Randall pointed to a weakness Dewey displayed in his inability to either properly assess or duly appreciate the institutional-sectarian side of religious history. Randall suggested that the reason for this weakness rested with Dewey's commitment to defend the "humanistic and naturalistic humanitarianism," which was fast becoming the operative religion among intellectuals in America. "There is about Dewey's views on religion," Randall wrote, "the kind of intolerance of other and alien religious values that springs from his own allegiance."[14] Indeed, Dewey was a polemicist at the point of *religious* conviction. He had no qualms in asserting "that the association of religion with the *supernatural* tends by its own nature to breed the dogmatic and the divisive spirit."[15] Dewey was convinced that Western "religions" with their historic links to supernaturalism were in radical tension with both the method of scientific inquiry and the forms of democratic association. His own polemics, over against this heritage, had constructive aims. To achieve the aim of naturalizing and humanizing the religious life, the "religious" had to be rescued from the supernaturalistic "religions." His naturalism, in effect, had a missionary side to it.[16] Dewey openly and vehemently sought to reassert the continuity of men and women with the natural and social worlds. "Religious qualities . . . are to be found in the ordinary and natural processes of living," according to Randall,[17] and therefore from Dewey's perspective it was the "religions" that are deeply *irreligious*. The separation of humankind from nature threatened to obliterate the authentically "religious" aspect of human life. It is in this context that one is to take Dewey's rather strident statement: "The opposition between religious values as I conceive them and religions is not to be bridged. Just because the release of these values is so important, their identification with the creeds and cults of religions must be dissolved."[18] Randall, therefore, appears to be quite correct when he commented that

Dewey is no religious liberal forced to the gradual abandonment of positions no longer intellectually respectable. His is rather a positive and aggressive critique of the religious tradition, in the interest not primarily of intellectual values, of theoretical consistency with scientific beliefs, but of the religious function itself. The things he wishes to get rid of are not just inessential parts of the tradition; it is essential to get rid of them if religion is to do its proper work. They belong, that is, to a competing faith that serves false gods.[19]

To put it even more forcefully, the traditions of the "religions" must be overcome and put behind us if the "religious" is ever to rearise in our midst.

When Dewey spoke of the "religious" he was not pointing to an experience which is itself religious. He deemed this favored tactic of late nineteenth and early twentieth century theological apologists to be a subterfuge that was then "used to validate a belief in some special kind of object and also to justify some special kind of practice."[20] The "religious" experience was never to be "marked off from experience as aesthetic, scientific, moral, political; from experience as companionship and friendship."[21] His position was that the religious is a quality of experience which may conceivably belong to any or all experiences as such. This meant that although the actual experiences underlying religion were not to be questioned, we must forever question the various interpretations of the religious which have been "imported by borrowing without criticism from ideas that [are] current in the surrounding culture." Dewey wanted an interpretation of the "religious" that arises "from the experience itself with the aid of such scientific resources as may be available."[22] His professed aim

is to indicate what happens when religious experience is already set aside as something *sui generis*. The actual religious quality in the experience described is the *effect* produced, the better adjustment in life and its conditions, not the manner and cause of its production. The way in which the experience operated, its function, determines its religious value.[23]

According to Dewey the "religious" was, at core, an attitude—a generic and enduring change in attitude. This involved the means whereby the more inclusive and deep-seated changes of our being in its entirety toward the world are effected. Dewey was willing to say that a religious outlook is discovered whenever and wherever such a change in attitude occurs. The "religious" arises out of the plethora of experience and is neither tied to a religion nor occasioned by any object regarded as intrinsically religious. According to Dewey the tradition of Western "religions" had prevented "the religious quality of experience from coming to consciousness and finding the expression that is appropriate to present conditions, intellectual and moral."[24]

Dewey considered "the religious attitude" as signifying "something

that is bound through imagination to a *general* attitude."[25] Following
Santayana's lead, Dewey saw the "religious" as a product of "intervening
imagination." That is, although it shared an imaginative base with
poetry, the religious, unlike poetry, enters profoundly into life rather
than merely playing upon it. In Dewey's pragmatic understanding of life,
facts rarely stand by themselves unrelated to human observation. Quite
to the contrary, "facts are usually observed with reference to some practical end and purpose, and that end is presented only imaginatively."[26] It
is important to realize that only in the context of imaginative extension
is human life experienced as teleological, as having aims and purposes.
The teleological is a product of the imaginative capacity to project ideas
of "wholes," be they the whole self or a universe, that is, the world envisioned as a "whole." Having aims and purposes is a unitive experience
and belongs to the province of imagination rather than to the domain of
knowledge. Dewey wrote that

> The connection between imagination and the harmonizing
> of the self is closer than is usually thought. The idea of a whole,
> whether of the whole personal being or of the world, is an imag-
> inative, not a literal idea. The limited world of our observation
> and reflection becomes the Universe only through imaginative
> extension. It cannot be apprehended in knowledge nor realized
> in reflection. Neither observation, thought, nor practical activ-
> ity can attain that complete unification of the self which is
> called a whole. The *whole* self is an ideal, an imaginative projec-
> tion. Hence the idea of a thoroughgoing and deepseated har-
> monizing of the self with the Universe (as a name for the total-
> ity of conditions with which the self is connected) operates only
> through imagination . .[27]

The interaction between "self" and "world," for Dewey, was neither
simple nor easily described. He pointed out, however, that the constitution of the self was dependent on the influx of sources from beyond the
self, sources which were not a matter of conscious deliberation. Dewey
felt it is "pertinent to note that the unification of the self throughout the
ceaseless flux of what it does, suffers, and achieves cannot be attained in
terms of itself." This is the case precisely because "the self is always directed toward something beyond itself and so its own unification depends
upon the idea of the integration of the shifting scenes of the world into
that imaginative totality we call the universe."[28]
    Although this was an acknowledgment of the complexities of
human selfhood, it did not require a religious appeal in the traditional
sense. On purely psychological grounds the penchant of religionists to

opt for supernatural sources for making sense of the self in harmony with the Universe may be understandable. However, it was an appeal that failed to add anything "intelligible" to our understanding of ourselves and our world. Experience, after all, was "the manifestation of interactions of organism and environment" and possessed a thoroughly "natural" meaning for Dewey. Indeed, any "philosophic theory of experience must proceed from initially linking it with the processes and functions of life as the latter are disclosed in biological science"—acknowledging, of course, that human beings are "acculturated organisms," and as human beings are further "subject to the influences of culture, including use of definite means of communication."[29] The upshot of this was that a viable theory of experience must adhere to empirical method, as long as one understands that Dewey's "empricism" was, in terms of both precognitive and cognitive experience, "connective" and "relational."

In terms of its practical and moral import, "religious" faith, for Dewey, acknowledged the "intimate connection of imagination with ideal elements in experience"[30] Although this was widely recognized, it required a proper interpretation. Mistakes occurred when faith was thought to possess epistemological status and was thus viewed as "a kind of anticipatory vision of things that are now invisible because of the limitations of our finite and erring nature."[31] Faith was mistakenly believed to be a kind of "knowledge" having certain contents guaranteed by an appeal to their alleged "supernatural" author. If one interpreted faith properly, that is, in naturalistic terms, it could be seen to express a belief that "some end should be supreme over conduct" and not a conviction that a being or an object "exists as a truth for the intellect."[32] Horace Friess expressed the issue in the following way: in "viewing the whole corpus of Dewey's writings, one can see his thought on religion as hinging upon a choice between a faith in natural possibilities still to be realized at risk, and a faith that values are secure in that 'antecedent reality' of the world, which rests on the already complete Being of a Supernatural Order."[33]

Dewey saw faith in terms of "the unification of the self through allegiance to inclusive ideal ends, which imagination presents to us and to which the human will responds as worthy of controlling our desires and choices."[34] It is a practical affair in that it has wholly to do with the "conviction that some end should be supreme over conduct."[35]

This was, in broad outline, a Feuerbachian interpetation. Both the origin and character of the "religious" aspect of experience and the source and locus of ideal ends belong solely to this world. Dewey held that ideals, whether they be in existence or not, are confined entirely to the domain of "experience" understood naturally and culturally. Moreover, as Steven C. Rockefeller points out,

Dewey agrees with Feuerbach's assertion that there is a malig-
nant principle at work in traditional theism and supernaturalism. He see progress toward democracy and amicable
cooperation between the peoples of the world as requiring the
abandonment of moral absolutism and the supernaturalism
and transcendentalism that have nurtured it.[36]

Not all moral faith in ideal ends was "religious" in quality for
Dewey. He saw the religious dimension as " 'morality touched by emotion' only when the ends of moral conviction arouse emotions that are
not only intense but are actuated and supported by ends so inclusive that
they unify the self. The inclusiveness of the end in relation to both self
and the 'universe' to which an inclusive self is related is indispensable."[37] Again, it is important to realize that religion or the religions
failed dismally to introduce genuine religious perspective into life.
Quite the opposite is the case, namely, "whatever introduces genuine
perspective is religious"; that is, "whatever introduces perspective into
the piecemeal and shifting episodes of existence."[38]

It was noted in passing that one of Dewey's trenchant indictments of
religion focused on religion as a false set of intellectual claims. We live in
a world, Dewey claimed, where "nothing less than a revolution in the
'seat of intellectual authority' has taken place," a world in which "new
methods of inquiry and reflection have become for the educated man
today the final arbiter of all questions of fact, existence, and intellectual
assent."[39] This revolution was so profound that it transcended all the
specific areas of conflict with religion pertaining to this or that particular item of belief. In the final analysis it was a conflict between allegiance to an open self-correcting method of inquiry and loyalty to the
notion of unmodifiable fixed beliefs. Dewey brooked no compromise here
with respect to the heritage of the religious tradition. Because of these
"fixed beliefs" the scientific revolution struck at the very core of the authority claims made by traditional religion, a matter far better understood by fundamentalists than by liberals within the religious spectrum.

There was not "but one sure road of access to truth—the road of pa-
tient, cooperative inquiry operating by means of observation, experiment, record and controlled reflection."[40] This was a revolution in
methodology and was not bound up with any particular item of intellectual assent. Conversely, no items of intellectual (or pseudo-intellectual)
assent were to be considered exempt from the kind of open public
scrutiny characteristic of the method of "freed intelligence"; that is, scientific method in the broadest sense of that term. Efforts to rationalize
specific items of belief were not only authoritarian in nature, but had
also resulted in tremendous expenditures of wasted energy.

It must be clearly seen that all dualisms, traditional or modern, imply epistemological dualism, for Dewey, however blatant or subtle their forms might be. The "general tendency to mark off two distinct realms," he contended, one over which "science has jurisdiction, while" the other over which "special modes of immediate knowledge of religious objects have authority,"[41] is intolerable and ultimately insidious. Newer forms of dualism have appeared in contemporary culture that employ variations of the two-realm language such as the terms *dimensions* or *aspects* of reality. These are nothing more than restatements "of the old dualism between the natural and the supernatural, in terms better adapted to the cultural conditions of the present time."[42] The type of reasoning underlying these terminologies was purely circular. The tactic was nothing less than an evasive attempt to reintroduce the very thing that the new method of determining truth had called into question. Dewey saw no viable option other than scientific intelligence. "Science," Dewey insisted,

is not constituted by any particular body of subject-matter. It is constituted by a method, a method of changing beliefs by means of tested inquiry as well as of arriving at them. It is its glory, not its condemnation, that its subject-matter develops as the method is improved. There is no special subject-matter of belief that is sacrosanct. The identification of science with a particular set of beliefs and ideas is itself a hold-over of ancient and still current dogmatic habits of thought which are opposed to science in its actuality and which science is undermining.[43]

Dewey saw the "matrix of human relations," that is, culture rooted in nature, as the sole source of ideal values. Humankind's "idealizing imagination" has generated such values out of the natural goods of life itself. The human being was seen as a moral agent whose values and ideals arose out of the domain of natural piety. Values and ideals did not require the supernatural for either authentication or explanation. They are neither to be considered outside this world as antecedent actualities, nor impossible of attainment—at least in the sense of approximation. Richard Bernstein writes that for Dewey

It is important to emphasize that ends or ideals are ultimately chosen by man; man chooses ideals he considers worthy of controlling the guidance of his life. As such, ends or ideals are not fixed parts of a reality that is completely independent of us. Ideals that are imaginatively conceived are real in the sense that they have an undeniable power in action.[44]

The ideals to which we aspire are not the products of fantasy; they are not will-o'-the-wisps pulled out of thin air. The ideals after which we strive are born of human imagination and are supported in the world of experience as real possiblities. Dewey claimed that "we are in the presence neither of ideals completely embodied in existence nor yet of ideals that are merely rootless ideals, fantasies, utopias. For there are forces in nature and society that generate and support the ideals."[45]

Dewey saw himself as a realist here, rather than as either a cynic or a romantic idealist. He knew that our control over nature was both partial and precarious at best. And although human beings rightly "strive to direct natural and social forces to humane ends . . . unqualified absolutistic statements about the omnipotence of such endeavors reflect egoism rather than intelligent courage. . . . Natural piety," Dewey remarks, "is not of necessity either a fatalistic acquiescence in natural happenings or a romantic idealization of the world."[46]

Quite aside from his persistent charge that Dewey was indeed the romantic idealist that he denied that he was, Niebuhr, overall, was quite consistent in finding justification for religion in the context of the overarching and haunting futility of a universe without meaning. Dewey posed the question as to whether the universe in which we are lodged is friendly to human beings. Aside from the problem as to whether questions regarding the "universe" made sense, his stated position was that in no matter what form this question was put, the answer was not an absolute or unqualified one. Following leads suggested by his reading of James Henry Breasted's *The Dawn of Conscience*, Dewey considered nature quite friendly with respect to the rise and development of "conscience and character" in human beings. Yet that was about the best that could be claimed.

For Dewey, "an intellectual view of the religious function" was finally based on the awareness "of continuing choice directed toward ideal ends" and we must rest content with that. If one is not an absolutist— and Dewey was clearly not that—then what remained was a belief in growth as the highest moral category pertinent to questions of valuation in human life. Such growth was "not confined to conscience and character" alone, but extended also "to discovery, learning and knowledge, to creation in the arts, to furtherance of ties that hold men together in mutual aid and affection."[47] Undoubtedly with individuals such as Niebuhr in mind, Dewey observed that "those who will have all or nothing cannot be satisfied with this answer. Emergence and growth are not enough for them. They want something more than growth accompanied by toil and pain. They want final achievement."[49]

Apart from the issue of wanting final achievement, Niebuhr's attitude toward Dewey's view of growth as the highest human value focused

on the elements of normativity and relativism in Dewey's thought. Writing fifteen years after *A Common Faith*, Niebuhr—utilizing passages
from Dewey's *Democracy and Education* (1916)—claimed,

> John Dewey's pragmatism is quite innocent of the taint of
> moral cynicism which is frequently levelled at it by the advo-
> cates of law. . . . he seems at times to believe that growth and de-
> velopment are themselves a norm to which life may conform.
> "Since there is nothing in reality to which growth is relative
> save more growth," he [Dewey] declares, "there is nothing to
> which education is relative save more education. . . . The criter-
> ion of value in education is the extent to which it creates the de-
> sire for more growth."[49]

Niebuhr, of course, detected normative elements in all of this which
exacerbated the circularity of Dewey's "evolutionary relativism." He
noted that "this confidence in growth as a norm of life is qualified by the
belief that historical development moved in a particular direction. For
Dewey the direction included both freedom and justice."[50] Niebuhr
might have added that for Dewey this direction also included an abiding
commitment to the value of scientific inquiry. His charge, however, was
that forms of modern relativism such as Dewey's "usually implicitly accept some version of the Christian norm which they explicitly deny."[51]
Five years earlier, while writing his "vindication of democracy,"
Niebuhr, in a somewhat expanded version of the same indictment, saw
Dewey as looking "forward to the cultural unification of the community
upon the basis of a 'common faith' embodied in the characteristic credos
of bourgeois liberalism."[52]

Dewey pondered whether a religion based on natural piety and devoted to the task of working toward this-worldly ideals with no assurance that such ideals would prevail could possess the moving power of
traditional religion. Certainly he was convinced that if there "were men
and women actuated throughout the length and breadth of human relations with the faith and ardor that have at times marked historic religions the consequences would be incalculable."[53] He maintained that
"there is no opposition between [intelligence] and emotion," and that not
only is intelligence—as distinct from the older conception of reason—
"inherently involved in action,"[54] but that "there is such a thing as faith
in intelligence becoming religious in quality."[55]

What intelligence could achieve, however, lacked the finality as-
pired to by traditional religion. Knowledge based on intelligence had a
tentative and hypothetical character, and it was always accompanied by
the doubts with which intelligence is moved. Such doubts "are signs of

faith, not of a pale and impotent skepticism. We doubt," Dewey exclaimed, "in order that we may find out, not because some inaccessible supernatural lurks beyond whatever *we* can know."[56] An intelligent faith, therefore, was basically positive although never certain. It was actively outreaching, however, and never paralized by the doubt that occasioned it. Intelligence seeking its way toward ideal ends within the context of human life itself, was, for Dewey, our "common faith."

In the final analysis as Dewey portrayed it, scientific intelligence and democratic structures and procedures constituted the substantive ideals commanding religious response. Dewey's position was uncompromising. The older options were simply no longer available to us in light of rational criteria, however much they might strike a cord with our psychological desires. The two cultural revolutions of science and democracy rendered the desirability of supernatural comforts a moot issue. Scientific method had made theology a nonissue insofar as philosophic inquiry was concerned. Moreover, the revolutionary alternative arising out of the sociopolitical "conditions under which human beings associate with one another" had undercut the types of religious and political control that, in the past, inhibited the freedom of "idealizing imagination."

Dewey's summation of the "common faith" reflected not only his own "religious" vision but also the ardor of his faith in that vision:

> We who now live are parts of a humanity that extends into the remote past, a humanity that has interacted with nature. The things in civilization we most prize are not of ourselves. They exist by grace of the doings and sufferings of the continuous human community in which we are a link. Ours is the responsibility of conserving, transmitting, rectifying and expanding the heritage of values we have received that those who come after us may receive it more solid and secure, more widely accessible and more generously shared than we have received it. Here are all the elements for a religious faith that shall not be confined to sect, class, or race. Such a faith has always been implicitly the common faith of mankind. It remains to make it explicit and militant.[57]

If Dewey's plan to write a major work on the subject of religion originally bothered some of his colleagues because of the undeserved attention he would be devoting to the topic, his published work bothered Niebuhr for just the opposite reason. It disturbed Niebuhr, not so much for its content and approach, but rather for its extrme brevity. In a review of Dewey's book for *The Nation* in September 1934, Niebuhr wrote that "this little volume . . . is something of a footnote on religion added by America's leading philosopher to his life work in philosophy." The effort "is disappointing only in the sense that it is too brief to do full justice to the problem or allow the author scope in elaborating his thesis on religion."[58]

Niebuhr's description of Dewey's effort as a "footnote" to a leading philosopher's life work was not a pejorative remark. In point of fact it was quite accurate in its representation of what Dewey's *A Common Faith* was attempting to accomplish. Niebuhr's statement was in line with Richard Bernstein's observation that those who see *A Common Faith* as Dewey's attempt to provide a "philosophy of religion" are quite mistaken. Instead, Bernstein contends, "it is rather an expression of what might be called Dewey's 'natural piety.' In this sense, Dewey's treatment of the religious attitude and quality is the culmination of his entire philosophy. We discover here how the pieces 'add up,' and how Dewey viewed man in relation to this universe that he encounters."[59]

The publication of *A Common Faith* occasioned a controversy over Dewey's willingness to employ the word *God*. Although Sidney Hook advised him not to use the term, Dewey chose to utilize it in spite of Hook's strenuous objections.[60] Niebuhr's review did not join the pseudo-issue as to whether Dewey was or was not a theist. Indeed, Niebuhr fully acknowledged that "Dr. Dewey's criticism of supernaturalism is most central to his own philosophical position."[61] Neither was Niebuhr of a mind to place Dewey in the pantheistic camp. He clearly recognized that "Dewey's empiricism and naturalism are in . . . obvious conflict with the presuppositions of the historic religions."[62]

Dewey, after all, had signed "A Humanist Manifesto" the year prior to the publication of *A Common Faith*,[63] and while claiming that "it is this *active* relation between ideal and actual to which I would give the name 'God,' " he immediately followed with the afterthought that "I would not insist that the name *must* be given."[64] Robert E. Fitch in his intriguing essay "John Dewey—the 'Last Protestant' " noted that whereas

> John Dewey's anticlericalism was implicit . . . his antisupernaturalism was explicit. If the anticlericalism was merely implicit, perhaps that was a part of his charity and tolerance towards all persons; and then, again, perhaps it was just a divine innocence on his part of the fact that the church really continued to exist in his day. Supernaturalism, however, he saw as one of the chief diseases to infect the human mind.[65]

Perhaps Fitch's view that the "God" language was a residual hangover from Dewey's religious affiliations with Protestant liberalism is an adequate account of its presence in the terminology of Dewey's philosophy. In effect, Dewey's proclivity to cling to such traditional forms of religious language exemplifies Fitch's image of the "last Protestant."

Although Niebuhr realized that Dewey stood in supreme conflict with the presuppositions of traditional religion, he agreed with Horace Friess that Dewey "associated this opposition of 'religion versus the religious' with the most pervasive and crucial issues in world-view, in method, in psychological attitude, in society and culture."[66] Niebuhr saw that for Dewey the "religious element in experience must be emancipated from the claim of monopoly of historic religions upon it" and that, furthermore, "this task of emancipation belongs to modern culture and philosophy."[67] According to Niebuhr, Dewey found this emancipation of the "religious" from "religion" and "the religions" to be necessary because

> (1) The religious element in experience is vital only when it is organic to the whole of man's experience and therefore atrophies when the effort is made to cultivate it as an end in itself. (2) Historic religions are all supernatural, implying that "ideals are real not as ideals but as antecedently existing actualities." Thus faith "that something should be in existence as far as lies in our power is changed into the intellectual belief that it is already in existence." (3) Historic religions suffer from an encumbrance of incredible mythical beliefs at variance with the facts revealed by modern science and a heritage of dogmatism in conflict with the freedom required by, and achieved in, modern science.[68]

Niebuhr discovered a certain pragmatic affinity with Dewey's view of the religious as "whatever introduces genuine perspective . . . into the piecemeal and shifting episodes of existence" and the religious quality of "any activity pursued in behalf of an ideal and against obstacles and in spite of threats of personal loss because of conviction of its general and enduring value." Such an admission (or conviction), Niebuhr thought, reflected a "kind of faith" that "is not arrived at by a scientific observation of the detailed facts of existence. It is an a priori involved in all knowledge and action, since both knowledge and purposeful action presuppose a meaningful world." To use Dr. Dewey's own phrase, Niebuhr concluded, "the imagination feels that [the world] is a 'universe.'"[69]

Dewey, in Niebuhr's interpretation, clearly accepted as legitimate aspects of religion both the transrational "poetic perspective which brings order and meaning into total experience and the moral vitality expressed in devotion to ideals." Niebuhr claimed that Dewey's emphasis brought him "closer to qualified theists than to humanistic dualists" because of his insistence upon the inclusion of "nature as a realm of value and meaning." He found it questionable whether the supernaturalism against which Dewey so persistently inveighed, namely, "a realm of being separate from the natural world and interfering in its processes, is really the kind of supernature about which really profound religion speaks."[70] Because Dewey's view of religion appreciated "the real world as a realm of value and meaning, that is, as a universe" he gives expression to a "kind of credo" which "comes closer than he is willing to admit to the primary tenets of prophetic religion."[71]

Niebuhr's position was that in assuming nature and history to be meaningful (as opposed to a denigration of the spatio-temporal order in Idealism or mysticism), Dewey's views simply reflected the influence of biblical faith on Western tradition. "Dr. Dewey," Niebuhr wrote,

> may insist that he does not believe in the ideals as "antecedently existing actualities," but he does believe in a world in which the possibility of realizing ideals exists. He believes in appreciating the world of nature as a realm of meaning even where it does not obviously support man's moral enterprise but is in conflict with it. This is the kind of faith which prophetic religion has tried to express mythically and symbolically by belief in a God who is both the creator and the judge of the world, that is, both the ground of its existence and its telos.[72]

From Niebuhr's perspective Dewey represented one among many forms of modern thought that has "surreptitiously insinuated something of a Hebraic-Biblical view of life into their naturalism, thereby making nature the bearer and even the artificer of a meaningful history."[73]

Niebuhr chose to see Dewey as a religiously sensitive naturalist who, in the context of his humanistic naturalism, voiced a profoundly pragmatic note that was congenial with the theistic vision of "prophetic faith." His attitude toward Dewey in this review of 1934 was much less strident, much less polemical, than that of *Moral Man* in 1932. Niebuhr, somewhat suprisingly, was even accommodating in tone and was not the least bit intent on pressing Dewey into a theistic or pantheistic mold as were some who offered interpretations of *A Common Faith*. One cannot help but speculate that Niebuhr's gentleness in responding to Dewey's work on religion could have been in compensation for the harshness with which he dealt with Dewey in *Moral Man and Immoral Society* two years earlier. Whatever might be the case in this regard, it is extremely unlikely that Niebuhr fell asleep at the switch when it came to dealing with Dewey's thoroughly "humanistic manifesto" on religion in *A Common Faith*.

Dewey was addressing those individuals who, in the aftermath of having rejected traditional theistic religion, nonetheless sought to find their way to a viable "religious" view of life.[74] He elected to seek emancipation from supernaturalism in the name of religious humanism, for supernaturalism was a potent symbol of both intellectual (dogmatic) and institutional (authoritarian) forms of irrationalism. The resulting freedom would significantly contribute to the two branches of one overriding revolution in the modern world: the experimental (scientific) method born of the demise of intellectual irrationalism, and the democratic process arising from the ashes of institutional irrationalism. Only as the prejudices of historically outmoded traditions yielded to the progression of science and democracy would "freed intelligence" come to full maturity. Dewey believed (or hoped) that intellectually respectable beliefs and the habit of rational flexibility would be the historical consequences of this emancipation. In such a climate two results could be expected: first, religious and moral sensitivities would make their necessary accommodations and, second, the associative conditions of the burgeoning democracies would result in voluntary associations in which antiauthoritarian habits would increasingly prevail.

6

A Broadening Out of the Issues

Ten years later Niebuhr pointed out that "the position of the most typical and greatest philosopher of American secularism, John Dewey, as expressed in *A Common Faith*" is one that "regards religious loyalties as outmoded forms of culture which will gradually disappear with the general extension of enlightened good-will." Dewey, Niebuhr went on to say, "looks forward to the cultural unification of the community upon the basis of a 'common faith' embodied in the characteristic credos of bourgeois liberalism."[1] Although his review of *A Common Faith* was mild by his previous standards of 1932, in the following years Niebuhr matured theologically and came to see the religious tradition itself as a vital resource on which to base an understanding of human life. Dewey, on the other hand, could see the historic faiths only as "a refuge, not a resource."[2]

It is on the matter of history that two of Niebuhr's major criticisms of Dewey came into focus; namely, criticisms of Dewey's "scientism" and his basically ahistorical view of history. It was Niebuhr's thesis in *The Self and the Dramas of History* that our tragic and widespread misunderstanding of *human* existence had increased with the burgeoning of nature studies since the time of the modern scientific revolution. He indicted modern empirical culture in general, and John Dewey, in particular, as the most visable spokesman of that culture. Niebuhr argued that "an 'empirical' culture was not prepared to deal with the problem of wide, rather than specific, conceptual schemes, that is, with presuppositions of inquiry which referred not to a specific type of being under scrutiny but with the very character of being itself." Instead of being open to "reexamination" these conceptual schemes "proved themselves powerful enough to determine the evidence by which they were to be tested." Somewhat ironically, although "Dewey, the most typical of modern naturalistic philosophers, never tired of insisting that the 'experimental method' must be rigorous enough to re-examine its own hypotheses," he mistakenly assumed "that the 'methods of science' could be transferred from the field of nature to that of history, and that only the intrusion of irrelevant religious and political authority prevented this consummation."[3]

Not only did Dewey seem uncritical of the basic metaphysical dogmas of modern science at crucial points, but these metaphysical blind spots led him to oversimplifications in his intepretation of history—and most specifically of religious history. In commenting on Dewey's *A Common Faith* in 1936, Niebuhr sarcastically noted that Dewey's desire to "eliminate conflict and unite men of goodwill everywhere" would supposedly be accomplished in part "by stripping their spiritual life of historic, traditional, and supposedly anachronistic accretions."[4] A decade afterward Niebuhr would again return to what he regarded as Dewey's typically modern combination of scientific naivete and historical ignorance, with its disasterous consequences for a rigorous assessment of the human condition. Niebuhr lamented that it was so typical of modern thought, beguiled as it was "by the tendencies of a scientific nominalism" that

> the most noted philosopher of America should attribute the egoistic corruption in moral and political judgments, which men of affairs take for granted and discount in their daily life, to the supposed compromise in the battle between science and authority, in which the fields of politics and morals were presumably declared immune to the beneficent sway of science, and kept under the traditional authorities of Church and state. In this case an elaborate theory is invented by a respected philosopher to account for a common phenomenon which the common sense of mankind has long since recognized as a universal characteristic, requiring no detailed explanations.[5]

Niebuhr's contention that Dewey embodied the "credos of bourgeois liberalism" was taken up again in September 1935, in an extended book review entitled "The Pathos of Liberalism." This review was a direct response to Dewey's recent book *Liberalism and Social Action*, which many thought to be a fairly realistic assessment of social existence. Niebuhr, in a strong but qualified sense, shared that judgment. He unequivocally stated that "no one in America has a more generally conceded right to speak in the name of liberalism than John Dewey." Moreover, as he had exhibited "a courageous willingness to extend both his theory and his practice beyond the limits set by traditional liberalism," Professor Dewey's newest volume in which he presents a "theoretic elaboration of his advanced position," offers us an "excellent opportunity to assess the resources of liberalism in the present social scene."[6]

Niebuhr applauded Dewey's call for an extension of liberty to the economic situation of the masses of individuals. He affirmed Dewey's willingness to advocate a conception of the state that would curtail legal liberties which often simply rationalized harsh inequalities of the status quo in society. Niebuhr thoroughly agreed with Dewey's realistic awareness that liberty often functioned as the ideological refuge of power and privilege in capitalistic social systems. Finally, he appreciated the recommendation for "thoroughgoing changes in the set-up of institutions and corresponding activity to bring the changes to pass" that lay at the center of Dewey's radical proposals. In effect, Niebuhr judged Dewey's "statement of faith" as "typical of a large body of intellectual liberalism, which resists the dishonest appropriation and corruption of the liberal creed by the plutocratic oligarchs of our society and which sees the problem of social change in larger terms than those of mere reformism."[7] Niebuhr, who only much later came to an appreciation of Roosevelt's pragmatic reforms, at this stage found encouragement in the fact that Dewey's position had very little "in common with the piecemeal reformism of the more timid liberals."[8]

Dewey's position in *Liberalism and Social Action*, as Niebuhr saw it, was excellent as far as it went. Dewey did seek to advance the cause of liberty in substantive ways by actually altering the social structure. There was a greater measure of realism here than in so much social thinking coming out of the liberal tradition. But Niebuhr found Dewey's second aim quite dubious, namely, that of making " 'freed intelligence' socially effective." He regarded Dewey's position as little more than a tedious continuation of the liberal penchant for romantic rationalism. For Niebuhr it was most especially "in his discussion of the function of intelligence in the process of social change that the limitations of Professor Dewey's liberalism appear."[9] Admittedly, chaos must be avoided if at all possible by giving intelligent direction to social change as Dewey suggested. Nontheless,

> every argument used in developing his theme of the function of "freed intelligence" in social change betrays a constitutional weakness in the liberal approach to politics. It does not recognize the relation of social and economic interest in the play of intelligence upon social problems. It does not perceive the perennial and inevitable interest in the social struggle. Its ideal of a "freed intelligence" expects a degree of rational freedom from the particular interests and perspectives of those who

think about social problems which is incompatible with the very constitution of human nature.[10]

Niebuhr's overriding objection to the liberal tradition surfaced once again. He increasingly diverged from the rather fatuous manner in which it dealt with "human nature." In Dewey, Niebuhr found the naive and sentimental view that, somehow and on some level, rational intelligence was exempt from the ambiguities of self-interest. Whatever the evolutionary scale of time portends, in the scale of historical time "human nature" was not as flexible or as maleable as Dewey believed. Certainly the most perennial characteristic of human community was conflict arising out of inordinate self-love. In Dewey's case, the transcendence of reason over particular involvements and interests was modeled after the striking "achievements of science in the development of technical civilization." Scientific technology, for Dewey, was a large-scale, historically documentable, and highly successful form of "organized intelligence in action." This manifestation of "organized intelligence," Dewey believed, demonstrated that incompatibilities between socioeconomic systems are not inevitable and will yield to rational suasion.

The reason Dewey gave for why such change had not yet come to fruition was, according to Niebuhr, invariably linked to some version of the "cultural lag" theory, as has been previously noted. Organized intelligence in the form of science gave rise to a remarkable technological civilization, but it had not yet generated a set of politicoeconomic arrangements compatible with its insights or dependent on its methodology. Quite obviously this failure was the result of institutions, remaining stubbornly unaffected by "the impact of inventive and instructive intelligence." In a book published in 1949, Niebuhr dealt with the notion of "cultural lag" in a somewhat expanded way. He wrote that

> even now we are not ready to measure the full depth of the problem of man's lack of strength to bring forth the historical newbirth required in a new age. The lack of strength to bring forth is usually interpreted as the consequence of a natural or cultural "lag." The common theory is that the mind is more daring and free in its comprehension of historical tasks than are the emotional and volitional forces which furnish the strength to do. Natural passions and cultural institutions supposedly offer a force of inertia against the more inclusive tasks which the mind envisages.
>
> This idea of a cultural lag is plausible enough, and partly true. But it does not represent the whole truth about the defect of our will. It obscures the positive and spiritual element in our

resistance to necessary change. The lower and narrower loyalties are armed not merely with the force of natural inertia but with the guile of spirit and the stubbornness of all forms of idolatry in human history.[11]

Cultural-lag theorists failed to take seriously enough that the self, even in its rational capacity, was never free from either partial perspectives or self-serving interests. Niebuhr belabored the point that it was precisely in the self's rational capacities, and preeminently in the freedom which results in the self's capacity for self-transcendence, that self-serving interests are compounded and rendered most dangerous. The danger was in the fact that the destructive possibilities in human life were equally indeterminate along with the creative possibilities. Niebuhr saw "the same inability to recognize the perennial enslavement of even 'freed intelligence'" to self-interest "revealed in Professor Dewey's discussion of violence and social change."[12] Niebuhr had no quarrel with Dewey's abhorence of violence or his desire to seek resolutions for social conflict short of overt conflict. What Niebuhr found so difficult was the lack of realism in Dewey's discussion of the possible ways of avoiding violence. Dewey, Niebuhr claimed, "sees violence only as a consequence of a social ignorance which a more perfect intelligence will be able to eliminate."[13] Because of the inclination of the self to serve its own ends, the only realistic expectation was that individual and collective self-interest were constant features of human life. Consequently, for Niebuhr, the fact of conflict was the starting point for any realistic assessment of political existence. A policy of balancing power against power and interest against interest, therefore, remained central to any meaningful hope of achieving a tolerable justice in the social arena.

Contrary to Niebuhr's sterotypical liberal, Dewey at least recognized "the coercive and even violent character of present society." As Niebuhr himself wrote, Dewey acknowledged that "it is not pleasant to face the extent to which, as a matter of fact, coercive and violent force are relied upon in the present social system as a means of social control."[14] Nonetheless, his rationalistic strategy for eliminating these deplorable social behaviors insisted on bringing conflicting interest under the spotlight of experimental intelligence where, under democratic methodologies, these conflicting claims "can be seen and appraised and where they can be discussed and judged in the light of more inclusive interests."[15] Niebuhr concurred that under very limited conditions conflicting interests were subject to arbitration in this "rational" manner. Two conditions must first be met, however. First, a relatively stable and cohesive social environment must exist. Second, only a marginal degree of conflict within that relatively stable setting can be present. In

Niebuhr's judgment conflicts of interest could yield, in part, to rational suasion only "when the contrast between them is not too sharp and when the contending parties do not absorb the total commmunity and therefore destroy the last remnant of impartiality and neutrality in the community with reference to a particular dispute."[16] Even then Niebuhr was somewhat amused to think that Dewey's method of convincing society that liberty is communal, and not just individual, "will supposedly soothe the savage beast of an imperiled and frantic oligarchy."[17] He rather sardonically suggested that the desired avoidance of violence and civil war "depends upon quite different considerations from those advanced by Professor Dewey."[18] A few years later he observed that " 'Reason' and 'force' may be the 'end terms' of human spirituality and vitality. But no sharp distinction can be made between any of the intermediate manifestations of human vitality, which history elaborates in endless variety."[19] Thus the balancing of various forms of political and social power in the community were absolutely essential for any hope of overcoming disproportions of power which constituted the very stuff of injustice.

Concepts such as the "cultural lag" and "freed intelligence" were hopelessly naive as resources for interpreting social change. Moreover, "in so far as a 'renascent liberalism' rests upon" such expectations, Niebuhr contended, "it will confuse the political problem." Sadly, therefore, "its stubbornness in maintaining [such concepts] imparts an aspect of pathos to even so courageous and honest a liberalism as that of Professor Dewey."[20]

Niebuhr once again turned his attention to Dewey's *Liberalism and Social Action* in 1939, when he was delivering his Gifford Lectures. He was convinced that Dewey's rationalistic social theories represented very little advance over those of the Enlightenment. In a lengthy, but considered reflection, Niebuhr wrote that Dewey

> has the same difficulty in finding a vantage point for reason from which it may operate against the perils of nature, and the same blindness toward the new perils of spirit which arise in the "rational" life of man. Dewey is in fact less conscious of the social perils of self-love than either Locke or Hume. In his thought the hope of achieving a vantage point which transcends the corruptions of self-interest take the form of trusting the "scientific method" and attributing anti-social conduct to the "cultural lag," that is, to the failure of social science to keep abreast with technology. . . . Professor Dewey has a touching faith in the possibility of achieving the same results in the field of social relations which intelligence achieved in the mastery of

nature. The fact that man constitutionally corrupts his purest visions of disinterested justice in his actual actions seems never to occur to him. . . . In common with his eighteenth century precursors, he would use the disinterested force of his "freed intelligence" to attack institutional injustices and thus further free intelligence. . . . No one expresses modern man's uneasiness about his society and complacency about himself more perfectly than John Dewey. One half of his philosophy is devoted to an emphasis upon what, in Christian theology, is called the creatureliness of man, his involvement in biological and social process. The other half seeks a secure place for disinterested intelligence above the flux of process, and finds it in "organized co-operative inquiry." Not a suspicion dawns upon Professor Dewey that no possible "organized inquiry" can be as transcendent over the historical conflicts of interest as it ought to be to achieve the disinterested intelligence which he attributes to it. Every such "organized inquiry" must have its own particular social locus. No court of law, though supported by age-old traditions of freedom from party conflict, is free of party bias whenever it deals with issues profound enough to touch the very foundation of the society upon which the court is reared. Moreover, there can be no "free co-operative inquiry" which will not pretend to have achieved a more complete impartiality than is possible for human instruments of justice. The worst injustices and conflicts of history arise from these very claims of impartiality for biased and partial historical instruments. The solution at which Professor Dewey arrives is therefore an incredibly naive answer to a much more ultimate and perplexing problem than he realizes. It could only have arisen in a period of comparative social stability and security, and in a nation in which geographic isolation obscured the conflict of nations and great wealth mitigated the social conflict within a nation.[21]

A new dimension of controversy between Niebuhr and Dewey began to take shape in the early 1940s. Dewey's *A Common Faith* had been addressed primarily to the religious liberal who was, in his estimation, a mere hairsbreadth away from secular humanism. He spoke to those persons whose religiosity was humanistic in substance and traditional only in form. Niebuhr's early religious orientation, although decidedly serious and committed, was liberal in ways that could have fit loosely into Dewey's audience. But between the publication in 1937 of *Beyond Tragedy* and his Gifford Lectures delivered in 1939, Niebuhr had moved into deeper theological waters. If the early 1930s found Niebuhr at odds with

Dewey's political liberalism, his ever-deepening theological formulations would prove to be unsettling to Dewey in the 1940s.

If Niebuhr's repudiation of social liberalism in *Moral Man* was an affront to Dewey, his rejection of religious liberalism, most evident in his
Gifford Lectures of 1939, was considered bewildering, dangerous, and,
above all, intellectually retrograde. This became evident in 1940 when
both men had occasion to respond to Niebuhr's former teacher, Douglas
Clyde Macintosh. The contexts in which they referred to Macintosh differed, although both of their reactions appeared in the same issue of *The
Review of Religion*, a publication sponsored by Columbia University. Two
additional facts are worthy of mention at this juncture. First of all,
Dewey and Niebuhr did not address each other directly or even indirectly by intent. Nonetheless, what each had to say to and about Macintosh provides us with a ready-made script for the key issues between
them. Second, Niebuhr was replying to a former teacher who had written what Niebuhr regarded as a "rigorous criticism" of his views. It is not
without a certain irony that the publication Macintosh was so troubled
by, Niebuhr's "The Truth in Myths," had appeared in 1937 in *The Nature of
Religious Experience*, which consisted of essays specifically in honor of
Douglas Clyde Macintosh! In any event, the particular manner in which
Niebuhr and Dewey responded to Macintosh in *The Review of Religion*
placed Niebuhr's growing departure from the liberal religious camp into
clear relief.

Niebuhr was replying specifically to Macintosh's criticism of his use
of myth in religious language. Macintosh had claimed that Niebuhr's
disavowal of literal truth with respect to religious concepts was equivalent to emptying religion of all truth. He thus saw his former student as
differing from *Als Ob* philosophers such as Feuerbach and Vaihinger only
in the degree of his "moral earnestness." Niebuhr sharply rejected this
indictment. He claimed that he sought a deeper and more profound understanding of the Christian faith—one that accepted the "poetic,"
"symbolic," and "mythical" insights of an admittedly transrational form
of language. Niebuhr repudiated both "the discredited dogmatism and
obscurantism of orthodoxy" and "the superficialities of liberalism."
Moreover, he saw very little in the type of liberal tradition Macintosh
represented "except the addition of pious phrases to the characteristic
faith of the bourgeois-liberal period, faith in the essential goodness of
man and in the idea of progress." Niebuhr found it "curiously ironic" of
Macintosh "to defend a Christian interpretation of life and history as
being 'literally true' [simply] because it is in essential agreement with
this liberal faith."[22]

In reviewing Macintosh's *Social Reform*, Dewey, on the other hand, suggested somewhat rhetorically that "Non-Christians may feel that the author's emphasis upon the strictly moral character of the principles set forth in the New Testament is more consistent with a naturalistic-cultural moral position than with one which gives a unique position to the Christian religion." In other words, perhaps, "Mr. Macintosh has gone so far in his 'liberalism' that he should go further."[23]

There is wonderful irony in all of this. Dewey expressed an appreciation for Macintosh's liberalism-*cum*-humanism while Macintosh was accusing Niebuhr of abandoning the literal sense of the tradition. Meanwhile, Dewey, along with Sidney Hook, would soon lament the dangerous degree to which anyone with Niebuhr's intellectual capacity and wide-ranging influence could conceivably lend credence to renascent forms of irrationalistic supernaturalism! This all made perfectly good sense if one came at it from the right direction. Dewey sympathized with Macintosh's religious liberalism precisely at the level where its substance—and not its residual traditional forms—was at one with the ethical character of religious humanism. Niebuhr, on the other hand, although jettisoning the literal—and thereby irrational—forms of religion, did so for the sake of the theological substance of the religious tradition. Finally, the very tradition Niebuhr had been rediscovering and reformulating in his theology was inimical to the kind of moralistic religion that Dewey *and* Macintosh—as humanistic and theistic liberals, respectively—represented.

It is worth one more excursion through the ironic convolutions in this three-way dispute. From the perspective of Niebuhr's emerging theological orientation the heart of Macintosh's religious liberalism merely echoed the sentiments of Enlightenment rationalism cloaked in pious phrases. From Dewey's perspective, however, Macintosh's religious liberalism could easily dispense with its theistic veneer and openly join the naturalistic camp. Yet from Macintosh's point of view, Niebuhr, in abandoning the literal meaning of religious language, was perceived as having abandoned any semblance of religious truth. At the same time, whereas Dewey found Macintosh's social sensitivity quite acceptable, Niebuhr viewed the social thought of both religious and secular liberalism as deplorably vacuous. Finally, as the fifth decade of the twentieth century began, Dewey found Niebuhr's theological turn which was so pronounced in *The Nature and Destiny of Man*, quite disturbing.[24] These complexities are especially important because they set the stage for the final developments in the relationship between Niebuhr and Dewey.

In the early 1940s Dewey would become increasingly distraught by what he deemed to be a resurgence of traditional religious belief. Indeed, as early as 1936, Dewey could agree that if not *the* problem, "the status of the supernatural" continued to be *a* "genuine and vital current problem for many persons." Moreover, among those multitudes who have "given up the supernatural" were many who were "wondering whether they must in consequence abandon also the religious."[25] Dewey had addressed that issue in *A Common Faith* two years earlier. In this time frame he had a somewhat hopeful confidence that traditional religious belief was on the wane. Instead of maintaining the mere shell of observances inculcated by the "great tradition," persons who had abandoned its operative center (supernaturalism) could derive meaningful observances elsewhere. They could embrace alternative traditions on which to organize their lives and base their values. With a measure of optimism Dewey wrote,

> We have at our disposal many traditions. There is the great tradition of autonomous literature, of music, of painting, of all the fine arts, in each of which, moreover, there are many significant traditions. There is the tradition of democracy; there is the tradition of experimental science, which if not thoroughly established is yet far from embryonic. For many persons it is a current problem whether from these traditions, apart from those of historic religions, there can not be extracted the equivalent of the observances derived from a tradition they no longer accept; observances which, indeed, no longer nourish their "hearts." Considering the variety of rich traditions that exist, there is something provincial in supposing that [meaningful responses] can be drawn only from a single confined tradition.[26]

Dewey's confidence that such provinciality would yield and that both supernaturalism and authoritarianism could be expected to give way to values based on the traditions of experimental science and democracy was at least partially intact. In his critique of Bertrand Russell's *Religion and Science*, Dewey stated that "ultimately, the conflict is between two opposed conceptions of the authority by which beliefs are to be formed and regulated, the beliefs in question affecting every phase of life from care of the body to moral endeavor."[27] The entire struggle between religion and science was seen as but one phase in the overarching conflict as to "whether and how scientific method, which is the method of intelligence in experimental action, can provide the authority that earlier centuries sought in fixed dogmas."[28] Dewey was convinced that a rationally authoritative direction to life was a basic requirement. Only to the extent that reason gained authority could authoritarianism be expected to decline. In spite of his qualified optimism, Dewey was quite disturbed by the fact that there had been a "sudden decline of faith in the method of free, experimental inquiry and of the recrudescence of dogmatic authorities, backed by physical force."[29]

Dewey was apprehensive of new "religious" ideologies loose in the world such as fascism, communism, and the various political nationalisms which had arisen. He rejected the notion that we just might have to resign ourselves to the possibility that "the method of intelligence is perpetually doomed to relative impotence because it is a feeble part of human nature in comparison with habit, emotion, and the impulses of some to power and of others to subjection."[30] We could not, however, simply ignore that "chaos and anarchy are with us," Dewey admitted. At least at that time there was some residual comfort in knowing that "scientific method is a newcomer on the scene" and that its status was that of "an infant struggling with adults generated and nourished through the long millennia of life on earth."[31] This partially explained why the technical application of science had, in the minds of many, totally submerged the tentativity, caution, and rational care of the scientific temper. Yet only in the nurture of scientific temper—frail reed that it was—was rational hope at all possible.

Russell showed that the political movements of our time had a decidedly religious character to them. Dewey concurred:

> They have their established dogmatic creeds, their fixed rites and ceremonies, their central institutional authority, their distinction between the faithful and the unbelievers, with persecution of heretics who do not accept the true faith.
>
> It is this situation which to my mind makes the issue of the social place and work of science so momentous and so urgent. We are in danger lest the only way out that will occur to men, even to us here in this country, will be the lining up of one creed and institution against the other and a consequent new type of religious war. . . . There are already among us groups of "intellectuals" who are fostering the external authoritarian doctrine and who are ready to become the official philosophers of the movement.[32]

Given such extreme apprehension, it was no wonder that Dewey reacted so strongly to a resurgence of traditional religion. Traditional religion was, by its own admission, transrational. Therefore, any appeals it might make on behalf of its "authoritativeness" were, ipso facto, "authoritarian" in Dewey's judgment. By way of both the emergence of these new political ideologies and the renascence of the older religious tradition, Dewey saw a particularly insidious threat to scientific intelligence. These concerns came to focus in the early 1940s in two very specific instances: first, with regard to incidents involving the newly formed Conference on Science, Philosophy and Religion; and, second, with respect to the kind of religious resurgence with which Reinhold Niebuhr—as leader and symptom—was associated.

7

Conflict in the Closing Years

Dewey played an important yet peripheral role in relation to what was called the *Conference on Science, Philosophy and Religion in their Relation to the Democratic Way of Life* (henceforth referred to as "the Conference").[1] This conclave met for the first time in September 1940. The Conference organizer, American Jewish Theological Seminary's Louis Finkelstein, had invited Dewey to join the organizing committee. Dewey declined the invitation and in a letter to H. A. Overstreet recounted that

> later as he [Finkelstein] pressed me I told him that while I could see good reasons for a move to combine persons of fundamentally different views for a definite practical object (I had in mind a consorting together of Jews, Catholics, Protestants and unbelievers to help check intolerance etc.), I thought it was a mistake to attempt to find common theoretical ground among those whose convictions were so different, many being committed by their positions to uphold their own doctrines. I said this was because he had emphasized as the object of the Conference the discovery of a common intellectual basis. The first Conference convinced me I was right, and that whether he so intended or not, theological fundamentalists were in control and were using the Conference for their own ends.[2]

Dewey continued to refrain from having anything to do with subsequent meetings of the Conference, despite successive appeals from Finkelstein and from men of such stature as Paul Weiss, Charles Morris, and H. A. Overstreet. For many of his contemporaries the very thought of a major conference on democracy's relationship to science, philosophy, and religion was unthinkable without Dewey's participation.[3] Therefore, Finkelstein implored Dewey to become actively involved. Recently in 1988 Finkelstein clearly recalled the protracted affair and pointed to the fact that Dewey had been, for quite some time, the special target of Catholic polemicists. He said that "I begged John Dewey to participate in the Conference . . . but he refused on the ground that he would not participate in any conference in which Jesuits participated. This was the attitude of several others at Columbia."[4]

Colleagues in the field of philosophy who were sympathetic to the Conference attempted to convince Dewey that, although Thomistic dogmatists like Mortimer Adler were both present and highly vocal, theirs was but one voice among many. Overstreet admitted that the Conference had some distasteful elements, including a few individuals "that strike me dumb with amazement (how can the human mind lift itself to such cosmic presumption?)," and felt that very little had yet been accomplished "unless one counts it much to have proponents of opposing views face one another and talk with at least a semblance of courtesy." He noted that he had "learned a good deal, particularly about the extent to which vocabulary gums up the situation." Nonetheless, Overstreet reluctantly accused Dewey of "sizing up the Conference wrongly." He believed that the issues were being openly and freely debated and that, in spite of some "bitterness and antagonism," people of diverse points of view were generally kind toward one another. Overstreet wished Dewey could have been present at this meeting (the third in 1942) and hoped he could "induce Dewey to join in the free-for-all" at the next year's meeting. He insisted that the Conference was planning to "turn altogether away from any attempt to find common ground among basic beliefs, and to try, instead, to discover what the various disciplines can offer on the problem of the kind of world we want to see built after the war." He believed that such a "turning away from the contemplation of our scholarly navels to the facing of a problem urgent and common to all of us will have a renovating effect."[5]

A year earlier fellow-philosopher Paul Weiss, too, had expressed regret over Dewey's continuing refusal to be party to the Conference. He was also personally saddened that Dewey declined to comment on Weiss's own paper, written expressly for the upcoming meetings. Weiss assured Dewey that the "coming conference will deal even less with theological and religious matters than the last one did." Moreover, he saw "nothing compromising in the attempt of the American philosophers to try to give a common statement of the meaning of democracy and to submit it for study and criticism by men in other disciplines" suggesting "that it may even be said to be our duty." Weiss recited names "like Brooks, Edman, Frank, Northrop, Overstreet, Rabi and Shapley" who were among the "founding and active members of the Conference." He implored Dewey:

Don't you think, in the light of the above, it will be possible for you to work with us who are trying to formulate a philosophy for democracy, apart from the pre-judgment of the various schools and creeds? If so, I do hope you will reconsider your decision regarding the conference and will at least join with us in this terribly difficult and important task of seeing what we philosophers hold in common. [6]

These strenuous appeals coming over a period of two years proved to be of no avail. Dewey's 1941 reply to Finkelstein was essentially the same as his response to Overstreet eighteen months later. Dewey claimed,

I explained to you last year why I was unable to take part. I could see the advantage of getting persons of different beliefs together with respect to some practical end they had in common; to try to make an intellectual synthesis where there are fundamental differences in intellectual attitude seemed to me a fundamental mistake. The actual conduct of the Conference [the initial one being in September, 1940] did more than confirm me in my belief. It was much worse than I could have anticipated. In the original call you mentioned exploration of the ground upon which theologians and scientific men could agree. When Einstein speaking for scientific men said that the two groups could operate on condition that theologians give up the supernatural you rebuked him for going outside his province as a scientist: This altho he was conforming to your own statement. I fail to see myself how any person of intellectual respect who is not ecclesiastical can take part in another such conference. [7]

Dewey's objections to the Conference were essentially twofold: first, the Conference apparently sought common ground between viewpoints which he believed to be fundamentally and irreconcilably at odds; and second, Dewey was convinced that there was a religiously based agenda designed to subvert Finkelstein's intentions to have an open conference. Specifically, Dewey was deeply offended by the treatment given Albert Einstein in the initial session and reacted sharply—as did Hook and others—to the arrogant "neo-thomistic authoritarianism" (to use Hook's description) of Mortimer J. Adler.

No doubt a large part of Dewey's information about the Conference came from Sidney Hook, who was present at the initial meetings. Hook, who described himself to me as "Dewey's bulldog,"[8] often had Dewey's ear and represented one school of influence upon Dewey.[9] The impact Hook had in helping shape Dewey's judgments regarding this Conference seems to have been extensive. After listening to Mortimer Adler, Hook angrily bid fellow humanists and other nontheistic liberals to walk out of the meetings.[10] He himself delivered a paper at the Conference which was published in the October 28, 1940, issue of *The New Republic* under the title "The New Medievalism." Eventually Hook issued a sharp public reaction in the Autumn 1942 issue of *The Humanist*, which he entitled "Theological Tom-Tom and Metaphysical Bagpipe."

Overstreet disagreed with Hook on his judgment of the Conference. "As to Sidney's fear," he wrote, "that we—the liberals—are being taken in by these fascist minded theologians, I think . . . is all nonsense."[11] Dewey, however, came to share both Hook's alarm and something of his anger and saw in the underlying premises of this Conference not only a form of intellectual dishonesty, but also an irrational subversion of all the values that characterize an open, tolerant, and liberal democratic civilization. Perhaps Dewey's most unguarded assessment came in a letter to his friend James T. Farrell, the American novelist. Dewey spoke rather caustically of both Adler and Walter Lippmann and seemed convinced that "the single worst case" of what Dewey called the "Jewish inferiority compensatory reaction" was to be found in "the abject surrender by Finkelstein of that so-called conference of theologians, philosophers, scientists to the rightwing of the Church last September."[12] There was no animosity towards Finkelstein in these remarks, for Dewey once mentioned to Overstreet that, in spite of finding good reasons to turn down Finkelstein's invitation to participate in the Conference, he "was rather attracted to him personally . . ."[13]

In the wake of this resurgence of what humanists saw as religious arrogance, Sidney Hook instituted a series of articles on the topic of what he called "the new failure of nerve." This series was published in two successive issues of the *Partisan Review* and included contributions from a prestigious group of individuals in addition to essays by both Hook and Dewey.[14] As the series organizer, Hook wrote the inaugural essay, which bore the title of the series itself. His thesis was that recent tendencies within contemporary culture paralleled those of the period between 300 B.C. and the end of the first century A.D. He found Gilbert Murray's characterization of that era as a "failure of nerve" to be an apt description of the current age. At that critical juncture, Hook argued, we were the dubious beneficiaries of a flight into asceticism and mysticism, together with a critical loss of self-confidence. This new "failure of nerve" had resulted in both shrill appeals for the credibility of absolute sources of truth beyond reason and nature and an abandonment of responsibility on the level of belief and action. In brief, the religious revival underfoot was an expression of wholesale intellectual panic. Obscurantism had become fashionable, Hook declared, and he openly focused upon Niebuhr as a representative of, and rallying point for, the move towards irrationalism within Protestant circles.[15]

Hook also continued his attack on the kind of neo-Thomistic fundamentalism which he believed both informed and largely controlled the proceedings of the Finkelstein Conference. The basic affront to both Hook and Dewey coming out of this conference was the notion that religious absolutism of the Christian variety was being advertised as the sole guarantor of democratic societies. They held that both history and logic would show that dogmatic totalitarianism is itself inimical to all of the hard-won freedoms of modern democratic cultures. Hook did not see Niebuhr as party to this type of arrogance, but Niebuhr was seen as embodying and reenforcing the obscurantism of our "new failure of nerve."[16] Thus the link was made when Hook wrote that this most recent theocratic tendency was partly a result of Catholic agitation and partly an expression of spiritual despair[17]—Niebuhr representing the descent into spiritual despair.

Clearly the issue of "Catholic agitation" occupied Dewey's attention. Dewey's feeling about the Conference and his reaction to conservative Catholic criticism of his philosophical position lay behind his essay "Anti-Naturalism in Extremis" written for the series. Hook claims that, whereas "Niebuhr's criticism of Dewey was essentially that he didn't recognize the strength of evil in human affairs and couldn't effectively cope with it by the methods of intelligence," the Catholic conservatives were Dewey's real nemesis and chief concern. They, Hook maintained, were "the most unscrupulous and outrageous critics of Dewey's pragmatism and naturalism [their criticism being] that Dewey's philosophy was itself an expression of an evil philosophy, indistinguishable ultimately from Hitler's etc."[18] The utter irresponsibilty of this type of indiscriminate attack as well as the pretentious arrogance on the part of Mortimer Adler who presented Catholic absolutism as the necessary condition of democracy, put Dewey on the offensive in Hook's *Partisan Review* series. Dewey's "Anti-Naturalism in Extremis" was, within the strictures set by Dewey's temperament and New England reserve, a forceful attack on supernaturalistic and rationalistic antinaturalisms. It was also an impassioned plea for a humanistic naturalism that would further the human quest for both rational understanding and a democratic form of life. Dewey, too, raised the specter of the Conference in responding to both religious and nonreligious types of antinaturalism. When he spoke about the supernaturalistic type, he directly broached Roman Catholic theology, referring to Thomas P. Neill, Jacque Maritain, and Cardinal Newman.

Dewey contended that the legacy of philosophical naturalism coming out of Aristotle was corrupted by the supernaturalism of medieval re-

ligious tradition. This tradition misrepresented Aristotle as one of the
founders of antinaturalistic philosophy. Dewey distinguished between
various types of antinaturalism in light of their respective tendencies to
reduce naturalism to materialism. He concluded that

> the view attributed to naturalism is simply another instance of
> a too common procedure in philosophical controversy: Namely,
> representation of the position of an opponent in the terms it
> would have *if* the critic held it; that is, the meaning it has not in
> its own terms but after translation into the terms of an opposed
> theory.[19]

Dewey claimed that the major task confronting us was to extend the
methodology of philosophical naturalism to the areas of psychology,
sociology, and politics, as well as to the domain of human values. Dewey
reversed the charge leveled at the Finkelstein Conference by some supernaturalists to the effect that theism alone can maintain a democratic
society. On the contrary, Dewey insisted that "Democracy cannot obtain
either adequate recognition of its own meaning or coherent practical
realization as long as anti-naturalism operates to delay and frustrate
the use of methods by which alone understanding of, and consequent
ability to guide, social relationships can be attained."[20] Consequently,
"the most pressing problem and the most urgent task of naturalism at
the present time is to work out, on the basis of available evidence, a
naturalistic interpretation of the things and events designated by the
words that now exert almost complete control of psychological and
societal inquiry and report"—words that bear the otherworldly or
dualistic orientation against which Dewey's entire philosophical program inveighed.[21]

The burden of Dewey's essay, therefore, centered on refuting the
charges brought against naturalism by the kind of Catholic thought he
and Hook believed to be so vocal at the Conference. Dewey vehemently
attacked the claim that religious dogmas are the primary basis for a free
and open society. He further castigated both those religious and rational
antinaturalists at Princeton who signed a statement to the effect that
naturalism, paying homage to a materialistic conception of human nature, threatens the dignity of the person and eliminates the domain of
values. Dewey wrote that

> It is probable that the signers of this statement belong to
> both the supernatural and the rationalistic varieties of anti-
> naturalism. Reference to our classic *and* religious heritage, to
> Greek *and* Hebraic-Christian sources, indicates that such is the

case. They agree for purposes of attack. But cross-examination would disclose a fundamental incompatibility. For example, philosophical anti-naturalists are obliged to confine themselves to dire prediction of terrible things to happen because of naturalism. Their companions of the supernatural variety are aware, however, of active and forcible means that were once employed to stay the spread of heresies like naturalism so as to prevent the frightful consequences from happening. If they are literate in their faith, they know that such methods are still required, but are prevented from now being put into execution by the spread of naturalistic liberalism in civilized countries. When members of this group think of the pains that were taken when the Church had the power to protect the faithful from "science falsely socalled," and from dangerous thoughts in scholarship, they might well smile at the innocence of their colleagues who imply that inquiry, scholarship, and teaching are completely unhampered where naturalism has not obtained a foothold. And they might certainly say of their merely philosophical confreres, that *they* are living off a capital derived from a supernatural heritage. A mere naturalist will content himself with wondering whether ignorance of history or complacency or provincialism with respect to the non-christian part of the world, or sheer rhetorical dogmatism is the outstanding trait of the pronounciamento.[22]

At bottom, according to Dewey, a radically negative view of human nature lay at the basis of "the asseverations that naturalism is destructive of the values associated with democracy, including belief in the dignity of man and the worth of human life."[23] In contradiction to such an interpretation Dewey insisted that

naturalism finds the values in question, the worth and dignity of men and women, founded in human nature itself, in the connections, actual and potential, of human beings with one another in their natural social relationships. Not only that, but it is ready at any time to maintain the thesis that a foundation within man and nature is a much sounder one than is one alleged to exist outside the constitution of man and nature.[24]

In Dewey's judgment the pessimistic and even cynical views of human nature which seem to accompany supernaturalist anti-naturalism, result in a rejection of those "resources that are potentially available for betterment of human life."[25] Supernaturalism has hind-

ered humankind's accomplishments precisely in direct relationship to
its own success in forming the views of a particular culture. By trumpeting
"higher truths" beyond the pale of scientific rationality, both the historic
accomplishments and the continuing pursuit of rational knowledge
were belittled or even repudiated. Consequently, in Dewey's words and
with his own emphasis, "*the fruit of anti-naturalism is then made the ground of
attack upon naturalism.*"[26] In the final analysis, the kind of dogmatic and
finalistic thinking that characterized the totalitarian mind belonged
not to scientific naturalism, but rather to supernaturalism. For it was
the supernaturalists who had a "lack of respect for scientific method,
which after all is but systematic, extensive and carefully controlled use
of alert and unprejudiced observation and experimentation in collect-
ing, arranging and testing facts to serve as evidence."[27]

Niebuhr, of course, did not proffer the type of position that Dewey
was attacking. In fact, Niebuhr strictly rejected any division of the
human community into two groups: those whose "spiritual view" of
humankind was a guarantor of democracy, and those whose naturalism
was implicitly totalitarian and inimical to the values basic to a democratic society. He was fully aware of the highly complex history that had fed
into the development of democracy in the West—a development in which
both religious and secular forces were at work. Moreover, in spite of his
substantive criticisms, he not only displayed a marked respect for scientific thought, he also valued the humane achievements among the best
resources of the secular tradition. Niebuhr, speaking out of a religious
framework, was arguably the most able and telling critic of religion in
the America of his day. He was highly adept at laying bare the pretensions and intolerance of the religious tradition in both its Catholic and
Protestant forms. To this extent he was as rigorously opposed as was
Dewey to the type of religious and political arrogance that both Dewey
and Hook were attacking.

The *Partisan Review* essays reflected a cause célèbre on the part of
American humanists in the early 1940s who felt that their elder stateman,
John Dewey, had been viciously and unjustly attacked. They also felt that
the nation itself was truly endangered by a resurgent wave of religious
obscurantism. Hook as much as admitted that there was a certain crisis
mentality about all of this in the minds of those who were embattled by
the kind of attacks represented by the worst of the Finkelstein Conference.
He also thought that Niebuhr, in an important sense—and, perhaps, in
spite of himself—was an ancillary part of the problem. In fact, Hook
acknowledged that in responding to the "new failure of nerve" Dewey took
on the task of criticizing the Catholic fundamentalists while Hook himself engaged Niebuhr for his unintended complicity in the situation.

At the point where obscurantism had beccome fashionable, Hook

openly focused on Niebuhr, who, given his prestigious position within
Protestant circles, had become a rallying point for the recent turn toward
irrationalism. There was a genuine note of disappointment there because
Hook admired and respected Niebuhr on many levels. The situation was
exacerbated by the fact that, although prejudicial arrogance was to be expected from certain conservative quarters within both Catholic and Protestant traditions, it was being reinforced—however indirectly and unin-
tentionally, Hook thought—by a man who not only symbolized personal
integrity, but who also commanded a high degree of respect among many
intellectually enlightened individuals in both secular and religious circles. The fact that Niebuhr could become caught up in such terrifying and
unnecessary "failure of nerve" revealed, to Hook, the sheer magnitude of
the problem. In taking Niebuhr on, Hook did not portray him as party to
the type of arrogance displayed by Adler or the kind of inanity coming out
of the Princeton group. Nonetheless, Niebuhr was viewed as embodying
and reinforcing the obscurantism of the "new failure of nerve."

Unlike Hook, Dewey did not directly identify Niebuhr as a source of
concern in this new crisis. However, Dewey would certainly have included Niebuhr within the boundaries of the phenomenon under attack
in his own article for *Partisan Review*. Niebuhr could not have been totally
outside of Dewey's purview; for example, when he spoke of "the chorus of
voices now proclaiming that naturalism is committed to a dangerously
romantic, optimistic, utopian view of human nature,"[28] he was obviously aware of Hook's attack on Niebuhr. Indeed, in a letter to Sidney
Hook written within two months of their *Partisan Review* articles, Dewey
commented that "Barnes expressed much admiration for your P. R. Failure of Nerve but said he thought it would be more effective with less
acerbity—then he laughed and said you'll think [that] a queer remark
coming from me!"[29] Dewey saw Niebuhr at the very least as a dualist and
as an advocate of a far too pessimistic view of human nature. Morever, he
had suffered Niebuhr's earlier attack on both him and the liberal tradition ever since *Moral Man and Immoral Society* in 1932. To the extent that
Niebuhr then provided a rallying point for the resurgence of religious
thought in America, Niebuhr clearly appeared to be in league with the
wave of antinaturalist hysteria— if in no other way than simple guilt by
association. This judgment was supported by the evidence of Dewey's correspondence with Farrell, Joseph Ratner, and especially Hook. Yet "socially and politically," as Hook maintained, "Niebuhr and Dewey were
so to speak broadly on the same side, members of an extended family.
These family quarrels were very important, too, because ultimately the
Niebuhrian confusions would play into the hands of reaction."[30]

According to Hook, Dewey clearly "recognized Niebuhr as a force—
as a formidable force on the contemporary scene." Both Hook and Dewey

saw Niebuhr as "the bellweather for American theology."[31] It was no wonder that Niebuhr's potent voice for theological renewal and reorientation and, most especially, his growing impact on influential individuals in the world outside theological circles, were viewed with a certain alarm by humanistic naturalists such as Dewey and Hook. Both men were deeply unnerved by the religious renascence occurring at that time. From their vantage point, as Hook put it, "many American intellectuals are losing their nerve. They are being swept away on a tidal wave of irresponsibility, bad logic and obscurantism." In Hook's account, "the Conference on Science, Philosophy and Religion is the foamy crest of the wave. To build bulwarks against this surging flood of irrationalism should be one of the specific tasks of the humanists and genuine democrats throughout the land."[32]

In the minds of the Dewey faction, Niebuhr's voice was solidly linked with the wave of irrationalism and obscurantism that had been recently unleashed in American life. In a letter to Dewey, James T. Farrell made this extended observation:

> I have just glanced through the first volume of Reinhold Niebuhr's GIFFORD lectures, THE NATURE AND DESTINY OF MAN. Niebuhr—whom incidentally, the corporation of Mumford, Frank Etc. touts highly—is a disgusting spectacle. You know, he is a man of keen intelligence, and broad background. He was the most intelligent man in the Socialist Party. His fiddling around with Christianity is abhorrent and repellent. You know, the man is really a Machiavellean. His book MORAL MAN AND IMMORAL SOCIETY tells us much, in its very title. He makes a polar opposition, man is moral as an individual, society is immoral as a group of men acting together for group purpose. Although such a premise is a bad one, that book is the product of a man of intelligence. Now, of course, he takes a different view. And again, his piddling around with a reformed Christianity in [sic] unworthy of him. But the man is no fool. You can't dismiss him the way you can Brooks and these people.[33]

Farrell echoed the view of many humanistic naturalists when he acknowledged that this man was indeed "a man of keen intelligence," who "is no fool" and whose "piddling around with reformed Christianity" cannot be easily dismissed. This, as we have noted, was precisely Dewey's and Hook's source of difficulty with Niebuhr. Even if Niebuhr's was a more tolerant brand of Christianity, the sheer power and effect of his voice lent credibility to religious authoritarianism. Their question was, "How, indeed, could a man of Niebuhr's intelligence and sociopolitical sensitivity give aid and comfort to this kind of intellectual obscurantism?"

The fact that Niebuhr was in Dewey's thoughts relative to these issues was seen in his brief note to Hook written late in 1942 relating to "two diagnoses of [C. D.] Joad."[34] These diagnoses reminded Dewey of Hook's own analysis of Niebuhr, which had to do with Hook's critique of the first volume of *Nature and Destiny of Man* appearing in the *New Leader* the year before. Hook had indicted Niebuhr for basing his analysis of evil on supernaturalistic grounds and made the charge that Niebuhr's problem was that he "wrestles valiantly with the problem created by his assumptions."[35] This apparently appealed to Dewey's sensitivities and largely reflected his own view of Niebuhr.

In the meantime, 1944 found Dewey writing to Niebuhr about the composition of the German Committee to which they both belonged. Whatever else transpired between them, Dewey and Niebuhr continued to share certain interests and activities pertaining to social issues. Dewey's initial letter to Niebuhr on this matter is missing. He had obviously expressed some apprehension regarding the German Committee, prompted, most likely, by the concerns of his friend and colleague Sidney Hook. Dewey was worried about allegations of communist affiliation, and Niebuhr's reply attempted to allay Dewey's fears:

Dear Professor Dewey:

Thank you for your letter. You will have seen Paul Tillich's answer in the most recent issue of *The New Leader*. There is not a single communist on our list of sponsors, and the organization has absolutely nothing to do with the Free Germany Committees organized by Moscow. The program warns against domination of Germany and of Europe by the West, or Russia, and opposes the dismemberment of Germany which the Russians are advocating.

The reason the German Committee included two communists in its organization was because they felt it was impossible to advocate a so-called East-West solution of the German problem without taking some communists in. Miss Ruth Fisher, herself an ex-communist, is merely engaging in libel when she declares that this Committee was sponsored and organized under Moscow directions.

I know the history of the Committee from the beginning. It first met under the Chairmanship of Thomas Mann. It, incidentally, includes some of the most prominent Catholic liberals.

Our sponsoring committee is made up of people who are determined not to have anything to do with the united front in this
country. But we do not believe that the conditions on the conti-
nent, particularly in view of the necessity of collaboration with
Russia, make it advisable to force our position upon the German Committee.

Sincerely yours,

Reinhold Niebuhr[36]

Dewey forwarded a copy of Niebuhr's letter to Hook in which he affixed
the remark, "I think I'll stay on the Council."[37]

The year 1944 also brought Dewey's eighty-fifth birthday. Niebuhr's
signature appears on a letter sent to Dewey from members of the
Philosophy Club of New York, reproduced in Figure 7.1.

Toward the end of 1945 the newly founded Jewish journal *Commentary* launched a series entitled "The Crisis of the Individual" to which
both Niebuhr and Dewey were invited to contribute. Niebuhr's article
"Will Civilization Survive Technics?" was the first in the series and appeared in the December issue. Dewey's essay "The Crisis in Human History" followed three months later in March 1946.

Niebuhr's essay was an interesting and extremely important piece
of writing in light of his relationship with Dewey. Niebuhr's article
seemed to reflect a clear awareness of the many concerns Dewey voiced
in "Anti-Naturalism in Extremis" two years earlier. In certain respects
Niebuhr appeared to be speaking directly to Dewey without once mentioning him by name. Moreover, the essay brought into focus many of the
issues and orientations that had separated Niebuhr from Dewey overall.
Dewey made a rather intriguing comment on Niebuhr's article in a letter to Joseph Ratner written soon after the appearance of his own contribution to the *Commentary* series. Dewey wrote:

I don't know whether Commentary, the new monthly, sent you
my piece in March where I had a chance to say something about
the revival of isolated individualism on an alleged "spiritual"
instead of material—economic—basis. The other articles before on the general topic, were pretty dreadful I thought—R.
Niebuhr's on the whole the best of the lot, but with his old
dualism—economic and spiritual.[38]

In his essay Niebuhr attempted to assess the current "crisis" on two
levels: the sociopolitical and the religiophilosophical. On the first level

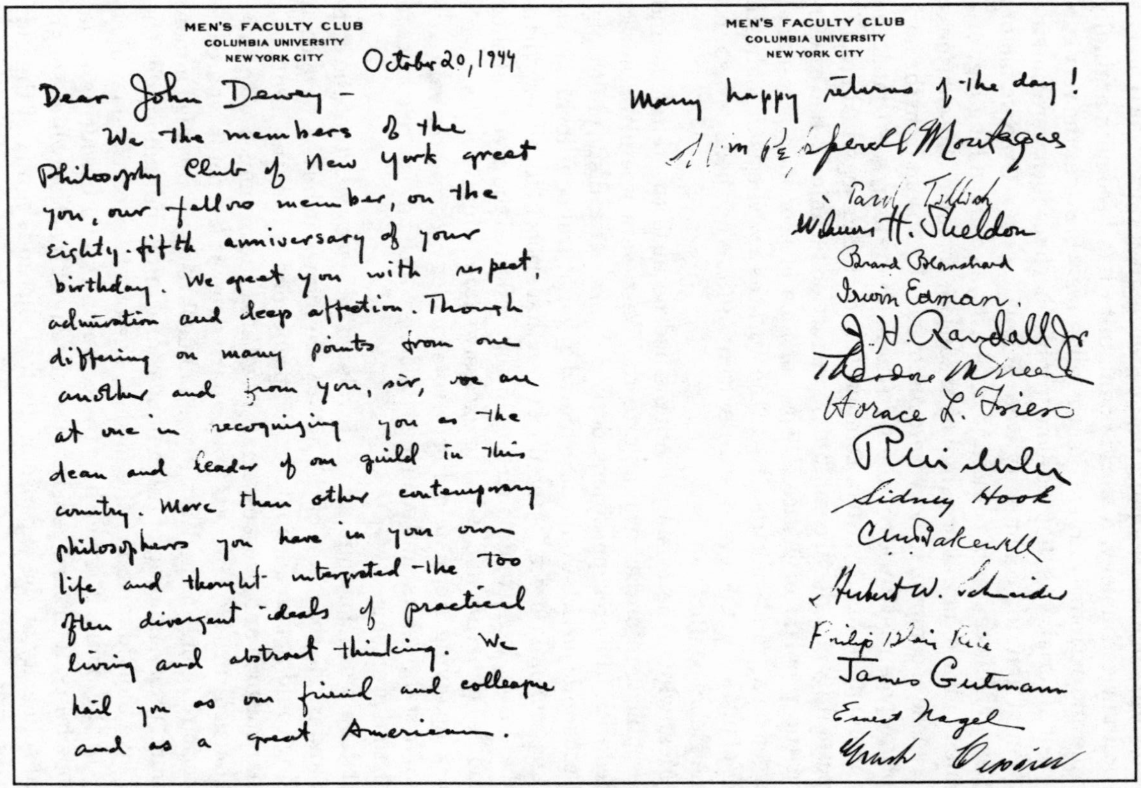

MEN'S FACULTY CLUB
COLUMBIA UNIVERSITY
NEW YORK CITY

October 20, 1944

Dear John Dewey—

We the members of the Philosophy Club of New York greet you, our fellow member, on the eighty-fifth anniversary of your birthday. We greet you with respect, admiration and deep affection. Though differing on many points from one another and from you, sir, we are at one in recognizing you as the dean and leader of our guild in this country. More than other contemporary philosophers you have in your own life and thought interpreted—the too divergent ideals of practical living and abstract thinking. We hail you as our friend and colleague and as a great American.

Many happy returns of the day!

I join F. J. E. Woodbridge

Parry Tiffin
Wilmon H. Sheldon
Bernard Bandsman
Irwin Edman
J. H. Randall Jr
Horace L. Friess
Philip Wiener
Sidney Hook
Charles Blakewell
Herbert W. Schneider
Philip Wiener
James Gutmann
Ernest Nagel
Ernest Dewey

Figure 7.1 From the John Dewey Papers, Special Collections, Morris Library, Southern Illinois University at Carbondale.

the crisis was to be seen in the inability "to develop political and social instruments which are adequate for the kind of society which a technical civilization makes possible and necessary."[39] Technology had placed the contemporary age in a quandry. In the aftermath of World War II and its concomitant technology, a world community had become marginally possible and extremely urgent. Yet the dilemma which was the very substance of the crisis was that the elements of cohesion which were the sine qua non of genuine community were simply lacking. Organic factors such as a viable center of power and authority, a common language or a common culture, moral or religious tradition, common consciousness, and a sense of common history were almost totally absent from the horizon of any potential world community. The supreme irony was that at the very moment in history when communication technology had created the possibility of a global community, production techniques had exacerbated the problem of justice. Disproportions of economic power had emerged on a grand scale relative to the world as a whole as the delicate forms of justice on the level of smaller communities had been devastated by the global conflict.

Meanwhile, the crisis was intensified because the religious and philosophical resources available to the West were woefully limited. Armed with "the presuppositions, derived from a naturalistic philosophy, that economic justice would be achieved by a natural equilibrium of social and economic forces,"[40] the West faced that crisis in its history virtually bankrupt. Persistent belief that history reflected the preestablished harmonies of nature and belief in excessive atomic individualism with its accompanying acommunal libertarian ideology, were at the very core of the "nostalgic social and economic theories which have no relevance to our actual problems."[41]

Niebuhr's major emphasis as it related to Dewey was that the complex and tragic character of the history through which they were then passing could not be adequately "comprehended within the limits of a secular culture" and, most especially, "without the resources of an older religious culture."[42] This was particularly true at the point where the "historic religions of the West, Jewish and Christian," revealed a more profound understanding of the unique character of individual life. The excessive individualism of the modern age emphasized freedom in society to the point of imperiling the community and obscuring social responsibility. It in turn generated a collectivist reaction which sought social solidarity at the expense of the freedom and dignity of the individual person.

The resources of a supposedly outmoded religious culture had seen that "in reality the individual has a form of constitutional spiritual freedom which makes it inevitable that even the best community will frustrate as well as fulfill the highest aspirations of the human spirit." This tradition knew that "love is the law of life for the individual, in the sense that no human being can fulfil himself within himself. He is fulfilled only in the community. But the same individual rises in indeterminate degree beyond all communal and social relevancies."[43] It is precisely here at the level of the transcendent freedom of the individual that Niebuhr found naturalism deficient and the "historic religions" of the West so valuable. Niebuhr then reflected at length on matters central to his ongoing debate with John Dewey. He wrote:

> The "naturalism" of our culture was celebrated as a great spiritual achievement in the heyday of our era. It was supposed to prevent men from being beguiled by false eternities. They would realize the highest historic possibilities the more certainly if they were no longer led astray by the illusions of eternal salvation and redemption. Actually there have been many forms of religious "other-worldliness" which were merely compensations for frustrations and expressions of social defeatism. It was good that men should be emancipated from them. There are also forms of "super-naturalism" which conceive the world as a kind of layer-cake affair, with two layers, the one natural and the other supernatural, the one physical and the other "spiritual." There is only one world; just as man in the unity of his physical and spiritual life is one. Religious dualism is an error. But so is a naturalistic monism that seeks to comprehend the full dimension of human existence from the standpoint of man's relation to nature.
>
> Man is undoubtedly a creature of nature, subject to its necessities and limitations. But an excessive emphasis upon this aspect of man's existence obscures the full dimension of human personality. It is by man's freedom over natural process and limitation that he is able to make history. But the same freedom which lies at the basis of man's historic creativity is also the root of human evil. Thus man, whose nature it is to be realized beyond himself in the life of his fellows, is also able to corrupt the community and make it the tool of his interests. The possibilities of evil as well as good are much greater than modern culture assumed.[44]

The issues that divided Dewey and Niebuhr over the years were superbly focused in their respective contributions to the *Commentary* series, even though they did not directly address one another in this forum. Dewey's concern in his article on "The Crisis in Human History" was to

avoid a wholesale retreat into individualism by overcoming the dangerous, yet artificial, split between the "individual" and the "social" that
plagued so much of Western intellectual history. Neither the individual
nor society existed in abstraction. It was far more proper to speak of the
"human being" recognizing therein the social character of humans in
their actual existence. Dewey contended that the "separation and opposition of individual and social," which were responsible for much of "the
chaos which is at the root of the present debasement of human beings,"
went far back into the historical past. "It was initiated," he argued,
"when man was linked to 'the next world' instead of to his fellows in this
world."[45] Although the origins of this debasement were exacerbated by
historical factors such as the rightful release from an oppressive tradition (Church and State), the metaphysical and religious dualisms of the
past were essentially responsible. Indeed, "no mistake is greater than to
overlook the substantial moral support given to Individualism in its laissez-faire Liberal career by the heritage bequeathed from certain religious traditions. These [traditions]," Dewey insisted, "taught that men as
singular or individual souls have intrinsic connection only with a supernatural being, while they have connection with one another only
through the extraneous medium of this supernatural relationship."[46]

Here we witness Dewey's attributing to the religious tradition responsibility for a fundamental bifurcation between the self and society,
whereas Niebuhr appealed to the same tradition as pointing to self-
transcendence as a barrier against all forms of naturalistic reductionism. Here we also have Dewey reading history in such a way as to require history's release from its religious past, whereas Niebuhr argued
that without the resources of an older religious culture the disasterous
oversimplifications of the present would remain with us.

A rather important insight into Dewey's attitude toward Niebuhr in
these later years found expression in a letter written to Robert V.
Daniels in 1947. Dewey wrote:

> A friend and former student of mine [Joseph Ratner]—who
> edited a collection or selection of my writings for the Modern
> Library "Intelligence in the Modern World"—has been reading
> Reinhold Niebuhr, and is writing a review, to be brought out in
> book form by the Beacon Press—the publisher of which says it
> is devestating. Well I have the impression that both he
> [Niebuhr] and Kierkegaard have both completely lost faith in
> traditional statements of Christianity, haven't got any modern
> substitute and so are making up, off the bat, something which
> supplies to them the gist of Christianity—what they find sig-
> nificant in it and what they approve of in modern thought—as

when two newspapers are joined. The new organ always says "retaining the best features of both."[47]

In spite of his ascerbic intentions, Dewey's observation was rather accurate and insightful. There was certainly a core of truth to his central observation. Niebuhr was indeed engaged in the tremendous cultural project of attempting to find a way of "retaining the best features of both" traditions that constituted the heritage of the contemporary Western world. Niebuhr was a firm advocate of a viable synthesis between the best insights of both Christian and secular culture. In 1936 he noted that in spite of its weaknesses and errors "the achievements of the Age of Reason" must not be overlooked. Indeed, "a prophetic religion which tries to re-establish itself in a new day without appropriating what was true in the Age of Reason," he contended, "will be inadequate for the moral problems which face our generation."[48]

Although Niebuhr's insights deepened and his sophistication grew both with regard to his understanding of religious as well as secular thought, his sentiment here never changed. Niebuhr became increasingly preoccupied with the diverging legacies of the Renaissance and the Reformation. Largely because of the impact of the Renaissance upon contemporary thought, he felt that "no alternative perspectives are available [with respect to the tragic character of our age] because the triumph of the Renaissance was so complete that it destroyed not only particular interpretations of the Christian religion, but submerged the Christian religion itself, as, in any sense, a potent force in modern culture."[49] It was not, in Niebuhr's estimation, a matter of the more authentic forms of Christian thought—the Reformation in particular—having been discredited. It was simply that they had been overwhelmed or rejected by the impact of the modern world. This made a viable synthesis between the religious and secular tradtions all the more imperative with respect to the truth they had to speak to one another. For the realities of the present age were so tragic that it was all the more pressing to begin "to chart the course by which we may emerge from them."[50] If it were possible to recover how and why "those aspects of the truth about human nature and destiny, in which the Renaissance and the Reformation contradict each other, represent valuable insights into human nature and history," then:

> a philosophy of human nature and destiny could emerge which would reach further into the heights and depths of life than the medieval synthesis; and would be immune to the alternate moods of pessimism and optimism, of cynicism and of sentimentality, to which modern culture is now so prone.[51]

The Ratner manuscript, mentioned earlier in Dewey's 1947 letter to Robert V. Daniels, never saw the light of day. The manuscript does exist in part and in various stages of editing; it is located in the Special Collections in the Morris Library at Southern Illinois University.[52] What is important here for our purposes is that Niebuhr's name came up periodically in a variety of contexts in the Dewey-Ratner correspondence between 1948 and 1950. These references to Niebuhr came within the space of a few short years before Dewey's death.

Dewey and Ratner were involved in an exchange of letters with regard to the difficulties a young man was having in his degree program at Columbia's Philosophy Department. Ratner claimed that this young man, in following the lines of G. S. Morris, was involved in doing much the same thing Niebuhr did. In a letter to Dewey he insisted that the young man

> reads like pages out of Niebuhr. As a Niebuhr specialist, I could see that right away—and that is what got me on the alert. But as I have told you—Niebuhr got his stuff from you. Niebuhr performs a double-operation. He first Deweyifies Jesus and then on [the] basis that Jesus is Dewey plus, criticizes Dewey. . . . In the case of Niebuhr, he does the double job all by himself. Except that what he takes out of Dewy and puts into Jesus, he then turns about and says it is not in Dewey but only in Jesus.[53]

A day later, on December 9, 1948, Dewey's reply simply contained the tempting observation that "What you say about Niebuhr and Morris is very interesting,"[54] Then he expressed his disagreement with Ratner over his interpetation of the young man's position.

The core of the corruption and dishonesty Ratner saw in American theology, in general, and Reinhold Niebuhr, in particular, related to what Ratner saw as deceitful maneuvers. An outmoded religious tradition sought to save itself by stealing the truth it claimed to possess from secular culture and then claiming that those truths belonged to religion from the beginning. Niebuhr was credited with most fully personifying this most recent stage in the warfare between theology and the rational sciences. Dewey might have agreed in some measure with whatever intellectual substance Ratner's indictment of Neibuhr contained, although there is no evidence that he shared Ratner's virulent attitude toward Niebuhr. Indeed, Niebuhr and Dewey had a real if perhaps somewhat grudging respect for one another on several levels, including common political orientations as well as intellectual prowess. Nonetheless,

Dewey's continuing unwillingness to give the "older religious culture" any credence whatsoever can be found in his September 6, 1950, letter to Ratner. Here Dewey wrote:

> It is my impression that your account of the present situation applies at the upper intellectual levels of the niebuhrs [sic]...I am not arguing however that my understanding is better than yours; though I think that because of having been brought up in evangelical Protestantism, it should be. Anything so incorporated in institutional culture as doctrines and techniques about saving "individual" souls will stand an awful lot of accommodations in its period of decline, and will keep a number of intellectuals, Niebuhrs say—busy, out of all proportion to its intrinsic significance.[55]

This basic orientation held for Dewey and was clearly reflected in his contribution to a symposium on Religion and the Intellectuals early in 1950. Returning to the very theme that Sidney Hook had defined as the "new failure of nerve" seven years earlier in the same journal, Dewey perceived a "coincidence *in time* between the loss of intellectual nerve, and the attendant reversion to a position not long ago discarded, and recent developments in human affairs." The series of shocks delivered by history against confidence in the easy progression toward a peaceful world order had also resulted in a widespread disillusionment with science. Unfortunately—and quite unnecessarily—this had resulted in some intellectuals' abandoning faith in science as such. This fact continued to be one of the major events of our times and it continued to be among the most deplorable events of the age insofar as it involved "a reversion to moral attitudes and beliefs which intellectuals as a class had abandoned." Not only must the scientific attitude gain a "place in the concerns and interests of highest importance to the mass of men" which it has never enjoyed, but a relapse into supernaturalistic modes of thought must not become the refuge of distraught intellectuals. "Not that anti-supernaturalism suffices," Dewey concluded, "but that freedom from it will provide an opportunity for a religious experience to develop that [in contrast to traditional religion] is deeply and pervasively human and humane."[56]

Niebuhr was but one of more than 1,000 signatures representing sponsors of a testimonial dinner held in honor of Dewey's ninetieth birthday. The ceremony was held in the Grand Ball Room of the Commodore Hotel in New York City on October 20, 1949. Prime Minister Jawaharlal Nehru of India had been invited as a special guest. As James Gutmann recounts it, Nehru was detained at a reception at the Indian Embassy to the United Nations. We waited around late in the evening, and when Nehru came to the hall, Dewey was among the first to see him coming, and at 90, rushed to the end of the platform to greet Nehru. It was something very moving, the representative of American philosophy, John Dewey and Nehru, who was not only the statesman but himself considered a philosopher, at least in a non-technical, but in significant sense, standing side by side . . . the symbolic value was quite striking.[57]

Within the space of three years John Dewey would be dead at age ninety-three. Reinhold Niebuhr, who was fifty-seven at that time, would live on until 1971 dying at the age of seventy-nine. Although Niebuhr wrote about Dewey on occasion throughout the remainder of his career, a series of strokes in 1952 left him physically impaired with partial paralysis. The engagement between these two men, although sporadic and often indirect, was significant on many levels, not the least of which was because it mirrored many of the major issues of an era in American intellectual history. In retrospect it seems fair to say, however, that Niebuhr and Dewey broke over what, in the final analysis, might be considered to be their respective versions—and visions—of what a pragmatic reading of the history of thought should or should not consider important for what Richard Rorty has called the ongoing conversation of a culture.

Plate 1. Reinhold Niebuhr at Union Theological Seminary in New York in the early 1930s near the time of the appearance of Moral Man and Immoral Society.

Plate 2. John Dewey in this early seventies in the early part of the 1930s.

Plate 3. Reinhold Niebuhr in the early to mid-1930s.

Plate 4. John Dewey surrounded by his children and his second wife, Roberta, on October 20, 1949, at his 90th birthday celebration at the Waldorf Astoria Hotel, New York.

*Plate 5. Reinhold Niebuhr at Union Theological Seminary at the zenith
of his career in the late 1940s.*

Plate 6. John Dewey in 1943 at the time the second volume of Niebuhr's Gifford Lectures, The Nature and Destiny of Man, *had been published.*

Plate 7. John Dewey at 90 relaxing at Maple Lodge in 1949.

Plate 8. Reinhold Niebuhr and friends sometime between 1953 and 1960 after Niebuhr's stroke.

Plate 9. Reinhold Niebuhr at the time of his retirement in 1960.

Part Two

The Major Issues

8

Conflict over Naturalism

The legacy of modern naturalism had deeply troubled Niebuhr beginning with his seminary and graduate school days at Yale and continuing, albeit with maturing assessment and shifting emphases, throughout his life. Indeed, in the course of the controversy between Niebuhr and Dewey, "naturalism" became a major point of contention. The issues involved here, however, were never as simple as they might have appeared to either man. Niebuhr was never comfortable with the burden of the naturalistic-supernaturalistic legacy, and if forced into that framework he usually, but not unequivocally, backed away from the language of supernaturalism. John Herman Randall, Jr., once depicted "Niebuhr's thought [as] a Christian naturalism."[1] Sidney Hook, in fact, confirmed that Randall teasingly regarded Niebuhr as, at heart, a "closet naturalist."[2] Although there might be some truth to this view, it is important to note that Deweyites Randall and Hook had a vested interest in seeing that their mutual and respected friend Niebuhr was sympathetic to the antidualism which their own shared pragmatic naturalism emphasized. Dewey, of course, also developed an uncompromising naturalism which was an antidote to the traditional metaphysical and theological dualisms of Western thought. But his formulation and defense of naturalism was, in addition, a sharp critique of reductionistic and sensationalistic empiricism. In this regard both Dewey and Niebuhr were equally adamant in their opposition to any formulation of naturalism that undermined either the complexity and uniqueness of human existence or the richness of experience.

Idealism as Ally

One clue to both Niebuhr's repetitive attacks on naturalism and Dewey's Herculean efforts to effect a reformulation of naturalism via a thoroughgoing reconstruction of philosophy can be found in their respective attitudes toward nineteenth century idealism. Idealism was both the context and ally of their early efforts to overcome classical empirical naturalism's vision of human nature. Both men labored early on in the vineyards of philosophical idealism. Indeed, when Dewey and Niebuhr were each in their twenties (the early 1880s for Dewey and 1914–15 in the case of Niebuhr), idealism had a magnetic, although qualified, attraction and provided the framework out of which each man's understanding of and antipathy towards naturalism would be formulated. As much as Dewey and Niebuhr later turned against idealism, they continued to acknowledge that, in important ways, idealism was superior to many of the leitmotifs of the philosophies against which it contended—most especially in idealism's recognition of what might be termed "the depth and complexity of human existence."

For Dewey "modern idealistic theories of knowledge have apprehended the fact that the object of knowledge implies that the found rather than the given is the proper subject matter of science."[3] The idealistic tradition rightly opposed the physicalistic reductionism of the sensational empiricists. Although idealism perpetuated the dualistic tradition of equating the real with the rational and then abstracted both from the world of nature, idealism did have a clear sense of the active-reconstructive role of intelligence. Moreover, in opposing tendencies toward either divesting nature of purpose and value or consigning them to the realm of subjectivity, idealism sought to reinstate both teleology and community—in spite of its disastrous reification of the transcendental moral and spiritual orders. As Paul Conkin put it when writing on Dewey: "Even the most speculative of idealists, with their wanton hyperbole in expression, came closer than the older empiricists to the wholeness of experience and more easily embraced a morally acceptable community."[4] Dewey, in fact, never relinquished his early appreciation of either idealism's insistence on the active role of intelligence or its sense of the relatedness of experience in spite of the fact that he strove to get around the problems of both idealism and early empiricism.

Even in his mature writings Niebuhr insisted that "Idealistic philosophy always had the advantage over naturalism in that it appreciates this depth of human spirit"—a depth that envisioned the self as "more than an organic unity."[5] But in his view of idealism the concrete particular self is ultimately lost to the abstract universal, and the domain of value—although clearly recognized—is safeguarded only by conceiving reason abstractly and by divorcing reason from nature, *nous* from *physis*. Like Dewey, Niebuhr saw that idealism's "dualism prevents it from understanding the organic relation between nature and reason and the dependence of reason upon nature."[6]

In Dewey's early years as a philosophical novice he defended the religious and moral tenets of his liberal Vermont Congregationalism against the implications of materialistic naturalism. Admittedly, for Dewey, in the early 1880s it was philosophy and not theology that constituted both foundation and guardian for whatever was worthwhile in religion and morality, and by 1890 all explicitly traditional religious language had disappeared altogether.[7] In one of his earliest efforts Dewey argued that a wholly materialistic theory of nature rested on an absolute monism which was inconsistent with its own metaphysical pretensions. In Dewey's account "materialism" itself depends on "a belief in the possibility of ontological knowledge of such objective reality, a claim that rules out the mind understood as only an effect of the phenomenal world. In a phrase, monistic materialism ends up taking for granted an "original irresolvable dualism" which, if held, "assumes things which thoroughly destroy the theory."[8] The vital issue behind this charge was that the reductionism implicit in a materialistic interpretation of nature undermined both purpose and value and afforded little, if any, room for human personality cum mental or moral agency. What is to be noted relative to Dewey's early polemic is that irrespective of the substantive changes in both his and Niebuhr's position over the years, they would both seek to frame broader and deeper accounts of the human situation consistent with their earliest critical instincts—however inappropriately these insights were uncritically linked with philosophical idealism.

Dewey would return to this issue of "materialistic naturalism" in a polemical essay published in 1943. In that essay he rigorously defended his understanding of naturalism against what he regarded as a clear and present danger arising out of a resurgent supernaturalism. By the time Dewey wrote "Anti-Naturalism in Extremis" he had formulated a pragmatic naturalism that resolved his earlier problems with classical empiricism. He could then maintain that both supernaturalists and other nonnaturalists (whom Dewey regarded as descendents of the former)

> identify naturalism with "materialism." They then employ the identification to charge naturalists with reduction of all distinctive human values, moral, esthetic, logical, to blind mechanistic conjunctions of material entities—a reduction which is in effect their complete destruction. This identification thus permits anti-naturalists to substitute name-calling for a discussion of specific issues in their proper terms in connection with concrete evidence.[9]

Early on, however, Dewey's own development led him to embrace idealism under the influence of his University of Michigan-based neo-

Hegelian mentor George Sylvester Morris, who taught at Johns Hopkins one semester each year. The convolutions in Dewey's thought during the idealistic period between his early intuitionism and his eventual instrumental naturalism need not concern us here.[10] Suffice it to say that while Dewey was enroute from the antidualistic and unitive vision of Hegelianism to his resting place in pragmatic naturalism, his underlying concern was with the formulation of a vision of the world that would be consonant with a view of experience that, although not limited to human experience, was recognizably human. That is to say, Dewey continued to resist a conception of nature that was the legacy of sensationalistic empiricism. The world as experienced was not accurately represented by discrete disconnected sensations and ideas devoid of relatedness. Neither was nature discontinuous and fundamentally value neutral. And because the Kantian compartmentalization of "theoretical" and "practical" knowledge was a woefully inadequate solution to the problem, it appeared to the young Dewey that idealism provided a way out of the dilemma. Eventually the legacy of Western dualism which persisted in force in idealism's bifurcation of reason and nature, human and Divine, body and spirit, the finite and the infinite, and the relative and the absolute led Dewey to Hegel, whose dialectical life-logic and concrete universal seemed, temporarily at least, to reknit what early idealism had driven assunder. Hegel's solution, however, became chimerical to Dewey. Dewey was finally convinced that

> The inherent vice of all intellectual schemes of idealism is that they convert the idealism of action into a system of beliefs about antecedent reality. The character assigned this reality is so different from that which observation and reflection lead to and support that these schemes inevitably glide into alliance with the supernatural.[11]

Thus, although idealism helped Dewey to overcome the materialistic and mechanistic views associated with sensationalistic empiricism, it could not reconnect the self with nature in a teleologically satisfactory manner. "Idealism," Dewey later noted, "is guilty of neglect that thought and knowledge are histories."[12] Permitting himself the locution that "nature . . . is idealizable," Dewey claimed that nature

> lends itself to operations by which it is perfected. The process is not a passive one. Rather nature gives, not always freely, but in response to search, means and material by which the values we judge to have supreme quality may be embodied in existence. It

depends upon the choice of man whether he employs what nature provides and for what ends he uses it.[13]

It was not until Dewey radically immanentized and relativized Hegel with the aid of Darwinian organicism that he was well on his way toward the pragmatic naturalism from which he launched his root and branch reconstruction of philosophy.

Reinhold Niebuhr's distrust of naturalism was clearly present from the very beginning. In his Yale B.D. thesis of 1914 on the topic of "The Validity and Certainty of Religious Knowledge," Niebuhr—in youthful fashion—set forth one of the major and perennially recurring concerns of his intellectual life: that naturalism fails to provide an adequate framework for explicating both the complexities and richness of selfhood. In the early groping language of the twenty-two-year-old Niebuhr, the difficulty with scientific naturalism was found in its inability to make room for "personality"—the deepest need of humankind that naturalism failed to meet. Religion's role had been to safeguard both personality and value in a world that scientific naturalism interpreted in impersonal and deterministic terms. Many of the later themes that Niebuhr would reformulate and develop were already nascent in the following remarks from the B.D. thesis: "In naturalism," he contended,

> the forces of external existence are supreme. With their little regard for what is dear to us they might at any time wipe out human existence. We would almost have to suppose that such indeed must some day be the case. Furthermore man would have no warrant that the relative perfection he had attained and which by his sacrifice was attained by future generations would have any degree of permanence. Why could not all for which we have labored be wiped out by a short period of human degeneracy. Any teleological faith, so necessary for the moral order, would be absolutely unjustified. . . .
>
> In the fight of personality for existence in the universe, a soul finds not only the conservation but an immediate appreciation of its values necessary. It wishes to be insured not only against the ultimate dangers of inimical forces but it wishes the assurance of aid in its most immediate struggles. It wishes in other words not only a strong God to insure success in the struggle of life but an intimate God to give aid in the struggles of life.[14]

Although Dewey's earliest reservations regarding naturalism were rooted in the liberal Protestantism of the Andover school, his defense of the concerns and values of that heritage soon took on a purely philosophical character. Niebuhr, on the other hand, strenuously defended "religion" as the solitary basis for grounding and sustaining personality, value, and hope in the world. And even though his theology would break loose from the older personalistic-liberal forms, demanding a reformulation of the issues overall, the fundamental interdependency between the "religious" and the "human" conceived in terms of meaning, purpose, and uniqueness would remain largely intact—although recast in terms closer to Martin Buber. Moreover, whereas Dewey disabused himself early on of the discontinuities embedded in classical or modern dualisms, the young Niebuhr of 1914 was only marginally troubled by the dualisms of the inherited tradition. In effect, the young Niebuhr took his idealism plain, but not straight. He was at this juncture unprepared to jettison the dualism that he held to be central to a defense of personality and value, yet he was rather doubtful of the metaphysical underpinnings on which such dualism had come to rest.

In his 1914 thesis Niebuhr identified with "the revolt of men like William James" against the mechanistic determinism of modern naturalism. He did so not only because of the intellectual difficulties associated with such naturalism but because James's revolt was "the revolt of a growing moral consciousness in men that is becoming increasingly impatient with a universe in which its struggles are without effect and its powers not its own. Man," Niebuhr claimed in Jamesian fashion, "wants to know that the battle of life is not a sham battle before he can be persuaded to take a real interest."[15] What Niebuhr here called *wanting to know* is the source of much difficulty with him. He struggled with the issue as to whether such a claim has epistemological grounding or whether *know* is to be construed as "belief" much in the fashion of James's *hope*. Niebuhr embraced a quite traditional theistic dualism, as he was convinced that some version and vision of a transcendent God were required as a basis both for personality and the viability of the moral life. He recognized that "this feeling of a need for an intimate God who appreciates our personal and moral values . . . is thought to be the result of an unwarranted 'tendermindedness.'" Yet with an eye to naturalists such as James and Dewey, Niebuhr noted that "these naturalistic thinkers who have accepted the demand [of resisting the implications of a too restrictive naturalism] as a legitimate one and have tried to meet it, are, very significantly, former adherents of traditional faith or have been strongly influenced by it."[16]

Niebuhr pointed to the fact that of all the various forms of naturalism which had involved themselves with the religious question, only pragmatism had come close to a genuinely sympathetic understanding of the issues. Yet throughout his career, although aware of

Dewey's attempt to secure the realms of personal and moral life on a naturalistic basis, Niebuhr clearly preferred the pragmatism of James over that of Dewey. For James not only appeared sympathetic to the kind of transcendental theism Niebuhr held to be crucial to both human personality and the moral struggle, he had also avoided engaging in a polemical defense of the type of naturalism that Niebuhr would come to see as metaphysically dogmatic. Certainly, the points at which James proved to be an embarrassment to fellow pragmatists were indicative of reasons why the Jamesian account of pragmatism held greater appeal to Niebuhr than Dewey's scientifically dominated account of naturalism.

The youthful Niebuhr recoiled from what he saw as the pragmatic severance of the Gordian knot of traditional epistemology. In his first book, published in 1927, he argued that "religion must be able to impress the modern world with the essential plausibility and scientific respectability of its fundamental affirmations."[17] As Niebuhr so aptly expressed it in a chapter significantly entitled "A Philosophical Basis for an Ethical Religion," it is crucial that "the values of personality are related to cosmic facts."[18]

It has been noted that Niebuhr took his idealism plain but not straight. Although he noted the fact that idealism appreciated the domain of personal life more readily than most forms of naturalism, Niebuhr never was convinced that idealism could deliver the goods promised in providing rational grounds for the dualisms which in his early years seemed so crucial. Aside from his tendency to regard idealism as susceptable to pantheism or determinim,[19] Niebuhr's call for the discovery of rational grounds for certainty acknowledged the tenuous metaphysics of idealism against which so much modern thought inveighed.

What was new in *Does Civilization Need Religion?* was a shift to socioethical considerations—a shift comparable to Dewey's increased commitment to matters of politics and social reform soon after his arrival at the University of Chicago in 1894. In the case of both Niebuhr and Dewey, religious and philosophical defenses of the importance of individual personality gave way to an intensified awareness of the social and political dimensions of modern industrial civilization. However, whereas this emphasis drew Niebuhr deeper into a search for the sense and relevance of the religious heritage, Dewey's emerging social consciousness resulted in his "distancing himself from [the] Congregationalism [of his youth]" and led to a lapse in church affiliation.[20]

In 1927 Niebuhr gave the ethical concerns occasioned by the crisis in society priority over the thirst for metaphysical consistency. In his judgment an adequate ethics was more important for religion than an adequate metaphysics. Niebuhr still wanted a dualism that, in offsetting the tendencies toward either monism or pantheism, would provide a basis for distinctions between man and God and the real and the ideal, which he believed were crucial for safeguarding certain truths. The truths thus safeguarded, however, were increasingly spelled out in terms of conflicting aspects within human nature rather than solely in terms of grounding personality as such. Niebuhr believed that "if a place for freedom and purpose in the cosmic order, however conditioned, is discovered the essential affirmation of religious faith is metaphysically verifed."[21] But he was content with what he called the *scientific and metaphysical virtues* of the pluralism of William James in spite of their inconsistencies. The reason is that Niebuhr had come to view such a qualified dualism as possessing greater moral potency than rival monisms or pantheisms, and as he saw it, "it is in fact better for religion to forego perfect metaphysical consistency for the sake of moral potency."[22]

Issues in "Naturalism"

If idealism supplied the historical and conceptual framework for Dewey's early discovery of the limitations and errors of the older naturalism as well as for focusing his storehouse of values, one must look to Dewey's mature position to grasp the type of naturalism he eventually claimed as his own. Most important, it was within this reformulation of naturalism that an understanding of how his storehouse of values was maintained becomes possible. Dewey's major concern became that of seeking to preserve such values in a strictly naturalistic framework from which the residues of dualism and transcendentalism had been exorcised.

Dewey, Paul Conkin noted, "transformed his youthful idealism into a tremendously broad and humane form of naturalism,"[23] and for all his criticism of Dewey's naturalism Niebuhr would certainly concur. Dewey's naturalism was, indeed, as humane as his humanism was naturalistic. This transformation came by way of an amalgamation of Darwin's vision of nature as organic, dynamic, adaptive, and emergent with a thoroughly immanentized Hegelianism that freed him from the dualistic, formalistic, and static categories which had been dominant in Western thought. Prior to his move into Darwinism, Dewey found in Hegelian syntheses a way of breaking down the barriers that had separated mind from matter, God from humanity, subject from object, and real from ideal. Not only was Hegel's vision restorative of a sense of unity within plurality, it also provided Dewey with a vision, as Richard Bernstein put it, of "life in all its forms as a dynamic interplay of interrelated and interdependent elements where distinctions are functional and changing rather than fixed and static."[24] It must be said parenthetically that Niebuhr, too, would eventually seek egress from his early defense of dualism by way of a more dialectical understanding of the relation of opposites. Moreover, it is from the vantage point of his later penchant for dialectical thinking (which alarmed both foe and some friends alike) that Niebuhr would be inclined to suspect that Dewey, while utilizing the synthesis of heretofore untenable oppositions in actual life, nonetheless failed to sustain the opposing tensions dialectically enough.[25]

A word here is in order regarding "mechanistic" naturalism. Dewey's theory of "transactions" was designed to expose the artificiality of drawing boundaries between the interacting organism and its environment. Thus, as he had shown as early as 1896 in his pivotal essay on "The Reflex Arc Concept in Psychology," organic interaction demands, on empirical grounds, a more functional, dynamic-holistic interpretation of human behavior than the mechanical-static-discrete event account of the stimulus-response psychology then coming into vogue. Dewey disapproved of mechanical accounts of life processes. Moreover, he and Niebuhr shared a common aversion to any understanding of naturalism that was "mechanical," as Dewey put it, "in the sense of assuming separate things acting upon one another purely externally by push and pull."[26]

At the same time Dewey did not use the pejorative epithet "mechanistic naturalism" as a scare tactic or as a summary dismissal of modern science.[27] Quite to the contrary, Dewey, in his seminal work of 1920 (*Reconstruction in Philosophy*), held that the reconception of nature as a set of mechanical interactions actually aided in the liberation of nature—and hence of human life within it—from the tyranny of fixed and formal ends set by nature that largely rendered foolish any human efforts to alter and direct change. This liberation meant that "observation and imagination were emancipated, and experimental control for scientific and practical purposes enormously stimulated."[28] Looking at the mechanical view as a requirement of experimental procedures by which control and redirection of nature can be achieved instead of as an extrapolated account of reality as such, dissolved the pseudo-problem of attempting a reconciliation of a totally mechanical universe with meaning and purpose in human life. Mechanism in this sense was simply a way of getting at physical nature so as to facilitate the human control of natural forces. In Dewey's acount, the mechanical view of nature was conceived pragmatically, not ontocosmologically. Looking at nature mechanically opened up the "natural" world to intelligent direction and thereby enabled human beings to introduce new ends and purposes into the process by means of intelligent action. At its core "the mechanization of nature," Dewey contended, "is the condition of a practical and progressive idealism in action."[29]

Niebuhr, on the other hand, was far less sanguine about Dewey's euphoria. He saw here the embodiment of a pre- and extra-scientific utopianism in the extreme and rather one-dimensional case that Dewey had made for scientific control of nature. A claim Niebuhr made in 1949 is simply typical of a viewpoint he expressed over and over again:

> History has taken a very ironic vengeance upon a culture which imagined that man's conquest of nature solved [its problems]. For the same technical instruments by which men have gained a comparative security against the perils and caprices of nature (though even here the security is not as absolute as they imagined) have created a technical civilization in which men are in greater peril of each other than in simple communities.[30]

Initially, as Bernstein pointed out, Dewey saw no real opposition between his Hegelianism and the experimental science of which, by the turn of the century, he would become an unqualified philosophical champion.[31] Only after his turn to Darwin was Dewey able to transform residual Hegelian elements into a reasonably consistent naturalism in which humankind was wholly fitted. Dewey had in effect to bring his Hegel to earth without totally discounting all that he had learned from him. Not least of all, Dewey came to insist that any unifying principle in existence belonged to nature as such. Moreover, to Dewey, whatever passed for spirit was nothing other than the product of the force of finite intelligence that gave direction and purpose to life understood as an everchanging nonultimate mundane affair. Dewey's mature thought was forged in the Darwinian age. And the clear and irrefutable lessons Darwinianism offered, according to John Herman Randall, Jr., were that any "antithesis between Nature and the Supernatural or Transcendental" was untenable and that a most important corollary of this, namely, that "the gulf between the nature of the 'natural scientist' and human life," is obliterated.[32] What is also true about Dewey's appropriation and use of Darwin is that in restoring human nature to "nature" he was able to recognize and resolutely oppose the early empiricism which not only particalized the world but which also erected an unbridgeable chasm between human experience and nature. On this point the thrust of Niebuhr's thought was in general agreement with Dewey's "naturalism."

The dominant and all-encompassing lesson Dewey learned from Darwin was that an organic biologistic model should be central to reconstructing a view of the human in nature. In his 1909 essay on "The Influence of Darwinism on Philosophy," Dewey not only regarded Darwin's contribution to be epochal with respect to the natural sciences, but also as destined eventually "to transform the logic of knowledge, and hence the treatment of morals, politics and religion."[33] For Dewey this came to represent even more than the poignant and far-reaching fact that Darwinian thinking forced a vision of development and change on all natural and historical aspects of existence. It first and foremost meant that a new paradigm was available for reconnecting humanness unequivocally and unreservedly to the natural world from which so much Western thought had severed it. Furthermore, the paradigm would govern the delineation of what, after all, it meant to be a human being qua human being. Dewey's reformulation of naturalism then—essential to his reconstruction of philosophy—was launched by way of Darwin yet trailing elements of Hegelianism. Darwin, in effect, was the linchpin for the immanentalization of Hegel.

As for Niebuhr, he had no problem with Darwinian science or with what he regarded as the empirical rather than the ontological side of modern science in general. Writing for a 1958 collection of anniversary essays honoring Darwin's *Origin of Species*, Niebuhr reiterated his view that "the resistance of the religious community . . . to the Darwinian discoveries in science was [both] stubborn and pathetic."[34] He acknowledged the foolishness and futility born of religion's rejection of Darwinian science as well as the methods by means of which certain theologies sought to defend the dignity of the self. Niebuhr nonetheless insisted that, given the absurdities spawned in the wake (and name) of Darwin in the areas of morality and history, "the religious impulse to defend the unique dignity of man [was] not as foolish as [it] seemed."[35] His conviction was that "the basic error introduced by Dawinian biology into historical studies" was not in maintaining "that natural as well as historical structures were subject to temporal development" (which Niebuhr saw as Darwin's main acheivement), but rather in the claim "that historical processes and natural processes were sufficiently identical to make the same scientific method applicable to both fields."[36]

As Niebuhr's critique of naturalism matured, he continued to abhor the obscurantism with which some versions of Christianity resisted modern science when that science conflicted with some cherished belief or other. What he had specifically to say on the issue of evolution applied across the board to all of the contributions of the natural sciences. Niebuhr, writing in 1955, was adamant in his repudiation of

> the pathetic efforts to refute undoubted discoveries about biological evolution by illicit appeals to the Biblical doctrine of creation, as if it were an alternative to scientific analysis of causes rather than a reference to the mystery which lies beyond all causal sequences and prompts reverence for the emergence

of any novelty in the temporal flux, particularly the emergence
of such a novelty as the human being. . . . There can be no question about the futility of the effort to guard the idea of the uniqueness of the human person by resisting and defying the evidence of the biological scientists in regard to the evolution of
natural forms.[37]

Niebuhr's naturalistic critics, both friendly and unfriendly, could
not help but think he had a hidden agenda. They saw him as seeking to
protect cherished illusions of his own against the encroachment of the
natual sciences, however much these illusions had been put into a demythologized guise. Niebuhr, of course, saw it differently. He again and
again acknowledged the historical achievement of the sciences in destroying "the partnership between piety and obscurantism, and between
religious faith and Aristotelian ontology," and praised the likes of
"Thomas Huxley who insisted on scrupulous honesty being in perfect
conformity to the great virtue of the scientific enterprise, which was and
is to 'follow the evidence.' "[38] Niebuhr saw his own attack on naturalism
and the scientific method as a frank attempt to get apologists for science
such as Dewey to be honest and open about science itself. His polemic
was twofold: first, Niebuhr claimed that neither the old nor the new
naturalism could fully or faithfully account for the full range of human
experience; and, second, he saw in Dewey's naturalism exaggerated
claims for a methodology that spawned its own species of dogmatism.
Such claims masked certain metaphysical presuppositions behind the
very naturalism out of which the sciences operated. Of equal importance
to Niebuhr was the uncritical assumption that the methods so productive in regard to the physical sciences could be equally fruitful in what
Vico had called the "new science" and Dilthey later labeled *Geisteswissenschaften*—the "human studies."

Method and Metaphysics

Niebuhr was not immune from the temptation to employ verbal hyperbole on occasion, a characteristic associated with his sometimes aphoris-
tic style of expression. One of the more notable instances along these
lines had been noticed by naturalists and received scathing criticism at
the hands of one of Dewey's staunchest defenders, Sidney Hook. Niebuhr
once remarked that "science which is only science cannot be scientifically accurate."[39] Dewey's self-described "bulldog" Sidney Hook, who on
many levels admired Niebuhr, severely indicted him for unwittingly

contributing to what Hook called the "new failure of nerve," a failure that Hook, Dewey, and others saw running rampant in the land during the early 1940s. Hook saw in Niebuhr's statement an "eloquent revelation" of the fact that "the attack upon scientific method, in order to be free to believe whatever voice speaks to us, is a flight from responsibility" and a capitulation to the regnant obscurantism.[40] While acknowledging that "science has known its dogmatism, too," Hook echoed Dewey's sentiments exactly when he suggested that "the cure of bad science is better science, not theology."[41]

If one takes the historical ambiguity of the term *science* to heart, taking into consideration both its recent meaning as referring to methodologies-operations characteristic of the modern natural sciences and its broader classical meaning as "wisdom," the point of Niebuhr's aphorism gains clarity. Niebuhr was saying, rather sharply, that the knowledge that comes from the natural sciences is not always wise insofar as it pretends to exhaust our understanding of the particular life we live as human beings. His choice of phrase was that "an object which has both surface and depth cannot be correctly interpreted in terms of one when it has in fact two [dimensions]."[42]

Although Dewey and his fellow naturalists were not unduly alarmed by resurgent forms of anti- or extranaturalism, Niebuhr saw in the then current adulation of naturalism and the incessant appeal to scientific method an exaggerated claim to be able to see experience plain and direct, unencumbered by prejudicial bias. Such a claim becomes insidious precisely at the point of its pretention to possess an unfiltered and therefore undistorted view of experience. As late as 1954 during an interview for Columbia University's Oral History Collection Niebuhr, specifically citing Dewey, stated that "presuppositions are the dogmas of our life. They are the spectacles by which we see things. Professor Dewey and all these other people talk about experience, nothing but experience should determine truth, but this is fantastic because we don't see except through our spectacles [which] color things very much."[43] Niebuhr was again focusing upon something he had long felt Dewey and many other naturalists within the orbit of Columbia University during the 1930s and 1940s were missing in their unrelenting defense of scientific method.

Dewey and his supporters represented a point of view that, in historical perspective, had been under prolonged political and doctrinal seige from religious quarters. Within the scope of a more recent history, Niebuhr saw himself doing battle on these issues against the myopia of *both* theological *and* scientific dogmatism. Two estimates of naturalism were in play. Dewey saw the broad strokes of an extended naturalism, via the language and methodology of the sciences, to be the only way of establishing a truly rational explication of the world—human as well as nonhuman. Niebuhr, however, saw recent naturalism as having taken leave of its empirical moorings. It did so by surreptitiously absolutizing a method and by indulging in ontological assumptions while denying it did so. Niebuhr insisted that "a justified empiricism in regard to the natural order may become so dominated by ontological (in this case naturalistic) presuppositions that it becomes impossible to be genuinely empirical about facts of a different order [pertaining to the uniqueness of human existence] which do not fit into the ontological presuppositions."[44] This opens onto the problem of what Niebuhr generally referred to as *scientism*.

By *scientism* Niebuhr meant the unwarranted belief in scientific method as the exhaustive approach for understanding human nature and as a curative solution for what Dewey called the *problems of men*, the title given to a book published in 1946 which included key articles published on that topic between 1935 and 1944. Niebuhr was referring to the understandable euphoria associated with the rise of scientific thought that resulted, however, in both serious miscalculations as to its own range of application and a new and sometimes stifling dogmatism in the modern world. Niebuhr's views echoed Whitehead's observation that "nothing is more curious than the self-satisfied dogmatism with which mankind at each period of its history cherishes the delusion of the finality of its existing modes of knowledge. Sceptics and believers are all alike." Whitehead claimed, "At this moment scientists and sceptics are the leading dogmatists," concluding wryly that "this dogmatic common sense is the death of philosophical adventure."[45]

Niebuhr noted that "naturalism never became a serious option for man throughout the history of Western culture until the phenomenal triumphs of modern science and its conquest of nature seemed to make it plausible."[46] What was really at issue for him was formulated in a series of rhetorical questions posed in 1949. Among these questions Niebuhr asked,

> Does it [the scientific culture] not incline to build metaphysical systems upon the erroneous confidence in natural cause as the final and adequate principle of meaning? Are not the historical sciences easily persuaded that the frameworks of meaning which they use as a loom upon which to weave the detailed facts of history into a pattern are the consequences, rather than the presupposition, of their scientific pursuit? And do not the various sciences pretending to be presuppositionless, insinuate

metaphysical presuppositions into their analyses which are most congenial to the type of reality subject to their analysis?[47]

Of course, Dewey maintained that a scientifically informed philosophy operated as a "critique of prejudices"[48] and that the "empirical naturalism" he was championing was the only solid foundation for the philosophical enterprise. Niebuhr, quite pointedly, thought otherwise. In his view, so common and deep-seated was the commonsensical view of scientific method among the intellectuals of the time, that Dewey was simply unable to see the need of the self-application of his own sine qua non of philosophy as a "critique of prejudices." Indeed, the scientific culture itself required "the criticism of wider philosophical disciplines." In essence, Niebuhr contended, it is precisely because of the inadequacies and pretensions of modern science that "there must be a movement from science to philosophy to counteract the movement from philosophy to science."[49] To put the most favorable light on it, Niebuhr did not see himself as pointing to some alternative nonscientific method, as it were, to be substituted for scientific method. Instead, he saw himself as resisting what he suspected to be the tyranny of methodology itself and was calling for a pragmatic antidogmatism in all directions at this very point. What Niebuhr seemed to be calling for is an intellectually open, rigorous and broadly based cultural criticism of the very claims on behalf of scientific philosophy that found both their supreme locus and advocacy in John Dewey!

Dewey, obviously, did not see things this way and was not quite as easily situated within Niebuhr's representation of science and scientific method as Niebuhr wanted him to be. In his Gifford Lectures published in 1929, Dewey displayed an awareness of the tendency toward "idolatry" to which science was prone. After all, the desire for certainty was part of the very fabric of Western history, and "the marking off of certain conclusions as alone truly science, whether mathematical or physical, is an historical incident."[50] For this reason it was historically understandable that the mystique of specialization and the temptation to treat itself "as an exclusive and esoteric understanding" resulted in a form of self-glorification in which nothing less than "truth" was at stake. It was thus, according to Dewey, that "'science,' meaning physical knowledge, became a kind of sanctuary. A religious atmosphere, not to say an idolatrous one, was created. 'Science' was set apart; its findings were supposed to have a privileged relation to the real."[51]

Dewey was critical of both the preceding view of science and the inordinate claims made for it. His understanding of the scientific attitude as "that which is capable of enjoying the doubtful"[52] meant that the kind of disciplined intelligence which enjoys the problematic is a "method operating within the world" and "places physical knowledge in respect to other kinds of knowing."[53] Experimental inquiry was such that "monopolies of the idea of science" were discounted. Dewey contended that "There is no kind of inquiry which has a monopoly of the honorable title of knowledge. The engineer, the artist, the historian, the man of affairs attain knowledge in the degree they employ the methods that enable them to solve the problems which develop in the subject-matter they are concerned with."[54]

Dewey's recognition of the possibility of an idolatrous science turned on both the tendencies to claim "a privileged relation to the real" and to see science as an "exclusive and esoteric" activity. But what he removed as an obstruction on the metaphysical level in the first tendency, he handed back as a methodological obstruction, in the second tendency. At least this is the judgment Niebuhr made in his suspicion that Dewey's naturalism trafficked off the presupposition that something called *the* scientific method existed and that this method operated as a model of rationality adequate for whatever is intended by the term "knowledge."

Niebuhr's suggestion that we needed a movement "from science to philosophy" as a corrective against the recent historical movement from "philosophy to science" should not be viewed simply as a nostalgic yearning for some metaphysical or religious past. It was, rather, indicative of his uneasiness with what William Shea more recently identified as the metaphysical and methodological implications of "the empirical principle."[55] Niebuhr's suggestion can be seen more profitably as a pragmatic point that needed to be made, even against the foremost pragmatist of the century. No less a Deweyite than Richard Rorty acknowledges that "the standard philosophical strategy of most naturalisms is to find some way of showing that our own culture has indeed got hold of the essence of man—thus making all new and incommensurable vocabularies merely 'noncognitive' ornamentation."[56] But Rorty goes on to exempt Dewey from this criticism when he writes:

> Dewey, it seems to me, is the one author usually classified as a "naturalist" who did not have this reductive attitude, despite his incessant talk about the "scientific method." Dewey's peculiar achievement was to have remained sufficiently Hegelian not to think of natural science as having an inside track on the essence of things, while becoming sufficiently naturalistic to think of human beings in Darwinian terms.[57]

Perhaps so—at least insofar as Dewey strove mightily to formulate a reconstruction in philosophy that would overcome essentialism in

Western thought. It is certainly clear that he left epistemological and ethical absolutism behind. It is dubious that Dewey's "reconstruction of philosphy" succeeded in the measure that either he had hoped or Rorty insists. Given the interplay between "nature" and "experience," on the one hand, and his commitment to "scientific method," on the other, Dewey's "naturalism" suggested, at minimum, a reluctance to give up entirely traces of "metaphysical" absolutism. Bruce Jannusch claims that, although it is true that "neo-pragmatism [of the type developed by Richard Rorty] views science as one genre of literature, the positivists erected Science as an idol to fill the place once held by God."[58] In my judgment there are sufficient positivistic tendencies in Dewey's conception of science that Niebuhr correctly picked up on. Certainly for Niebuhr it was precisely Dewey's "incessant talk about 'scientific method'" that suggested a problem. After all, it was Dewey who penned the lines: "new methods of inquiry and reflection have become for the educated man today the final arbiter of all questions of fact, existence and intellectual assent."[59]

Niebuhr would not only insist that there are other ways of talking than the scientific way, he would also maintain that these other ways of talking were crucial in penetrating the premature closures that scientific talk had been busily erecting. Most important is the recognition that Science and *the* scientific method constituted the lingering shadow of foundationalism in both Dewey and Dewey's time. In this respect it is quite fair to say, albeit, on different grounds, that both Dewey and Niebuhr were not quite ready to give up the metaphysical ghosts of the past.

What had characterized the period since the triumph of the scientific conquest of nature was, in Niebuhr's phrase, a "naturalistic ontology." The treachery in all of this lay in the fact that modern naturalism's "animus against 'dogma'" in the form of either classical rationalism or religious authoritarianism was made "in the name of [an] 'empiricism'" that contained hidden dogmas of its own and out of those dogmas spawned its own set of illusions.[60] Blindness to one's own illusions and the conviction that an allegedly neutral *empirical* inquiry had overcome the vestiges of prejudiced judgment were, in Niebuhr's view, the hallmarks of the kind of naturalism Dewey and his followers propagated. What Niebuhr specifically called the *hidden dogmas* of naturalism were both plentifully evident and consistently masked by the claims made on behalf of scientific inquiry. Thus by his use of the term *naturalistic ontology* Niebuhr sought to call attention to the presuppositions associated with inquiry as such. Relying on James Conant's *Science and Common Sense*, Niebuhr equated his use of the term *presuppositions* with Conant's *conceptual schemes*, which, in Niebuhr's judgment, constituted the "hidden dogmas" of science. These "hidden dogmas" or frames of meaning that governed inquiry were drawn from sources other than an allegedly pure and neutral science. Moreover, being presupposed and therefore hidden, "they are usually more potent for being implicit rather than explicit."[61]

The assumption among natural scientists was that such conceptual schemes were kept to a minimum and prevented from having a distortive effect by being open to an ongoing process of critical self-correction. Indeed, from the time of Francis Bacon this had been assumed to be a relatively simple procedure, although "practically," Niebuhr contended, these assumptions "proved themselves powerful enough to determine the evidence by which they were supposed to be tested."[62] Niebuhr made the following charge against Dewey in whom this tradition had come to preeminent focus:

> Thus professor John Dewey, the most typical of modern natural-istic philosophers, never tired of insisting that the "experimental method" must be rigorous enough to re-examine its own hypotheses. But it never occurred to him that his insistence that the "methods of science" could be transferred from the field of nature to that of history, and that only the intrusion of irrelevant religious and political authority prevented this consummation, rested upon an erroneous and, unexamined presupposition. That was the universally held belief of modern culture that the realm of history was essentially identical with the realm of nature.[63]

Niebuhr would ask that Dewey turn his own astute observation back upon himself when Dewey noted that

> the *ways* in which we believe and expect have a tremendous affect upon *what* we believe and expect. We have discovered at last that these ways are set, almost abjectly so, by social factors, by tradition and the influence of education. Thus we discover that we believe many things not because the things are so, but because we have become habituated through the weight of authority, by imitation, prestige, instruction, the unconscious effect of language, etc.[64]

Quite obviously, Dewey was making his own, and quite another point, when he penned those lines. Yet Niebuhr felt that Dewey was attempting to exempt scientific inquiry, if not the sciences themselves, from the relativities of "social factors" and "tradition," in spite of

Dewey's insistence that all that passes for science was to be viewed as a sociocultural phenomenon.

Both Niebuhr and Dewey sought a broader, deeper and more highly textured view of "human nature" than any reductionist version of naturalism would allow. In point of fact, Dewey's philosophical program had as one of its leading aims the formulation and defense of a conception of nature that was more textured and available than that provided by classical rationalism or modern idealism. Such a view of nature was also more flexible and complex than that allowed by the earlier empiricism. Niebuhr, unfortunately, did not acknowledge this fact and thereby failed to credit Dewey for his rather remarkable achievement.[65] One reason for this is that there is precious little evidence that Niebuhr was aware of the radical nature of Dewey's program to "reconstruct" the philosophical tradition. Moreover, it is doubtful if Niebuhr ever read *Experience and Nature* or, if he had, that he grasped its importance. Niebuhr, it seems, was far more preoccupied with Dewey's evangelism in advocating the extension and application of scientific method to "man and his problems" than he was with Dewey's reinterpretation and refinement of naturalism.

Dewey denied that his efforts to overcome the separation of humankind from nature were reductionistic. In rescuing "experience" from the domain of mere subjectivity Dewey insisted that experience was both *in* and *of* nature. His entire philosophy was a refutation of the objection "that to view experience naturalistically is to reduce it to something materialistic, depriving it of all ideal significance." Dewey's contention was that "if experience actually presents esthetic and moral traits, then these traits may also be supposed to reach down into nature, and to testify to something that belongs to nature as truly as does the mechanical structure attributed to it in physical science."[66] Dewey found this to be not a product of wishful thinking, but rather the outcome of an empirical method whose purpose was to take seriously what is, in fact, found in experience itself. This, in essence, was Dewey's version of James's "radical empiricism," and it was anything but "reductive." What Shea says of the naturalists, in general, certainly applies to Dewey:

> Naturalism is materialist neither in intention nor in its achievement. The distinctions naturalists make and the arguments they commonly offer for the reality of mind and values ought to preclude the charge. More accurately, the naturalists limit being or reality to the world proportioned to human knowing, but exclude nothing from existence or significance that is within that world. It is no more materialist in fact or logic than the human sciences are. While it might be argued more justly

that they so limit being or reality without sufficient reason, their failure to justify their position philosophically does not entail a denial of the reality of mind or spirit, nor the view that "all that is, is material."[67]

Dewey summarized what might be termed his "comprehensive naturalism" in the early part of *Experience and Nature* when he claimed that

> The history of the development of the physical sciences is the story of the enlarging possession by mankind of more efficacious instrumentalities for dealing with the conditions of life and action. But when one neglects the connection of these scientific objects with the affairs of primary experience, the result is a picture of a world of things indifferent to human interests because it is wholly apart from experience. It is more than merely isolated, for it is set in opposition. Hence when it is viewed as fixed and final in itself it is a source of oppression to the heart and paralysis to imagination. . . .
>
> When objects are isolated from the experience through which they are reached and in which they function, experience itself becomes reduced to the mere process of experiencing, and experiencing is therefore treated as if it were also complete in itself. We get the absurdity of an experiencing which experiences only itself, states and processes of consciousness, instead of the things of nature. Since the seventeenth century this conception of experience as the equivalent of subjective private consciousness set over against nature, which consists wholly of physical objects, has wrought havoc in philosophy. It is responsible for the feeling mentioned at the outset that "nature" and "experience" are names for things which have nothing to do with each other.[68]

Niebuhr, indeed, failed to pay homage to Dewey's achievements in enlarging and humanizing the traditional boundaries of naturalism, although he did appreciate Dewey's own personal *humanitas*. Yet, Niebuhr's own set of concerns led him to the conviction that for all its disclaimers Dewey's "empirical naturalism" involved ontological commitments about nature that significantly affected an adequate understanding of the nature of human existence. Dewey's anthropology was, as Niebuhr read it, Dewey's Achilles' heel. In Niebuhr's account the boundaries of Dewey's reflections on the "nature of man" were determined, in part, by his naturalism and, in part, by the optimistic illusions he shared with the wider liberal culture which his naturalism proved ill-equipped to criticize. Niebuhr's charge that Dewey's social thought bought into the entire range of liberal illusions about the "nature of man" was the focal point of his criticism of Dewey. He was of the opinion that the social and political illusions under which Dewey labored were not simply the result of an uncritical mirroring of the "funded experience" of America's liberal culture. Rather Niebuhr saw such illusions endemic to what Morris Eames called *pragmatic naturalism*[69] insofar as that tradition embodied a theory of experience which carried excess metaphysical baggage that a more rigorous pragmatic self-criticism should have prevented. Where Niebuhr fundamentally departed from Dewey was over what could be called a metaphysics of experience which, however broadly conceived, seemed to result in linguistic or "conversational" closure. To use a more recent nomenclature, Niebuhr was of the opinion that certain aspects of experience either came into focus or else failed to do so in accordance with the context of the language being employed. In his judgment, the prevailing language of "naturalism" either ignored such aspects of experience because they simply did not emerge within the constraints of the language allowed or else rejected or distorted them because they were found offensive.

In 1955 Niebuhr restated for the *Bulletin of the Atomic Scientists* what had become a perennial theme of his; namely, that the "Comptean thesis that no more than an extension of the scientific method would be required to comprehend and master the mysteries of history, as well as of nature" is "one of the pathetic illusions of our culture"—an illusion "propagated more assiduously by the social than by the natural scientists."[70] Although Niebuhr penned these lines several years after Dewey's death, the indictment was clearly aimed at those whose hero and model was John Dewey.

In attempting to too consistently "understand man *ex analogia naturae*," Niebuhr insisted, the "empirical method which unlocked the mysteries of nature so well" became "the basis of an implicit dogma which obscured the salient facts about the human situation."[71] Dewey came to epitomize for Niebuhr the very tendency of modern culture since the Renaissance to move "towards an ironic climax of misunderstanding man by the same alleged methods which helped it to understand nature, and to cover up the significant failure in one field by a phenomenal success in another."[72] The "obvious facts" which had been overlooked by modern culture had precisely to do with human nature and history—facts that when ignored or misunderstood had ominous consequences. The situation was a dangerous one, according to Niebuhr, because a failure to deal with such facts directly and realistically left the present generation exposed to face a perplexing and perilous age "with nothing but the soft illusions of the previous two centuries to cover their spiritual nakedness."[73]

In the final analysis it would be a mistake to see Niebuhr and Dewey battling over metaphysical issues—making points, pro and contra, relative to naturalism, on the one hand, and extranaturalism on the other. The deeper issue in all of this is that there was a sense in which both men failed to let loose entirely of foundational thinking, a kind of thinking so characteristic of Western tradition in which the credibility of convictions were seen to require grounding in something beyond the uncertainties and relativities of tradition itself. Dewey never brought the force of his pragmatic critique to bear against the myths of the "scientific method" and "rational inquiry" that functioned as the still-point in the vortices of time, nature, and history. Niebuhr, on the other hand, never entirely abandoned his early view that meaning and value required certainties which he couched, if not in supernatural, at least in transcendental terms, even if those terms demanded an act of faith. In a word, both Niebuhr and Dewey, in quite different ways, drew back from the nihilistic implications of their own pragmatism.[74] In this aspect of their respective work, Dewey and Niebuhr were representative of what Bruce Jannusch refers to as the "old" pragmatism versus the "new" pragmatism of the Rortian model. Jannusch put it this way: "In my view, the early pragmatists often spoke the language of relativism in ethics and the language of skepticism in epistemology. My question to Rorty is this: 'Where do we find the early pragmatists speaking the language of nihilism?'"[75]

Still, on another level, Niebuhr's point about the ontological assumptions associated with naturalism was not itself an ontological point in the sense that he had a better ontological gift to give.[76] Rather his point was a pragmatic one—as, indeed, was Dewey's counterpoint against super-, supra-, or extranaturalisms. Niebuhr's central dispute was over what, exactly, got distorted or overlooked or ruled out by means of the terms the new naturalism set forth as boundaries that enclose inquiry. What made Dewey such an attractive target for Niebuhr was the combination of Dewey's prestige and influence, on the one hand, and his being *the* preeminent advocate of a *social science* naturalism, on the other. Dewey's naturalism, after all, was not directed primarily toward nature, but rather towards a reassessment of *the human* in nature and the *human* in social contexts. It was precisely on matters of self-understanding and the political order that Niebuhr found the social science naturalism of Dewey so wanting.

9

The "Human Studies"

Naturalism and the Human Studies

Ironically, the "facts" that advocates of social science naturalism such as Dewey had obscured, according to Niebuhr, were anthropological in nature, facts that Niebuhr held to be crucial to an adequate understanding of the self and community. In Niebuhr's account these facts included "the self's freedom, the self-corruption of the self in self-concern" and, finally, "the self's historical character."[1]

Niebuhr's development and interpretation of these themes was both probing and extensive, ranging throughout his writings, particularly from the period of his 1939 Gifford Lectures down to the publication of *The Self and the Dramas of History* in 1955. His descriptions and analyses of self-understanding in terms of the self's freedom, self-centeredness, and historical character were central to his theology, and should be investigated by any reader who wishes a deeper and more detailed picture than can be provided here.[2] The purpose and scope of this present work, which is to focus on the controversy between Niebuhr and Dewey, simply do not allow for the kind of systematic and comprehensive analysis these Niebuhrian topics deserve. They will, however, be considered in respect to the issues at stake between these two men.

It was because of his claim that naturalism was unable either to recognize or properly assess these aspects of human existence, that Niebuhr was not nearly as sanguine about the success of the social sciences as he was about the indisputable productivity of natural science. Whatever else disturbed him about Dewey, Dewey's role as the undisputed champion of the cause to extend the methods of the natural sciences to the personal and social life drew the most intense fire from Niebuhr's pen.

In the latter stages of his life, Dewey, in an introduction written for a collection of essays published in 1946 as *Problems of Men*, summed up his long-standing position:

Today social subjects, as far as concerns effective treatment in inquiry, are in much the same state as physical subjects three hundred years ago. The need is that there be now the kind of systematic and comprehensive methods and habits and the same projection of generous hypotheses as, only a few hundred years ago, set going the revolution in physical knowledge. The opportunity is as great as the need. The obstacles to understanding the work in social questions are greater than they ever were in dealing, say, with the heavenly bodies.[3]

Dewey, in effect, vehemently believed that the social sciences could achieve a truly *scientific* character and that they should be given the inside track in guiding human affairs. In *Reconstruction in Philosophy* Dewey had written that "These four facts, natural science, experimentation, control and progress have been inextricably bound up together"[4] and that up until then scientific methodology had affected human life only in an accidental way. Niebuhr clashed with Dewey over epistemology relative to science and experimentation as we have seen in Niebuhr's charge of scientism. But he also divided sharply with Dewey over an understanding of history, as the controversy between them over social control and progress reveals—a controversy that will occupy our attention in due course.

Dewey persistently argued that the rather technical and largely accidental successes science had had in the domain of the social world could be transformed and expedited only when the "directed intelligence" of science qua science was systematically and comprehensively applied in such a way as to foster a genuinely *social science*. For Dewey the "initial step" in carrying through a "revolution" in relationship to "social subjects" comparable to the one launched centuries ago with respect to "physical knowledge," involved promoting "general recognition that knowing, including most emphatically scientific knowledge, is not outside social activity, but is itself a form of social behavior, as much so as agriculture or transportation."[5] The conclusion Dewey drew from this was not quite the radical Kuhnian and neo-pragmatist view that science qua science is a sociocultural phenomenon, reflecting all the relativities and interests of temporal existence all the way down to, and including, method. Instead he drew the methodologically monistic conclusion that what worked so well in the natural sciences would, given time and dedication, work equally well as a basis for the development of social science.

William Shea has suggested that the "chief significance of evolution for the naturalists lies in its methodological implications rather than in any hypothesis about the cosmos."[6] His point is that,

For them [the naturalists] Darwin's work definitively established that nature can no longer be taken as a term of distinction setting humankind over against a nature that somehow exludes it. Darwin showed that humankind can only be understood as an outcome of natural processes and that it is subject to the same methods of analysis that are used to understand the rest of nature. Thus the significance of Darwin for naturalist philosophy is methodological monism: Humanity is subject to methodological study under the canons of scientific method.[7]

Niebuhr was not only suspicious of the quasi-Comptean reading of history implicit in Dewey's position, but he was also convinced that, behind this notion of the transferability of the method of the natural to the social sciences, there lurked a variety of ontological commitments. In other words, the universality of method that Dewey espoused so strongly was not neutral, but presupposed all sorts of things about the nature of things.

Professor John E. Smith was also of the opinion that for Dewey, "The term Nature is far from innocent."[8] According to Smith,

For all of his criticism of absolutes and of an ultimate context, Dewey's naturalistic empiricism does not avoid a vantage point from which it interprets reality as a whole. A great deal of the power of Dewey's thought in American life has in fact been due to the circumstance that he did not follow his own prescriptions. Dewey's thought is deeply involved in a differential principle governing the interpretation of the whole of nature and of man's place in it; the biological situation—the interaction of organism and environment plus the mutual adjustment required for survival—furnishes the key to understanding the human predicament; experience in the form of science provides us with the exclusive instrument for coping with it.[9]

In line with Shea's point, Niebuhr saw the "basic error" of the Darwinian model (which, in the final analysis, operated as the basis of Dewey's methodological monism) expressed in the claim "that historical processes and natural processes were sufficiently identical to make the same scientific method applicable to both fields"[10]—a claim that will be treated in some detail at a later point in this chapter.

In the opening pages of his early major work *Moral Man and Immoral Society*, Niebuhr stated his objection to the transference of the methodology of the natural to the social sciences in a manner that brought several themes to light. He argued,

The idea that we cannot be socially intelligent until we begin experimentation in social problems in the way the physical scientists experimented fails to take account of an important difference between the physical and the social sciences. The physical sciences gained their freedom when they overcame the traditionalism based on ignorance, but the traditionalism which the social sciences face is based upon the economic interest of the dominant social classes who are trying to maintain their special privileges in society. Nor can the difference between the very character of social and physical sciences be overlooked. Complete rational objectivity in the social situation is impossible. The very social scientists who are so anxious to offer our generation counsels of salvation and are disappointed that an ignorant and slothful people are so slow to accept their wisdom, betray middle-class prejudices in almost everything they write. Since reason is always, to some degree, the servant of interest in a social situation, social injustice cannot be resolved by moral and rational suasion alone, as the educator and social scientist usually believes. Conflict is inevitable, and in this conflict power must be challenged by power. That fact is not recognized by most of the educators, and only very grudgingly admitted by most of the social scientists.[11]

Dewey, aside from his scathing criticism of "general moral causes,"[12] was certainly not oblivious to the facts of self-interest, the ideological taint, or class prejudices as we shall note in due time. What is important here, however, is Niebuhr's strenuous rejection of Dewey's oft-repeated charge that among the obstacles to the social sciences the most prominent are an authoritarian institutional history and a pattern of obscurantism and recalcitrance promulgated by religious superstition, ignorance, and language.

Dewey's position is framed largely in terms of the last stage in the Comptean reading of historical progression. According to Dewey, the early warfare between science and religion resulted in a premature and distorted jurisdictional compromise—a division of fields, as it were—that gave rise to new dualisms in the modern world. Recently this "compromise" had broken down, and the reconstructive work of philosophy must attend to the task of applying "scientific intelligence" to the domain of morals as a result of this breakdown.[13] Dewey saw great strides having been made in extending the scientific method; first, through "its application in astronomy and general cosmology" in the seventeenth century; then, "in physics and chemistry" in the eighteenth century; and most recently, in "geology and the biological sciences" in the nineteenth century. "Does it not seem," Dewey wrote rhetorically, "to be the intellectual task of the twentieth century to take [the] last step" of making "the new ideas and method . . . at home in social and moral life?"[14]

Niebuhr was very much aware of the obscurantism associated with the religious tradition. His own position was in agreement with certain charges Dewey leveled against religion in his analysis of what Dewey called traditional religion's role in the "social reign of accident."[15] Niebuhr was also aware of the quietistic feature in otherworldly supernaturalism as well as of the difficulty in achieving toleration within the framework of traditional religion. He and Dewey were equally critical of the excessive and misconceived individualism of much of Protestantism. It should be recognized, however, that Niebuhr's theological acumen resulted in more substantive and detailed critical analyses of defeatism and obscurantism within Christianity than Dewey's tangential and largely unsympathetic perspective allowed him.[16]

Scientific Method and the "Cultural Lag"

The crucial point is that Niebuhr saw something of mythological proportions in Dewey's own representation of history. He was most disturbed by Dewey's use of a "cultural lag" mythology as both an indictment of the past and as an explanation for the delay in Dewey's much desired future. "According to Dewey," Niebuhr noted, "the divisive elements in human culture are vestigial remnants of outmoded religious prejudices which will yield to the universal perspective which modern education will inculcate." With an unmistakable note of sarcasm, Niebuhr concluded his observation by noting that "Modern culture was generating new and fierce ideological conflicts, not remotely connected with traditional religious concepts, while Professor Dewey was writing this book."[17]

Dewey, whom Niebuhr categorized as a "rationalistic naturalist" (more naturalist than rationalist in that he did not split "the human spirit into a speculative and a pragmatic intelligence" as the "purer rationalist" did), arrives "at a 'cultural lag' theory of human evil" and hopes "for a society which will ultimately be governed purely by rational suasion rather than force."[18] As Randall put it, Dewey saw natural science to be the most "distinctive trait" and "greatest achievement" in Western culture. Science, for Dewey, was

> primarily a cultural phenomenon: it is an institutionalized habit of thinking and acting, a way whereby that culture conducts many of its tasks and operations. It is essentially a social method of doing and changing things, a complex technique that

has proved both extraordinarily successful and extraordinarily disruptive of the older pattern of life. It is a method of inquiry, of criticizing traditional beliefs and instituting newer and better warranted ones.[19]

It followed from his view of the cultural lag that Dewey would regard past history, overall, to be both overwhelmingly authoritarian and anti-progressive. Dewey, after all, had been prompted by the desire to "break away from current and established classifications of the world" that had been productive of "a system of belief, recognitions, and ignorances, of acceptances and rejections, of expectancies and appraisals of meanings which have been instituted under the influence of custom and tradition."[20] Dewey expressed open appreciation to Randall for observing that his (Dewey's) role in relation to Western cultural heritage was that of "a critic and reconstructor of tradition" who "is forever bringing men's past experience with ideas to the test of present experience."[21]

Because Dewey saw the scientific method as the "best intellectual method" ever constructed, he deemed it to be *the* "cultural method" by which society "operates on its inherited and traditional materials."[22] This meant two things: first, the past is to be read (both in terms of the lessons it bestowed and the folly in which it was engaged), by the lights of this new cultural method; and second, the relationship between present and past is essentially one of struggle and conflict between "the active force of scientific knowledge and technical power, and the deflecting force of the lag and inertia of institutionalized habits and beliefs."[23] This struggle was so central in Dewey's reading of history that the success of the scientific method became the very purpose and force of education. "Lag in mental and moral patterns," Dewey wrote in 1935, "provides the bulwark of the older institutions; in expressing the past they still express present beliefs, outlooks and purposes. Here is the place where the problem of liberalism centers today," and liberalism's "work is first of all education, in the broadest sense of that term."[24]

Although Niebuhr acknowledged an aspect of truth in the theory of a "cultural lag,"[25] he was of the opinion that,

> The error embodied in the theory of the cultural lag is the modern assumption that the "cultural lag" is due merely to the tardiness of the social sciences in achieving the same standards of objectivity and disinterestedness which characterize the natural sciences. This belief embodies the erroneous idea that man's knowledge and conquest of nature develops the wisdom and the technics required for the knowledge and the conquest of human nature. . . . Scientific knowledge of what human nature

is and how it reacts to various given social situations will always be of service in refashioning human conduct. But ultimately the problems of human conduct and social relations are in a different category from the relations of physical nature.[26]

As the basis for a "reading" of history, the cultural lag theory was made to do far more work than its partial truth warranted. The uses Dewey made of it involved, among other things, a rather facile and one-dimensional interpretation of traditional religion. After all, Dewey, whom Niebuhr regarded as "the most typical and greatest philosopher of American secularism," was seen by Niebuhr to have regarded "religious loyalties as outmoded forms of culture which will gradually disappear with the general extension of enlightened good-will."[27] This, of course, prevented Dewey, in Niebuhr's view, from having anything but a "thin" analysis of the religious tradition. So Dewey's own prejudices, disinterest, and harsh polemic left him without the ability or the willingness to discern within that tradition anything of constructive or critical value.

The crux of Niebuhr's view was that he saw Dewey's use of the cultural lag theory in the light of a Comptean positivism, a position that failed on several counts. Its overexaggeration of the possibility and innocence of rational control left it incapable of properly gauging both the character and extent of evil. Conversely, it overestimated the prospects for hope, espousing an inordinate optimism, sometimes bordering on utopianism. It also perpetuated the myth of "scientific objectivity" in matters of personal and historical life, and sought to ground this alleged objectivity in its quasi-empirical naturalism. Finally, the rationalistic excesses of its own naturalism resulted in misgauging the complexity and recalcitrance of the natural-historical processes.

Niebuhr found special irony in the fact that a naturalism such as Dewey's, which prided itself on rescuing the self from all sorts and sundries of dualisms, ended up advocating a type of rationalism that ought to have been prevented by naturalistic, if not pragmatic, restraints. In an early response to Dewey's *A Common Faith*, Niebuhr remarked that Dewey's exposition of his own religious faith betrayed the "pathos of modern spirituality" in its failure to adequately gauge the factors of power and conflict in historical life. Dewey, he went on to say, sought—in excessively idealistic fashion—to "eliminate conflict and unite men of goodwill everywhere by stripping their spiritual life of historic, traditional, and supposedly anachronistic accretions." With his penchant for irony, Niebuhr saw the extravagance of Dewey's proposal as representing "a striking example of the faith of modern rationalism in the ability of reason to transcend the partial perspectives of the natural world in which reason is rooted,"[28] a most unbefitting prospect for a rigorous pragmatic naturalist. This all became quite understandable to Niebuhr because he saw an inordinate "confidence in the power of reason," rooted in Greek culture, to be "a strong motif in our culture"—a motif that expressed "itself in even such strong and anti-Aristotelian philosophers as John Dewey."[29]

In Dewey's highly reputed antitotalitarian defense of liberal democratic society published in 1935, he had stated that the fact that coercion and oppression on a large scale exist, no honest person can deny. But these things are best seen as "the product . . . of the perpetuation of old institutions and patterns untouched by scientific method." Whereas it is true "that the social order is largely conditioned by the use of coercive force, bursting at times into open violence," what "is also true is that mankind now has in its possession a new method, that of cooperative and experimental science which expresses the method of intelligence."[30]

Niebuhr's reaction to Dewey's position appeared in his Gifford Lectures where he wrote:

> The thought of a typical naturalistic philosopher of the twentieth century, John Dewey, advances remarkably little beyond the perplexities and confusions of the previous centuries. He has the same difficulty in finding a vantage point for reason from which it may operate against the perils of nature, and the same blindness toward the new perils of spirit which arise in the "rational" life of man. Dewey is in fact less conscious of the social perils of self-love than either Locke or Hume. In his thought the hope of achieving a vantage point which transcends the corruptions of self-interest takes the form of trusting the "scientific method" and attributing anti-social conduct to the "cultural lag", that is, to the failure of social science to keep abreast with technology.[31]

In this, one of his more extended commentaries on Dewey's thought, Niebuhr criticized Dewey for holding to the view that "The failures of the past and present are due to the fact that the scientific method 'has not been tried at any time with use of all the resources which scientific material and the experimental method now put at our disposal'."[32] Niebuhr found incredulous the fact that "Not a suspicion dawns upon Professor Dewey that no possible 'organized inquiry' can be as transcendent over the historical conflicts of interest as it ought to be to achieve the disinterested intelligence which he attributes to it."[33] Dewey's belief that the traditional mind-body dualism was responsible for a faulty pedagogy which prevented us from discerning the need to employ the disinterested force of "freed intelligence" in an effective attack upon institutional injustices, was, in Niebuhr's account, patently absurd. He deemed the "solution at which Professor Dewey arrives" to be "an incredibly naive answer to a much more ultimate and perplexing problem than he realizes." Niebuhr conjectured that Dewey's solution "could only have arisen in a period of comparative social stability and security, and in a nation in which geographic isolation obscured the conflict of nations and great wealth mitigated the social conflict within a nation."[34]

Dewey, in an article specifically directed against Niebuhr's early attack on him in *Moral Man and Immoral Society*, countered Niebuhr by pointing out that those who question the use "of the method of intelligence to control social change" merely "perpetuate the present confusion."[35] Although he acknowledged that the role of intelligence in directing social affairs could easily be made to appear ridiculous, Dewey admitted that would be the case only in relation to the past. He proposed to critics that specific "success of this method [of intelligence] in obtaining control over physical forces and conditions has been offered as evidence that the case for trying it in social matters is not altogether desperate nor yet illusory."[36] Dewey argued that when the alternatives were considered— namely, "dogmatism, reinforced by the weight of unquestioned custom and tradition, the disguised or open play of class interest" or "dependence upon brute force and violence"[37]—then perhaps what Niebuhr deemed to be the "illusion" of social-scientific intelligence ought to be tried even more strenuously. Specifically chiding Niebuhr, Dewey noted,

In view of the influence of collective illusion in the past, some case might be made out for the contention that even if it be an illusion, exaltation of intelligence and experimental method is worth a trial. Illusion for illusion, this particular one may be better than those upon which humanity has usually depended.[38]

Yet Dewey's poignant charge that we have, in human affairs, either the influence of intelligence or a capitulation to habit, custom, and tradition, somewhat missed Niebuhr's point. The issue for Niebuhr was not between intelligence or the absence thereof, as Dewey seemed to suggest. Rather it was between a view of scientific rationality that Niebuhr took to be extremely naive, and a more circumspect intelligence that gauges the facts of sociopolitical life more realistically and more in line with the complexity and type of experience being considered. Dewey denied that he held either the view that "the particular techniques of the physical sciences are to be literally copied—though of course they are to be utilized whenever applicable" or the view "that experimentation in the laboratory sense can be carried out on any large scale in social affairs." Rather, he was advocating the position that it was "the attitude of mind exemplified in the conquest of nature by the experimental sciences" which is of crucial importance, and that that attitude and the "method involved in it . . . should be carried into social affairs."[39]

The Question of Experience

Niebuhr had no difficulty concurring with the judgment that the "attitude" generated by the scientific revolt was of great importance to a better understanding of experience, both in its human and non-human forms. But he found significant irony at the point where "the 'spirit of science' as 'humility before the fact' is transmuted into a denial of obvious 'facts' so that the inconvenient facts will not seem to invalidate the 'methods of science.' "[40]

Niebuhr saw the assumption of rational objectivity behind Dewey's view of the applicability of science to the arena of human studies as disastrously mistaken. Although Dewey defended scientific rationality in the social sphere as decidedly "not something laid from above experience," Niebuhr believed that a too simple transference of scientific method onto the social world resulted in a "tyranny" of method which tended to falsify the very experience it sought to clarify and interpret. The transposition of method was disturbingly unconvincing. It was disturbing not only because of the broader illusions of liberal culture reflected in such claims, but also because of what Niebuhr took to be an exaggerated continuity between humankind and nature in Dewey's very undialectical naturalism. For Niebuhr, the self as an object *in* nature—in the manner Dewey tended to place it—missed the self as one whose "nature" defies such simple placement. The issue finally came down to the nature of experience, or more aptly put, the issue turns on just what presuppositions about experience lie behind the supposedly neutral word *experience*—a word, as Whitehead noted, that "is one of the most deceitful in philosophy."[41]

An observation by Nancy Frankenberry sheds light on the tension between Niebuhr and Dewey on this matter of "experience." She wrote, "The selection of what is to count as empirical criteria is, of course, never philosophically neutral. Empiricism has always stood for the justificatory need to ground all knowledge in experience. But as such it is a thesis in search of an adequate *theory* of experience."[42] The problem, as Langdon Gilkey put it, is that

Every mode of empirical inquiry has presuppositions: about the nature and structure of "reality" or actuality; about the possibility, the conditions and the nature of our knowledge of it; and about the worth, use, and so goal, of such knowledge. The mode of inquiry does not produce these presuppositions but depends on them; and they in turn are neither self-evident nor universal. Thus, no inquiry is purely empirical.[43]

Niebuhr was clearly convinced that there were aspects of experience that were either ignored or distorted through the lens of the type of naturalistic empiricism Dewey's thought represented. The question, in effect, was, "What should such alleged 'facts' of experience suggest about the theory Dewey employed to portray experience?" On this issue Niebuhr held that Dewey's theory of experience had serious inadequacies.

The question of how "experience" is best understood in Dewey's thought is a serious candidate for the thorniest question in all of Dewey studies. This investigation does not pretend to address the complex and formidable problems involved in Dewey's concept of experience, much less to engage in a discussion of the differences among Dewey scholars.[44] An attempt will be made, however, to consider the question of experience in relation to specific conflicts at issue between Dewey and Niebuhr.

Dewey saw his own interpretation of experience as a *via media* between the extreme atomistic pluralism of early sensationalistic empiricism and block-universe holisms.[45] It is also clear that he sought to avoid both the subjectivism of the experienc*er* which followed from early empiricist assumptions and the simplistic position of certain versions of philosophical realism regarding experienc*ed* objects. Dewey's view of experience encompassed both the fact of experienc*ing*—an assuredly psychological matter, in part—and the fact of the experienc*ed*. In opposition to idealism, experience, for Dewey, was more extensive than "knowing." At the same time it was not identical to nature as such, because there is more to nature than we either experience or know (although Dewey's *theory* of experience has to do only with existence within the reach of experience). As Gail Kennedy pointed out, "by 'experience' [Dewey] means *all* of the complex series of transactions which occur between the live creature and its environment,"[46] so long as one understands that Dewey's use of *transaction*—in place of *interaction*—deliberately points to the fact that there are no clear boundaries between the experiencing organism and its experienced environment. Experience, for Dewey denotes the planted field, the sowed seeds, the reaped harvests, the changes of night and day, spring and autumn, wet and dry, heat and cold, that are observed, feared, longed for; it also denotes the one who plants and reaps, who works and rejoices, hopes and fears, plans, invokes magic or chemistry to aid him, who is downcast or triumphant. It is "doubled-barrelled" in that it recognizes in its primary integrity no division between act and material, subject and object, but contains them both in an unanalyzed totality.[47]

Experience is *of* nature and is not, as in the legacy of early empiricism, a subjective barrier that closes the self off from nature. Epistemological skepticism is rejected by the realization that in experience nature discloses something of itself. In the case of the rather abstract experience known as "scientific inquiry," for example, "the inner nature of things" is not available, "but only those connections of things with one another that determine outcomes and hence can be used as means. The *intrinsic* nature of events is revealed in experience as the immediately felt qualities of things."[48]

Dewey's theory of experience, in accordance with his radical empiricism, saw nature as experienc*ed* having qualitative features correlative to the qualitative experiences of the experienc*er*. Because qualities are a given in experience, for Dewey, they are, as such, a feature or trait in nature itself. Nature is not reducible, in his judgment, to mechanisms devoid of values and ideals. In Dewey's words: "If experience actually presents esthetic and moral traits, then those traits may also be supposed to reach down into nature, and to testify to something that belongs to nature as truly as does the mechanical structure attributed to it in physical science."[49] Experience, for Dewey, although it included knowledge at an abstract level, meant primarily ways of doing and suffering. As John E. Smith pointed out, therefore, "there is an ineradicable teleology in Dewey's conception of things; nature turns out to be a most human affair."[50]

Dewey's conception of experience is best seen as a form of naturalism strongly governed by a combination of organicism and behaviorism. Niebuhr insisted that the "naturalistic version of the ontological structure" stemming from Darwinism received a "spurious triumph over the 'empirical' reality which can be attested to by any honest 'experience.'"[51] The terms set by Dewey's organistic positivism, as I choose here to call it, constitute the basis for Niebuhr's oft-repeated charge that Dewey's naturalism failed to do justice to both the depth and diversity of experience—most especially *human* experience. Niebuhr, in effect, early on saw the point of William Shea's comment on a remark made by Sidney Hook. Shea wrote:

> Sidney Hook, in his introduction to the new edition of Dewey's *Experience and Nature*, suggests that what Dewey there called a metaphysics is in fact a philosophical anthropology. The remark could be extended to cover the work of other naturalists as well. . . . Naturalism is a theory of humankind and culture rather than a theory of nature. Indeed, it is a philosophical anthropology before it is a metaphysics, if it is a methphysics at all. If one is to learn from Naturalism, it will be from its understanding of humankind; if one is to question Naturalism, it will have to be at this point as well.[52]

Although Niebuhr acknowledged the biological evidence in support of the evolution of natural forms, he was concerned that the biological model had become the primary, and therefore inordinate, basis for anthropological theorizing. According to Niebuhr, "Darwinian conclusions did materially influence the modern estimate of man's nature so that it seemed impossible to conceive of man as a unique creature."[53] Difficult, perhaps but not impossible, for it cannot be gainsaid that Dewey knew something of the uniqueness of the human creature. After all, his entire theory of inquiry and "freed intelligence," not to mention his theory of experience and views on value, presupposed it. As Dewey put it in his later recollections:

> For many years I have consistently—and rather persistently— maintained that the key to a philosophic theory of experience must proceed from initially linking it with the processes and functions of life as the latter are disclosed in biological science. So viewed, I have held that experience is a matter or an "affair" (*pace* Mr. Santayana) of interaction of living creatures with their environments; *human* experience being what it is because human beings are subject to the influences of culture, including use of definite means of intercommunication, and are what in anthropological jargon are called *acculturated* organisms.[54]

Nonetheless, the content of such concepts as the "interacting organism," "transactions," "experience *in* and *of* nature," as well as his abiding sense of the organic relationship between subject and object, was clearly the language of a studied and programmatic naturalism tightly linked to the biological and organic metaphors from which it sprang. This language intended that any discussion of the nature of the self and community, however complex and richly textured, be both conducted within flexible naturalistic presuppositions and governed by a scientific theory of inquiry. Consequently, where Niebuhr fundamentally departed from Dewey was in what might be called the metaphysics of experience which, in Dewey's case, resulted in a view of experience expressed in terms of a far too linear and undialectical naturalism.

The Problem of Self-Understanding

Niebuhr insisted that ours was a time of tragic and widespread misunderstanding of human nature, and that this misunderstanding had been exacerbated by the burgeoning of nature studies since the time of the scientific revolution of the seventeenth century. Niebuhr's view was that the legacy of this tradition

> has been so serviceable in our understanding and "conquest" of nature and has won such increasing prestige by these accomplishments that it has threatened to discredit the Hebraic component more and more, relegating its characteristic insights to outmoded "superstitions" *at the precise moment in history in which its insights would be most serviceable* in understanding man's history; and the more consistently a proud Hellenic culture tended to misinterpret that tragic drama, the more its philosophies and sciences became "empirical" and more intent upon the "facts."[55] (Italics mine.)

Niebuhr believed that "the same Greek component in our culture which is responsible for laying the foundations of all our philosophy and sciences" was "also responsible for all our most serious misunderstandings about man and history."[56] This judgment also revealed the core of his disagreement with his friend and colleague Paul Tillich. In his dispute with Tillich Niebuhr set himself apart from the rationalistic metaphysics of the classical tradition. The essence of his reply to Tillich is of importance in understanding his thinking and the approach he took on matters basic to his conflict with Dewey. Niebuhr remarked

> ontology is the "science of being" [and] has its limitations in describing any being or being *per se* which contains mysteries and meanings which are not within the limits of reason. Among these [is] the human self in its mystery of freedom within and

beyond the rational structure of mind. . . . My point is simply
that when we deal with aspects of reality which exhibit a freedom above and beyond structures, we must resort to the Hebraic
dramatic and historical way of approaching reality. . . . I do not
believe that ontological categories can do justice to the freedom
either of the divine or of the human person, or to the unity of the
person in his involvement in and transcendence over the temporal flux or that the sin of man and the forgiveness by God of
man's sin or the dramatic variety of man's history can be comprehended in ontological categories.[57]

Niebuhr's response to Tillich is important here because what
Niebuhr saw as the radical difference between humans and the other
creatures had led him, as noted in the previous chapter, to level a similar
criticism of what he conceived to be Dewey's "naturalistic ontology." Will
Herberg once noted that with respect to Niebuhr's use of Martin Buber's
language of the dialogic life, Niebuhr clearly maintained that

The very texture of this threefold dialogue of existence [of the
self with itself, others, and at least as imagined, with God] is
historical. Niebuhr would not go so far as Ortega y Gasset in asserting that "man has no nature, what he has is history"—after
all, Niebuhr does stress the natural and social coherences in
which human existence is embedded—but he would certainly
go along with the Spanish philosopher in insisting that "to comprehend anything human, be it personal or collective, one must
attend to its history." This direction of Niebuhr's thinking,
which seems to be both biblical and existential, has of course
brought him into conflict with the basic ontological outlook
championed by Paul Tillich. . . . Where Tillich asserts that "all
problems drive us to an ontological analysis," Niebuhr insists
that "the human person and man's society are by nature historical, and the ultimate truth about life must be mediated historically."[58]

Niebuhr interpreted the Western mind as having moved between
two divergent poles of thought, and the main lines of thought since the
rise of modern science, including idealism and naturalism, were of the
same fabric as the dominant tradition stemming from Hellenistic culture. In many respects Dewey and Niebuhr were working in the same
vineyard when, from somewhat different directions, they sought both to
overcome a dualistic anthropology and to reconceive the self in sociocul-

tural and historical terms rather than as having a fixed and static "nature." Nonetheless, whereas Dewey was preoccupied with overcoming the rampant dualisms in both classical and Christian sources, Niebuhr focused on finding a way out of the rationalistic ontologies endemic to classical as well as modern philosophy. The irony for Niebuhr, as we have noted, was that this rationalistic culture culminating in modern science which was so "intent upon understanding nature and boasting of ever more impressive achievements in the 'conquest' of nature, has become involved in ever more serious misunderstandings of human nature, of the self and its uniqueness, and in its dramatic-historical environment."[59]

Over against what he regarded as the ontological mainstream, Niebuhr set the dramatic-historically minded tradition, which he usually called the *Hebraic* and sometimes *Biblical tradition*, fully recognizing that elements in both late Judaism and Christianity reflected Hellenistic culture. Niebuhr contended that

> The Hebraic tradition, which is allegedly more crude and less rational, is still relegated to the sphere of "pre-scientific" or "pre-philosophical" thought. *It is*, despite these prejudices, *more "empirical"* than the Greek tradition. Its superior accuracy consists in its understanding of the wholeness of the human self in body, mind and soul, in the appreciation of the dramatic variety of the self's encounters with other selves in history, and in the discontinuity between the self and God.[60] (Italics mine.)

Niebuhr appealed to a "dramatic-historical approach" and an imaginative-poetic language because he believed they more adequately captured both the uniqueness of the self and the self's ambiguous relationship to nature than did the naturalistic languages then in vogue. The very center of the self is the mystery of the self in its freedom. This is far better represented in the nonrational and nonscientific languages of poetry and drama. Niebuhr was here pointing to what he called *self-transcendence*, a capacity which he saw in terms of the self's ability to make itself its own object in the sense of discerning itself as an actor in a drama of which it is a part.

The radical character of the self's capacity for self-transcendence was the basic source for the reason why the self's relationship to nature and reason ought to be understood more dialectically than was the case with most philosophical traditions, including naturalism. The dimension of self-transcendence, Niebuhr wrote, was seen in the self's capacity to transcend "not only the processes of nature but the operations of its own reason, and to stand, as it were, above the structures and coherences

of the world." This pointed to the essential mystery of the self that made
it, in part, impervious to "all purely rationalistic interpretations, not to
speak of purely naturalistic ones."[61] The self, Niebuhr contended, was
"'soul' insofar as it has an experience of [its organic] unity."[62] And
"spirit" was the "self itself in its awareness of its freedom over its functions," which might best "be regarded as the ultimate freedom of the self
over its inner divisions."[63] He was not denying the self's standing in nature in using such terms. For Niebuhr "all the structures of history are a
complex unity of the natural and the spiritual, even as individual man
exhibits this unity. History is thus a proof of the creatureliness of man as
well as of his freedom."[64] Niebuhr thus approached the self's relation to
nature dialectically. In one of his most familiar reflections found at the
beginning of his 1939 Gifford Lectures, Niebuhr pondered,

> Man has always been his own most vexing problem. How
> shall he think of himself? Every affirmation which he may
> make about his stature, virtue, or place in the cosmos becomes
> involved in contradictions when fully analyzed. . . .
>   If man insists that he is a child of nature and that he ought
> not to pretend to be more than the animal which he obviously
> is, he tacitly admits that he is, at any rate, a curious kind of ani-
> mal who has both the inclination and the capacity to make such
> pretensions. If on the other hand he insists upon his unique and
> distinctive place in nature and points to his rational faculties as
> proof of his special eminence, there is usually an anxious note
> in his avowals of uniqueness which betrays his unconscious
> sense of kinship with the brutes.[65]

Niebuhr actually found a certain irony in the fact that what he took
to be extravagant claims on behalf of reason in Dewey contradicted the
notion that the self is continuous with nature. Yet, overall, his position
was that naturalism, especially in its romantic forms, tended "to ascribe
to the realm of the biological and the organic what is clearly a compound
of nature and spirit, of biological impulse and rational and spiritual freedom."[66]

Dewey definitely found objectionable all self-descriptive language
that hypostatized functions into antecedent and transcendent entities.
Thus, he was wary of terms like *consciousness, self-consciousness,* and most
especially *spirit,* because of their essentialistic and supernaturalistic
connotations. In fact, as Bruce Kuklick points out, "Consciousness was,"
for Dewey, "a function of an active organism's relation to a problematic
environment."[67] Dewey would simply not abide any position that resulted in a "gratuitous breach of continuity between nature, life, and

man."[68] He obviously recognized and was quite willing to talk about activities and forms of existence which were uniquely present in human life. But Dewey could not tolerate concepts of human nature that either assumed things "beyond" nature or saw within nature irreconcilably discordant elements. S. Morris Eames, for example, noted that the pragmatic naturalists uniformly rejected the tendency to take "the function of consciousness as an emergent in human life" and transform it "into an entity, into a substance which is thought to be vital to the notion of personal identity and the basis for individuality." Eames rightly contended that for pragmatic naturalists "the act of transforming a function into an entity is one of the greatest errors in the history of philosophy."[69]

Dewey quite obviously knew something of the "uniqueness" of the individual within human life and, most especially, of the distinctive and qualitative differences between human life and the pre- or subhuman biological life forms. He neither interpreted nature materialistically nor the self's place within nature mechanistically. *Materialism* referred to a metaphysical theory about nature that Dewey had consistently rejected. And although he certainly accepted "mechanisms" in nature, Dewey held a qualitative and teleological view of experience that disallowed the reduction of human life to mechanistic interpretation.[70]

What governed any viable descriptions of human existence, for Dewey, even its distinction from other forms of life, was what he called the *biological matrix* of inquiry. Dewey stated that "The primary postulate of a naturalistic theory of logic is continuity of the lower (less complex) and the higher (more complex) activities and forms." At minimum, he went on to say, this principle "excludes complete rupture on one side and mere repetition of identities on the other; it precludes reduction of the 'higher' to the 'lower' just as it precludes breaks and gaps."[71]

The viewpoint Dewey maintained involves two claims. The initial claim is that experience, naturalistically understood, provides the parameters for any intelligible self-descriptions. But, as Eames points out,

> experience [here] is anything and everything which can be pointed to or denoted. Experience includes feelings, sensations, concepts, psychical events, physical things, relations, actualities and ideals, harmonies and disharmonies, common sense and science. Experience includes memories and imaginations, past and projected futures, present awareness, illusions and hallucinations; it includes truths and falsehoods, objects of beauty and ugliness, good and evils; it includes language and events; it includes "death, war, and taxes." In other words, ex-

perience includes all that is, has been, and has potentiality of
becoming. For pragmatic naturalists [and most certainly for
Dewey], experience is ultimate reality.[72]

The clue here is to understand that Dewey believed himself to be employing the terms *nature* and *naturalism* in the broadest sense possible. Although acknowledging that "No one philosophical theory has a
monopoly on the meaning to be given Nature," Dewey also admitted that
"it is the meaning given Nature that is decisive as to the kind of
Naturalism that is put forward." Although giving extremely broad scope
to terms like *experience* and *nature*, Dewey was nonetheless clear that his
"Naturalism is opposed to idealistic spiritualism [and] is also opposed to
super-naturalism and to that mitigated version of the latter that appeals to transcendent *a priori* principles placed in a realm above Nature
and beyond experience."[73]

The second claim Dewey made was that within the governing
parameters of this naturalism, those aspects of human life that differ
from lower life forms be clearly visible, duly acknowledged *and*
adequately interpreted. As Dewey had put it in the quotation already
cited from his *Logic*, the continuity of lower and higher activities and
forms precludes "reduction of the 'higher' to the 'lower' just as it precludes complete breaks and gaps." In point of fact Dewey's case for the
"distinctively human" was made very clear in the subsequent chapter in
his *Logic* which focuses on the "cultural matrix" of inquiry in contradistinction to the purely "biological" matrix. As Dewey had insisted in his
reply to Henry W. Stuart's essay on "Dewey's Ethical Theory," it is precisely the shift from the biological to the cultural matrix in which he,
Dewey, dealt "expressly with the radical change wrought when biological conditions and activities are taken up into the distinctively human
context of institutions and communication."[74]

While Dewey refused to see even the highest forms and expressions
of human life—including "inquiry" itself—in terms other than "a development out of organic-environmental integration and interaction,"[75]
he fully understood that a cultural as well as biological matrix was
operative in understanding and interpreting human beings. Dewey
stated it this way:

> The environment in which human beings live, act and in-
> quire, is not simply physical. It is cultural as well. Problems
> which induce inquiry grow out of the relations of fellow beings
> to one another, and the organs for dealing with these relations
> are not only the eye and ear, but the meanings which have

developed in the course of living, together with the ways of forming and transmitting culture with all its constituents of tools, arts, institutions, traditions and customary beliefs.[76]

Dewey exercised caution and restraint just at the point of this awareness, however. On the one hand, it was surely true that everything culture meant and involved demanded that any naturalistic theory "face the problem of the extraordinary differences that mark off the activities and achievements of human beings from those of other biological forms."[77] On the other hand, it is precisely "these differences which have led to the [erroneous] idea that man is completely separated from other animals by properties that come from a non-natural source."[78] Dewey concluded his line of thought with the observation:

> The conception to be developed . . . is that the development of language (in its widest sense) out of prior biological activities, is, in its connection with wider cultural forces, the key to this transformation. The problem, so viewed, is not the problem of the transition of organic behavior into something wholly discontinuous with it—as is the case when, for example, Reason, Intuition and the A priori are appealed to for explanation of the difference. It is a special form of the general problem of continuity of change and the emergence of new modes of activity— the problem of development at any level.[79]

Dewey went on to develop a theory of language and culture so unique and pervasive, that it, along with his wholesale effort to reconstruct philosophy by overcoming essentialism, led the neo-pragmatist Richard Rorty to cast Dewey as a precursor of deconstructionist tendencies in recent philosophy ranging from Gadamer to Derrida.[80]

Whatever differences there were between humankind and the rest of nature, Dewey insisted that these differences were "not the problem of the transition of organic behavior into something wholly discontinuous with it." Niebuhr would certainly have agreed with the emphasis on "wholly" discontinuous in the sense Dewey's examples suggested. Yet for Dewey, as for Niebuhr, the *difference* between the human and the rest of nature did, indeed, make *all* the difference. Niebuhr saw profound paradoxes in human existence. This led him to express the differences between the "self" and the natural world dialectically so as to highlight those features which were distinctively human. For Dewey, on the other hand, as significant and indeed radical as such differences were, the tendency to perpetuate or reintroduce one of "the greatest errors in the history of philosophy," as Eames expressed it, required a strong and uncompromising emphasis on the self's continuity with nature.

Dewey stated that "Transformation from organic behavior to intellectual behavior, marked by logical properties, is a product of the fact that individuals live in a cultural environment."[81] Niebuhr would clearly take such a formulation as question begging. Instead of being a reasonable explanation of the difference between humans and nature, Niebuhr would view it as simply a recognition of a difference that needed accounting for. The same would be true for Dewey's recognition of language and symbolization in the human being as the key to the transformation from the lower forms of organic life to the human form. These types of facts pointed to a discontinuity that needed to be adequately explained instead of simply reiterating the obvious fact of the self's organic unity with the vitalities of nature—a fact with which Niebuhr had no dispute.

There is an unavoidable and irreconcilable aspect to this conflict between Niebuhr and Dewey. Dewey sought to remain strictly within a functional-behavioral account of human nature. In his reply to Gordon Allport he remarked,

> from the standpoint of a biological-cultural psychology the term "subject" (and related adjectival forms) has only the signification of a certain kind of actual existence; namely, a living creature which under the influence of language and other cultural agencies has become a person interacting with other persons (concrete human beings).
>
> In my theory of experience and of the experiential continuum, this way of regarding the subject (or self, or personal being, or whatever name is employed) is fundamental. For, although the psychological theory involved is a form of Behaviorism, it differs basically from some theories bearing the same name.[82]

The differences that Dewey cited were not insignificant ones for him and included a rejection of the kind of "behavioristic" thinking that conceived of behavior essentially in terms of "something taking place in the nervous system or under the skin of an organism," rather than in environmental terms. Dewey also separated himself from the kind of behaviorism that disregarded the interaction of persons, both with respect to present and past cultural histories. Dewey's "behavioral" approach, as he preferred to call it, was more situational and gestalt than the "behaviorism" of J. B. Watson, for example. As Lewis Hahn puts it, it is "the contextual, situational, contractual or field character of experience" that "stands out in [Dewey's] account."[83]

Nonetheless, Dewey's behavioral and functional approach to self-description would render suspect the frequency and ease with which Niebuhr employed the terms he did to intepret the "nature of man." Although Dewey was specifically discussing the use of subject-object language in epistemology in response to a critical essay written by Hans Reichenbach, a statement that Dewey made there gains general importance because it illustrates the bearing he held toward this entire subject. Dewey wrote, "By way of further clearing up my own position I would point out that I hold that the word 'subject,' if it is to be used at all, has the organism for its proper *designatum*. Hence it refers to an *agency of doing*, not to a knower, mind, consciousness or whatever."[84] This, in brief, summarizes not only Dewey's behavioral procedures but also his fundamental biological orientation.

In the wake of Gordon Allport's critique of Dewey in his article on "Dewey's Individual and Social Psychology," Dewey admitted to having "failed to develop in a systematic way my underlying psychological principles" which, if they had been developed, would certainly have been a "socio-biological psychology."[85] He also acceded to Allport's criticism that he (Dewey) lacked "an adequate theory of personality." In accepting this charge, however, Dewey reiterated one of his perennial concerns:

> In a desire to cut loose from the influence of older "spiritualistic" theories about the nature of the unity and stability of the personal life (regarded as a peculiar kind of substantial-stuff), I failed to show how natural conditions provide support for integrated and potentially equalibrated personality patterns.[86]

Niebuhr's language of dialogue, freedom, and self-transcendence was a language that sought to highlight aspects of the personal and interpersonal life often ignored in the dominant strand of Western intellectual history. This was his way of inveighing against the same metaphysical commitments to "substance" and "essence" that Dewey had sought to "deconstruct." However, Niebuhr performed a similar function by employing what might be termed a "relational ontology" drawn in large part from the kind of approach taken by Martin Buber. From Niebuhr's perspective Dewey's biologistic naturalism had elements in it that made this task more difficult than an approach which appealed to the poetic, dramatic, and historical forms of language available in the "Hebraic" tradition.

To a limited extent, at least, the type of language Niebuhr used (although perhaps not in the way he used it) could conceivably be noted, acknowledged, and reformulated in a way that would be congenial to a fruitful dialogue with certain forms of naturalism. The psychologist Carl Rogers, for example, in a review of *The Self and the Dramas of History*, discovered some of Niebuhr's insights into the dialogical life of the self to be in accord with his own therapeutic experience. This was no doubt based on Rogers' profound appreciation for Martin Buber.[87] Admittedly, the accord Rogers found with Niebuhr was somewhat reluctantly granted. For, overall, he found much fault with Niebuhr's position and was mostly "offended by Dr. Niebuhr's dogmatic statements," to the point of feeling "ready to turn back with fresh respect to the writings of science."[88]

Perhaps a somewhat more congenial form of naturalism might be found in the social psychology of Dewey's fellow-pragmatist, George Herbert Mead. Mead, of course, was a consistent naturalist with whom Niebuhr also took issue.[89] It is nontheless worthy of note that Martin Buber, the very person from whom Niebuhr drew inspiration for his *Self and the Dramas of History*, has been compared with Mead in a manner that would suggest overlapping agreement, in spite of serious divergences.[90] Indeed, it appears that Buber and Mead came to similar forms of sociodialogic descriptions of the self quite independently of one another at about the same time, in spite of the fact that Buber's was a religious vision and Mead's was not.

The fact that Niebuhr's understanding of the nature of the self contained accents present in certain naturalistic approaches to the problem should be of no great surprise. After all, a common cultural heritage was available to otherwise divergent voices. It might even be suggested that despite Dewey's disclaimers he and Niebuhr were on much of the same ground at the point where Dewey focused on "culture," "language," and "meaning" as manifestations of a distinctly human form of life.

Nature and History

In a review of Edwin Conklin's *Man: Real and Ideal*, Niebuhr commented that,

> When dealing with the scientific aspects of the human situation and studying man's relation to the natural world, Professor Conklin gives us a very competent analysis of the natural basis of man's moral and spiritual life. He holds to a teleological view of nature and opposes all mechanistic views. In common with most scientists he is inclined to define the difference between men and animals as one of degree rather than kind. "Fear, suffering, antagonism, joy, affection fidelity, even responsibility,"

he declares, "are manifested in greater or less degree by some animals. . . ." This familiar error of a "scientific" view of man can be easily refuted. If the difference between men and animals is only one of degree and not of kind then it ought to be possible to point to some history of animal institutions. Animals have no such history. Their mode of life is bound by nature and is therefore involved in endless repetition. Only man has a history because he only has the freedom to rise above nature and fashion and refashion the modes of his life and the forms of his society.[91]

Niebuhr, of course, included Dewey at the very center of this indictment:

it had never occurred to [Dewey] that his insistence that the "methods of science" could be transferred from the field of nature to that of history, and that only the intrusion of irrelevant religious and political authority prevented this consummation, rested upon an erroneous and, unexamined presupposition. That was the universally held belief of modern culture that the realm of history was essentially identical with the realm of nature.[92]

Historical and cultural life constitute the fabric and setting of life that is distinctively unique to human existence. Nature may well have a history, but the "self" is its history, for history is in the self and the self is in history in ways that have no comparison in subhuman nature. "Historical time," on Niebuhr's view, "is to be distinguished from natural time by the unique freedom which enables man to transcend the flux of time, holding past moments in present memory and envisaging future ends of actions which are not dictated by natural necessity."[93] The character, unity and ambiguity of the self were, according to Niebuhr, obscured in the "modern belief that 'scientific objectivity' may be simply extended from the field of nature to the field of history."[94] It is "the freedom of the human spirit over the natural processes" that "makes history possible,"[95] Niebuhr contended. Moreover, "the significant unit of thought and action in the realm of historical encounter is not a mind but a self."[96]

In an article written in 1953 Niebuhr gave a highly abbreviated version of a position he would fully develop by 1955 in *The Self and the Dramas of History*:

The simple fact is that philosophies, whether naturalistic or idealistic, fail to understand man insofar as they try to fit him into a system. The system obscures the height of his spirit, the uniqueness of his being, and the egoistic corruption of his freedom. That is why the dramatic historical approach to human and divine reality validates itself despite the prestige of modern science.[97]

The solution Niebuhr found to the limitations and distortions of both idealism and naturalism, therefore, was to insist on a discontinuity between "nature" and "history." This approach was, in the final analysis, at the very center of his criticism of Dewey on the issue of scientific methodology and the "human studies." At bottom, Niebuhr believed that a strictly *social science* was not as complete a possibility as Dewey believed it to be, because the historical character of human existence meant that the self's relationship to nature must be conceived in far more radical and dialectical terms than Dewey's naturalism allowed.

The degree of objectivity achievable or desirable in the natural sciences was simply untranslatable to the realm of human events. In such a realm the self is both situated within, and is an interested participant in the events that define its being as historical. The self qua self has an existential, and not a spectator-observer, relationship to the realities that human studies themselves address. Niebuhr was not being irrationalist or even antirationalist here. He did not consider it

superfluous for man or scientist to gather all relevant data pertaining to the solution of a human or historical problem as diligently as possible; and to correlate evidence as honestly as the prejudices of the individual or of an age will permit. There are innumerable scientific elements in history. What is insufferable is that elaborate claims should be made for the resources of "science" in the clarification of our perplexities, when it is obvious that a most rigorous application of the methods of science means a denial of everything which is characteristically human.[98]

Although Niebuhr insisted that the "scientific spirit in history is desirable if all viewpoints are not to degenerate into a consistent rationalization of conflicting interests," he, nonetheless, contended that such objectivity was, in the final analysis, not a "scientific" achievement at all. Rather, "this objectivity or disinterestedness is not so much an intellectual as a moral and spiritual achievement" in which "the 'self' must detach itself from its interests because there is nothing in any scientific method which would compel the mind to do so."[99] There was, in effect, a profound fallacy in the "modern belief that 'scientific objectivity' may be simply extended from the field of nature to the field of history," and that fallacy "obscures the unity of the self which acts, and is acted upon by history. It also obscures the ambiguity of the human self" and the dialectical relationship the self has to history. For "the self as the creature of history is the same self which must be the creator of history."[100]

What is important to realize is that Niebuhr found the distinction in Dilthey between *Naturwissenschaften* and *Geisteswissenschaften* to be a most crucial one. In discussing psychology as a natural science just after the statement he made about science that Sidney Hook found so objectionable (namely, "science which is only science cannot be scientifically accurate"), Niebuhr wrote:

> This is particularly true of *Geisteswissenschaft* in contrast to physical science. . . . (The real profundities of self-consciousness, the complex problems of personality, in the breadth of its relations to the world of nature and history on the one hand and in the depth of its dimension as self-conscious ego on the other, are the concern of only those schools of psychology which frankly leave the confines of natural science and regard psychology *as a cultural science*, which means that their psychological investigations are guided and prompted by philosophical and therefore semi-religious presuppositions.[101] (Italics mine.)

Niebuhr's view of the discontinuity between nature and history was prompted by the deficiencies he discerned in the naturalist's position, as we have already seen. The way in which he conceived of that discontinuity between nature and history rested largely on the pioneering work of Wilhelm Dilthey and his successors, including R. G. Collingwood. This is true in spite of the obvious reliance Niebuhr had upon Ernst Troeltsch, according to Wilhelm Pauck.[102] Niebuhr, along with Troeltsch, had a profound interest in the practical sociopolitical setting of human spirituality that went beyond Dilthey. Thus, what finally gave shape to the Diltheyean *Geisteswissenschaft* in Niebuhr was what Langdon Gilkey calls Niebuhr's "fundamental dialectic"—a dialectic "between transcendence and creatureliness, between eternity and time (in his earlier works), between God and world,"[103] although Gilkey noted that Niebuhr was interested in the "ethical and political" rather than the "ontological meaning" of this veridical concept.[104]

Niebuhr did not accept the Diltheyean tradition uncritically, however. Indeed, his criticisms of this historicist "pole of historical epistemology" were, themselves, instructive. Niebuhr dissented from what he regarded as "Dilthey's profound study of historical relativism" at the point where Dilthey "finds escape from scepticism by the assumption that a common participation in 'objective spirit' allows the observer of historical phenomena an affinity with the observed phenomena, transcending the different contingencies in which the observers and the observed are involved."[105] Thus, Niebuhr criticized the Diltheyan school for its attempted escape from the consequences of its radical temporal-historical position by way of an "'idealistic' interpretation," an interpretation that resulted in a very unhistorical rationalization of history.[106] Of course, Niebuhr's attempt to safeguard the "self" from what he regarded as the denigrating effects of a too consistent naturalism by an appeal to the "history-nature" dichotomy could, itself, be construed as a hangover from Idealism.

On the other side of the ledger, Niebuhr had little more than contempt for the supposedly "scientific" epistemologies of history that he found in Maurice Mandelbaum's *The Problem of Historical Knowledge* and, to a lesser degree, in Karl Mannheim's *Ideology and Utopia*. Mannheim's overall contribution was provisionally striking to Niebuhr "because his 'sociology of knowledge' is so much more conscious of the all-pervasive character of ideology than most similar analyses."[107] However, he made precious little of this insight having come under the inordinate influence of "the modern confidence in science." In the final analysis Mannheim believed that a sociology of knowledge could be achieved "which will, in infinite regression, refine historical knowledge by isolating and excluding the conditioned perspectives of persons, classes, interests, and periods until the real truth is reached."[108] Niebuhr's real scorn, however, was reserved for the American philosopher, Maurice Mandelbaum, who sought

> to escape historical relativism by exalting "facts" and minimizing their valuation, through which the historian betrays his own relative viewpoint. "Every historical fact," he declares, "is given in some specific context in which it leads to some other fact. . . . Thus when an historian makes a statement it is not with an isolated fact but with a fact in a given context that he is concerned. And in that context the fact leads on to further facts without any intermediation or selection, based on the historian's valuational attitudes, class, interests, or the like."[109]

For Niebuhr the claim that philosophers and historians could "eliminate 'evaluations' in order to get rid of 'evaluational distortions,' " was an expression of the sort of nonsense fostered by the illusion of an objective "scientific" history. Niebuhr held that "all the structures of meaning which furnish the principle of coherence for historiography are contained in these 'evaluations,'" and thus "historical events are established in terms of coherence by precisely the 'evaluations' which are so embarrassing philosophically."[110]

It is well that Niebuhr, for all his criticism of Dewey's "scientism," did not simply identify Dewey with his type of positivistic historicism. In his *Logic* Dewey presented what John Herman Randall, Jr., saw as "a brilliant analysis of the historian's method." Dewey wrote that,

> As culture changes, the conceptions that are dominant in a culture change. . . . History is then rewritten. Material that had formerly been passed by, offers itself as data, because the new conceptions propose new problems for solution, requiring new factual material for statement and test. . . . All historical construction is necessarily selective. . . . If the fact of selection is acknowledged to be primary and basic, we are committed to the conclusion that all history is necessarily written from the standpoint of the present, and is, in an inescapable sense, the history not only of the present but of that which is contemporaneously judged to be important in the present. . . . Intelligent understanding of past history is to some extent a lever for moving the present into a certain kind of future. . . . Men have their own problems to solve, their own adaptations to make. They face the future, but for the sake of the present, not of the future. In using what has come to them as an inheritance from the past they are compelled to modify it to meet their own needs, and this process creates a new present in which the process continues. History cannot escape its own process.[111]

Putting Dewey's instrumentalist reading of the use of history aside, it is certainly true that his remarks showed a clear awareness of the evaluational character of both historical interpretation and appropriation. Dewey, after all, spent much of his time striving to overcome the bifurcation of "fact" and "value." In 1920, arguing for "moral reconstruction," Dewey maintained that, "When the consciousness of science is fully impregnated with the consciousness of human values, the greatest dualism which now weighs humanity down, the split between the material, the mechanical, the scientific and the moral and ideal will be destroyed."[112] Once science is viewed instrumentally, as bearing on human life, then science "becomes itself humanistic in quality" and the "moral meaning of natural science" is recognized. Dewey's denial of the separation of "fact" and "value" was stated in 1948 in the introduction to the republication of his *Reconstruction in Philosophy*:

Now the simple fact of the case is that any inquiry into what is deeply and inclusively human enters perforce into the specific area of morals. . . . When "sociological" theory withdraws from consideration of the basic interests, concerns, the actively moving aims, of a human culture on the ground that "values" are involved and that inquiry as "scientific" has nothing to do with values, the inevitable consequence is that inquiry in the human area is confined to what is superficial and comparatively trivial, no matter what its parade of technical skills.[113]

The problem, for Niebuhr, was not any difficulty in accepting Dewey's awareness of the evaluational dimension of historical interpretation, or in acknowledging his repudiation of any separation of "fact" from "value" so far as "nature as experience" was concerned. Rather the problem was that such insights failed to penetrate to the depth they ought to have. Dewey was not about to put in radical question either his conviction that nature and history were ontologically continuous or that a scientific method was somehow inappropriate as *the* way into understanding the radical historicity of human existence. Dewey was firm in his convictions on this matter. If we could overcome the "superstitious awe" in which science is held, he wrote, "it would be clear enough that what makes any proposition scientific is its power to yield understanding, insight, intellectual at-homeness, in connection with any existential state of affairs, by filling events with coherent and tested meanings."[114]

Dewey rejected a view of history exemplified in Wilhelm Windelband which had come to the point where *Historismus* left us with the conclusion that "the only attitude which can be taken toward historic situations and characters is non-intellectual, being esthetic appreciation, or sympathetic artistic rehabilitation."[115] If this is the case, we are left with the impression that it is clearly "a waste of time to discuss whether there can be such a thing as a science of history because "history and science are by definition at opposite poles."[116] We must then face the curious, awkward, and totally unacceptable position that, "if all natural existences *are* histories, divorce between history and the logical mathematical schemes which are the appropriate objects of pure science, terminates in the conclusion that of existences there is no science, no adequate knowledge."[117] Dewey held the position that such a conclusion could only result from a conception of "knowledge" that identified knowledge with mathematics and formal logic. This left the temporal world either meaningless or explainable only by abstracting from the concrete to transhistorical and transtemporal entities. Dewey's instrumental view of knowledge and his historical interpretation of nature led him to a different conclusion:

Aside from mathematics, all knowledge is historic; chemistry, geology, physiology, as well as anthropology and those human events to which, arrogantly, we usually restrict the title of history. Only as science is seen to be fulfilled and brought to itself in intelligent management of historical processes in their continuity can man be envisaged as within nature, and not as a supernatural extrapolation. Just because nature is what it is, history is capable of being more truly known—understood, intellectually realized—than are mathematical and physical objects.[118]

Niebuhr never came to grips with this profoundly cultural and even existential-pragmatic manner in which Dewey dealt with the historical character of nature.[119] Yet it can still be said that even Dewey's extended and extensive "naturalism" gave Niebuhr problems. His difficulty was not so much with the relativistic epistemology seemingly occasioned by the historicization of nature. Rather it was with what he judged to be a failure to deal with the discontinuities occasioned by the naturalization of history in Dewey's thought.

Dewey, of course, had couched the historicotemporal character of nature in Darwinian categories. So, although he saw both nature and history in "historical" terms, Dewey had no reason to see any serious tension between them. It can be said, therefore, that in spite of viewing nature in historical terms, Dewey most properly placed history solidly within the framework of naturalism. In spite of its uniqueness and complexity, human existence was a thoroughly "natural" phenomenon as was evidenced in the claim that the methods which governed inquiry into the world of nature applied equally well to *human* nature. In Dewey's account, it would make precious little sense to talk otherwise. Attempts to do so would have to be seen as futile at best. At worst they would be looked upon as rather pathetic attempts to reinstate some variation of metaphysical or theological dualism in order that human nature be viewed as somehow "outside" or "beyond" nature.

From Niebuhr's perspective, Dewey's naturalism obscured the fact that history is not quite as "natural" as an organismic model dictates. Niebuhr recognized that, for whatever its limitations, the idealistic epistemology of history generated by Dilthey and his followers reflected an earlier awareness of the temporal, cultural, and historical character of self-knowledge than did the thought of those working out of a strict allegiance to the scientific model. Moreover, the language of history used by that tradition was more adequate to the task of delineating what was distinctive about human life.

It is quite obvious that on some level the residue of metaphysics in

Dewey's "naturalism" and in Niebuhr's "theism" is beyond resolution so long as the problem is pushed back into the province of fundamental assumptions. Perhaps if the focus were shifted in the direction advocated by the neo-pragmatists, then Rorty's contention that preserving "the opposition between the natural and the human sciences" in the Diltheyan sense of a split between the *Natur-* and the *Geisteswissenchaften* would serve no interesting point.[120] Of course, such would be the case only if dogmatic claims for science and scientific method were put aside. That Dewey was unprepared to consider this has been more than evident. As John E. Smith put it, Dewey believed that "method is neutral and does not of itself commit us to special theses about the nature of things." Smith goes on to confess:

> It is difficult to understand what leads anyone to suppose that methods remain free of assumptions and that they invariably enjoy protective neutrality. When someone tells us *how* to obtain something, he is assuming that he knows the general sort of thing he is after and has some idea of where it is to be found. To suppose that one-sidedness and special pleading attach only to results and conclusions and not to methods has been one of the most cherished fancies of the entire pragmatic tradition.[121]

Niebuhr's own pragmatic instincts were at their best here in discerning this, one of pragmatism's "most cherished fancies." In the context of Niebuhr's *pragmatic historicism*, the "pragmatic naturalism" of Dewey provides us with a conception of "nature and experience" wherein both "nature" and "experience" are largely devoid of historical awareness in Niebuhr's use of that term. Recognizing that "nature" as experience in both the classical and modern periods took predominantly ahistorical, essentialistic, and commensurating forms (to use Rorty's language), Niebuhr's deliberate and strategic shift from "nature and experience" to "history and experience" was intended to make room for a broader range for "cultural conversation."

Overall, Niebuhr was at his weakest at the point where he equivocated on the degree to which his alternative to strict naturalistic language was rationally compelling. That is to say, he moved between two poles in his apologia; namely, that of attempting to argue for empirical validation, on the one side, and appealing to the transrational "mysteries of faith," on the other. Critics would say he wanted it both ways. All too frequently his tactic was to hurl thinly veiled "religious" perspectives or insights against the quandaries and deficiencies of rival schools of thought. Niebuhr rarely, if ever, *argued* his case; that is, he did not engage in philosophically recognizable procedures of argument, much less in serious and sustained analysis of the writings of his adversaries. This latter point is widely recognized and was partly offset both by his specific aims and his rather brilliant capacity for intellectual synthesis. The point about his failure to engage in careful philosophical reasoning was pointed out rather severely by Julian Hartt of Yale.[122] Because of this weakness, much of what Niebuhr had to say about the nature of the self and history was not developed in a manner that would either give the terms of his position clarity or seriously commend them to the "cultured despisers" (a phrase Niebuhr borrowed from Schleiermacher) of religion among the philosophically sophisticated. Niebuhr, as is generally known, was much more adept at pleading his case to the "cultured de-spisers" within circles populated by historians and political theorists-practitioners, than he was among the philosophers. Generally the philosophers of that day, especially those in the Columbia-Union Semi-nary axis, had much more "philosophical" contact—happy or unhappy, as the case may be—with Niebuhr's colleague Paul Tillich, than with Niebuhr.

One additional matter should be mentioned. Niebuhr did, after all, give expression to a religiously committed point of view. In the final analysis, he interpreted the radical freedom of the self in its self-trans-cendence as well as the self's historical character in a theological framework. However open some naturalists might be to Niebuhr's con-tributions on one level, they would most certainly balk at any hint of a claim that the insights he had to offer them either pointed to, or derived from, a transcendent divine source.

Niebuhr strongly advocated the worth and availability of "Hebraic" modes of thought as a much needed corrective to the legacy of "Hellenis-tic" culture. Dewey, not entirely without reason, was deeply antagonistic to the religious tradition to which these modes of thought were, in great measure, related. This antagonism, along with a distinctly different set of loyalties and interests, rendered him basically closed—and therefore somewhat blind—to the possible resources such modes of thought might have to offer. Niebuhr found this fact to be both unfortunate and, indeed, irrational in its own way. When all is said and done, Niebuhr had a recog-nizably Western religious orientation. Dewey, on the other hand, saw himself as a religious naturalist; that is, he openly espoused a religious vision of his own that he believed to be thoroughly consistent with naturalisitic assumptions and values.

10

Approaches to Religion

Dewey and Religious Naturalism

Dewey saw the institutionalized religions of Western tradition inhibiting the achievement of religious values within the confines of natural experience. Historically, as well as conceptually, the "religions" had prevented the emergence of the "religious," that is, of whatever was capable of introducing genuine perspective into human life. To facilitate the liberation of the "religious" in experience, Dewey pressed for an abandonment of the position that there were special truths of a religious nature and the correlative notion that there existed special avenues to such truths.

Because Dewey saw "religion" as having contributed substantially to the widespread *antireligious* attitude of the modern world, Dewey's basic distinction between the adjective *religious* and the noun *religion* in *A Common Faith* was sharply polemical. The decline of the "religious" in American life was, on Dewey's account, a direct result of the intransigence and absurdity of "religion."[1] Dewey's aim, therefore, was to separate (and thereby rescue) the religious dimension in human experience from the traditional religions that had obscured the genuinely "religious" in experience.

Religious life, as Dewey saw it, was thoroughly compatible with a naturalistic interpretation of the world. Moreover, following the contours outlined by Feuerbach, Dewey insisted that an authentic religious life was possible *only* on the basis of a naturalistic interpretation because only within such an intepretation could human *nature*'s self-alienation be overcome. What Dewey was attempting to do in *A Common Faith*, acccording to Richard Comstock, was to designate "the naturalistic equivalents to those ultimate concerns of man that religion has in the past put into a supernatural framework."[2] This meant that Dewey's concern, as Randall put it, was "with making explicit the complete compatibility between the religious values in experience and whatever beliefs may be intellectually warranted."[3]

Dewey gave voice to what William Shea termed a *hard* naturalism,[4] inasmuch as he neither tolerated compromise with traditional theistic supernaturalism nor displayed even a hint of immanentalistic theism, such as Henry Nelson Wieman sought to impose on him both in a 1934 review of *A Common Faith* and again in a debate sponsored by *Christian Century* entitled "Is John Dewey a Theist?"[5] Wieman insisted that Dewey's idea of "God" as that which "holds the actual and the ideal together" involved "forces in nature and society" beyond the integrative power that originates and sustains those ideals. Dewey steadfastly resisted Wieman's representation of him and saw Wieman's efforts as an attempt to read "his own position into his interpretation of mine." Because of Dewey's general respect and admiration for Wieman, he was visably disappointed with the position Wieman imputed to him.[6] Dewey openly agreed with Edwin Aubrey whose position in the dispute supported the view that Dewey was neither a theist nor a pantheist and could be represented as such only by severe distortion of Dewey's words and intentions. Aubrey's judgment was that "the integrative power binding actual and ideal is still restricted, in Mr. Dewey's thought, to human imaginative intelligence."[7]

A large measure of the problem that enveloped Dewey rested with his determination to employ the word *God* in *A Common Faith*. Sidney Hook, for example, was not only taken back by the fact that Dewey would devote the time and energy to write on religion, but was also utterly dismayed by his intention to use the term central to classical theism. Hook predicted that a great danger of misunderstanding would accompany Dewey's use of the term *God,* whatever nontheistic sense he planned on giving the word.[8] The various meanings that the term received at Dewey's hand are found in the section of *A Common Faith* entitled "Faith and Its Object."[9] Basically, Dewey used the term *God* to point to the "*active* relation between ideal and actual"—a unifying, by means of imagination, of ideal ends which arouse us to a desire and action. The crucial point was that Dewey did not identify the term with a Being, nor with antecedent realities (realities existing prior to and independent of experience), nor, finally, with mystical forces within nature that allegedly generated and sustained such ideals.[10] The imaginative union of which Dewey spoke was not a given. Rather it was conceived as a process—an active and practical *uniting* achieved by disciplined thought and action solely on the part of human beings in relation to a natural world which was sometimes supportive and sometimes not. Dewey did want to make it clear that the "ideal possibilities unified through imaginative realization and projection [are] connected with all the natural forces and conditions—including man and human association—that promote the growth of the ideal and that further its realization."[11]

In *A Common Faith* Dewey gave as one reason for his use of the term *God* his desire to overcome the preoccupation with "man in isolation" which he found common to both militant atheism and supernaturalism alike. The despair of the militant atheist and the otherworldliness of the supernaturalist undermined humankind's continuity with nature and resulted in a denigration of the natural world. Both supernaturalism and militant atheism lacked what Dewey called "natural piety." He wrote that "A religious attitude . . . needs the sense of a connection of man, in the way of both dependence and support, with the enveloping world that the imagination feels is a universe." Because of this need the "use of the words 'God' or 'divine' to convey the union of actual with ideal may protect man from a sense of isolation and from consequent despair or defiance."[12] This type of consolation, perhaps, makes the best sense if it is taken as one of the lingering elements of Dewey's Protestant heritage as Robert Fitch noted in his interpretation of Dewey as the "last Protestant."[13]

Sidney Hook shed interesting light on Dewey's rationale for resisting strong advice that he avoid theistic language. According to Hook, among the reasons why Dewey believed the word *God* could be used with impunity was an explanation that Hook claimed "men like [Betrand] Russell or [Morris R.] Cohen would never have dreamed of presenting." Hook reported Dewey to have said: "Besides there are so many people who would feel bewildered if not hurt if they were denied the right to use the term 'God.' They are not in the churches, they believe what I believe, they would feel a loss if they could not speak of God. Why then shouldn't I use the term?' "[14]

However curious this episode over the use of the term *God* was, Dewey suffered increased frustration over the fact that the controversy had detracted from his main point. He attempted to make that point clear in his response to Wieman:

> There is a fundamental difference between that to which I said, with some reservations, the *name* God might be applied and Mr. Wieman's attribution to me of something "that holds the actual and ideal together." What is said was that the union of ideals with *some* natural forces that generate and sustain them, accomplished in human choice and action, is that to which the name God might be applied, with of course the understanding that that is just what is meant by the word. I thought the *word*

might be used because it seems to me that it is this union which has actually functioned in human experience in its religious dimension.[15]

Dewey's frustration was recorded in an intermittent correspondence with Corliss Lamont between 1935 and 1941, a fact Lamont made public only in 1961. Dewey exclaimed to Lamont in 1935 that "What I still don't get about your reaction to my book . . . and the same is true of reviews from the conventional religious angle—is why there is so much more concern about the world 'God' and so little attention to that which I said was a reality to which the world *might* be applied."[16] At the close of their correspondence on this matter, Dewey wrote to Lamont on May 31, 1941, "I think it important to help many people to realize that they can save what it actually meant to them free from superstitious elements." Lamont proved gratified that Dewey's letters constituted

> decisive evidence for settling the long argument as to his use of the term "God." He did not incorporate that word into his "common faith" or into his philosophy, as outstanding naturalist philosophers have often done—Aristotle and Spinoza, for example—to the lasting befuddlement of their readers for centuries, and indeed right down to the present day. John Dewey was not, then, in any sense a theist, but an uncompromising naturalist or humanist thinker who saw the value of a shared religious faith free from outworn supernaturalism and institutional fanaticism.[17]

In a more informal setting, with a group of individuals meeting at Lamont's apartment in New York City in 1959 to reminisce about Dewey, Horace Kallen spoke of the loss of the soul in Dewey's psychology. Kallen pointed out that there was both a "replacement of the soul by the body under the influence of George Herbert Mead [and] a replacement of God by ideals under the influence of Edward Scribner Ames of Chicago."[18]

Perhaps what is central to all of this is that the term *God* simply represented the last echo of a tradition that Dewey could not quite let go. The reason for his retention of the word might mean little more than a last gesture of nostalgia—an eye to a past that, on one level, was quite irrecoverable. On quite another level, however, this same past was by choice received into an unwelcoming and unfamiliar present, but only on the condition that its incarnation be emptied of its prior meaning. Dewey, in this sense, is preeminently one of the very "last Protestants" on the deepest and most persistent level. He was among that special breed for whom the presence of the holy, "like Alice's Cheshire Cat," according to Sidney Mead's image, "threatened to disappear altogether, or, at most, to remain only as a disembodied and sentimental smile."[19]

Whatever the influences on Dewey's reconception of the meaning of the term *God,* his identification of the word with "ideal possibilities unified through imaginative realization and projection"[20] had as its proper context a "hard" naturalism directed toward the religiously disenfranchised element within the liberal-modernist wings of the Protestant tradition. *"A Common Faith,"* Dewey insisted in 1939,

> was addressed to those who have abandoned supernaturalism, and who on that account are reproached by traditionalists for having turned their backs on everything religious. The book was an attempt to show such persons that they still have within their experience all the elements which give the religious attitude its value.[21]

The "religious" dimension of life, as Dewey saw it, required neither a transcendental object nor some experience intrinsically and uniquely religious. Religious experience was not in some class by itself (determined as much by the nature of its object—the numinous—as by the inner structure of the experience—mysterious tremendum—as had been maintained within Protestantism via the tradition of Rudolph Otto and Frederick Schleiermacher). The religious "denotes attitudes that may be taken towards every object and every proposed end or ideal." In other words, it is "a quality of experience" as such, which may belong to any or all spheres of experience, be they "aesthetic, scientific, moral, political," including "companionship and friendship."[22]

In seeing the "religious" as a dimension within and open to all experience, Dewey affirmed that the *religious,* properly understood, was not incompatible with naturalism, properly understood. In spite of Lamont's inclusion of "intelligent theologians as Reinhold Niebuhr" among those who chose to make "capital" out of Dewey's use of the term *God,*[23] Niebuhr's brief review of *A Common Faith* conceded that Dewey's position manifested the rigorous "empiricism and naturalism" Dewey intended it to be. Several years later in a review of Arthur Dakin's *Man the Measure,* Niebuhr, consistent with his honest recognition of Dewey's religious naturalism, alluded to Dewey as one of the "great philosophers" who understood "the implications of their own position."[24]

If Niebuhr made "capital" out of Dewey's position, it related to Dewey's refusal to cut the "religious" off in any way from the immediacy of the present world. The vehemence with which Dewey applied this consequence of his naturalism appealed to Niebuhr for its iconoclastic value. He saw Dewey as a religiously sensitive naturalist who failed to compromise with any religious conception that was world denigrating. The "capital" Niebuhr made of Dewey's *A Common Faith* was not to press him into an unholy alliance with theism, but rather to stress that Dewey's *naturalistic* position was closer to what Niebuhr held to be the world-affirming orientation of biblical thought as contrasted with the dualistic tendencies of Hellenistic thinking. Niebuhr saw that with his emphasis on "nature" and the "real world" as "realms of meaning," Dewey's view was closer to the world-affirming character of "prophetic religion" than even Dewey realized. Niebuhr was nonetheless quite open about the fundamental difference between Dewey's naturalism and Niebuhr's own religious orientation:

> Dr. Dewey may insist that he does not believe in the ideals as "antecedently existing actualities," but he does believe in a world in which the possibility of realizing ideals exists. He believes in appreciating the world of nature as a realm of meaning even where it does not obviously support man's moral enterprise but is in conflict with it. This is the kind of faith which prophetic religion has tried to express mythically and symbolically by belief in a God who is both the creator and the judge of the world, that is, both the ground of its existence and its *telos*.[25]

Nonetheless, from the vantage point of Niebuhr's "biblical faith," Dewey's naturalism was open to the charge of impiety, if not idolatry, for having emptied "its world of references to the transcendent source of life and meaning, thus arriving at its self-contained and self-sufficient history."[26] The issue for Dewey, of course, was simply a question of evidence and not at all a matter of impiety.

With respect to the values associated with much philosophical idealism, Dewey's humanistic naturalism sought to preserve its valuational insights, while at the same time divorcing those insights from the metaphysics with which they had become attached. Dewey once wrote that "the school of objective idealism" had borrowed certain traits from aesthetic experiences and had

> illegitimately extended them till they became categories of the universe at large, endowed with cosmic import. I am not prepared to deny to writers of this school genuine esthetic insights; and in so far as these insights are genuine, it is the task of an empirical pragmatic esthetics to do justice to them without taking over the metaphysical accretions.[27]

This, of course, was indicative of the manner in which Niebuhr eventually came to view idealism. Idealism, for both Dewey and Niebuhr, included more of the complexities of the self and displayed a greater insight into the religious, ethical, and aesthetic sides of life than did narrow versions of empiricism and naturalism. The polemical thrust of Dewey's pragmatic naturalism against the truncated form of mechanistic naturalism was based on such realizations as he sought to remedy the situation within the boundaries of naturalism. Both Dewey and Niebuhr insisted that the "depths" in things be taken seriously in any account of *human* existence. Both were also of the opinion that such an account was *not* intrinsically connected to the metaphysical commitments of idealism. Although some might see in this an example of claiming one can sit at a common table without partaking of the meal, Dewey's and Niebuhr's pragmatic instincts suggested that such metaphysical food was both unobtainable and unnecessary for a "deep" understanding of the human situation.

Dewey sought an "empirical pragmatic" religion that would do justice to the religious and moral aspects of experience. Not only did he *not* wish to take over the "metaphysical accretions" associated with idealism and traditional theistic supernaturalism, but he also saw those accretions as substantive detractors from the task of bringing the authentically *religious* quality of all experience into the light of day. Dewey, in effect, saw the need to clear the ground prior to generating what he called "a more humane, more liberal, and broader religious attitude."[28]

Dewey also had his problems with the term *humanism* as applied to his religious convictions. Uncomfortable with the subjective turn given to the term *humanism* by Schiller, Dewey insisted that his philosophical position, if properly interpreted, was that of a naturalist. Goaded by Corliss Lamont to label his position *humanism,* or at least *naturalistic humanism,* Dewey firmly declined. He preferred *cultural* or *humanistic naturalism* as a more adequate designation of his point of view. Dewey allowed the term *humanism* as an adjective prefixed to *naturalism* essentially as a *religious* counterpoint to supernaturalism. He was adamant about this limited use of the term *naturalism* for another reason. Aside from humanism's subjectivistic connotations—that is, its tendency to conceive religious experience as "inner" experience—Dewey was also convinced that "some humanists are inclined to minimize the natural basis of human life in comparison with what is contributed by the distinctively human factor." Expressing this concern in a response to Bernard Meland in 1935, Dewey showed his central concern to be with the "danger of 'anthro-inflation' [borrowing Meland's term] in any theory that isolates man from his natural matrix."[29] Even though Dewey had no compunction about affixing his name to "The Humanist Manifesto" of 1933, he consistently backed away from the term *humanism* because, as he put it in *A Common Faith*, "A humanistic religion, if it excludes our relation to nature, is pale and thin, as it is presumptuous, when it takes humanity as an object of worship."[31]

Dewey's naturalism, as John E. Smith noted, possessed a "vantage point from which it interprets reality as a whole," and most especially the human being's place within it. This vantage point Smith rightly called "the biological situation—the interaction of organism and environment plus the mutual adjustment required for survival" that, he held, "furnishes the key to understanding the human predicament" for Dewey's thought.[23] This "vantage point" indicates the specific character of Dewey's naturalism and accounts for the kind of resistance he offered against other forms of naturalism. What is of particular importance here is Dewey's opposition to fellow naturalists Henry Nelson Wieman and George Santayana. Dewey's disclaimer of Wieman's attempt to ascribe anything smacking of theism, pantheism, or mysticism to Dewey's use of the term *God* has already been noted. However, it was Dewey's controversy with Santayana that really illuminated both the naturalistic commitment in Dewey's interpretation of the "religious" and Niebuhr's criticism of that interpretation.

The Role of Santayana

Santayana inaugurated the controversy in a major review of Dewey's *Experience and Nature* which was published in 1925. Dewey's response came more than a year later, and the dispute was taken up again in the initial volume of The Library of Living Philosophers.[33]

Santayana brought into sharp relief a core problem that had bearing on the religious quality of Dewey's naturalism. In describing Dewey's naturalism as accidental, "half-hearted and short-winded,"[34] Santayana accused Dewey of exclusively stressing the "foreground" of nature-as-experience and thus ignoring the depth and independence of nature's "background."[35] Dewey countercharged that Santayana had introduced a "structural dislocation of non-human and human existence" that resulted in an unnatural break between humankind and nature. To conceive of nature in terms of such radical discontinuity was, in brief, to reintroduce the kind of dualism "reminiscent of supernatural beliefs,"[36] thus abandoning that continuity which Dewey regarded as *the* fundamental postulate governing the very logic of naturalism.[37]

Santayana, according to Dewey, failed to discern the continuity between nature's background (i.e., its general traits) and nature's foreground in experience. Generic traits such as stability and instability, harmony and disharmony, order and disorder render life problematical. The stituational "problematic" engendered by these traits of existence give rise to problem-solving reflections. Such experiences are "had" and "known"; that is, they are to be understood as traits *in* nature as well as elements in cognition.

A far more crucial point relevant to the issue of religion is to be found in an ancillary charge Santayana leveled against Dewey. According to Santayana, Dewey's ethicopragmatic emphasis on *techne*, as well as the activism of individual and social life, was linked to Dewey's disregard for "the mysterious but momentous background" of natural realities encountered in human action. This led Dewey to give expression to a form of naturalism that was "half-hearted," a naturalism that simply failed to go deeply enough. The "background," in Santayana's account, was orphaned and resulted in a fundamental act of *natural* impiety on Dewey's part.

It is somewhat ironic that Santayana's charge came in spite of Dewey's own strenuous advocacy of a "natural piety" that he found expressed in a humble but "intelligent courage" associated with the human task of extending control over nature. Dewey's rejection of the title *humanism* was based on precisely the sort of anthropocentrism (Meland's "anthro-inflation") that Santayana attempted to lay at Dewey's own doorstep. Of course, Dewey saw natural piety in different terms than did Santayana. Dewey viewed "natural piety" as having due respect for the fact that the natural environment both "supports our undertakings and aspirations as much as it . . . defeats . . . us." Such piety avoids the extremes of both a "fatalistic acquiescence in natural happenings" and a "romantic idealization of the world" that gives vent to egoistic pretensions about controlling nature. For Dewey, then, natural piety was "an inherent constituent of a just perspective in life" which enables us to humbly "strive to direct natural and social forces to human ends."[38]

Santayana's sense of "natural piety" was quite different. As he saw it, natural piety was more than a mere recognition that nature sometimes cooperates with, and sometimes confounds, our strivings. It was, rather, an expression of a sense of the mysterious and nonhuman character of the natural "background." In other words, the root of Santayana's vision of natural piety lay in the irresolvable and uncontrollable mystery of nature *as background* in its relation to the *foreground* that is nature-as-experienced.

The contrast here is both sharp and divergent. For Dewey "natual piety" ought to lead to a "sense of the permanent and inevitable implication of nature and man in a common career and destiny." In the context of such an understanding an "increased knowledge of nature" could be seen, not as "irreligious," but rather as "potentially much more religious than all that it is displacing."[39] Moreover, Sterling Lamprecht's observation represents Dewey's fears. Lamprecht claimed that "Piety toward some precious existence and reverence before some fine event may at times add to the beauty and the moral worth of men's lives. But as soon as such piety and reverence lead men to attribute an effect to an origin outside the natural world, they become deplorable occasions for obscurantism."[40] For Santayana, on the other hand, "natural piety" was a reverential attitude before the impenetrable mystery of nonhuman nature that ought to give rise to a religious vision of the natural world. In Santayana's judgment, Dewey lacked this deeper piety primarily because his "half-hearted naturalism" was, at bottom, governed by a pragmatic activism for which naturalism was merely an accident of historical timing.[41]

The elements of mystery and a somewhat mystical reading of the nonhuman which gave Dewey such offense, were at the very center of Santayana's naturalism. For Santayana these were the elements that both kept nature from being reduced to the pragmatist's easy domestication and opened up genuine religious possibilities. Santayana, in Richard Comstock's words, believed "that a wise piety will recognize the inherent limitations of human symbols gleaned from the forground to dispel the mysterious character of the background."[42] This was analogous to Niebuhr's criticism of Dewey's particular breed of naturalism. Niebuhr, of course, shared Dewey's activism rather than Santayana's quietism. That is to say, both Dewey and Niebuhr saw life in this world in terms of social responsibility and not in terms of passivity or withdrawal from political action. Moreover, Niebuhr resolutely opposed any mystical naturalism that suggested pantheistic or acosmic tendencies. The appeal Santayana had for Niebuhr was that his general criticism of Dewey focused on the fact that Dewey's naturalism was entirely closed to genuine transcendence.

From Santayana's viewpoint Dewey's position was the ultimate in an anthropocentric attitude toward nature. "The dominant foreground which [Dewey] calls Experience," he insisted, is "filled and bounded not so much by experience as by convention. It is the social world."[43] This interpretation of Dewey—correct or incorrect—is a telling and revealing one. It would have applied equally well to Niebuhr on one level. For although Niebuhr acknowledged the "mysterious" in a way that Dewey did not, he, like Dewey, shared—with some differences—the sociocultural focus of Dewey's pragmatic outlook. The most significant difference between them, as previously examined, lay in the fact that Niebuhr turned toward "history" and away from "nature" to present the self's dialectical relationship to nature more fully than he believed possible within Dewey's naturalism.

Santayana responded to the "unfathomableness of the world" as the deep source and meaning of "natural piety." Dewey dismissed such a position as obscurantist, lending credibility to the perpetuation of unintelligible discourse. Moreover, for Dewey such an attitude led to a mystification of nature that diminished, if not dismissed entirely, the importance of human action. The "spirtuality" associated with Santayana's "natural piety" emphasized a contemplative detachment that undermined the very activism which both Dewey and Niebuhr thought central to a responsible life. Santayana's "spiritual" dimension, in Dewey's account, tended toward escapism based on a disparagement of the historical and natural processes. This tendency toward passive acquiescence based on a denigration of the world was precisely what both Dewey and Niebuhr abhorred. Writing in this vein, Niebuhr noted that "In the conception of such religion [as acosmic pantheism] Santayana's judgment, that creation was really the fall, expressed the religious feeling precisely. The sense of sin is a sense of finiteness before the infinite, a feeling in which the metaphysical emphasis imperils the ethical connotation."[44] That Santayana exhibited such tendencies was seen by Dewey as a byproduct of Santayana's "broken-backed" naturalism—an obscurantistic naturalism that ushered in a world-denying dualism after all. For Niebuhr, also, Santayana's religious vision revealed how closely certain forms of naturalism were related to mysticism. In 1936 Niebuhr claimed:

> Modern naturalism is really a form of expansive pantheism, while the more rigorous types of rationalistic religions are contractive and result in an acosmic pantheism. In such pantheism the difference between good and evil is identical with the meta-physical distinction between the eternal and the temporal and between the spiritual and the material world.[45]

Early on Niebuhr had known the ambiguous tension in the relationship between the religious impulse and ethical responsibility. Dewey, who was inclined to see supernaturalistic religious belief as necessarily expressive of a fated acquiescence, judged that Christian social activism was something of an anomaly—illogically conducted in spite of the logical tendencies of its own metaphysics. Niebuhr saw the problem in more paradoxical terms. "Religious hope," he wrote in 1934, "always tends to encourage moral energy by promising victory to a seemingly hopeless enterprise, but it also enervates moral energy by guaranteeing victory too unreservedly." Niebuhr went on to express the judgment that "Generally the vital period of a religion extracts resources of energy from its hope while the later more conventional eras use it to escape responsibility for action."[46]

Niebuhr was in total agreement with Dewey's contention that "otherworldliness" in either its rational, mystical or theistic forms ought not to be regarded as a "refuge" from the world. Dewey's alternative to this tendency on the part of the *religions* was entirely singular, however. His solution was to turn toward a "religious faith which attaches itself to the possibilities of nature and associated living [and] would, with its devotion to the ideal, manifest piety toward the actual."[47] Niebuhr, on the other hand, drew inspiration from a prophetic faith that knew the law of love required a quest for justice. At the same time Niebuhr's vision of faith was one that encouraged responsible action, while maintaining an attitude of "nonchalance" without which "all moral striving generates a stinking sweat of self-rightousness and an alternation of fanatic illusions and fretful disillusionments."[48]

Santayana's dispute with Dewey helps focus and illuminate Niebuhr's fundamental differences with Dewey on the question of religion. Niebuhr's contention with the implications of Dewey's naturalism was that Dewey excluded the sense of openness to transcendence that naturalists such as Santayana allowed. From his earliest years, quite often shifting context as well as language, Niebuhr stressed what could be called the tangents between "time and eternity," the "finite and the infinite," and, respecting the life of the self, between the self as both "in" and "beyond" nature and history.[49] Niebuhr, in effect, consistently bought into a tradition-based commitment to "transcendence." However, he did not understand or accept these terminologies in the traditionally dualistic fashion as suggested in both traditional metaphysics and supernaturalism. In fact, in his review of Dewey's *A Common Faith*, Niebuhr remarked that "It is questionable whether the supernature against which Dr. Dewey protests, a realm of being separate from the natural world and interfering in its process, is really the kind of supernature about which really profound prophetic religion speaks."[50] Accepting "the paradox of man and history fundamentally," Niebuhr claimed,

> is to understand that man is, even in the highest reaches of his transcendent freedom, too finite to comprehend the eternal by his own resources. But it is also understood that man is, even in the deepest involvement of process and nature, too free of nature to be blind to the possibilities of a disclosure of the Eternal which transcends him.[51]

By the time Niebuhr gave his Gifford Lectures in 1939, he had come to emphasize biblical symbols rather than the more general symbolism of the philosophy of religion. He stressed Hebraic-dramatic metaphors rather than either ethico- philosophical or Hellenic-ontological ways of thinking. He also emphasized dialectical tensions within the self, and between the self and the world, all of which reshaped the ways in which he expressed the notion of "transcendence." Whatever difficulties Niebuhr had in giving expression to the idea of "transcendence," it was his conviction that the substantive meanings of religious symbols depended on something more than self-transcendence. Niebuhr thus sought to stress the oppositions, tensions, and cross-purposes within the fabric of the world in a way that would avoid the pitfalls of radical monism and radical dualism. For Niebuhr, Dewey's naturalism, in its legitimate resistance to religious and philosophical dualisms, overstated "continuity" in such a way as to err on the side of monism and thus oversimplified the complexities or "depths" of existence. Dewey's position, according to Niebuhr, glossed over the discontinuities that Niebuhr's dialectical approach sought to emphasize as a way of speaking more "truly" about both the mystery of the self and the mystery of the world. Niebuhr returned to a favorite illustration of the diverging half-truths represented by idealism, on the one hand, and naturalism, on the other—both of which mistakenly demanded a too "rationally conceived system of meaning" for the world. The "configurations and structures which stand athwart" such attempts, Niebuhr insisted, are best exemplified

> in man himself, who is both in nature and above nature and who has been alternately misunderstood by naturalistic and idealistic philosophies. Idealism understands his freedom as mind but not his reality as contingent object in nature. It elaborates a history of man as if it were a history of mind, without dealing adequately with man as determined by geography and climate, by interest and passion. Naturalism, on the other hand, tells the history of human culture as if it were a mere variant of natural history.[52]

All "natural and rational structures of the world," for Niebuhr, were confounded by the capacity of "genuine freedom" to defy their expected schemes of order and coherence. The mystery of freedom which is the self's capacity for self-transcendence and pointed to a transcendence beyond itself, was most clearly recognized early on by Pascal. Niebuhr wrote:

This mystery of human freedom, including the concomitant
mystery of historic evil, plus the previous incongruity of man
both as free spirit and as a creature of nature, led Pascal to
elaborate his Christian existentialism in opposition to the
Cartesian rationalism and Jesuit Thomism of his day. Pascal
delved "in mysteries without which man remains a mystery to
himself"; and that phrase may be a good introduction to the consideration of the relation of the suprarational affirmation of the
Christian faith to the antinomies, contradictions, and mysteries of human existence.[53]

Niebuhr believed that this Pascalian insight into the depth of
human grandeur and misery, and the paradox of their common root in
the self's freedom, had largely been lost to modern thought. It is surely
the case that such thinking was lost on Dewey and many of his fellow-
naturalists. Minimally, it must be said that whatever truth Pascalian
thinking contributed with respect to the complexity of human existence
was both sacrificed to irrationalistic language and lost to unnecessary
transcendental intimations. Whatever truth was in Pascal, Kierkegaard
and their theological descendents could better be stated in naturalistic
terms. In fact Dewey linked Niebuhr to Kierkegaard in 1947 when he
suggested that "he and Kierkegaard have both completely lost faith in
traditional statements of Christianity, haven't got any modern substitute and so are making up, off the bat, something which supplies to them
the gist of Christianity—what they find significant in it and what they
approve of in modern thought."[54]

For Niebuhr, on the other hand, the forms of naturalism that simply
reduced the self to the dimensions of nature or, conceiving nature itself
in religious terms, had underestimated the paradoxes of Pascalian
thought. According to Niebuhr, man is "not just a slighly more clever animal. He is unique not only in the degree of his practical intelligence or in
his inventive genius. His real uniqueness consists in the fact that he can
make himself and the world the object of his thought and inquire into the
relation of his self to the world." In the final analysis, for Niebuhr, the
"dignity of man is his freedom, his capacity to make and remake history,
to search out all things and to inquire after the meaning of existence."[55]

Although naturalism better understood the limits of the self's
creatureliness, idealism more properly gauged the depth of human existence and the transcendence to which such depth pointed. In the controversy between Dewey and Santayana, it was the naturalism of Santayana—in spite of its dualistic and world-denigrating tendencies—
that was attuned to the mystery in things. To see the mystery in the self

and the world, for Niebuhr, was crucial to a genuine and more complete sense of the "religious."

Symbolism and Religion in Niebuhr

Both Dewey and Niebuhr would agree with Santayana's judgment that "to hypostatize . . . human symbols, and identify them with nature or with God, is idolatry." Santayana's subsequent judgment would, however, be more akin to Niebuhr's religious outlook. Santayana concluded that "the remedy for idolatry is not iconoclasm, because the senses, too, or the heart or the pragmatic intellect, can breed only symbols. The remedy," as Santayana saw it, "is rather to employ the symbols pragmatically, with detachment and humor, trusting in the steady dispensations of the substance beyond."[56] Aside from the fact that Niebuhr would not speak in terms of "the steady dispensations of the substance beyond," his major departure from Santayana—and, of course, from Dewey—was that Niebuhr insisted on the central *religious*, rather than merely literary or aesthetic, importance of biblical symbolism. Niebuhr's way of making this point can be seen in his reaction to the "purely aesthetic and non-religious" view of myth that is "sceptical about values in the ultimate sense." In taking note of Santayana's notion that "Poetry is religion which is no longer believed," Niebuhr observed that "Religion, to transpose Santayana's phrase, is poetry which is believed. Religion seeks mythically to grasp life in its unity and wholeness"—something which cannot be expressed in purely rational terms.[57]

It must be noted that "unity" and "wholeness" are categories that played a central role in Dewey's account of the aesthetic. In his book *Art As Experience* he wrote, for example,

> A work of art elicits and accentuates this quality of being a whole and of belonging to the larger, all-inclusive, whole which is the universe in which we live. This fact, I think, is the explanation of that feeling of exquisite intelligibility and clarity we have in the presence of an object that is experienced with esthetic intensity. It explains also the religious feeling that accompanies intense esthetic perception. We are, as it were, introduced into a world beyond this world which is nevertheless the deeper reality of the world in which we live in our ordinary experiences. We are carried out beyond ourselves to find ourselves. I can see no psychological ground for such properties of an experience save that, somehow, the work of art operates to deepen

and to raise to great clarity that sense of an enveloping unde-
fined whole that accompanies every normal experience. This
whole is then felt as an expansion of ourselves.[58]

What is of interest here is that Dewey seemed to concur with Niebuhr's
point that the sense of unity and wholeness in life—any perspective on
life that gives a sense of meaning to life as such—is both "trans-rational" and yet utterly central to the deepest levels of human life. Dewey,
of course, came close to providing an aesthetic theory of the religious, a
notion that also surfaced in *A Common Faith* but was generally subsumed
under a more pedestrian socioethical religious vision. As has previously
been noted, Steven Rockefeller, while acknowledging the dominance of
the socioethical in Dewey's religious writings, nonetheless sees fit to
make the most of these "trans-rational" elements even to the extent of
arguing on behalf of a more consistent and prominent mystical dimension in Dewey's thought than has heretofore been offered.[59] Whatever
else was being suggested by Dewey's religioaesthetic language, his
image of the noncognitive unities that arise out of the immediacy of experience were not reasonably open to what Niebuhr meant by "transcendence" (except nominally as self-transcendence) or by any traditional
sense of the "eternal." Whereas it might have been fair had Niebuhr
suggested that Dewey was verging on descriptions that, in Niebuhr's
view, were best intepreted in the perspective of faith, it would have been
equally fair of Dewey to politely but firmly refuse the embrace. After all,
as Dewey both understood and presented it, such experiences, although
psychologically complex, fell entirely within the pale of *natural* experience and required nothing more than a *natural* explanation.

The curious three-way exchange involving Niebuhr, Dewey and
Niebuhr's former teacher Douglas Clyde Macintosh, has already been
surveyed.[60] Macintosh's criticism of Niebuhr's treatment of myth has an
important bearing on the question of myth and symbol. He was convinced that Niebuhr's deliteralization of biblical religious symbols had
emptied religion of any claim to truth. Macintosh was disturbed not so
much that Niebuhr had left the emperor without his clothes but rather
with whether or not, after Niebuhr got through, there was any emperor
at all. At best Macintosh saw Niebuhr as a "morally earnest" version of
Feuerbach or Vaihinger.

Niebuhr's core conviction was that the insights of the Biblical faith
could be salvaged only by taking biblical symbols "seriously," but not
"literally." His aim was to get at the "permanent" as opposed to the
merely "primitive" in mythic language. Only in this way could the substantive "truth" in myths be distinguished from the unacceptable story
forms in which such "truth" was couched. The issue of "truth" here is a

thorny one. For Dewey myths were simply prescientific. For Niebuhr they were both pre- and suprascientific. By insisting upon such a distinction Niebuhr maintained that biblical myths are far more than simply morale-boosting and therefore motivationally useful fictions. They are also ways into the truth about the human condition, with respect to both self-understanding and life's ultimate meaning. Myths do not explain events in the world in the causal sequences as does science, but they do "illuminate" both the breadth and depth of human existence as well as the "end of existence." What Niebuhr chose to call the "truth" in myths defied rational confirmation. He believed, however, that the discernment of mythic "truth" was not simply arbitrary but made sense within the orbit of interpersonal (not private) life. Indeed, for Niebuhr, not only was "the genius of true myth" suggestive of the "dimension of depth in reality,"[61] but the sense of "the world as a realm of coherence without denying the facts of incoherence" was a mythic portrait.[62] In Niebuhr's account, Dewey's awareness of the fact of the "feeling of exquisite intelligibililty and clarity" associated with the "larger, all-inclusive whole which is the universe in which we live" was accompanied by a blissful unawareness on Dewey's part that he was in the province of mythic imagination.

Niebuhr's treatment of myth and symbol involved a three-sided polemic. First he rejected outright the obscurantism of religious conservatives whose defensive strategies had exacerbated the discrediting of myth in the modern world. Niebuhr once remarked that insisting on the literal meaning of religious symbols resulted in a "corruption of religion into a bad science" and had aroused the "justified protest of a scientific age." Unfortunately, such a tactic had "also helped to tempt science to become a bad religion."[63] His only lament concerning orthodoxy was that its symbols contained a profoundly important element which, in being concealed by a literal rendering, had been overlooked or rejected by liberalism. Niebuhr, however, was also put off by those who turned to religious conservatism out of disillusionment with the vacuity of liberalism. He confessed that "As a matter of fact, nothing fills me with more dismay than the tendency of some theologians to flee from the superficialities of liberalism to the discredited dogmatism and obscurantism of orthodoxy."[64]

The second side of his polemic was directed against religious liberalism. Niebuhr wanted to separate himself from those religious liberals for whom the classical religious tradition had precious little substantive meaning. The liberals, of course, were Niebuhr's natural, albeit uncomfortable, constituency—the community that he took seriously enough to direct the brunt of his theological polemics. The "superficialities of liberalism" left Niebuhr with the conviction that there was not "very much in most liberal theology except the addition of pious phrases to the characteristic faith of the bourgeois-liberal period, faith in the essential goodness of man and in the idea of progress."[65] For all intents and purposes, liberalism had maintained at best a residual nostalgia for the very religious tradition whose central convictions and ongoing relevance it itself had eroded by means of a progressive and largely uncritical accommodation to the "wisdom of the world." The result was that, while rightly rejecting the literal truth in religious symbols, liberalism found neither a way nor a reason to probe mythic language for what, in Niebuhr's view, was "permanent" as opposed to what was "primitive" in myth.[66]

The third side of Niebuhr's polemic involved Dewey's broader constituency that, in addition to self-professed humanists and religiously inclined naturalists, included disillusioned members within the liberal and liberal-modernist camps. To this somewhat polyglot community of religious voices Dewey offered the refuge of his "common faith" without mythotheistic trailings. Niebuhr was well aware that this segment of the religiously sensitive community was largely without a frame of reference, much less an inclination, to take religious myths in any sense other than that provided by the Feuerbachian paradigm of "projection." This allowed only a reductionist approach, in which the meaning of myths was taken under the jurisdiction (and authority) of literature, sociology, or psychology. Niebuhr saw that such an option eliminated the possibility of taking myths "seriously" at all for the obvious reason that their openness to "transcendence" was denied from the very start.

An openness to "transcendence"—with the ancillary commitment that there are, what Niebuhr called "tangents toward the eternal" in the self's awareness of both its finitude and in sin as the perplexing depths of all morality[67]—is precisely what, at bottom, separated Niebuhr's understanding of the "religious" from that of Dewey. In reversing Santayana's phrase "Poetry is religion which is no longer believed" into "Religion is poetry which is believed," Niebuhr was maintaining that there are "aspects of reality which are supra-scientific rather than pre-scientific."[68] Such aspects would include "value . . . in the ultimate sense," the "unity and wholeness" of life, and "the dimension of depth in existence."[69] What Niebuhr called the "religious essence" that validates the "permanent" as opposed to the "primitive" in myth is nothing less than those suprarational tangents within experience which point to the "dimension of eternity in time"[70] and which can be expressed only in the poetic language of myth. The "primitive" in myth, on the other hand, referred to the "part of mythology which is derived from pre-scientific thought" and "does not understand the causal relations in the natural and historical world." Such *literal* readings of myth "must naturally be sacrificed in a scientific age."[71] Niebuhr's reaction to Rudolph Bultmann's radical interpretation of myth is apropos here. Writing in 1955, Niebuhr took issue with Bultmann, stating that

> Bultmann's desire to cleanse the Scripture of "pre-scientific" myths is in accord with a responsible attitude toward the dangers inherent in the dramatic and poetic attitudes towards reality. . . . But [his] failure to guard the truth in the *kerygma* [having reduced it to "the message of existentialist philosophy"], despite his professed concern to leave it untouched, proves that he has not made a sufficiently sharp distinction between pre-scientific and permanent myths. Pre-scientific myths disregard what may have already been known, or have not become known, about the ordered course of events in the world. Permanent myths (it would be better to use the word "symbol" to avoid the sceptical connotation of the word "myth") are those which describe some meaning or reality, which is not subject to exact analysis but can nevertheless be verified in experience. The experience which verifies it and saves the myth from caprice is usually in the realm of history and of freedom beyond the structures and laws of existence.[72]

The precise interpretation Niebuhr gave to specific myths in biblical tradition (e.g., creation, fall, resurrection, the "end-time," etc.) are interesting and very important in certain contexts. However, the major consideration here is of the *religious* rationale Niebuhr gave for his notion of "permanent myth" in contrast to Dewey's position on religion and myth.

Niebuhr quite obviously had a deep convictional relationship to the "biblical faith"; whereas, Dewey did not. Dewey interpreted religious faith in wholly naturalistic terms and allowed it essentially a "practical" meaning. He denied religious faith any epistemological or ontological status; that is, he dismissed the notion that faith has a noetic meaning. He viewed faith in terms of its moral and aesthetic aspects. "I should describe . . . faith," Dewey said, "as the unification of the self through allegiance to inclusive ideal ends, which imagination presents to us and to which the human will responds as worthy of controlling our desires and choices."[73]

For Niebuhr, on the other hand, Christian faith involved taking biblical symbols (permanent myths) "seriously but not literally," That is to say, along with all bona fide religions, faith affirms the presence of the "eternal in the temporal." In much the same way as he opposed orthodox literalism, Niebuhr also repudiated Barthian fideism. In "The Truth of

Myths," Niebuhr claimed that "The modern reaction against naturalism and rationalism expressed in Barthianism fails, significantly, to escape dogmatism." Although "it is superior to the older dogmatisms of orthodox religion in that it does not insist on the scientific and rational validity of the mythical details of its tradition," it nonetheless asserts "the total truth of the biblical myth . . . dogmatically with no effort to validate Christianity in experience against competition with other religions."[74]

The radical opposition between Niebuhr and Dewey on religion and myth manifested itself in the fact that, whereas Dewey's aim was a *reconstruction* of religious language, Niebuhr strove to *rehabilitate* that language. In a phrase, Niebuhr sought to reformulate and reassert the specific ways in which biblical symbols represented the "eternal in time." Dewey, on the other hand, sought to translate the religious tradition into terms appropriate to what he called "humanistic naturalism." From the vantage point of "humanistic naturalism," Niebuhr was vulnerable to Dewey's query set forth in *A Common Faith*:

> It is sometimes held that beliefs about religious matters are symbolic, like rites and ceremonies. This view may be an advance upon that which holds to their literal objective validity. But as usually put forward it suffers from ambiguity. Of what are the beliefs symbols? Are they symbols of things experienced in other modes than those set apart as religious, so that the things symbolized have an independent standing?" Or are they symbols in the sense of standing for some transcendental reality—transcendental because not being the subject-matter of experience generally? . . . The conception that faith is the best available substitute for knowledge in our present estate still attaches to the notion of the symbolic character of the materials of faith; unless by ascribing to them a symbolic nature we mean that these materials stand for something that is verifiable in general and public experience.[75]

Sharing a view akin to Tillich's position that symbols "participate" in the reality that they symbolize, Niebuhr saw mythic symbols as "standing for some transcendental reality," to use Dewey's phrase. Niebuhr, of course, would have denied the either-or terms in which Dewey put the issue. In a real sense he wanted it both ways. Niebuhr wanted to strip religious language of its literal absurdities for the excellent reason of attempting to rescue what he took to be its deeper meaning. At the same time he insisted that religious symbols were not simply free floating—they actually pointed to "an aspect of reality." He was convinced that what was involved in the notion of "transcendence" defied the limits of rational language and he found the poetic-dramatic language of the Hebraic tradition preferable to the kind of metaphysical terminologies Tillich employed. In stating his position in response to Tillich, Niebuhr made the following confession:

> If it is "supernaturalistic" to affirm that faith discerns the key to specific meaning above the categories of philosophy, ontological or epistemological, then I must plead guilty of being a supernaturalist. The whole of the Bible is an exposition of this kind of supernaturalism. If we are embarrassed by this and try to interpret Biblical religion in other terms, we end in changing the very character of the Christian faith.[76]

The terms of the claims and counterclaims involved between Niebuhr and Dewey cannot be fully explored, much less resolved here, for the parameters are far too broad and wide-ranging. What is worthy of mention, however, is that their basic opposition respecting religion reveals a peculiarly twofold recognition characteristic of the modern Western world. This involves both mythological self-consciousness and a hazy awareness of the possible inescapability of mythic forms of thought.

Put quite simply, the first recognition is that myth has come to discern its own mythological character; that is, the mythological consciousness is conscious of itself as mythical. To employ a biblical image, the modern world is somewhat "east of Eden," aware of its loss of innocence and wholly outside the sacred places looking in—in spite of a sometimes fervent desire to be *inside* the region from which one has been exiled. Niebuhr represents the agony of this situation far more grievously than Dewey by the obvious fact that he wished to maintain the transcendental meaning of religious symbols. Dewey, on the other hand, proved quite willing to walk away and find his "sacred places" in a desacralized world, a dilemma that posed its own problems, not the least of which was evident in those humanists who not only saw no reason to continue to use the term *God*, but also saw no reason to even use the term *religion* in a naturalist context.

Another part of the issue is the question as to the avoidability or unavoidability of mythological thinking. Niebuhr was acutely aware of what has been more recently termed the *mythology* of modern thought. His terminology, however, was more rationalistic inasmuch as he spoke of the "presuppositions" governing all world-views and of the "act of faith" in back of all convictions as to the meaning of life. Nonetheless, Niebuhr knew that the variant forms of naturalism constituted *the* operative faith of the modern Western world. He also knew that what is allowed to stand as "factual," "meaningful," and noetically significant in experience is largely determined by trans- or suprarational commitments with respect to the world. In conjunction with the fact that Niebuhr saw all "suprarational" commitments to be, at core, "religious," this had all the makings of a view of unavoidable, yet historically relative, "mythologies."

In this context the interesting question is whether, in turning his back on even the nostalgia of religion's mythology, Dewey took up residence, quite without notice, within the prevailing, and highly compelling, mythology of the modern world. Perhaps the constellation of images, concepts, symbols, and models that make up "naturalism and modern science" was Dewey's mythology, and provided the vantage point from which he insisted on a demythologized "religion" based on his vision of a "common faith." Strictly speaking, of course, one would have to play with an expanded sense of myth as self-referential instead of transcendentally referential, which, after all, was the classic religious sense of myth.

Niebuhr saw "permanent myths" as symbols that expressed the mystery of the "eternal in time." This is precisely what the scientific world-view which Dewey represented had ruled out. Mysteries, in Dewey's account, were not fundamental in pointing to the interstices between time and eternity. Rather mysteries were merely as-yet-unsolved problem areas in an otherwise rational, that is, demystified, universe. Dewey's naturalism, it will be recalled, would not even permit the credibility of a Santayanian "background" sense of mystery *in* nature as such. There is the distinct possibility that with Dewey we are left with an antimythological mythology, characterized by a broken symbol-system that fails to symbolize in the traditional sense. Of course, this would be putting things in a form favorable to a Niebuhrian outlook. In Niebuhr's account, the hallmark of the "religious" was a view as to the unity and meaningfulness of life and of the world for which the requisite is an "ultimate" meaning involving the dialectic of time and eternity. "Man's historic existence," Niebuhr believed, "can not have meaning without faith" in this sense.[77]

Meaning and Existence

In *The Nature and Destiny of Man* Niebuhr maintained that

> Implicit in the human situation of freedom and in man's capacity to transcend himself and his world is his inability to construct a world of meaning without finding a source and key

to the structure of meaning which transcends the world beyond his own capacity to transcend it. The problem of meaning, which is the basic problem of religion, transcends the ordinary rational problem of tracing the relation of things to each other as the freedom of man's spirit transcends his rational faculties.[78]

This question concerning the meaning of existence was, for Dewey as well as Niebuhr, central to the problem of religion as Niebuhr suggested. They divided sharply, however, about what role the question of meaning had and how the problem of meaning was to be handled.

From the time of his Yale B.D. thesis to the very end of his career, Niebuhr consistently sounded the note that "There is no meaning in this whole historical process at all if it is not held together by a higher sovereignty and governed by a stronger power than any force to be detected in either the nature below man or the mind within man."[79] From Niebuhr's perspective this conviction led to the conclusion that the force of skepticism and despair can be overcome only by means of a faith in the transcendent meaning of life. In the context of such faith, time and history are not annuled as they are in either mysticism or radical dualism. Because Niebuhr saw the meaning of time and history negated in both mystical and dualistic traditions, he was more sympathetic to the naturalists than to either the dualists or the mystics. Yet the logic of naturalism, in opposition to the excessive optimism and even utopianism with which it has often flirted, led to either skepticism or despair. Naturalists such as Joseph Wood Krutch and quasi-naturalists such as Bertrand Russell acknowledged this in directly confronting what they took to be the naturalist's situation. Although Niebuhr knew very well that the open and consistent skepticism of the "tragic humanists" was a rarity, he saw that "complete scepticism [which] represents the abyss of meaninglessness [is] a pit which has constantly threatened modern culture and into which it occasionally tumbles."[80]

Niebuhr felt that unless the central symbols of biblical faith were taken "seriously," Christianity, too, tended to degenerate into either "Platonism" [i.e., metaphysical dualism] or utopianism, as evidenced in otherworldly tendencies of medievalism and the liberal-humanist tendencies of modern Protestantism, respectively. "Creation," in relating existence to the ground of existence, points to both the dependency and goodness of the temporal world. Under the myth of creation the world is neither self-sufficient nor evil. In the symbol "of the Resurrection the Christian faith hopes for an eternity which transfigures, but does not annul, the temporal process." And the "symbol of the Last Judgment . . . emphasizes the moral ambiguity of history to the end [thus negating] utopian illusions in progressive interpretations of history as rigorously as the symbol of the Resurrection rejects the Platonic flight into an eternity of 'pure' being." In Niebuhr's account the "eschatological symbols . . . do justice to the temporal and the eternal dimensions of man's historic existence,"[81] whereas all Christian myths, "in one way or another, [express] both the meaningfulness and the incompleteness of the temporal world, both the majesty of God and his relation to the world."[82]

The sphere of actual life, interpreted in light of the biblical myths, was held to be meaningful in spite of appearances to the contrary—but only by the power and providence of God who stands as both the basis and fulfillment of the world. Niebuhr claimed that,

> We do not believe that the human enterprise will have a tragic conclusion; but the ground of our hope lies not in human capacity but in divine power and mercy, in the character of the ultimate reality, which carries the human enterprise. This hope does not imply that fulfillment means the negation of what is established and developed in human history. Each moment of history stands under the possibility of an ultimate fulfillment. The fulfillment is neither a negation of its essential character nor yet a further development of its own inherent capacities. It is rather a completion of its essence by an annihilation of the contradictions which sin has introduced into human life.[83]

Dewey, of course, rejected the type of alternatives posed by Niebuhr. Skepticism and despair were certainly incompatible with Dewey's temperament. Although he steadfastly denied he was the rampant optimist cum utopian as sometimes portrayed, with equal fervor he repudiated the notion that the logic of experience without transcendental hope led inexorably into hopelessness and desperation. Dewey definitely separated himself from the heroic humanism of Russell whose sense of the tragic in life portrayed man as "A weary and unyielding Atlas, who sustains for a moment the world which his own ideals have builded against the trampling march of unconscious power."[84] Although Dewey's temperament might have led him to regard such expressions as so much exaggerated emotional posturing at the very least, he himself was not unaware of the tragic implications of a consistent naturalism. In his Gifford Lectures of 1929 Dewey recognized that our actions in this world were accompanied by no guarantees and grounded in nothing "approaching absolute certitude." Modes of action governed by intelligence provided "insurance but no assurance."[85] He saw "a pathos, having its own nobility, in philosophies ["all traditional philosophical idealisms"] which think it their proper office to give an intellectual or cognitive certification to the ontological reality of the highest values."[86] Dewey observed:

> The thing which concerns all of us as human beings is precisely the greatest attainable security of values in concrete existence. The thought that the values which are unstable and wavering in the world in which we live are eternally secure in a higher realm . . . that all the goods which are defeated here are triumphant there, may give consolation to the depressed. But it does not change the existential situation in the least.[87]

Dewey did not believe that "consolation to the depressed" ought to be offered at the expense of "the existential situation." Yet a major element in Dewey's *Quest for Certainty* underlined the fact that humankind, as T. S. Eliot remarked, really can't abide too much reality. Humankind seemed virtually incurable with respect to its "quests for certainty." Dewey, however, could not identify with James Joyce's opinion (expressed through Stephen Dedalus) that "history is a nightmare from which I am trying to awake."[88] In what is perhaps his most poignant, personal, and self-revealing "religious" confession, Dewey ruminated at length:

> Men move between extremes. They conceive of themselves as gods, or feign a powerful and cunning god as an ally who bends the world to do their bidding and meet their wishes. Disillusioned, they disown the world that disappoints them; and hugging ideals to themselves as their own possession, stand in haughty aloofness apart from the hard course of events that pays so little heed to our hopes and aspirations. But a mind that has opened itself to experience and that has ripened through its discipline knows its own littleness and impotencies; it knows that its wishes and acknowledgments are not final measures of the universe whether in knowledge or in conduct, and hence are, in the end, transient. But it also knows that its juvenile assumption of power and achievement is not a dream to be wholly forgotten. It implies a unity with the universe that is to be preserved. The belief and the effort of thought and struggle which it inspires are also the doing of the universe, and they in some way, however slight, carry the universe forward. A chastened sense of our importance, apprehension that it is not a yard-stick by which to measure the whole, is consistent with the belief that we and our endeavors are significant not only for themselves but in the whole.

Fidelity to the nature to which we belong as parts however
weak, demands that we cherish our desires and ideals till we
have converted them into intelligence, revised them in terms of
the ways and means which nature makes possible. When we
have used our thought to its utmost and have thrown into the
moving unbalanced balance of things our puny strength, we
know that though the universe slay us still we may trust, for our
lot is one with whatever is good in existence. We know that such
thought and effort is one condition of the coming into existence
of the better. As far as we are concerned it is the only condition,
for it alone is in our power. To ask more than this is childish; but
to ask less is a recreance no less egotistic, involving no less a
cutting of ourselves from the universe than does the expectation that it meet and satisfy our every wish. To ask in good faith
as much as this from ourselves is to stir into motion every capacity of imagination, and to exact from action every skill and brav-
ery.[89]

Virtually everything is present here. Dewey's naturalism was one of
balance between an earthly hope and an ultimate resignation that refused to give voice to disconsulate and paralyzing despair. His was not a
temperament that fit well with the existential mood. Neither was his a
vision of pure stoic resignation, although he viewed the lot of human beings as having to accept the fact that their "human situation falls wholly
within nature."[90] Dewey, who only subsequent to his death was widely
discovered to have tried his hand at poetry, penned the following lines
which seem to be both serious and mockingly humorous at the same
time:

Because the plan of world is dim and blurred
Not some wise God's clear utter'd word,
Shall I resentful stand in scorn
Or crushed live dumb in mood forlorn?
Or suppose there's no plan at all
But things chanced as did befall,
Shall I frown in offish censure
Because it's all a vast adventure?

Not till I take a Stoic pose
Because ungardened grows the rose;
Not till flowers smell foul to me
And the briar rose is unfair to see.
Not while racing rivers run to sea
Bearing on their bosom this unbounded me.

Wag if you wish your gloomy head
Because some man hath solemn said
"The world just happ'd by accident,
Whose good and beauty were never meant"—
But ask not me to join your wail
Till loving friendships pass and fail;
Till wintry winds do lose their glee
And singing birds no more are free.[91]

Niebuhr would no doubt have respected the profound religious sensitivies in Dewey's confessed naturalism while at the same time seeing in it a measure of an ingrained American sentiment that refused to gauge the dark side of things in sufficient measure.

Dewey's pragmatic-behavorialist view of "mind" saw the activity of intelligence engaged in attempting to resolve the problematical,[92] but this did not involve moving from situations of doubt to certainty of a metaphysical or theological kind. Dewey knew very well that the "natural man dislikes the dis-ease which accompanies the doubtful and is ready to take almost any means to end it" and that "uncertainty is got rid of by fair means or foul."[93] Nonetheless, such certainties are simply not humankind's to have. This does not mean, however, that Dewey narrowly conceived *life* as a problem to be solved, as some suggest to be the logical outcome of his instrumentalist theory.[94] Nor does it suggest that Dewey overlooked the dark side of life in its wholesale effects upon either individual action or destiny. Dewey, after all, knew that "when all is said and done, the fundamentally hazardous character of the world is not seriously modified, much less eliminated."[95] The generic traits of the universe, after all—such as the stable and the unstable, harmony and disharmony, continuity and discontinuity, and order and disorder—are in both "man and nature." Thus, for example, Dewey could write:

If disharmony were not in both man and nature, if it were only between them, man would be the ruthless overlord of nature, or its querulous oppressed subject. It is precisely the peculiar intermixture of support and frustration of man by nature which constitutes experience. The standing antitheses of philosophical thought, purpose and mechanism, subject and object, necessity and freedom, mind and body, individual and general, are all of them attempts to formulate the fact that nature induces and partially sustains meanings and goods, and at critical junctures withdraws assistance and flouts its own creatures.[96]

Dewey was neither oblivious to the ambivalence of nature relative to humanity striving nor to the fact that nature's outcome for humanity was a tragic one. Living occurs within a precarious world. Both Dewey and Niebuhr understood something of the context of pathos and tragedy within which life and its problems occur. The important difference between them is that Niebuhr addressed that context, and its impact upon the question of meaning, on its own merits as *the* fundamental problem of all religion, and therefore, of human existence. Dewey, on the other hand, turned away from the problem of life's overall meaning as a futile, if not meaningless, venture and turned toward the kind of problems that life does permit us to constructively address. Pursuit of the question of *"the* meaning of life," as Dewey saw it, usually resulted in following one's private desires or abandoning the quest to a mood of despair. He saw other alternatives; however, "There is no need of deciding between no meaning at all and one single, all-embracing meaning. There are many meanings and many purposes in the situations with which we are confronted—one, so to say, for each situation." Dewey was convinced that "belief in a single purpose distracts thought and wastes energy," and he saw "the future of religion [to be] connected with the possibility of developing a faith in the possibilities of human experience and human relationships." His position was that "Such happiness as life is capable of comes from the full participation of all our powers in the endeavor to wrest from each changing situation of experience its own full and unique meaning."[97]

The doubts in life with respect to which resolution is possible are strictly those proximate and temporary situational doubts accompanying specific problems. In spite of the precariousness of life, Dewey believed that many experiences can be found which "have the force of bringing about a better, deeper and enduring adjustment in life," which was, in his view, the very aim of the religious function. The fact that such experiences "are not so rare and infrequent as they are commonly supposed to be" and "occur frequently in connection with many significant moments of living,"[98] constitute Dewey's version of "common grace." To the extent such an awareness prevails, Dewey wrote, "The idea of invisible powers would take on the meaning of all the conditions of nature and human association that support and deepen the sense of values which carry one through periods of darkness and despair to such an extent that they lose their usual depressive character."[99]

Dewey's attitude at least dulled the edge of Santayana's charge that in his instrumentalist view of humankind's relation to nature Dewey was culpable of "natural impiety." Dewey, after all, noted that "statements about the omnipotence of [human effects to direct natural forces] reflect egoism rather than intelligent courage."[100] Indeed, he maintained that it is only "where egoism is not made the measure of reality and value" that we become "citizens of this vast world beyond ourselves, and any intense realization of its presence with and in us brings a peculiarly satisfying sense of unity in itself and with ourselves."[101] Perhaps Horace Kallen gave the best summation of Dewey's attitude when he wrote: "If this calls for a loyalty to our own being, it does so conditionally, as a function of the nature in which we live and move and have that being. It assigns to that nature a certain providential harmony with the human creature which is one of its own multitudinous diversifications."[102]

Dewey's pragmatic naturalism led him to the conviction that the overriding problem confronting philosophical endeavors was that of reintegrating beliefs regarding the world and beliefs about value and purpose that supply direction for human life. Because value and purpose were considered to be quintessential aspects of experience—a matter ascertained via Dewey's "radical empiricism"—a correlative problem for Dewey was to overcome any false division between beliefs about common experience and beliefs resulting from the natural sciences. As Dewey put it in his Gifford Lectures, "The problem of restoring integration and cooperation between man's beliefs about the world in which he lives and his beliefs about the values and purposes that should direct his conduct is the deepest problem of modern life."[103] Dewey, in effect, sought to forge a naturalism that would both acknowledge and properly assess the ethicoreligious as well as the scientific facts about the world of experience.

Dewey believed the major function of religion was to "bring about a better, deeper and enduring adjustment in life." He recognized that the particular interpretation of the "complex of conditions that have operated to effect an adjustment in life, an orientation, that brings with it a sense of security and peace," was not a part of such experiences themselves, but was "derived from the culture with which a particular person has been imbued."[104] This sociocultural view led Dewey to severely criticize those who sought a revitalization of the religious through an appeal to individual consciousness. In commenting on the sharp decline of traditional religion "as a vitally integrative and directive force in men's thoughts and sentiments," Dewey wrote:

> there are those who urge that in order to obtain a recovery of a center and totality in life, we must begin with a regeneration of religion in the individual consciousness. But aside from the fact that there is no consensus as to what a new religious attitude is to center itself about, the injunction puts the cart before the horse. Religion is not so much a root of unity as it is its flower or

fruit. The very attempt to secure integration for the individual, and through him for society, by means of a deliberate and conscious cultivation of religion, is itself proof of how far the individual has become lost through detachment from acknowledged social values. It is no wonder that when the appeal does not take the form of dogmatic fundamentalism, it tends to terminate in either some form of esoteric occultism or private astheticism. The sense of wholeness which is urged as the essence of religion can be built up and sustained only through membership in a society which has attained a degree of unity. The attempt to cultivate it first in individuals and then extend it to form an organically unified society is fantasy.[105]

Dewey held that a viable adjustment in life demanded an allegiance to open inquiry as a way of establishing "warranted belief" as opposed to an uncompromising loyalty to fixed beliefs. This is essentially Peirce's distinction between "science," on the one hand, and "authority" or a priori commitments, on the other, as the proper way of settling belief.[106]

Effective adjustment wherein an individual brings about an accord between his or her values and purposes with what can be known about experience and nature, is, overall, dependent on an acceptance of scientific attitude and methods. This is precisely what William A. Clebsch held to be Dewey's "original ideal"; that is, the idea of holding "the universe, or the physical and social realities with which persons were related, open to improvement by critical examination and positive reconstruction via the scientific method."[107] It is in this vein that Dewey observed "There is such a thing as faith in intelligence becoming religious in quality," and he further noted that such a fact "perhaps explains the efforts of some religionists to disparage the possibility of intelligence as a force. They properly feel such faith to be a dangerous rival."[108] "Freed intelligence," or the operation of reason in accordance with the assumptions and procedures of the sciences, is one of two pillars underlying the function of religion.

Because scientific rationality can thrive only without dogmatic and authoritarian restraints, and because individual selves are "selves" only within sociocultural reality, Dewey felt that democracy, itself, was crucial to the religious function. Freed intelligence can exist only in a free society; that is, within a democratic structure that allows free inquiry its proper reign. Moreover, Dewey's "common" faith was necessarily a "shared experience," to borrow Randall's phrase.[109] In this context, "democracy," for Dewey, "is but a name for the fact that human nature is developed only when its elements take part in directing things which are common."[110]

It might be accurate to say that, because the very Western values found in science and democracy were seen as the context for the religious function, they operated as metareligious elements in Dewey's understanding of the "religious." They were not so much the substance of religious belief, as they were the conditions on which religious life could best thrive. In other words, the changes that take place to compose *the* religious attitude, for Dewey, can best take place within a framework constituted by science and democracy.[111] In writing of the growth of science and democracy in the modern world, Dewey claimed:

> As the new ideas find adequate expression in social life, they will be absorbed into a moral background, and thus will the ideas and beliefs themselves be deepened and be unconsciously transmitted and sustained. They will color the imagination and temper the desires and affections. They will not form a set of ideas to be expounded, reasoned out and argumentatively supported, but will be a spontaneous way of envisaging life. Then they will take on religious value. The religious spirit will be revivified because it will be in harmony with men's unquestioned scientific beliefs and their ordinary day-by-day activities.[112]

The manner of promoting the values of science and democracy was the responsibility of education—one of the most consistent and urgent matters in all of Dewey's life work. Indeed, science, democracy, and the education on which they depend have often been identified as the substance of Dewey's religion.[113] As merely representative of his vast efforts here, the following is a quote from Dewey's 1908 article "Religion and Our Schools":

> So far as education is concerned, those who believe in religion as a natural expression of human experience must devote themselves to the development of the ideas of life which lie implicit in our still new science and our still newer democracy. They must interest themselves in the transformation of those institutions which still bear the dogmatic and the feudal stamp (and which do not?) till they are in accord with these ideas. In performing this service, it is their business to do what they can to prevent all public educational agencies from being employed in ways which inevitably impede the recognition of the spiritual import of science and of democracy, and hence of that type of religion which will be the fine flower of the modern spirit's achievement.[114]

Whether these tender shoots, science and democracy, be the substance of Dewey's religion or whether the "deeper and enduring adjustment in life" which effects fundamental "changes in ourselves in relation to the world in which we live that are much more inclusive and deep seated[115] than mere adaptations is the core of Dewey's religious vision is of some importance. At bottom the religious attitude was a matter of self-realization for Dewey and not merely a life adjustment to the world. Because the Deweyian "ideal" was actualizable (as nature itself was idealizable),[116] the actual self was in relationship to its own ideal ends as a genuine possibility. In contrast to idealism, this means that for Dewey the self was a process of realization through actualization that alone gave expression to whatever meaning existence might have. The self was seen as a project in the existential sense of making itself via its possibilities being actualized through its own futurity. That is, for Dewey, there was no "human nature" as such. There was only self-creation consonant with and congruent to the evolutionary process expressed through and actualized by the self's self-forming transactions with the social and natural worlds.

In *A Common Faith* Dewey made this rather remarkable comment when writing about the changes that go on "in ourselves in relation to the world." These changes

> relate not to this and that want in relation to this and that condition of our surroundings, but pertain to our being in its entirety. Because of their scope, this modification of our ourselves is enduring. It lasts through any amount of vicissitude of circumstances, internal and external. There is a composing and harmonizing of the various elements of our being such that, in spite of changes in the special conditions that surround us, these conditions are also arranged, settled, in relation to us.[117]

The statement is of special interest because Dewey was focusing not on the self's interaction with its environment in expressly instrumentalist terms, but rather on what he termed the "organic plentitude of our being," whose attitude is active and "more ready and glad" than a "mere Stoical resolution to endure unperturbed throughout the buffetings of fortune."[118]

In Dewey's treatment of the relationship of imagination to the "religious" he generally concurred with Santayana's conviction that "Poetry is religion which is no longer believed," except that Dewey, unlike Santayana, showed no particular nostalgia for specific symbols within the historic faith. Poetry, Dewey once wrote, was the "emotional kindling of reality," a resource that could "deliver truth with a personal and passionate force which is beyond the reach of theory painting in gray on gray."[119] He saw poetry and religion as motivational resources which, if pursued in harmonious conjunction with the cognitive sciences, could supply the necessary zeal for accomplishing desired change in the world. "Poetry, art, religion are precious things," Dewey once wrote. They

> are an out-flowering of thought and desires that unconsciously converge into a disposition of imagination as a result of thousands and thousands of daily episodes and contact. They cannot be willed into existence or coerced into being. The wind of the spirit bloweth where it listeth and the kingdom of God in such things does not come with observation. [Our task is] to expedite the development of the vital sources of a religion and art that are yet to be. . . . We are weak today in ideal matters because intelligence is divorced from aspiration. . . . When philosophy shall have co-operated with the course of events and made clear and coherent the meaning of the daily detail, science and emotion will interpenetrate, practice and imagination will embrace. Poetry and religious feeling will be the unforced flowers of life. To further this articulation and revelation of the meanings of the current course of events is the task and problem of philosophy in days of transition.[120]

Dewey approvingly cited Sanatayana's claim that "Poetry is called religion when it intervenes in life, and religion, when it merely supervenes upon life, is seen to be nothing but poetry," but he concluded that "The difference between intervening *in* and supervening *upon* is as important as the identity set forth."[121] In commenting upon the "penetrating insight of Mr. Santayana," Dewey took exception to Santayana's notion that only imagination in its intervening function overcomes mere observation of brute fact. Dewey held instead

> that the difference between imagination that only supervenes and imagination that intervenes is the difference between one that completely interpenetrates all the elements of our being and one that is interwoven with only special and partial factors. There actually occurs extremely little observation of brute facts merely for the sake of the facts. . . . Facts are usually observed with reference to some practical end and purpose, and that end is presented only imaginatively.[122]

Dewey's understanding of the religious involved the intimate combination of aesthetic and ethical components. Religion was linked to a form

of imagination that entered profoundly into life, rather than merely playing upon it. Fundamental here is the awareness that religion has to do
with a sense of the unity and wholeness of things. Niebuhr saw this emphasis in Dewey when, in his review of *A Common Faith*, he suggested that
Dewey recognized that "The two legitimate aspects of religion are . . . the
poetic perspective which brings order and meaning into total experience
and the moral vitality expressed in devotion to ideas."[123] This means, as
James Martin, Jr., put it, that "Unlike Santayana, Dewey believes that
the religious, esthetically described, may provide the basis for valuable
and enduring changes in the human condition."[124]

Imagination, for Dewey, was the source by which "all possibilities"
in life reached us. It was also the basis for a sense of unity. Because ideal
ends in life have a reality "vouched for by their undeniable power in action," the imaginative function is not simply fanciful or doubtful.[125] Because these ideals are found within experience, Dewey was not alluding
to anything "transcendental" here, except as Donald H. Meyer uses the
term "secular transcendence"[126] to suggest a self-transcending relatedness to a natural world beyond the self and its inner experiences. "The
aims and ideas that move us," Dewey insisted, "are generated through
imagination" and "are made out of the hard stuff of the world of physical
and social experience."[127] Dewey's rationalistic naturalism would have
been perfectly comfortable with Roy Wood Sellars's judgment that the
"*imaginative* interpretation of human living" is truly at work only "after
mythology and superstition have been quietly and firmly put to one side
as no longer a thoroughfare for an adult humanity."[128]

The unity of ideals and the unity of the world understood as a universe are "felt" realities in the sense of being imaginative constructs.
The religious attitude is also closely tied to a sense of the relatedness of
a particular person to the world which that individual imaginatively en-
visions to be a universe, a totality. When Dewey considered the wisdom
of using the term *God* he depended heavily on his conviction that

> A religious attitude . . . needs the sense of a connection of man,
> in the way of both dependence and support, with the enveloping
> world that the imagination feels is a universe. Use of the words
> "God" or "divine" to convey the union of actual with ideal may
> protect man from a sense of isolation and from consequent de-
> spair or defiance.[129]

Dewey maintained that the "*whole* self is an ideal, an imaginative
projection" and only through imagination does "the idea of a thoroughgoing and deepseated harmonizing of the self with the Universe (as a
name for the totality of conditions with which the self is connected)"

come to expression.[130] Traditional religion was quite correct in seeing that the composition of the self was not an achievement of voluntary resolution, but was, instead, involuntary—"an influx from sources beyond conscious deliberation or purpose." The self does not constitute itself in its unity either voluntarily or in isolation. Dewey insisted:

> it is pertinent to note that the unification of the self throughout the ceaseless flux of what it does, suffers, and achieves, cannot be attained in terms of itself. The self is always directed towards something beyond itself and so its own unification depends upon the idea of the integration of the shifting scenes of the world into that imaginative totality we call the Universe.[131]

The "beyond itself," however, was constituted by the natural and social worlds, for Dewey, and did not involve a traditional understanding of "transcendence." Dewey clearly recognized the self's yearning for a transcendence in the traditional religious sense but it is equally certain that he found such yearning to be futile. In its utter futility it ended up distracting from the legitimate human quest. What Dewey called *"moral faith"* had, in fact, been diminished by the various attempts to convert the moral realities of practical faith into speculative faith, or "matters of intellectual assent." Faith, for Dewey, was also connected to imagination in much the same way as ideal elements in experience. Such imaginings were not articles of knowledge pointing to antecedent realities beyond or behind the natural world. He insisted that

> Apart from any theological context, there is a difference between belief that is a conviction that some end should be supreme over conduct, and belief that some object or being exists as a truth for the intellect. Conviction in the moral sense signifies being conquered, vanquished, in our active nature by an ideal end; it signifies acknowledgment of its rightful claim over our desires and purposes. Such acknowledgment is practical, not primarily intellectual. It goes beyond evidence that can be presented to *any* possible observer. Reflection, often long and arduous, may be involved in arriving at the conviction, but the import of thought is not exhausted in discovery of evidence that can justify intellectual assent. The authority of an ideal over choice and conduct is the authority of an ideal, not of a fact, of a truth guaranteed to intellect, not of the status of one who propounds the truth.[132]

Dewey, of course, would hope that the ideal ends one strove to realize in life and allowed to "conquer and vanquish" the active nature were arrived at through an intelligent assessment of natural possibilities. Nonetheless the imaginative basis of "self," "universe," and the "unity of ideals" suggests that Dewey's more practical and ethical conceptions of religion which he sought to bring under the control of rational life, were themselves under the sway of supra- or transrational commitments.

This suggests that the character and role Dewey had assigned to imagination in the religious life as the foundation of religion's ethical function had certain affinities with Niebuhr's interpretation of myth and symbol as "poetic" forms of expressing the sense of unity, depth, and meaning of life in this world. Both Niebuhr and Dewey seem to have shared, in varying degrees, the realization that the basis of imaginative construction and purposeful action presupposes a meaningful universe and, as Niebuhr put it, "man's historic existence can not have meaning without faith."[133] The depth of life which is the very core of the religious vision, Niebuhr wrote,

> is concerned with life and existence as a unity and coherence of meaning. In so far as it is impossible to live at all without presupposing a meaningful existence, the life of every person is religious, with the possible exception of the rare sceptic who is more devoted to the observation of life than to living it, and whose interest in detailed facts is more engrossing than his concern for ultimate meaning and coherence. Even such persons have usually constructed a little cosmos in a world which they regard as chaos and derive vitality and direction from their faith in the organizing purpose of the cosmos.[134]

Although Dewey might well have agreed with Niebuhr that human beings generally presuppose a meaningful existence and derive both "vitality and direction" from faith, he would not have accepted Niebuhr's notion of the need, much less the availability, of some *ultimate* meaning and coherence. Dewey was quite content with particular meanings attached to life's moments. Because of their imaginative nature, such notions as "ultimate" coherence or meaning in *the* universe simply lacked cognitive significance. Of course, throughout his later writings, Niebuhr moved between the poles of suggesting that to be human is to need such ultimate meaning and coherence while saying, also, that what we require is not rationally attainable. Niebuhr, of course, insisted that, although intimations of such meaning are available to all, the assurance of an ultimate meaning to life comes only by faith. Contrary to Dewey, Niebuhr not only wanted the mystery of existence in this final and totalistic sense left in tact as a kind of transrational boundary for reason to ponder, but he also held to the specifically Christian belief that in the divine scheme of things such coherence and meaning will involve the redemption (and thus fulfillment) of the fragmentary character of our existence in this world.

According to Niebuhr every effort to find unity and meaning to life overall involved suprarational commitments that confirmed the "religious" character of those commitments. The presence of such acts of faith in schemes of meaning led Niebuhr to claim that "Bertrand Russell is right, therefore, when he declares that philosophies which ascribe meaning and value to external reality are rationalized mythologies."[135] In the light of this claim Niebuhr commented: "It is interesting that even the strong naturalistic emphasis in modern culture, which ostensibly prompts the modern mind to view human life from the standpoint of its dependence upon nature, does not prevent even the most consistent naturalists from envisaging an ultimate triumph of the rational over the irrational."[136] He saw a mythical aspect to this type of faith to which all naturalistic faiths, in Niebuhr's account, were susceptible. There is a tendency, Niebuhr claimed,

> to introduce mythical and transcendent elements covertly (usually unconsciously) into the supposedly scientific accounts of life and history. Our modern culture has maintained its spiritual life by such a covert myth: the idea of progress. It is possible to speak of progress in interpreting the endless changes of life only if some measuring rod of value can be found with which to gauge the process. But the rod must not be a part of the process. It must transcend it. The rod taken by modern culture has usually been some ethical ideal, inherited from religion. The confidence that the processes of nature support and contribute to the victory of this ethical ideal is really a rationalized version of the Christian myth of salvation. Unfortunately it is more optimistic and really less credible than the Christian myth.[137]

Niebuhr's criticisms of modern naturalism are sometimes unfairly, or at least carelessly, applied to Dewey by implication only. Niebuhr did explicitly charge Dewey with being a "rationalistic naturalist," whose views were consistently expressed in the optimistic expectation that both the recalcitrant views of the "religions" and the desired goals of scientific reason and democractic community would be brought about through education.[138] Whereas Niebuhr was correct in crediting Dewey with certain naive hopes and expectations common to Enlightenment rationalism, he was incorrect in suggesting that Dewey's brand of naturalism was "religious" in the sense of the worst case scenario

Niebuhr gave to modern naturalism. Many of Niebuhr's most trenchant criticisms of naturalistic religion are more appropriately leveled against men like Wieman or Santayana whose brands of naturalism were open to charges of pantheism or acosmism. The religious dimensions of Dewey's naturalism did not include any commitments to "ultimate" meaning, "ultimate" hope for a human victory over nature, or "ultimate" anything else. Dewey could certainly be naively optimistic about science, reason, education and even democracy. But he did not assign to the world any final coherence or utopian destiny.

Back in 1922 Dewey did give voice to a rather unusual expression of hope, which has been often cited: "Within the flickering inconsequential acts of separate selves dwells a sense of the whole which claims and dignifies them." He concluded with the words, "In its presence we put off mortality and live in the universal."[139] When Niebuhr quoted this passage in 1949, he remarked with mild sarcasm that "Since men live in particular communities, whose existence is even more contingent than that of the individuals who are able to survey their relations to them, this is a rather inadequate triumph over life's ambiguities."[140] Dewey resigned himself without too much fanfare, but not without his share of sentimentality, to the notion that "The acts in which we express our perception of ties which bind us to others are" the "only rites and ceremonies" of the "life of the community in which we live and have our being," which is, itself, the only "fit symbol" of man's relationship to the universal.[141]

This is, indeed, an "inadequate triumph over life's ambiguities." But it was the only one Dewey could honestly envision, and it did reflect the limits of a naturalism that took its naturalism *all the way down* and refrained from indulging in "wholesale" questions about the meaning of life. It is clear that Dewey's sense of the unity and meaning of life were spelled out in minimalist terms. There is, in all of Dewey's thought, not a modicum of openness toward what Niebuhr regarded as a *genuinely mythical* "grasp of life in its unity and wholeness." That in itself would leave Niebuhr to automatically include Dewey among those who "obscure the ultimate issues of life and . . . give shallow answers to ultimate questions."[142]

11

The Liberal Tradition

The General Situation

Social liberalism in America had become a muted force since the advent of New Era business idealism in the early 1920s, particularly as that idealism reached a state of euphoria with Herbert Hoover's overwhelming presidential victory in 1928. The fortunes of the early social gospel–progressivist days, which had sought to establish a new course for American democracy against the rampant laissez-faire ideology of the Gilded Age, had come to a virtual standstill during the decade following World War I. The 1920s witnessed a return to normalcy in which the aims of social liberalism to democratize American industrial society suffered a sharp but temporary reversal. A resurgence of laissez-faire liberalism (America's "conservatism" according to Niebuhr), cloaked in a less Darwinian and more noble sense of its social role, occupied center stage during a time of prosperous and often self-indulgent complacency between the administrations of Warren G. Harding and Herbert Hoover.

To a small group of intellectuals, who, as Arthur Schlesinger, Jr., noted, were recipients of social liberalism's "ideological residue"— Dewey being prominent among them—fell the task of "reorganizing the liberal mind and reconstructing the liberal tradition"[1] during the time of its eclipse. Between 1920 and 1930 Dewey engaged in a reconstruction of the nature and function of philosophy itself—bringing to systematic fruition what Morton White has termed a general "revolt against formalism"[2]—through the major works *Reconstruction in Philosophy* (1920), *Experience and Nature* (1925), and *The Quest for Certainty* (1929). From the perspective of social and political life, Dewey's reconstruction of philosophy established a view of the intellectual life that transcended the dichotomy of theory and practice. Therefore, it demanded a reconception of philosophy as, in Cornel West's view, "a mode of cultural critical

186 The Major Issues

action that focuses on the ways and means by which human beings have, do, and can overcome obstacles, dispose of predicaments, and settle problematic situations."[3]

At the same time, Dewey was busy giving specific social and political focus to his ideas in a work on social psychology (*Human Nature and Conduct*, 1922) and an exploration of the meaning of "public" in relation to both community and the state (*The Public and Its Problems*, 1927). Dewey's role in the endeavor of liberal reconstruction was monumental and would come to explicit critical focus with a series of six essays written on "Individualism: Old and New," published between January 22 and April 2, 1930, in the *New Republic* just after the beginning of the Great Depression. Dewey's efforts to rethink and reformulate the liberal tradition would gain increasing force and urgency in the early 1930s through a profusion of articles as well as in his most important book on the subject, *Liberalism and Social Action*, published in 1935.[4]

The crisis of industrial America in the Depression environment propelled Dewey's concern with both the meaning of and prospects for the liberal tradition. While writing on Justice Holmes in the year before Niebuhr arrived in New York and prior to the overt crisis within capitalism, Dewey noted the "seeming eclipse of [social-democratic] liberalism," and assigned that eclipse in part to the "disillusionment as to the power of ideas and ideals."[5] In this setting, as Paul Kurtz pointed out, Dewey "sought to work out a new definition of liberalism" in which he "was attempting to break away from the traditional nineteenth-century conception of classical liberalism."[6]

Both Dewey and Niebuhr agreed that a social-democratic liberalism responsive to the requirements of justice in a complex industrial society required a sharp critique of what Dewey had termed "pseudo-liberalism."[7] According to Dewey, classical eighteenth century liberalism, which had a genuine liberal spirit in its quest for liberty and individuality, had, through nineteenth century permutations, abdicated the spirit of liberal social idealism. In effect, Dewey and Niebuhr were adamant in their attacks upon laissez-faire liberalism which, as Niebuhr eventually explained it, was identified in America with a conservatism that "is not conservative at all," but rather "is a part of the traditional liberal movement and . . . exhibits the defects of its creed [while failing to retain] many of its virtues."[8] This "spurious liberalism," to employ Dewey's term,[9] had abandoned both the generosity of spirit and the desire to enlarge the scope of freedom for those industrial workers who then required emancipation from oppression—features that Dewey took to be the very hallmarks of authentic liberalism. Dewey charged that "pseudo-liberalism" had so "ossified and narrowed generous ideas and aspirations" that

Even when words remain the same, they mean something very different when they are uttered by a minority struggling against repressive measures and when expressed by a group that, having attained power, then uses ideas that were once weapons of emancipation as instruments for keeping the power and wealth it attained. Ideas that at one time are means of producing social change assume another guise when they are used as means of preventing further social change.[10]

Niebuhr also saw that America's "wide variety of political creeds explicate on the various facets of the liberal ethos in such a way that the term 'liberal' has become almost meaningless among us because it is claimed with a measure of validity for the most contradictory programs."[11] Both he and Dewey knew the changes that had taken place with respect to the term *liberalism* since it came into vogue in the nineteenth century. On one level, it is accurate to say that the liberal creed had remained constant and that massive changes in the economic environment occasioned by the industrial revolution had rendered the creed obsolete. On another level, the change was ideological and thus altered the meaning of the creed itself. That is to say, what began as legitimate and just aspirations for individualism and liberty by an industrial and commercial class against undue restrictions against economic activity imposed by feudal aristocracies in Europe was later transformed into an inflexible and self-serving ideology of the highly expanded and concentrated propertied classes in capitalistic society. The force of this twofold change was seen clearly by both Dewey and Niebuhr. As a constant set of commitments to the creed of individualism and liberty, classical liberalism had become irrelevant by virtue of the altered character of industrial society. In association with its emergence as a creed of the business community, liberalism metamorphized into the self-serving ideology of a powerful capitalistic class that set liberal values against the economically weak and disenfranchised. As George Geiger stated the issue, "it was a tragedy for political liberalism that the negative character of rights was frozen, as it were, on the very eve of the Industrial Revolution and so has yielded only with the greatest difficulty to the economic and technological changes which have made so much of laissez-faire simply an anachronism."[12]

The rational enlightenment of the eighteenth century which had, according to Dewey, promulgated a "strenuous demand for the liberty of mind, freedom of thought and its expression in speech, writing, print, and assemblage,"[13] in the nineteenth century, had largely collapsed into a theory of economic liberty dogmatically grounded in a conception of natural law. Two things had happened according to Dewey: first, "governmental action and the desired freedoms were placed in antithesis to each other" and, second, a view of natural law developed in relation to "social matters as well as in [relation to] physical, and these natural laws [were also viewed as] economic in character. Political laws, on the other hand," Dewey went on to say, were seen as "man-made and in that sense artificial. Governmental intervention in industry and exchange was thus regarded as a violation not only of inherent liberty but also of natural laws—of which supply and demand is a sample."[14] The ingredients for a laissez-faire ideology were basically in place, awaiting only the rise of a *social* Darwinism to transform the earlier idealistic economic libertarianism into a cynical and self-justifying law of the survival of the fittest. Instead of being a mere anachronism, economic liberalism became an ideology—the creed of American conservatism. Dewey's importance here, of course, was that he turned the Spencerian conjunction of inevitable progress with the gospel of enterprise totally around. With Dewey social Darwinism became a *social* gospel of pragmatic possibilities in which the potentialities of intelligence rendered the human species fit to modify the environment to better serve socially desirable ends.[15]

Niebuhr agreed with Dewey's observation that "the word [*liberalism*] came into use to denote a new spirit that grew and spread with the rise of democracy."[16] Niebuhr wrote

"Liberalism" in the broadest sense is . . . synonymous with "democracy." Its strategy is to free the individual from the traditional restraints of a society, to endow the "governed" with the power of the franchise, to establish the principle of the "consent of the governed" as the basis of political society; to challenge all hereditary privileges and traditional restraints upon human initiative, particularly in the economic sphere and to create the mobility and flexibility which are the virtues and achievements of every "liberal society" as distinguished from feudal ones.[17]

The rise of industrial capitalism, however, had radically altered conditions since the entrepreneurial days when laissez-faire theory arose. Not only were those groups within society who once had legitimate reason to appeal to liberty as a requirement of justice now immensely powerful, but they were appealing to the virtues of liberty as a way of denying justice to the ever-expanding legion of the powerless spawned by the industrial revolution. Throughout their careers both Niebuhr and Dewey forcefully spoke to the crises precipitated by those radical changes. They both clearly recognized that the predominant crisis was a crisis of democracy itself. This crisis came at the very point where the transformations within the liberal tradition had turned liberalism, if not into an outright antidemocratic creed, at least into a severely truncated and misguided one. The laissez-faire ideology emphasized the freedom of economic life from political constraints. Aside from having become a doctrinaire and self-serving ideology of the business classes, its view of liberty saw danger almost exclusively in terms of political power and control. According to its doctrine, whereas the political world was in some sense artifactual, the economic world obeyed "natural laws." Thus, the conservative-liberalism that Niebuhr identified as "the old liberalism of the Manchester School,"[18] was, at best, somewhat aware of the problems of power and self-interest in the political sphere while remaining naively oblivious to such realities in the economic sphere where self-interest was supposedly regulated by natural harmonies. These regulated harmonies of the marketplace within classical liberalism were, of course, thought to be the benign and beneficent harmonies of a Newtonian natural order and not the virulently competitive natural law of social Darwinism. The upshot of such a view was that "power, in the thought of the typically bourgeois man," as Niebuhr once wrote, "is political."[19] Thus,

> The "liberal" society which gradually emerged out of the disintegration of the medieval culture and the feudal-agrarian economy is generally characterized by democratic political institutions and by an organization of economic life which dispenses, as far as possible, with the political, and even the moral, control of economic activities.[20]

The issue, as Niebuhr told a predominantly business audience during World War II, was one of recognizing that "where power is disproportionate, power dominates weakness and injustice results."[21] The problem with the conservative-liberals was not so much that they espoused the pursuit of economic self-interest. Rather the real problem was that they were either naive or deceitful about the nature of self-interest. Although self-interest had a creative and energizing role in the life of economic society, unbridled self-interest had led to greater inequalities in the economic sphere and thus exacerbated the problem of injustice. Justice, in Niebuhr's view, demanded equality as well as liberty and, as each of these principles was in tension with the other, he regarded both as regulative principles of justice with neither principle being the sum of justice.[22] Consequently, democracy required the kind of liberalism that "preferred security to absolute liberty and which sought to bring economic enterprise under political control for the sake of establishing minimal standards of security and welfare."[23]

Dewey, who had been acknowledged within intellectual circles as the preeminent voice of American liberalism since before World War I, labored in the very midst of what Gary Bullert described as the "retrenchment" of liberalism in the 1920s.[24] His efforts at liberal reconstruction prior to the Depression years took place in the generally apolitical age of enchantment and excess that characterized the 1920s, an age that spawned a far broader malaise, as Schlesinger pointed out, "than simply the exhaustion of liberalism."[25] The ostentatious display of wealth, coupled with an increasingly vulgar and pervasive hedonism attendant upon a self-congratulatory business culture, occasioned revulsion among diverse members of the intellectual community. Some intellectuals abandoned even the semblance of political responsibility; whereas others of a literary bent could only satirize what they saw as the vulgarity and cruelty of an aggressively self-serving culture.

As the malaise turned to skepticism with the collapse of the financial markets in 1929, antiliberal sentiment reached new heights and expressed itself in ever-more radical forms. Therefore, the resurgence of liberalism, following the lead of Dewey's reconstructive labors, took place within an increasingly hostile environment. The revival of social-activist liberalism not only faced the intensified scorn of a highly defensive business community, it also confronted a deepening alienation from romantic critics among the literati whose swing from apoliticalism to utopian politics rendered them all the more cynical as the democratic crisis progressed. Democratic sympathizers among the literary social critics such as Waldo Frank and Louis Mumford virtually abandoned the hard business of forging a liberal response to the crisis of industrial capitalism. Instead they tended to retreat into a politics of nostalgia, either pining away for a pretechnological age of idealized innocence, fashioning some spiritual utopia that was believed to have once been America, or indulging in romantic and even mystical mythologies of community.[26]

Far more severe, however, was the onslaught against liberalism stemming from both reactionary and radical sources. Dewey clearly recognized this state of affairs when, in a 1937 review of Walter Lipmann's *Good Society,* he commented that that work "comes at a time when the liberal movement is under fire from both Conservatives and Revolutionaries."[27] The chorus of voices abandoning or denouncing liberalism wholesale reached its zenith in the mid-1930s. Even Dewey and Niebuhr, who ended up as the two most important reconstructive voices in the liberal tradition, flirted with the notion of an irredeemably decadent American society in which the spoils of impending revolution would belong either to the communists or the fascists.

In their own ways, both Dewey and Niebuhr had been attracted to Marxism. To the degree that Marxism appealed to Dewey, it did so not because of its catastrophism or even its diagnostic assessment of power and conflict. Its appeal in the years between Dewey's visit to Russia in 1928 and the Moscow trials of 1936–1937 was confined largely to its emphasis on societal planning and the enthusiasm Dewey detected in the Russian people. However, because Niebuhr, as Arthur Schlesinger, Jr., noted, "was more tempted by Marxism than the others [he] was more articulate in explaining both its immediate attraction and its ultimate unacceptability. Rebounding from the liberal belief in the inevitability of progress, Niebuhr was for a moment [circa, 1933–1934] susceptible to an extreme belief in the inevitability of catastrophe."[28] In the short run Niebuhr would back off from his catastrophism. In the long run, however, he benefited from a critical appropriation of Marxist realism with respect to power, conflict, and the "ideological taint." The way Niebuhr chose to put it in 1939 was "that though I express my opposition to liberal civilization politically in terms of Marxian politics, I regard Marxian culture as participating essentially in all the liberal illusions."[29]

In the context of that tumultuous era Niebuhr became as cynical as he ever would be with respect to the democratic prospects in both the West in general and America in particular. In *Reflections on the End of an Era,* published in 1934 during his most radical phase, Niebuhr's despair over the onslaught of reactionary and radical forces found him suggesting that American politics might very well polarize into extreme factions:

> When it becomes apparent (as it must in the long run) that political control of private capitalism cannot produce sufficient equality of income to eliminate overproduction and unemployment the stage will be set for a sharper delineation of the social struggle in our American life. The vague liberalism of the Roosevelt administration which has achieved a temporary unity in our national life, challenged only by a few reactionaries on the right and radicals on the left, will then disintegrate into a more obvious conservatism and radicalism.[30]

Niebuhr's despondent mood was even echoed in the normally unflappable and less apocalyptic-minded Dewey, whose 1937 review of Stephen Spender's *Forward From Liberalism* warned

The conclusion I personally draw from this sincere and courageous book is that unless there is organized assertion of
economic and cultural democracy in this country, liberals here
may find themselves in a position where they see only a choice
between fascists and the communists of the official stripe.
Furthermore, there may not be a great deal of time in which to
make the assertion.[31]

Of course, Dewey and the rational liberalism he so ably represented
were on the defensive, having come under scathing attack from the Left.
Two years earlier Dewey had spearheaded an attempt to clarify and defend the American faith in liberal democracy against the illiberal faiths
threatening it from all sides. Ostensibly devoted to the theme "The Future of Liberalism," the "common theme" at the symposium held at the
American Philosophical Association meetings in December 1934, as
John Herman Randall, Jr., pointed out, "was not so much the future of
'liberalism' as the faith in intelligence and reason, which the participants proposed to salvage as the core of the liberal tradition and oppose
to the new faiths that are pressing it."[32]

The year of the APA symposium, of course, was the year before
Dewey's *Liberalism and Social Action* appeared—his major work on the
crises within liberalism and his remedy for them. During this period
Dewey wrote a spate of essays in defense of what he believed to be a radical, yet rational, democratic liberalism.[33]

Dewey "placed his ideas," as R. Alan Lawson said, "at the service of
radical reform efforts more fully than other notable philosophers before
him [in the American tradition] had done."[34] But his ideas, however radical to him, were reformist in the sense that Dewey sought to salvage
both liberalism and democracy and not abandon them. His vision of a
"renascent" liberalism, therefore, involved a critical diagnosis of traditional liberalism, a strenuous defense of contextually redefined liberal
values such as individualism and liberty, an ever-present conviction as
to the need for social planning based on the rational direction of political
action, and an educated public whose ongoing vigilance would preserve
and expand the conditions on which the survival of democracy depended.

Diverging Views on Liberalism and Liberal Reconstruction

Niebuhr eventually came to the judgment that not only was classical
liberalism defective, but the various formulations being given to the socially responsible liberalism that sought to address the changed conditions of the industrial age were fundamentally flawed. Because Dewey

became the lightning rod of Niebuhr's attack on social liberalism, the widening appeal of Niebuhr's criticism placed Dewey in a rather unique position. Dewey who had found himself assailed from all sides—from the laissez faire liberals as well as from the radicals—now found himself under attack from within the liberal household. This is important to realize, not only for understanding Dewey's dilemma and the anger some disciples of Dewey displayed toward Niebuhr, but also for a proper understanding of the dilemma into which Niebuhr was placed in the course of his critique of liberalism. Niebuhr, who was also increasingly scorned by the radicals as well as by laissez faire liberals, would eventually have his liberal credentials questioned by both liberals and conservatives alike in the declining years of his influence on the American scene. These matters will occupy our attention at a later point. Suffice it to say here that Niebuhr was a liberal critic of liberalism, a household critic whose criticism went deeper than most and who did not hesitate to draw on the wisdom of *classical* conservatism in bringing about his own *liberal* reconstruction.

By the time Niebuhr burst upon the scene in 1932 with his indictment of liberalism and of John Dewey as the quintessential liberal in *Moral Man and Immoral Society*, Dewey possessed an almost legendary status and reputation within the American liberal community. The eminent American historian Henry Steele Commager wrote at mid-century that "more fully than any other philosopher of modern times, Dewey put philosophy to the service of society. More, he formed a whole network of alliances—with science, with politics, with education, with aesthetics, all directed toward advancing the happiness of mankind."[35] Niebuhr paid homage to "Professor Dewey's great interest in an understanding of the modern social problem."[36] Yet to the degree Dewey was "regarded as a typical and convenient example" of the prevailing social philosophers who embodied liberal naivete, Niebuhr singled Dewey out as the central figure in the lexicon of those individuals who represented all that was flawed in the liberal tradition.

Niebuhr forged his criticism of Dewey and liberalism beginning in earnest in 1932 and pressed the attack with both constancy and intensity beyond the mid–1930s.[37] The gravity of liberalism's internecine strife, therefore, is vividly portrayed in the fact that Niebuhr's assault on the liberal tradition was reaching a full head of steam at very moment when Dewey, who lamented that "the liberal movement is divided within itself at a most critical period," pleaded his case that "the future depends to a large extent upon its unification."[38]

In a preface written for the republication of *Moral Man and Immoral Society* in 1960, Niebuhr claimed that he still believed in and was committed to the central thesis of that book. "The central thesis was, and is,"

Niebuhr wrote, "that the Liberal Movement both religious and secular seemed to be unconscious of the basic difference between the morality of individuals and the morality of collectives, whether races, classes or nations."[39] He believed that, although the role of self-interest in collective life ought not lead to cynicism, it certainly should result in a wholesale refutation of the kinds of simplistic moralism and rationalism which governed so much liberal thinking about politics. To the extent that social scientists, educators and religious moralists indulged in such naivete, they sewed nothing but confusion in the arena of political action. The "polemical interest" of *Moral Man*, therefore, was openly set against

> the moralists, both religious and secular who imagine that the egoism of individuals is being progressively checked by the development of rationality or the growth of a religiously inspired goodwill and that nothing but the continuance of this process is necessary to establish social harmony between all the human societies and collectives.[40]

Niebuhr saw as one of his major objectives in *Moral Man* the "deflation of liberal social idealism,"[41] a task that required exposing the roots of secular and religious liberalism's confusion about the "relation of coercion to moral idealism."[42] Niebuhr's friends and critics alike were shocked by both the form and substance of his attack on the liberal tradition. In retrospect the shock felt within secular liberal circles was not so much due to a sense of betrayal (as it often was for those within religious liberal circles[43]) as it was due to a startling recognition of just how deep the rift ran with respect to the struggle over liberalism itself.

Niebuhr's book was a profoundly telling missile aimed at the very heart of the liberal creed by one who was, and always would be, an insider, a liberal in spirit. The substance of *Moral Man*, as Arthur Schlesinger, Jr. observed long ago, was "a somber and powerful rejection of the Social-Gospel-Dewey amalgam with its faith in the politics of love and reason."[44] The impotency of liberal politics in its advocacy of "love" and "reason" represented, in shorthand, the bankruptcy of the religious idealism of Protestant liberalism and the rational idealism of secular liberalism, respectively. Appeals to love and reason as substitutes for the hard work of the politics of justice were simply two sides of the same liberal coin. On the religious side Niebuhr found a shallow and noxious sentimentalism to be "the peculiar voice of liberal Protestantism," a voice that by uncritically "adjusting its faith to the spirit of modern culture imbibed the evolutionary optimism and the romantic overestimates of human virtue, which characterised [sic] the thought of the Enlightenment and of the Romantic Movement."[45]

The sentimentality of liberalism was most evident in its "hope for the redemption of society in the possibility of making the love-universalism, implicit in religious morality, effective in the whole human society"[46]—a hope whose fundamental weakness becomes "increasingly apparent as one proceeds from ordinary relations between individuals to the life of social groups."[47]

Niebuhr saw himself poised between two undesirable alternatives to religious social thinking. From the one side he had nothing but scorn for the stratospheric eschatology of a Karl Barth which manifested an unwillingness to engage in the relative, yet utterly crucial, judgments regarding justice in sociopolitical life. Barth's surprisingly undialectical insistence on the absolute transcendence of God issued in a heretical dualism that utterly obscured "the foothills where human life must be lived."[48] Yet, if there was paralysis on the Barthian side, there was dangerous naivete on the Protestant liberal side. Niebuhr saw the sentimentalized love-universalism of religious liberalism virtually identifying the kingdom of God with historical processes in such a way as to give vent to a moral perfectionism utterly irrelevant to political life.

Niebuhr chastised religious liberalism largely because, as he put it in 1929, it was "so busy adjusting itself to the modern mind that it can find no energy to challenge the modern conscience."[49] Ten years later, although acknowledging that liberal Christianity had rightly accepted "the achievements of modern culture," Niebuhr claimed that it had also "quite obviously accepted the prejudices as well" and was "pathetically eager to justify itself before the 'modern world.'"[50] Religious liberalism, therefore, was largely seen as a reflection of the broader secular liberal tradition to such a degree that it lost its critical edge. In other words, religious liberalism had forsaken its "prophetic" role by having lost touch with the unique resources of its own special history, a history in which both self-critical and culture-critical perspectives were based. As Niebuhr put it in a book critique published in 1939, "Unfortunately 'liberal' Christian thought has been so busy trying to prove that it does not mean or imply anything in its doctrines except what the modern man already believes, that it has made no contribution to an understanding of the Christian position."[51]

In effect, the "dangers seem equally great," Niebuhr lamented, between both neo-orthodox and liberal tendencies. There is obvious danger in the "tendency of Barthianism to sharpen the contrast between the human and the divine in one minute so that all the world lies in hopeless sin and in the next minute to 'justify' the hopeless world in its imperfections." But there is equal danger in "the liberal tendency to find the divine in every little human virtue."[52] Pondering the quandary he discovered here, Niebuhr wrote:

As one who bears a few wounds from doing battle against complacent liberalism, I must confess that this appropriation of Barthian thought by reaction almost persuades me to return to the liberal camp as a repentant prodigal. Fortunately there are alternatives which make it unnecessary to embrace liberal illusions for the sake of avoiding orthodox confusions.[53]

Although Niebuhr began acquiring a shift in theological orientation after the mid-1930s, his identity—both in theology and in politics—remained that of a reconstructed liberal. In his avoidance of "liberal illusions" and "orthodox confusions," Niebuhr never returned "to the liberal camp as a repentant prodigal." Fundamentally, he had always remained in the liberal camp as one of its sharpest and most unrepentant critics. This remained the case in both theology and politics. The unrepentent criticism he applied to both religious and secular liberalism for their naivete about the possibilities of love and reason was based on his conviction that, at bottom, they shared common illusions. In general, as has been noted previously, Niebuhr saw religious liberalism in terms of its reliance on secular liberalism.

Niebuhr's sensitivity to the assault upon liberalism coming from the side of radical political thought led him, in 1936, to distinguish between the "creed" and the "spirit" of liberalism. He condensed the creed of liberalism, which he found justifiably assailable, as follows:

a. That injustice is caused by ignorance and will yield to education and greater intelligence.

b. That civilization is becoming gradually more moral and that it is a sin to challenge either the inevitability or the efficacy of gradualness.

c. That the character of individuals rather than social systems and arrangements is the guarantee of justice in society.

d. That appeals to love, justice, good-will and brotherhood are bound to be efficacious in the end. If they have not been so to date we must have more appeals to love, justice, good-will and brotherhood.

e. That goodness makes for happiness and that the increasing knowledge of this fact will overcome human selfishness and greed.

f. That wars are stupid and can therefore only be caused by people who are more stupid than those who recognize the stupidity of war.[54]

There are numerous elements here, some descriptive and others prescriptive. In essence, when Niebuhr differentiated between the "spirit" and the "creed" of liberalism he was attempting to draw a distinction between the normative values of liberalism, which he shared, and the relative ease with which liberals tended to believe such values could be attained, which he openly disavowed. Although Niebuhr fundamentally shared the virtues and ideals of liberalism, he scorned the lack of realism he saw in liberalism's assessment of the conditions and possibilities relative to the ideals espoused. He firmly believed that the "spirit" of liberalism—the virtues of tolerance and fairness, as well as love, justice, and brotherhood—was crucial to the humaneness of human community. But the ideals that were central to the liberal "spirit" required less of an idealistic and far more of a realistic assessment if they were to have genuine bearing on the political process. In effect, Niebuhr insisted that the "creed" as such, because of its lack of realism, placed the "spirit" of liberalism at grave risk. He regarded the liberal "creed" as blind to "the perennial difference between human actions and aspirations, the perennial source of conflict between life and life, the inevitable tragedy of human existence, the irreducible irrationality of human behavior, and the tortuous character of human history."[55]

Looking back upon a decade of struggle against the liberal "creed" for the sake of the liberal "spirit," Niebuhr once summarized that creed in the following manner: "I should say" that the liberal creed is

> primarily faith in man; faith in his capacity to subdue nature, and faith that the subjection of nature achieves life's final good; faith in man's essential goodness, to be realized either when man ceases to be spiritual and returns to nature (romanticism), or when he ceases to be natural and becomes rational; and finally, faith in human history which is conceived as a movement upward by a force immanent within it. Whether this faith rests upon Darwin or upon Hegel, that is, whether nature is believed to guarantee progress or whether progress is conceived of as man's "gradual spiritualization" and his emancipation from natural impulses, prejudices and parochial attachments, the optimistic conclusion is the same.[56]

Niebuhr, who in the area of politics, J. David Hoveler, Jr., saw as "probably the most important twentieth-century critic of Dewey,"[57] found in Dewey far too many signature elements of the liberal creed. Niebuhr isolated for special criticism what he took to be Dewey's inordinate confidence in rational solutions to political problems, his penchant for overestimating social science engineering in addressing social ills and directing social solutions, and his optimism in the possibility of a "common faith"; that is, the rationally based cooperative democratic community. Niebuhr had once commented that "the faith of modern man contained two related articles: the idea of progress and the idea of the perfectability of man," of which "the latter is frequently the basis of the former article."[58] Although Niebuhr ran roughshod over certain qualifications in Dewey's position that separated him from the stereotypical liberal Niebuhr was targeting, those qualifications did not, in Niebuhr's judgment, seriously alter or mitigate the fact that Dewey perpetuated many of liberalism's grievous errors.[59] Dewey, in effect, still held to a too simplistic confidence in "rational man" to satisfy Niebuhr's sense of what was judicious for the validation of democracy. And following from this, Niebuhr also felt that Dewey had an excessive confidence in the progressive achievement of history as a result of his confidence in the progressive extension of the work of "freed intelligence," a matter that will be taken up in the next chapter in connection with a discussion of Dewey's "democratic religion."

Dewey's social and political expectations provided the context for Niebuhr's choice of the term *naturalistic rationalism* as descriptive of Dewey's position.[60] In spite of toughness suggested by Dewey's identification with naturalism, he was enough a stepchild of the Enlightenment that he sought refuge in a " 'free cooperative inquiry' which is involved in the natural-historical process and yet somehow has a vantage point of pure disinterestedness above it."[61] Niebuhr saw Dewey's social and political optimism as a legacy of the overconfidence in reason stemming from the Enlightenment and the identification of that overconfidence in more recent times with a model of social-scientific engineering. In R. Alan Lawson's words, Dewey's role, if not that of "the acknowledged leader of pragmatic rationalism . . . was surely its guiding spirit."[62]

Niebuhr's criticism of Dewey's "social engineering" did not take aim at the sterile technocratic mentality that often goes under the label of "pragmatic rationalism."[63] Niebuhr was fully aware of Dewey's humanistic commitments as well as his efforts to overcome the unfortunate severance of science from value. He would have known what Dewey's virulent scholastic critics either did not know, or stubbornly refused to admit, that Dewey's "humanistic naturalism" had also to pose the question, as George Nash framed it, "On what basis could we erect a 'moral foundation for democracy'?" And as Nash went on to point out, "The very appearance of the notion that democracy required a 'moral basis' was a sign of the times."[64] Niebuhr's major objections involved both an attack on the naive optimism behind Dewey's view of the translatability of method from the natural to the social sciences and the refusal to seriously entertain a wisdom in human affairs at odds with the scientific model to which Dewey made incessant appeals. This latter objection was not so much an objection to science as such as it was to a pervasive rationalism in the history of liberal culture that paraded itself as scientific.

Dewey had published an article on "Science and Society" in 1931 in which he claimed that "it is our human intelligence and human courage which are on trial" by those who continue to use science in a "half-way and accidental" way. Although he knew that the social sciences had come onto the horizon too late to directly influence the formation of early liberal social theory, Dewey nonetheless found it "incredible that men who have brought the technique of physical discovery, invention, and use to such a pitch of perfection will abdicate in the face of the infinitely more important human problem."[65] Quoting extensively from the last few pages of this work,[66] Niebuhr's *Moral Man* accused Dewey of mentioning " 'our predatory self-interest' . . . only in passing without influencing his reasoning, and with no indication that he understands how much social conservatism is due to the economic interests of the owning classes."[67] According to Niebuhr,

> The very terms in which they [the educators and, by implication, Dewey himself on whom they rely] state the political problem proves that they are themselves bound by middle-class perspectives, which will naturally increase in force and narrowness in proportion to the distance from the ideal of the educator. . . . It would be pleasant to believe that the intelligence of the general community could be raised to such a height that the irrational injustices of society would be eliminated. But unfortunately there is no such general community. There are many classes, all of them partially deriving their perspectives from, or suffering them to be limited by, their economic interest. The failure of modern socially minded educators to realise [sic] this fact proves that their very educational theory, which partly transcends the impulses of the dominant economic groups by force of sheer intellectual honesty and penetration, is also partly bound and limited by the environment of their own class, the middle class. For this class, living in comfort and security, is unable to recognize the urgency of the social problem; and, living in a world of individual relationships, is unable to appreciate the consistency with which economic groups express themselves in terms of pure selfishness. The conception that what society needs and, if intelligent enough, will be able to secure, is "trained and experienced specialists" [quoting Harold Rugg] to

perform the "expert functions" of government, betrays an additional class prejudice, the prejudice of the intellectual, who is so
much the rationalist, that he imagines the evils of government
can be eliminated by the expert knowledge of specialists.[68]

Dewey, who finally responded to Niebuhr in 1933, opened his essay
on "Unity and Progress" with a declared attempt to "make some connection between my own article and that of Dr. Niebuhr's which opened this
series."[69] Claiming to be neither negative nor personal, Dewey's various
criticisms of Niebuhr amounted to a repudiation of Niebuhr's identification of Dewey with a liberal view which, in politics at least, Niebuhr had
dubbed as a spent force. Dewey was somewhat sensitive in his insistence
that his

> method of considering, on the one hand, urgent needs and ills
> and measures which will cope with them, and, on the other
> hand, of forming an idea of the kind of society we desire to bring
> into existence, which will give continuity of direction to politi-
> cal effort, is very different from that which Dr. Niebuhr
> criticizes under the name of "liberalism." It has nothing in com-
> mon with the sentimentalism to which he gives that name. . . .
> I am not questioning either the existence or the futility of what
> Dr. Niebuhr calls liberalism. I am concerned only to point out
> the irrelevancy of his description and condemnation to the kind
> of procedure which I am proposing.[70]

Niebuhr's own contribution to the *The World Tomorrow* series published a week earlier, did, of course, lambaste social liberalism as a
"spent force" in politics and pointed out that "educational and religious
idealists shrink from the conclusions to which a realistic analysis of history forces the careful student," cautioning that "social intelligence can
have a part in guiding social impulse only if it does not commit the error
of assuming that intelligence has destroyed and sublimated impulse to
such a degree that impulse is no longer potent. This," Niebuhr concluded, "is the real issue between liberalism and political realism."[71]
Although Dewey replied only marginally to Niebuhr in his 1933
essay "Unity and Progress," he responded abruptly to Niebuhr's attack
on both himself and what Niebuhr took to be the core of social liberalism
in his article "Intelligence and Power," published in April 1934. Dewey
denied that his conception and advocacy of social intelligence ignored
the power and persistence of self-interest in human affairs. If Niebuhr's
correct, but highly abstract, notion of the faults of rationalism was the
entire story, then Dewey too would "more than agree with the critics who

doubt that intelligence has any particular role in bringing about needed social change."[72] Dewey in effect returned to his point in "Unity and Purpose"; namely, that although what Niebuhr called *liberalism* indeed had a futility about it, it was at best an abstract stereotype and at worst actually hindered the task at hand. Dewey reiterated his earlier charge that Niebuhr's view of liberalism was irrelevant to both Dewey's own position and program. Dewey was incensed that Niebuhr imputed to him "middle-class prejudices in ignoring the role of class interest and conflict in social affairs" and "a great exaggeration of the potentialities of education."[73]

Somewhat condescendingly Dewey heartily agreed with Niebuhr's claim that the social sciences faced a traditionalism based on the economic interests of dominant classes who sought to maintain their privileges. But he chided Niebuhr for thinking that the traditionalism which natural science had to overcome was simply one of ignorance and not self-interest. "It is a naive view of history," Dewey wrote, "that dominant class interests were not the chief force that maintained the tradition against which the new method and conclusions in physical science had to make their way" or that "the new scientific method would have won its way . . . unless it had found a lodgment in other social interests than the dominant ones and been backed by the constantly growing influence of other interests."[74]

Niebuhr might well have agreed that there was also self-interest at work in resistance to the advance of the natural sciences, but he would see such evidence as an additional demonstration of his major contention that the *fact* of the conflict of interests was not truly confronted by the rationalism of the social liberals, Dewey's disclaimer notwithstanding. Niebuhr's point was that, most especially in the political and economic spheres, where the "social intelligence" of the social scientist must make its way, the problem of self-interest was exacerbated.

Although Dewey thought David Hume exaggerated the case from the opposite side, he expressed qualified agreement with Hume's notion that " 'reason is and always must be the slave of passion'—or interest."[75] What Dewey saw himself asking for was not the conflict-free world of Niebuhr's hypothetical liberal who was oblivious to the ways of self-interest in the world, but rather an alignment of "strong interests now active which can best succeed by adopting the method of experimental intelligence into their struggle [instead of continuing to] rely upon the use of methods that have brought the world to its present estate, only using them the other way around."[76]

From Niebuhr's perspective Dewey's way of putting the matter revealed the very liberal naivete that remained at the core of Dewey's position.[77] Pushing this position to its extreme, there seemed to lurk in

Dewey's way of putting the matter his own mythology of history. This mythology assumed that we were once situated in a time of institutional forms, customs, and illusions ruled by ignorance and superstition. And now we find ourselves on the edge of the dawning of a new age symbolized by the notion of "freed intelligence," which ideally can extricate itself from the older methods and overcome the ill-conceived ways of adjudicating conflicts. Because Dewey acknowledged that "the old and the new have forever to be integrated with each other" and that the "function and meaning" of liberalism was in making the necessary adjustments between the stabilities of the past and the disturbing changes of the present,[78] Niebuhr's judgment might seem unfair. After all, in Dewey's account, it was precisely "the remaking of the old through union with the new" that is the hallmark of "intelligence."[79] Yet, for Dewey, armed with the salutary virtues of scientific rationality which, at bottom, constituted the meaning of intelligence as such, the present had precious little to learn from the past except for a legacy of error. Dewey's one-way view of the desirability of historical influence saw the "wisdom" of the past as little more than some deposit of common sense. He virtually removed the possibility of seeing that the past might house a "wisdom" that, if heeded, could conceivably penetrate the rationalistic and optimistic fog of the present.

From Niebuhr's perspective, it was the state of liberal thinking that was the problem needing rectification. It seemed as if Dewey had fashioned a mythology of the modern world situated in an "in-between-time" in which the transition from authoritarianism to freedom was being actualized both by the determined course of evolutionary history and the voluntary efforts of dedicated human beings. This was precisely the kind of romantic dichotomy Niebuhr abhorred and contested from both sides: past tradition was not without its wisdom and the future would not be without its illusions any more than any present is in its own time. Niebuhr wanted to assure that the present was also open to all creative pasts, and thereby open to self-criticism to the extent the wisdom of the past was allowed to speak against the foolishness of the present. Without gainsaying the constructive power of science, Niebuhr wanted fervently to remind Dewey that the future would also have its power politics, a fact of life requiring a more serpentine understanding of reason than the myth of scientific rationality provided. Niebuhr was left in somewhat of a quandary because of all the incessant preaching about the place of science in human affairs. He wrote

One may well wonder how the social and psychological sciences which have proved their value on so many levels of human experience, should generate so many naive miscalculations on the ultimate level of political wisdom. Perhaps the miscalculations are the fruits of two errors which characterize all merely naturalistic approaches to the problems of human behavior. It is not understood that the "nature" which is to be mastered and manipulated contains the self, with all of its guile of spirit; and the mind which is supposed to master nature, is also involved in this same self, with all of the capacities of self-deception. Most of the pretentious analogies between the mastery of natural and of historical evil, are therefore misleading.[80]

Because they began with a different set of assumptions about human beings, conflict, power, and self-interest, Dewey and Niebuhr diverged sharply on what constituted a "rational" view of reason and the limit of its possibilities in the collective life. This, of course, constituted the framework for their clash over liberalism itelf. Dewey, reacting with desperation to the long-standing "domination of the methods of institutional force, custom and illusion," cast about for some other "method." And he saw "the effort to stimulate resort to the method of intelligence" as perhaps the only one yet to be tried with any degree of seriousness.

In one sense, of course, Dewey was quite correct in stressing the point that liberalism as a social philosophy "signifies the adoption of the scientific habit of mind in application to social affairs."[81] Even Niebuhr would have held this as indisputable if all that was meant was the kind of "wisdom" that was hypothetical, empirical, and always open to self-correction. But Niebuhr was also correct in pointing out that the more extravagant rationalism in Dewey's view of reason too easily overlooked the fact that we are "a society in which the power factors are obscured" and that quite mistakenly such a democratic society "is assumed to be a 'rational' rather than coercive one."[82] Niebuhr always thought it rather strange to set the problem up as a contrast of methods, as Dewey was inclined to do. Instead he urged Dewey to be more circumspect regarding his mythology of the rational life and more realistic about the perennial problem of conflicting self-interest. And an additional measure of "realism" was urgently needed for discerning the tendency of reason to serve ends other than purely rational ones—a tendency most evident in the fact that reason continually deceived itself into thinking that it was so engaged. The liberal tradition, in effect, had never taken seriously, in its grandiose view of intelligence, the stubborn fact that intelligence was always "interested intelligence."[83]

Niebuhr's exchange of letters with Morton White between May and July of 1956 is instructive here. White had sent Niebuhr a copy of "Orig-

inal Sin, Natural Law and Politics," which appeared as an "epilogue" in
the 1957 edition of *Social Thought in America: The Revolt Against Formalism.*
In one of Niebuhr's responses to White, he wrote,

> You admit that Dewey was rather too optimistic about
> human nature, but you do not cite the chief criticism I made of
> his social theory. That was the criticism of his opinion that the
> "scientific method" could be applied with the same validity in
> the historical as in the natural realm, if only, in the warfare be-
> tween science and religion, a truce had not been made prema-
> turely delivering the historical sciences to to the interference of
> "State and Church" and therefore condemning them to perma-
> nent inactitude. I think this is the root error of modern culture,
> resting on the failure to recognize the intimate relation be-
> tween reason and interest and passion in all historical judg-
> ments.
>   I have been called an "irrationalist" for holding to this con-
> viction, though I would not think it irrational to call attention
> to empirical evidence of the taint of interest upon the purity of
> reason. I know of no political scientist or historian, many of
> whom share my convictions, who are accused of irra-
> tionalism.[84]

Niebuhr was somewhat chagrined by the widespread charges of irrationalism leveled against him by the secular liberals whose naivete
about reason he found as burdensome as the naivete of religious liberals
regarding the possibilities of love. As Niebuhr saw matters, he was defending a far more "rational," that is, circumspect, view of reason than
his adversaries. In line with that view he strenuously objected to all
forms of "obscurantism," as he told Morton White,[85] but resented the
fact that "in the polemics of modern culture it is simply assumed that
anyone in the religious camp is an obscurantist, or if he is not he must
have recently repented."[86] Niebuhr deplored what he regarded as the
need "to have absolute faith in the purity of reason in all situations to be
admitted into the camp of the 'rational' men, who may be very unreasonable in defending their own faith," and he claimed in response to White:

> I am persuaded that you still misunderstand my criticism
> of Dewey. If I criticized him for using intelligence in solving his-
> torical problems, what would I do with all the political science
> and the historical inquiries with which I have spent my life? . . .
> My criticism of Dewey is that he follows the Comptean thesis
> that it is comparatively easy to transfer the objectivity of the

natural sciences to historical inquiries, if only these sciences can be freed of the heavy hand of "church and state." In short he attributes the ideological element in all historical inquiries to overt corruption and obscures the covert corruption of interest and passion in our historical judgments. If one has empirical objections to this kind of faith in reason, one is called an "irrationalist." I find this mode of reasoning almost as obscurantist as reason subject to religious dogma.[87]

Niebuhr found the naive rationalistic tendencies in modern culture preeminently manifested in American society, a society which was, in his estimate, *the* paragon of bourgeois liberal culture. He saw that to one degree or another liberal social thought shared the vain hope that the selfishness of self-interest would yield if only people could be reasoned out of their selfishness. He believed that, however sophisticated Dewey might otherwise have been, he had, at bottom, bought into this central liberal illusion. Morris Raphael Cohen who, as Sidney Hook reported it, admitted "that Dewey's faith in the use of intelligence and its imaginative projection to widen the circles of shared experience, was the true faith of the liberal" nonetheless agreed that "Dewey seemed to underplay, if not ignore the darker sides of human nature." Hook then went on to relate a personal anecdote. "Reinhold Niebuhr persistently made the same kind of criticism of Dewey. When I once related the gist of that criticism to Dewey, he plaintively asked, in an idiom he rarely used, 'Do I have to believe that every man is born a sonofabitch even before he acts like one, and regardless of why and how he becomes one?' "[88] The answer, of course, is no. But the answer from Niebuhr's point of view simply begs the question at issue.

Such liberal hopes were vain, Niebuhr contended, precisely because they were expressions of hope and not the result of a firm evaluation of the facts of experience. Niebuhr, therefore, in his dispute with Deweyite educator George A. Coe in 1933, urged "placing every possible social and inner check upon" the egoism of human beings as *the* truly rational procedure with respect to political life. As he said to Coe, it is only as "rational and religious idealists stop fooling themselves and recognize the basic fact of a social struggle in society" that "they will be the more able to direct it morally and rationally."[89] Niebuhr's expression here of the possibility of giving moral and rational direction to the social struggle might well have reflected too liberal of a tone, suggesting a greater ease than he would later consider judicious. Because of the self's inordinate self-interest, a prudent *political* rationality is guided by something quite different from rational or moral suasion to secure justice. Nonetheless, as Niebuhr put it much later, because a human being has a capacity for justice as well as an inclination towards injustice,[90] political rationality should both allow for a wideranging free play of competing interests and appeal to disinterested sources of judgment on conflicting interests to achieve the greater equity justice requires.

Curiously enough, Richard Fox, who was correct in claiming that Dewey had "some reason to insist that the radical movement commit itself to a belief in 'intelligence' if it was to build a social order,"[91] also insisted that Niebuhr's statement to Coe was "a sentimental hope quite at odds with the dominant tone of Moral Man."[92] It was certainly not contradictory to the notes Niebuhr sounded in Moral Man on power and self-interest, nor was it merely a sentimental hope. Although Niebuhr would put the matter somewhat differently and more guardedly in subsequent years, the statement was quite consistent with his own critique of the nature and place of reason in life—a critique whose cardinal tenet was that reason's first task is to discern the limits of its own rational claims. Far from being "sentimental" about rational and moral suasion, Niebuhr was arguing for a far more circumspect and serpentine view of reason than that of the views of the dominant liberal tradition on which he had launched such a vehement attack. He strove for a more balanced view of reason than he found in the liberal tradition. He knew, as he once put it, that "because reason is something more than a weapon of self-interest it can be an instrument of justice." But he knew also that "since reason is never dissociated from the vitalities of life, individual and collective, it cannot be a pure instrument of [any] justice."[93]

In the midst of the heightened assault on the liberal tradition taking place in the 1930s, Dewey's Liberalism and Social Action was published. This small but important volume was an eloquent defense of liberalism that grew out of a series of lectures delivered at the University of Virginia. In spite of Dewey's observation that such a brief treatment did not afford either the time or space necessary to say all that needed to be said, this book constituted Dewey's most concentrated and powerful defense of liberalism. Niebuhr, who was also struggling with liberalism at that time, had expected much more from Dewey's effort.

Dewey focused on "an inner split in liberalism" caused by "the ambiguity from which liberalism still suffers," an ambiguity between those who tended to dichotomize "organized social action and the province of purely individual effort" and those who were "committed to the principle that organized society must use its powers to establish the conditions under which the mass of individuals can possess actual as distinct from merely legal liberty."[94]

Dewey pointed out that liberalism was at an impasse. His aim was to find out the "way in which liberalism may resolve the crisis, and emerge as a compact, aggressive force."[95] The crisis of liberalism was that the creative forces of its fundamental values—liberty, "the development of the inherent capacities of individuals made possible through liberty, and the central role of free intelligence in inquiry, discussion and expression"[96]—were "ineffective when faced with the problems of social organization and integration."[97] These values, which Dewey regarded as the very marks of liberalism's continuing relevance in the modern world, were values that found their expression in "an enduring social organization . . . in which the . . . forces of productivity are cooperatively controlled and used in the interest of the effective liberty and the cultural development of the individuals that constitute society."[98] Such a goal was possible only if the earlier liberal ideal of the unplanned activities of separate atomic individuals, either personal or corporate, was abandoned. Dewey rallied forces on behalf of a "renascent liberalism" which, as he saw it, depended entirely on a firm commitment "to the use of freed intelligence as the method of directing change,"[99] a method made available by the resources of modern science and the experimental method and that only very recently had begun to be incorporated into the social sciences.

Niebuhr's disappointment was evidenced in the form of an extended review of Dewey's book. In "The Pathos of Liberalism," Niebuhr mixed praise with disillusionment regarding Dewey's effort and pointed out that the much needed support for liberal self-criticism would not be forthcoming from the single most important spokesman of the liberal community. Niebuhr exclaimed that

> No one in America has a more generally conceded right to
> speak in the name of liberalism than John Dewey. He has been
> for many years not only the leading philosophical exponent of
> liberal doctrine but the fountain and source of liberal pedagogical theory and method. He has furthermore been active in a
> score of political and social movements in which he has proved
> not only his interest in the practical application of his theories
> but also a courageous willingness to extend both his theory and
> his practice beyond the limits set by traditional liberalism.[100]

Because of Dewey's stature within the liberal world, Dewey's book could have been "an excellent opportunity to assess the resources of liberalism in the present social scene, particularly since the book is a theoretic elaboration of his advanced position."[101] Niebuhr, however, found such resources severely lacking. Dewey had claimed that the most pressing need was to extend the two major contributions of liberalism, liberty and intelligence, in such a way as to both create a social structure that would extend liberty to the general populace and to render freed intelligence more effective in the social sphere. Niebuhr's retort was that "all that is good in a modern advanced liberalism is revealed in the development of the first point and all that is dubious betrays itself in the second."[102] He did not dispute the broad outlines Dewey made in his appeal for "an intelligent direction of social change" to avoid a "drift into chaos." Rather Dewey's approach was wrong, according to Niebuhr, because it continued to reveal and repeat the systemic flaws in traditional liberalism.

For all the occasional insights into self-interest and social conflict shown in Dewey's assessment of historic liberalism, the prognosis for a "renascent liberalism," with which Dewey concluded his book, tediously reiterated the naive and exaggerated rational expectations so characteristic of liberalism. After all was said and done, Dewey persisted in trafficking off the more generalized illusions of liberal culture as a whole. Dewey's reconstructed liberalism, in Niebuhr's account, simply failed to probe the core difficulties of the entire liberal creed or to subject them to the kind of rigorous self-criticism a genuinely reconstructed liberalism demanded. Dewey remained the quintessential liberal "committed to the organization of intelligent action as the chief method,"[103] and although he paid lip service now and again to the fact that "coercive and violent force" must be directly and openly faced, such realistic moments were merely judged to be a temporary nuisance preliminary to grasping "the meaning of dependence upon intelligence as the alternative method of social direction."[104]

According to Niebuhr, Dewey persisted in confusing hopes with realities so that there was an abysmal lack of realism in his discussion of the issue because "Professor Dewey" continued to see "violence only as a consequence of a social ignorance which a more perfect intelligence would be able to eliminate."[105] And when Dewey urged that those who held power and privilege might be dissuaded from violently resisting the loss of their power and privilege if only liberalism would "assume the responsibility for making it clear that intelligence is a social asset and is clothed with a function as public as its origin" instead of being merely an individual possession,[106] Niebuhr quipped

> A liberalism which defends liberty as a public necessity rather than a private right will supposedly sooth the savage breast of an imperiled and frantic oligarchy, while the older and more individualistic liberalism merely succeeded in maintaining liberty "as long as it did not menace the status quo." One might as well expect to beguile the gentlemen of the Liberty League to modify their touching devotion to the Constitution by proving to them logically, rationally, and intellectually that the flexibil-

ity of the Constitution is a necessary prerequisite of orderly social change.[107]

Such a naive understanding of reason was a feeble reed, indeed, against the endless conflict, coercion, and rival contests of self-interest that were part and parcel of the political process. Justice in the world unhappily depended on a balance of power and a constant adjudication of conflicting interests. Even though Niebuhr himself held that there were elements of goodwill in human life that prevented justice from merely being cast in terms of a power conflict—elements that shall receive a closer examination in the next chapter—he looked on in dismay as Dewey voiced the hope that a day would arrive in which party disputes would yield to impartial, scientifically guided inquiry. Niebuhr concluded his review of *Liberalism and Social Action* by insisting Dewey's notion that

> "The idea that the conflict of parties will, by means of public discussion, bring out necessary public truths" has nothing "in common with the procedure of organized cooperative inquiry, which has won the triumphs of science in the field of physical nature." We are back, in other words, where we began, on the thesis that nothing but a cultural lag prevents men from viewing the social policies in which they are involved with the same degree of objectivity they use in delving into the mysteries of biochemistry or astronomy. Whatever the possibilities and necessities of social intelligence in social action, that thesis is a hopeless one. In so far as a "renascent liberalism" rests upon it, it will confuse the political problem.[108]

The pathos Niebuhr saw in what he took to be Dewey's stubbornly overstated view of the rational life was compounded by the fact that Dewey's liberalism was, as Niebuhr said, both "courageous and honest."[109] One is left with the distinct impression that for Niebuhr, John Dewey possessed such talents and stature that he, above all others identified with liberalism, should have known better. Niebuhr clearly hoped that, in his efforts to bring about a renascence of liberal tradition, this most influential and highly respected voice of social liberalism would have engaged in a more fundamental critique of those liberal premises that had rendered the tradition so otiose.

What Niebuhr called "the new liberalism" in the context of a position paper written for Americans for Democratic Action, was a liberalism that had "profited by the experience of the whole western world" and could ideally express a wisdom wiser than its earlier historical creed. Whereas Dewey saw liberalism antedating the very scientific intelligence which he believed alone could render liberalism a viable force in the modern industrial age, Niebuhr viewed the liberal creed in terms of a 400 hundred year legacy that required a sweeping historical and self-critical analysis. Whereas Dewey saw the history of liberalism, overall, as a movement from out of the shadows of authoritarianism toward the light of critical openness and free inquiry, Niebuhr saw the same liberal tradition as inextricably linked to a virtual catalogue of self-vitiating illusions. To some extent, of course, both Dewey and Niebuhr were correct. Liberalism was indeed related to a history of emancipation as Dewey's position assumed, although his rather romantic account of that emancipation rendered him incapable of seeing anything constructive coming out of a very complex and diverse religious tradition. Moreover, his romanticized report of the struggle of science with the weight of tradition, as Niebuhr saw it, blinded him to the illusions borne by the liberal creed itself. The crux of Niebuhr's dispute with Dewey over liberalism turned precisely on this claim. For, as we have seen, Dewey's case for scientific rationality was, in Niebuhr's judgment, bound up with some of the most central and persistent illusions of the liberal tradition as a whole and severely limited the force of his otherwise remarkable contributions to liberal-democratic culture.

Niebuhr and Liberal Reconstruction

The relationship of Reinhold Niebuhr to the liberal tradition is of some interest and importance. Any definitive answer to what, on it its own terms, this relationship might be is made all the more complex in light of the fact that liberalism itself had been undergoing a disputatious reassessment. One thing is sure: Niebuhr was never even tempted by either political or religious conservatism, both of whose core convictions were not only offensive to him but also lacked the pragmatic realism so important to his own thought.

It would be quite beside the point to enter the labyrinthian passageways of more than thirty years of liberal and conservative misappropriations of Reinhold Niebuhr. A few remarks on this complex subject, however, do seem to be in order. Since as early as the 1950s, and most especially through the 1960s and 1970s, Niebuhr, along with Niebuhrianism, have been subjected to a rash of critical hyperbole and downright distortion. Far too much ideological posturing and propagandizing was in the air. Certainly the *conservative* label given to Niebuhr was always ill-fitting at best. As first chairman of the Union for Democratic Action formed in 1941 (later passing over into Americans for Democratic Action in 1947), Niebuhr was a leader of a group that, as James Wechsler put it, pressed "for liberal causes while vigorously supporting the Allied cause abroad."[110] The pragmatic tone of Niebuhr's liberal realism and his institutional affiliations during the 1940s and 1950s offended radicals and conservatives alike. And that fact alone should be sufficient to give pause to anyone seriously considering the conservative garb for Niebuhr.

It has to be acknowledged that Niebuhr's long-time friend Will Herberg did a great disservice when his 1961 essay "Reinhold Niebuhr: Burkean Conservative" was published in his "Religion" column in William F. Buckley's *National Review*.[111] It is not so much what Herberg said there that is the source of the disservice, although the fact that he chose to affiliate his own burgeoning conservative ideology with Niebuhr raises some interesting questions. The real source of the problem is that Herberg placed his offering in a journal whose editorial policies and staff writers were utter anathema to Niebuhr's political philosophy as well as his judgments on concrete political action.

Niebuhr had attempted to make his views as clear as possible in 1955. He wrote

It is obviously necessary to make the most careful distinctions between the conservatism and liberalism which are merely moods or ideologies according to which one defends a status quo or seeks to leave it behind, and the conservatism and liberalism which are cogent political philosophies. We can dismiss the sort of conservatism and liberalism which are dispositions towards some staus quo very simply by giving an *a priori* preference for liberalism over conservatism on the grounds that it is not reasonable to defend any status quo uncritically; and that it is certainly not reasonable to do so in the rapidly changing conditions of a technical society in which "new conditions teach new duties and time makes ancient truth uncouth." If being for or against change were the only issue involved, any critical person would be bound to be a "liberal."[112]

Niebuhr, as Robin Lovin noted, held a "dialectical relationship between justice and order" that required "the statesman always to regard justice both as a support for the existing social order and as a threat to it."[113] In line with this understanding, ten years later Niebuhr reiterated his "strong conviction that a realist conception of human nature should be made the servant of an ethic of progressive justice and should not be made into a bastion of conservatism, particularly a conservatism which defends unjust privileges." He felt strongly enough about the matter that he went on to say that "I might define this conviction as the guiding principle throughout my mature life of the relation of religious responsibility to political affairs.[114]

Quite obviously Niebuhr had learned something from realists such as Augustine and David Hume as well as from cynics like Thomas Hobbes and Sigmund Freud. He certainly gained insights from bona fide conservatives such as Edmund Burke. Together this set Niebuhr apart from, and over against, what he often called the *creed* of liberalism. What Niebuhr learned from conservatives such as Burke set him in strident opposition to what passed for American conservatism as well as to many of the views of the social liberals. His appropriation of conservative-realist insights into the limits of human nature and the force of historical traditions set him at odds with the whole of liberalism, be it classical laissez-faire or social-progressive. Niebuhr learned to be skeptical about human goodness and historical progress and, consequently, to look more seriously at the force of self-interest and power in human affairs. Niebuhr, too, learned to give more weight to history and tradition, and especially to what he recognized as the *organic* factors that entered into the fabric of human communities. Indeed, among the virtues he found in the rough vitalities of life, while always balanced in his mind by the anarchical dangers such vitalities posed, included liberty as a perennial virtue of civil society. On this basis Niebuhr was never tempted, as so many liberals were (and are), to sacrifice the conflicting cross purposes of such liberty in the name of some idyllic social conformism. With the wisdom of the conservative tradition at its best Niebuhr's reconstructed liberalism was, to borrow Michael Walzer's term, "an anti-ideology."[115] Drawing further from Walzer, Niebuhr's answer to the question "What is the preferred setting, the most supportive environment, for the good life?" was clearly along the lines of Walzer's notion of a "critical associationalism" with respect to "civil society," with society's requisite "uncoerced associations and also the set of relational networks . . . that fill this space." Niebuhr's vision of liberalism involved a necessary pluralism that provided an antidoctrinaire view of society.[116] What Niebuhr did not learn from the realist-conservative heritage was either an orientation toward the status quo or a cynicism regarding the possibilities of social justice. In effect, Niebuhr did not learn to abandon the "spirit" of liberalism wherein, in his account, an authentic concern for liberty and social justice were to be found. As William Lee Miller so rightly saw, after discerning certain facts about life that came out of the best of the conservative tradition, Niebuhr's position proved to be diametrically opposed to that of the self-appointed conservatives. "The conservative," Miller wrote,

> gives one answer, Niebuhr gives another. The conservative takes the traditional and existing relationships not just as fact but also as norm; Niebuhr sees them as facts that must be taken into account in action that finds its norm elsewhere, in a Biblical understanding of justice. Niebuhr understands man and history realistically, not to discourage any challenge to the status quo but so that a challenge will be more effective.[117]

Misappropriations, of course, have surfaced over the years from the side of the liberal Left as well, a fact that Miller, in informal discussion, passed off as "partly due to that dynamic, unstable mixture of ingredients in [Niebuhr's] thought and partly the dependence, in the end, on the original political insight (and moral commitment)" that were Niebuhr's alone.[118] In point of fact, challenges to Niebuhr from the Left have been far more numerous and significant than those coming from conservatives seeking to claim Niebuhr as one of their own. From the Left, liberal criticism of Niebuhr has been quite diverse. Niebuhr has been accused of betraying liberalism outright (thus charging him with the greatest of all illiberalities, that is, of *being* a conservative at heart); of softening his social criticism while allegedly playing the role of the Cold Warrior; and of being a "corporate liberal," incapable of leveling substantive criticism at either America's socioeconomic policies or its imperialistic ventures.

The other part of the "reason" for such misappropriations that Miller left unspoken lay in the fact that many of the leftist criticism of Niebuhr was ideological to the core and vindictive in tone, if not intent. Actually both Niebuhr and Dewey have come in for a share of sharp criticism from the Left, not the least of which came as a result of the antiideological character of their fundamental pragmatism. Moreover, because Niebuhr and Dewey had overlapped so extensively over the years in their concrete political attitudes and actions, both radicals and a variety of Left-liberals have had a field day castigating them for a variety of sins. The list is extensive. It includes their days as socialists, their early rejection of Rooseveltian pragmatism, Niebuhr's outright support of American intervention in World War II (as well as Dewey's belated and begrudging acceptance of the war), their eventual anti-Stalinist position during the "Cold War," their attempts in the postwar environment to occupy the "vital center" (to employ a term Arthur Schlesinger, Jr., coined) between the pro-Communist Left and reactionary Republicanism, and finally their efforts to defend the fundamental liberties of liberal tradition against the attempted suppression of those liberties from both Left and Right. In effect, Dewey and Niebuhr's sin in the eyes of the radical Left was that they were unabashedly committed to the fundamentals of democratic liberalism and were so with a far more pragmatic temperament than so many on the Left or the Right. From Niebuhr's perspective, of course, the bone in the throat of both his conservative and liberal critics was his sometimes strident quest for a consistent realism. And as Roger Shinn once pointed out, "the opposite of realism is romanticism and illusion, whether left or right."[119]

Ronald Stone pointed to something important about the relationship between Niebuhr and Dewey when he remarked that "there is sufficient reason to regard the Niebuhr-Dewey controversy of the 1930's as an intramural affair."[120] Stone correctly saw that, within the context of that intramural affair, Reinhold Niebuhr, every bit as much as John Dewey, was a self-correcting voice within America's liberal-democratic tradition. This perspective has gained increasing support in spite of Niebuhr's broadside against liberalism and the sharp disagreements he and Dewey had over the issue of liberal reconstruction. It is thus that Richard Fox could claim that "in retrospect it appears clear that even in his most radical period Niebuhr was in fact struggling not so much to destroy liberalism as to transform it into a philosophy that was realistic — as he believed Marxism to be — about the role of power, self-interest, and political mobilization in the social arena."[121] There was, among moderate supporters and critics of Niebuhr, a broad consensus on this issue going back to 1956 when Arthur Schlesinger, Jr., who vividly portrayed Niebuhr's wholesale assault on the liberal tradition, nonetheless saw Niebuhr's role as that of helping to bring about "a revolution in the bases of American liberal political thought."[122]

To see Niebuhr as a sharp and unrepentent critic within the social liberal tradition is to put his fundamental struggle with himself as well as with Dewey and the entire liberal community into proper perspective. Niebuhr was seeking to bring a much needed realism to the pressing requirements of liberal reconstruction. His approach was based on a broad appeal to both religious and secular traditions within whose resources he could garner ammunition aimed expressly at his reconstructive efforts. Niebuhr saw what might best be termed *pragmatic realism* as an antidote for the "pragmatic rationalism" of the prevailing social liberalism of his day. Shifting the metaphor somewhat it can be said that Niebuhr's relationship to liberalism was not one of a virus attacking an organism as an alien from without. Rather he worked feverishly as an antibody from within, aiming its defense against what Niebuhr took to be both internal and external diseases. In effect, the issues were in-house. The only subtantive issue with respect to the question of Niebuhr's liberal credentials is whether or not, or to what degree, the Niebuhrian anti-dote was a needed remedy. Understood from this vantage point it can be affirmed that, although in sharply diverging and adversarial ways, Dewey and Niebuhr were both involved in a reconstructive rehabilita-tion of the liberal tradition which none of their fellow-liberals could ig-nore. In speaking specifically of Niebuhr's case, Paul Merkley recorded that

> From that time [1930] to this, the liberal-intellectual camp had been divided three ways on the question of Niebuhr's signifi-cance: that he made sense in spite of his theologizing (which I submit is a delusion); that he made sense because of his theol-ogy (which is a tribute to the missionary impact of Niebuhr within the liberal-intellectual community since the 1930's); and that he makes bad sense. Liberal-intellectuals who tried simply to ignore him altogether had their cards taken away from them long before the thirties were out.[123]

12

Democracy

Van A. Harvey correctly classified Niebuhr, along with Paul Tillich, as one of "the last two public theologians in this country, that is, theologians whose names were recognized because they contributed to those types of discourse that seriously engage American intellectuals."[1] Of course, Niebuhr and Tillich engaged in different kinds of discourse so their audiences among American intellectuals diverged accordingly. Niebuhr's audience was especially populated by political scientists, historians, and social philosophers, many of whom were thoroughly secular with respect to their personal confessions and affiliations. Indeed, there were so many secular thinkers among Niebuhr's audience that the philosopher Morton White, a sharp yet respectful critic of Niebuhr, saw him as "courageous, shrewd, and sensitive"[2] and even suggested an official gathering of "atheists for Niebuhr."[3]

Whether professed atheists or not, those from a secular orientation who held Niebuhr in high regard were legion. Although far too numerous to name, included among those individuals who identified Niebuhr as a unique voice within American liberal-democratic debate were historians Perry Miller and C. Van Woodward,[4] and political thinkers Kenneth Thompson and the quintessential realist Hans Morgenthau. Indeed Morgenthau, in an oft-repeated accolade, claimed that Reinhold Niebuhr "was the greatest American political philosopher since Calhoun."[5]

Acclaim for Niebuhr coming from political scientists and historians focused on Niebuhr's "political theology" (to borrow Langdon Gilkey's phrase[6]), most particularly on his reflections on democracy and the liberal tradition. Arthur Schlesinger, Jr., identified these foci when, within the space for four years' time, he both labeled Niebuhr's work as involving a "penetrating reconstruction of the democratic faith"[7] and referred to Niebuhr himself as "the most searching critic of the rationalism and utopianism of the official liberal tradition."[8] Certainly over the entire range of tenure of his dispute with John Dewey, Niebuhr's prestige at the point where he challenged Dewey's liberal ideas and ideals was highly appreciated in some quarters and sharply contested in others. And, as we have already noted, for Niebuhr, a defense of democracy required a far more penetrating criticism of the liberal creed than Dewey thought necessary. This dispute was raging at the very time both men sought desperately to fashion a viable defense of democracy amidst the crisis of the 1930s and 1940s.

Democratic Vistas

Niebuhr and Dewey never engaged one another directly on the subject of democracy, as they had so forcefully on the question of liberal reconstruction. Their confrontation over liberalism, however, had important implications for their respective interpretations of democracy and for identifying its core issues. Indeed, their differing accents on democratic life and institutions were largely consistent with their attitudes toward the liberal tradition itself. Specifically, from Niebuhr's perspective, "one of the real tragedies of our era is that the very democracy which is the great achievement of liberalism cannot be maintained if liberalism is not transcended as a culture."[9] That is to say, given the transformation of early libertarian liberalism into a capitalistic class ideology amid the drastically altered circumstances of the technoindustrial age, democracy's survival required, above all else, overcoming what Niebuhr had seen to be the wholesale limitations of the liberal "creed."

Dewey's view of democracy was both expansive and visionary. His understanding of democracy had vision inasmuch as Dewey foresaw that the very survival of democracy was inextricably bound up with the survival of a reconstructed liberal tradition. Dewey's defense of this vision against those who were prepared to abandon democracy, as well as against the profoundly illiberal history of what Dewey called "pseudo-liberalism," was both powerful and forthright. Niebuhr, too, had attacked the liberalism of the "bourgeois world"—a world that, "in dreaming of achieving 'liberty, equality, and fraternity,' [had] developed such monstrous disproportions of social and economic power as to threaten not only the security of those who lacked power but the stability of society itself."[10]

Dewey's emphasis on sociocommunal, rather than simply "political," democracy meant that he was also highly expansive in his representation of the democratic ideal. Robert Westbrook, a recent biographer, whose aim was to examine "Dewey's career as an advocate of democracy,"[11] describes Dewey's vision of democracy as one that "calls

upon men and women to build communities in which the necessary opportunities and resources are available for every individual to realize
fully his or her particular capacities and powers through participation in
political, social, and cultural life."[12] What had negative as well as positive overtones, in Niebuhr's opinion, was Dewey's particular rendition of
the Jeffersonian faith in reason and the rational methods that Dewey,
along with Jefferson, held to be—as Westbrook puts it—"intrinsic to
democracy."[13]

Dewey's view of democracy was also expansive in the sense that for
Dewey democracy came as close as anything to qualifying as a way of
life—and a religious way of life at that, as was noted in Chapter 10. In
both form and substance, as the context for permanent liberal values,
democracy embodied the framework for the realization of the highest
values attainable in human life. Given Dewey's moral convictions here,
there is no small measure of irony in the fact that *the* noted instrumentalist who insisted on operationalism as a guide for meaning, in point of
fact, scorned any strictly operationalist view of democracy that would
tend to see democracy as merely a set of procedures conducive to achieving desired consequences. The irony, of course, is due to the persistence of
some critics to drape Dewey in positivist clothing. What must be remembered is that Dewey was a value theorist and decried the positivist separation of science from values while conducting a tireless battle against
those who included him among the positivist ranks.[14] The fact that
Dewey spoke quite seriously of democracy in religious and metaphysical
terms gave the lie to those such as Santayana and Russell who saw
Dewey's pragmatism as little more than a reflection and sanctification of
what was crass in American commercialism. It also gave the lie to critics
like Lewis Mumford whose pejorative and ubiquitous term *pragmatic
liberalism* purported to dismiss as simply utilitarian the bloodless and
abstract rationalism bereft of values often associated with Dewey.[15]

Dewey saw democracy in a symbiotic relationship to core liberal values. For Dewey the enduring liberal values included "liberty, the development of the inherent capacities of individuals made possible
through liberty, and the central role of free intelligence in inquiry, discussion and expression."[16] Conversely, the attainment and preservation
of these core liberal values were possible only in a democratic society. In
effect, those liberal values that served to guarantee democracy were
themselves guaranteed only by democracy itself. This is the burden of
Westbrook's claim that "in Dewey's metaphysic, democracy was the full
realization of the possibilities of human society as such. . . . Since perfection was impossible in a precarious, uncertain world, democracy was a
regulative ideal, not a fact, yet it was an ideal rooted in the most essential features of human experience."[17]

Democracy, for Dewey, was not just one form of human association among others. As Dewey put it, "Regarded as an idea democracy is not an alternative to other principles of associated life. It is the idea of community itself. It is an ideal in the only intelligible sense of an ideal: namely, the tendency and movement of some thing which exists carried to its final limit, viewed as completed, perfected."[18] Dewey regarded democracy as the quintessential form of association rooted in the very features of human nature; that is, expressive of and conducive to that liberty which allows for the development of inherent human capacities.[19] When this notion gets joined with the last of Dewey's enduring liberal values, namely, "the central role of free intelligence or inquiry, discussion and expression"—that is, the scientific method in the broadest sense—the circle is closed. As Horace Friess stated it forty years ago, "Dewey's recipe for social inquiry does read in part like a program for democratic action, and this seems to trouble some who feel that philosophy and special pleading are here confused."[20]

Certainly Dewey had no compunction about articulating and defending his vision of democracy as a way of life. He did so eloquently in an address delivered by Horace Kallen at Dewey's eightieth birthday celebration in New York and published soon thereafter, in 1940.[21] Dewey saw that "at present, the frontier [our democratic society now faced] is moral, not physical."[22] Dewey turned the exhausted spatial frontier of Frederick Jackson Turner 180 degrees around into a new frontier, an inner space that was now to be won. This inner space was the space of self-creation and social transformation. "The period of free lands that seemed boundless in extent has vanished," Dewey noted. But the "unused resources are now human rather than material." Dewey said that "what I mean when I say that we now have to re-create by deliberate and determined endeavor the kind of democracy which in its origin one hundred and fifty years ago was largely the product of a fortunate combination of men and circumstances" is that the really untapped resources "are found in the waste of grown men and women who are without the chance to work, and in the young men and women who find doors closed where there was once opportunity."[23] For all the creativity required of those who trecked the earlier frontier, Dewey saw the pressing need of his own era to be that of surpassing those efforts in creative genius. With the power of a genuine but studied visionary, Dewey continued:

> If I emphasize that the task can be accomplished only by inventive effort and creative activity, it is in part because the depth of the present crisis is due in considerable part to the fact that for a long period we acted as if our democracy were something that perpetuated itself automatically; as if our ancestors had suc-

ceeded in setting up a machine that solved the problem of per-
petual motion in politics.[24]

Then Dewey, eighty years old and ever hopeful for the democratic prospect, implored his unseen audience, as well as those who would later
read his words, to fully understand—and understand deeply—that

> in thought and act . . . democracy is a *personal* way of individual
> life; that it signifies the possession and continual use of certain
> attitudes, forming personal character and determining desire
> and purpose in all the relations of life. Instead of thinking of our
> own dispositions and habits as accommodated to certain insti-
> tutions we have to learn to think of the latter as expressions,
> projections, and extensions of habitually dominant personal
> attitudes.
>   Democracy as a personal, an individual, way of life . . . signi-
> fies that powerful present enemies of democracy can be success-
> fully met only by the creation of personal attitudes in individual
> human beings; that we must get over our tendency to think that
> its defense can be found in any external means whatever,
> whether military or civil, if they are separated from individual
> attitudes so deep-seated as to constitute personal character.[25]

Democracy, therefore, was not primarily an administrative or pro-
cedural matter for Dewey. Indeed, in Dewey's account, what he called
"political democracy" denoted as "a mode of government, a specified
practice in selecting officials and regulating their conduct as officials
[was] not the most inspiring of the different meanings of democracy
[being that it was] comparatively special in character."[26] He scorned the
view that democracy was primarily a set of procedures conducive to delivering a set of desired consequences.

Dewey wanted always to stress the customary rather than the institutional side of democracy. The fact that "the underlying and genera-
tive conditions of concrete behavior" are even more social than organic,
those ideals, attitudes, and habits that ultimately "mirror a state of
civilization"[27] make democracy as a *way of life* far more important than
the machinery of political democracy. Indeed, Dewey fervently believed
that the only things that can conceivably secure and perpetuate political
democracy are the customary patterns of democratic behavior in the life
of a people. What Dewey called the "democratic convergence,"[28] which
was the product not so much of thought or planning as it was the result of
complex social forces, meant for him the optimistic judgment that the
historical "current has set steadily in one direction: toward democratic

forms."[29] The structures of democratic politics, "that government exists
to serve its community, and that this purpose cannot be achieved unless
the community itself shares in selecting its governors and their policies.
. . . marks a well-attested conclusion from historical facts."[30] Therefore,
Dewey argued,

> We have every reason to think that whatever changes may take
> place in existing democratic machinery, they will be of a sort to
> make the interest of the public a more supreme guide and
> criterion of governmental activity, and to enable the public to
> form and manifest its purposes still more authoritatively. *In this
> sense the cure for the ailments of democracy is more democracy.*[31] (Italics
> mine.)

But, because Dewey felt "the primary difficulty" of the times lay
elsewhere—namely, in "discovering the means by which a scattered,
mobile and manifold public may so recognize itself as to define and express its interests"—then his conclusion was that

> This discovery is necessarily precedent to any fundamental
> change in the machinery. We are not concerned therefore to set
> forth counsels as to the advisable improvements in the political
> forms of democracy. Many have been suggested. It is no deroga-
> tion of their relative worth to say that *consideration of these
> changes is not at present an affair of primary importance.* The problem
> lies deeper; it is in the first instance an intellectual problem:
> the search for conditions under which the Great Society may be-
> come the Great Community. When these conditions are
> brought into being they will make their own forms. Until they
> have come about, it is somewhat futile to consider what politi-
> cal machinery will suit them.[32] (Italic mine.)

In his important chapter on the "Search for the Great Community"
in *The Public and Its Problems*,[33] Dewey insisted on the priority of the conditions for the transition from the "Great Society" to the "Great Community" over attempts to reform the political machinery. The "Great
Society," whose "impersonal and mechanical modes of combined human
behavior" Dewey saw as "the outstanding fact of modern life,"[34] undermined the viability of a democratic community that could exercise control over these new behavioral forms. Dewey wanted a reconstitution of
local communities and direct democracy to facilitate the transition to
the "Great Community" in which democracy would again be viable. As
Robert Westbrook has maintained, Dewey recognized the intellectual

problem of and need for the "interdependence of local communities with the Great Community," but gave precious little direction toward solving the matter.[35]

For Dewey democracy was essentially a belief system involving a deeply held conviction that a rationally based associative life could give expression to a set of values which would lead to self-realization through individual growth. Dewey's democratic vision was, in a word, Jeffersonian, except that it strove mightily to adapt democracy to the changed conditions of an industrial and technological age, an endeavor the scale of which Jefferson's agrarian vision could neither have envisioned nor thought possible. In good Jeffersonian fashion Dewey's vision centered upon "the development of the higher capacities of individuals," and in the context of the present age this meant that

> The problem of democracy becomes the problem of that form of social organization, extending to all the areas and ways of living, in which the powers of individuals shall not be merely released from mechanical external constraint but shall be fed, sustained and directed. Such an organization demands much more of education than general schooling, which without a renewal of the springs of purpose and desire becomes a new mode of mechanization and formalization, as hostile to liberty as ever was governmental constraint. It demands of science much more than external technical application—which again leads to mechanization of life and results in a new kind of enslavement. It demands that the method of inquiry, of discrimination, of test by verifiable consequences, be naturalized in all the matters, of large and of detailed scope, that arise for judgment.[36]

The expansive vision Dewey had when he wrote in defense of democracy was clearly evident in the fact that he saw the issues attending the crisis of liberalism and democracy in broad cultural terms. And, because he saw his philosophy as a form of culture criticism, Dewey necessarily treated democracy as having far broader vistas than its strictly political meaning as a system of government. The crisis of liberalism in the modern age was not merely that of readjusting liberty to the conditions and consequences of the industrial age. It cut into far wider and deeper channels than that. It was, for Dewey, "the problem of humanizing industrial civilization, of making it and its technology a servant of human life."[37] This, in effect, involved the problem "of creating a genuine culture" in America out of the very fabric of that civilization precisely because its developments of technology and industrialism had made America a paradigm for the entire industrial world.

Dewey was talking here not of culture as "interest in art, science, and philosophy (areas where he believed the United States was doing tolerably well), but rather of "the type of emotion and thought that is characteristic of a people and epoch as a whole, an organic intellectual and moral quality."[38] The spiritual meaning of America did not, in his account, entail an overlay of "high personal cultivation" in condescendingly superior contradistinction to its technicoindustrial character. Rather the spiritual meaning of America must emerge out of "our own material civilization itself. . . . by turning a machine age into a significantly new habit of mind and sentiment, or it will not come at all."[39] The question, for Dewey, was, "Can a material, industrial civilization be converted into a distinctive agency for liberating the minds and refining the emotions of all who take part in it? Thus, the cultural question is a political and economic one before it becomes definitely cultural."[40] In true Jeffersonian fashion, democracy, for Dewey, was a spiritual reality having as its task both cultural transformation and individual liberation.

Dewey clearly saw democracy as a "shared experience" within which growth was enhanced along the path of life. And growth, for Dewey, was among the highest values attainable in the natural life. After stating "the democratic faith in the formal terms of a philosophic proposition," he defined democracy as "belief in the ability of human experience to generate the aims and methods by which further experience will grow in ordered richness—[in effect it is] a faith that the process of experience is more important than any special result attained, so that special results achieved are of ultimate value only as they are used to enrich and order the ongoing process."[41]

The problem of what criteria governed Dewey's notion of the "growth" and "enrichment" of life in relation to the "ongoing process" has been a recurrent one. In his chapter on "Education as Growth" in *Democracy and Education* (1916) Dewey had written

When it is said that education is development, everything depends upon *how* development is conceived. Our net conclusion is that life is development, and that developing, growing, is life. Translated into its educational equivalents, this means (i) that the educational process has no end beyond itself; it is its own end; and that (ii) the educational process is one of continual reorganizing, reconstructing, transforming.[42]

Education was, for Dewey, the very meaning of growth and the very heart of democracy. It was the meaning of growth in the sense that the educative process is a nurturing and cultivating process, and thus is involved in enhancing the conditions whereby growth itself is made possible. "The educative process," as Dewey said, "is a continuous process of growth, having as its aim at every stage an added capacity for growth."[43] It is proper on the grounds Dewey laid out to say, as quoted earlier, that "the educational process has no end beyond itself" precisely because, as Dewey insisted four years later, "growth itself is the only moral 'end.'"[44]

The context for all of this, of course, was personal growth in the kind of community that only a democratic way of life made truly possible. In the brief address Dewey personally delivered at his ninetieth birthday gala in New York, he implored his listeners one last time to realize

> that democracy is an educative process; that the act of voting is in a democratic regime a culmination of a continued process of open and public communication in which prejudices have the opportunity to erase each other; that continued interchange of facts and ideas exposes what is unsound and discloses what may make for human well-being.
>
> This educational process is based upon faith in human good sense and human good will as it manifests itself in the long run when communication is progressively liberated from bondage to prejudice and ignorance. It constitutes a firm and continuous reminder that the process of living together, when it is emancipated from oppressions and suppressions, becomes one of increasing faith in the humaneness of human beings; so that it becomes a constant growth of that kind of understanding of our relations to one another that expels fear, suspicion, and distrust.[45]

The circularity of Dewey's core liberal values and the democratic way of life suggest that, in spite of his view that facts properly faced and assessed alone point the way to arrive at value conclusions,[46] Dewey entered the fray of fact with quite an array of values already in hand. The deck out of which Dewey dealt his liberal-democratic values was constituted by none other than the liberal-democratic tradition itself.[47]

Niebuhr was certainly aware of the predicament surrounding these issues. In 1949, while writing on the problem of relating his own norm of agape to the relative demands of justice, Niebuhr commented on Dewey. He noted that

> the relativism of both the older romanticism and of modern pragmatism is [usually] only provisional. . . . John Dewey's pragmatism is quite innocent of the taint of moral cynicism which is frequently levelled at it . . . [Dewey] seems at times to believe that growth and development are themselves a norm to

which life may conform. "Since there is nothing in reality to which growth is relative save more growth," he declares, "there is nothing to which education is subordinate save more education. . . . The criterion of value in education is the extent to which it creates the desire for more growth." [*Democracy and Education*, pp. 60–62] Actually this confidence in growth as a norm of life is qualified by the belief that historical development moves in a particular direction. For Dewey the direction includes both freedom and justice. If one were to make a charge against modern evolutionary relativists it would be that they usually implicitly accept some version of the Christian norm which they explicitly deny.[48]

One might wish that Niebuhr had followed up this matter instead of mentioning Dewey almost incidentally in passing. Details are not given, but clearly Niebuhr, too, contended that Dewey came to his discussion of growth, education, and value with a stacked deck, and not in the strictly empirical manner Dewey would have had us believe. Given the broad and complex history of democracy, the values with which Dewey came armed were themselves an admixture of religious and secular values that entered into the fabric of the very democracy Dewey prized so highly.

Dewey not only saw democracy in moral terms, he also saw it in spiritual terms under his religious notion of a "common faith." The thrust of Dewey's humanistic naturalism, in an age in which traditional supernaturalistic faiths were becoming incredulous, focused on the community of living men and women. And while Dewey could wax eloquently on the fact that the "community of causes and consequences in which we, together with those not born, are enmeshed is the widest and deepest symbol of the mysterious totality of being the imagination calls the universe," it was actually the concrete communal life in which "all the significant achievements of men in science and art and all the kindly offices of intercourse and communication"[49] that occupied the true center of his religious vision. After all, in his credo of 1930, Dewey had confessed "I would suggest that the future of religion is connected with the possibility of developing a faith in the possibilities of human experience and human relationships that will create a vital sense of the solidarity of human interests and inspire action to make that sense a reality."[50]

The cosmic "matrix," as he called it, merely gave a residual, but quite sincere, religious sense of awe to the history of human life on the planet. In so doing it also suggested the very thing Niebuhr mentioned previously; namely, that somehow the core values of the human project are, for Dewey, connected to the very natural course of things. The real heart of Dewey's "common faith" was democracy itself seen as the set of conditions wherein the liberty and rationality so central to the values of the moral imagination could flourish and grow. The idea and ideal of democracy were the ultimate historical heritage, and the values democracy both expressed and promoted were ours to conserve, expand, and transmit. "Here," Dewey wrote in the closing lines of *A Common Faith* are "all the elements for a religious faith that shall not be confined to sect, class, or race. Such a faith has always been implicitly the common faith of mankind. It remains to make it explicit and militant."[51] It requires no great stretch of the imagination to link these closing lines of *A Common Faith* with the closing sentences of Dewey's *Liberalism and Social Action*, published only one year later, where he wrote:

> the cause of the liberty of the human spirit, the cause of opportunity of human beings for full development of their powers, the cause for which liberalism enduringly stands, is too precious and too ingrained in the human constitution to be forever obscured. Intelligence after millions of years of errancy has found itself as a method, and it will not be lost forever in the blackness of night. The business of liberalism is to bend every energy and exhibit every courage so that these precious goods may not even be temporarily lost but be intensified and expanded here and now.[52]

Niebuhr cautioned numerous times against making a religion out of democracy, focusing his objection on the failure of secular naturalism to adequately gauge the heights and depths of existence to which the traditional religions, Christian and non-Christian alike, had always attested. However, George Geiger was both intemperate and wrong when, in company with "the most pontifical of the new conservatives, Russell Kirk [and] in some of the more 'liberal' conservatives like Peter Viereck and Clinton Rossiter," he found Niebuhr to be "the apocalyptic source of the idea" that "the final weakness of the liberal is his religious dereliction."[53] Geiger's charge properly belonged to the litany of conservatives who endlessly appealed to religion as a mainstay of social stability. An even truer target for his arrows would have been the virulent coterie of reactionary Catholics who, in league with Mortimer Adler in the early 1940s, castigated and maligned Dewey not only for his irreligious humanism but also for the alleged totalitarian danger his type of secular humanism portended. Niebuhr, on the other hand, tended to focus largely on what he took to be the "political deficiencies" of Dewey's liberalism. Niebuhr, of course, did have religiously based criticism of humanistic naturalism, but he was not sanguine about the virtues of the religious tradition or unaware of the contributions of secular culture to the rise of modern democracy. As a result he was far too appreciative of the diversity of history's creative forces in general and the profound humanism of John Dewey in particular to preoccupy himself with the secular goblin of political and religious reactionaries.

Niebuhr strongly resisted those secular visions of life, including some advocates of democracy, who were prone to idolatrize the nation or values within the social processes. Without a more inclusive religious faith, Niebuhr believed, "we tend to identify our particular brand of democracy with the ultimate values of life," a tendency he saw as especially characteristic of American democracy.[54]

Of course, as Dewey, at worst, indulged only slightly in romanticizing democracy and not in idolatrizing the nation, Niebuhr's criticisms of Dewey's "religious" view of democracy centered on what Niebuhr regarded as his typically naturalistic myopia toward the deeper spiritual aspirations of human beings that, Niebuhr felt, no sociopolitical community could fully express or satisfy. Niebuhr knew that Dewey abhorred absolutes in the truth-telling activities of life just as Niebuhr himself spent much time resisting absolutistic claims within historic Christianity. This meant that Niebuhr refused to engage in the kinds of attacks leveled at Dewey by those who saw Dewey's version of secular naturalism to be a prima facie threat to democracy itself, or those who, like Mortimer Adler, the most uncompromising of that species of critic, took such criticism to absurd lengths.

Niebuhr's criticisms of the religionization of democracy were real and quite sincere. But his rather astute sense of the historical influences on democracy, not to mention his mutually respectful friendship with Deweyites such as Friess, Randall, and Hook (who vigorously defended both Dewey and himself against the odious charade of the Adlerites), meant that Niebuhr knew and respected the genuine democratic character of both Dewey and his political philosophy.

Niebuhr assiduously set himself apart from the polarized claims and counterclaims of those who either credited religion with the rise of democracy and saw secular thought as its undoing or who saw religion as democracy's nemesis and credited only secular forces with its emergence and preservation. In many instances he had dealt openly and judiciously with the mixed legacy of democratic thought and the relative strengths and weaknesses of both secular and religious sources within that convoluted history. In fact, on balance—because he was more open to the contributions of the secular tradition than Dewey was to the normative religious tradition—Niebuhr's record was better than Dewey's on this score. He noted at one point that

For a long time a debate has been waged between Christian and secular leaders on the question whether democracy is the product of the Christian faith or of a secular culture. The debate has been inconclusive because, as a matter or history, both Christian and secular forces were involved in establishing the political institutions of democracy; and the cultural resources of modern free societies are jointly furnished by both Christianity and modern secularism. Furthermore there are traditional non-democratic Christian cultures to the right of free societies which prove that the Christian faith does not inevitably yield democratic historical fruits. And there are totalitarian regimes to the left of free societies which prove that secular doctrine can, under certain circumstances, furnish grist for the mills of modern tyrannies. The debate is, in short, inconclusive because the evidence for each position is mixed.[55]

Because in Niebuhr's account the individual human being has its ultimate end in God, democracy or any other societal arrangement simply cannot meet the needs of the human spirit. Of equal importance, democracy as a religion, however rationally articulated, always flirts with the long-standing tradition of idolatrizing the state, the nation, or the community. Such a suggestion, of course, would make no strict *theo*logical sense to Dewey in light of the rationally based humanistic naturalism he offered. Nonetheless, sensitive naturalists such as Dewey and Hook surely understood the tendency of humankind to absolutize the relative.

Whereas Dewey was always trying to play down or deflate religion (but not the "religious"), Niebuhr was ever aware of its potency in life. Dewey wished to transform religion into a very manageable affair based on the rationality of science coextensive with the idealized "common faith" of democratic life. Dewey's rather tepid ideal of religion led him to see no special difficulty in identifying religion with the democratic way of life. His nice compartmentalization between religion in its dogmatic-authoritarian past and the "religious" in its liberated and liberating future, might well have blinded him to the full gravity of one of Niebuhr's warnings; namely, that "As politics deals with the proximate ends of life, and religion with ultimate ones, it is always a source of illusion if the one is simply invested with the sanctity of the other."[56] It was quite clear to Niebuhr that, given the fury of secular religions in the modern world, such a warning was just as apropos in the twentieth century as it ever was in the past.

Although Niebuhr's work did deal with what Gordon Harland described as "the cultural formulations and conditions for the proper functioning of democracy,"[57] his writings on democracy neither were as expansive as Dewey's nor did they celebrate the glories of democracy as a way of life. Whereas one might wish Niebuhr had dealt more expansively with the conditions for democracy, it is both unfair and inaccurate to suggest, as Robert Westbrook did, that Niebuhr's shortcoming was that his "argument for democracy . . . was not only . . . shortsighted as a description of American society, but that, as an ideal, it stripped democracy of most of its moral implications and reduced it to little more than a mechanical equilibrium of power."[58] It is unfair because Niebuhr's reassessment of democracy was never intended as an overall "description of American society." Westbrook's remark is inaccurate to the extent that even a cursory reading of Niebuhr shows that his discussions of the equilibrium of power as an essential ingredient of justice did not strip "democracy of most of its moral implications."[59]

Niebuhr's reflections on democracy rested upon two dominant anthropological motifs: first, an attempt to affirm both the indeterminate heights of the individual's self-transcending freedom and the inordinate depths of its corruption of that freedom; and, second, a lifelong effort to apply the norm of love (agape) to the historical and political task of achieving justice, a task whose outlines were already taking form in *Moral Man and Immoral Society*.[60] In working through these motifs against the backdrop of both cynical and romantic conceptions of democracy, Niebuhr cautioned against a too grandiose vision of democracy's historical possibilities. He pointed instead to the ironic fact that the very freedom so characteristic of viable democratic societies has made "for a fortunate confusion in defining the goal towards which history should move; and the distribution of power in a democracy prevents any group of world savers from grasping after a monopoly of power."[61] As an antidote to a tendency to idealize democracy, Niebuhr emphasized what he saw to be the pragmatic virtue of democracy as "a method of finding proximate solutions for insoluble problems."[62] He saw that the problems of adjudicating between the requirement of order and the need for justice in community were perennial ones, thus belying any permanent solutions. There is at least a modicum of irony in the fact that Niebuhr was the one who stressed the pragmatic note of "proximate solutions for insoluble problems" while Dewey, the instrumentalist, would devote so much energy to providing a devotional rhetoric for democracy!

In the context of his effort to relate love and justice, however, Niebuhr quite consistently saw the struggle of democracy to balance power in moral terms. In relation to a discussion of international problems in 1959, he urged that

> The educational enterprise for this nation, in short, must include a thorough re-examination of the problems of political

morality, which will help the new generation to understand that any consideration of power and interest in analyzing the peace within a nation and among the nations need not be a cynical defiance of the moral order but can well be what responsible statesmanship has always been: an effort to coerce competitive and contradictory human aspirations and interests into some kind of tolerable order and justice. Such a task is a highly moral one.[63]

Although the anthropological basis of Niebuhr's analysis of democracy and power politics had profound "moral implications," he did, indeed, focus his attention more narrowly on certain deficiencies within American liberal-democratic faith. From Niebuhr's standpoint the very last thing a defense of democracy required in its embattled position between internal bourgeois liberal illusions and external denunciations by cynical fascists, utopian Marxists, or disillusioned radicals was another ritual celebration and reassertion of the type of sentimental idealism that had been so thoroughly discredited by contemporary history. The pressing need, as Niebuhr saw it, was to launch a rigorous critique of those very creeds and illusions on which the traditional defense of democracy had come to rest and then provide a more realistic vindication of democracy against idealists and cynics alike. In this endeavor the judgment of Arthur Schlesinger, Jr., seems quite correct when he claimed that in showing "that the refutation by history of democratic illusions need not turn into a refutation of democracy," Niebuhr did effect a "penetrating reconstruction of the democratic faith."[64]

Niebuhr knew full well that "democracy in the West is both a political system and a way of life. It requires a high degree of literacy among its citizens, a sense of the dignity of the individual but also a sense of his responsibility to a wider community than [the] family."[65] Along with Dewey, Niebuhr held that democracy embodied broad fundamental values that gave fuller expression to the self's *humanitas* than alternative political systems. As he once put it, "ideally democracy is a permanently valid form of social and political organization which does justice to two dimensions of human existence: to man's spiritual stature and his social character; to the uniqueness and variety of life, as well as to the common necessities of all men."[66] As a form of social organization that maximizes liberty, the relative freedom of its social and political life corresponds to, and allows for, the endless elaboration of individual and collective vitalities that rise "in indeterminate degree over all social and communal concretions of life."[67]

Democracy, for Niebuhr, was both the fruit and cause of religiocultural pluralism. Historically, as he put it, "The new wine of humanistic science, of autonomous national cultures and of religious sectarianism could no longer be contained in the old bottles."[68] The democracies learned, in part by the force of events of which they were the product and in part as a sign of developing political wisdom, to understand that "the more imagination develops, the more it becomes possible and necessary to allow life to express itself variously within one community."[69] There was a reverse side to this, however, a side to which idealist interpreters of the democratic way of life failed to do justice. For, although the "indeterminate creativity" of human life "validates the idea of a free or democratic society, which refuses to place premature checks upon human vitalities," it is equally the case that the "destructive possibilities of these vitalities prove democracy to be a more difficult achievement than is usually supposed."[70] In effect, because of the "peril of disharmony" stemming from such vitalities, "democracy must find a way of allowing them to express themselves without destroying the unity and life of the community."[71] Niebuhr was thus ever insistent that the "twin evils [of] tyranny and anarchy, represent the Scylla and Charybdis between which the frail bark of social justice [in a democracy] must sail."[72]

The major errors of modern democratic civilizations (particularly in the United States, which Niebuhr saw as the paradigm of bourgeois liberal culture) included both the extravagant individualism of liberal culture which gave rise to modern democracy and a touching faith that conflicting tensions between self-interest and the general interest were easily resolved. In the context of democratic history, the attempt of utilitarians to derive a sense of obligation from a hedonistic analysis of morals (wherein Bentham argued that the prudential wisdom of the egotist would serve wider interests than his own) was joined with the earlier notion of Adam Smith whereby the actions of the egotist were rendered harmless by virtue of the control of the "invisible hand" of natural law (whether Nature's law or God's law was of little account). As a result the ideological bent of laissez-faire political philosophy, when it was not overtly committed to the survivalist doctrines of social Darwinism, was covertly wrapping its own inordinate self-interest in the tenuous reasoning of these liberal attempts to explain away or deny the force of self-interest in human communities. The consequence, Niebuhr noted, was an encouragement of "an unrestrained expression of human greed at the precise moment in history when an advancing industrialism required more, rather than less, moral and political restraint upon economic forces."[73]

The problem endemic to liberal thought was twofold. In addition to an unwillingness to adequately gauge the power of self-interest, the liberal tradition was also "unconscious of the corruption of self-interest in all ideal achievements and pretensions of human culture,"[74] most especially of liberal idealists themselves. Given this fact, Niebuhr could ironically point out "how much more plausible and dangerous the corruption of the good can be in human history than explicit evil."[75] Thus "democracy as a political system," Niebuhr wrote, "is important precisely because liberalism as a culture . . . is fallacious and too optimistic" in "its interpretation of human nature."[76]

Taking the relatively harmless and "natural" limitation of the survival impulse "as the normative form" of the egoistic drive in human nature, liberal democratic culture failed to see that "the most significant distinction between the human and the animal world is that the impulses of the former are 'spiritualized' in the human world."[77] Niebuhr saw this "spiritualization" of the survival impulse as illustrative of the self's capacity for both good and evil. This "spiritualization" takes two forms. First, there is the "will-to-live" or "will-to-live-truly" that embodies "the desire to fulfill the potentialities of life and not merely to maintain its existence." This "will to self-realization" is complex precisely because the self is social, never completing itself in itself, but only in and through others. Thus "self-realization involves self-giving in relations to others" and is, therefore, profoundly paradoxical.[78] Second, the "will-to-power" or the "desire for power and glory" that moves human conflict involves something more than a competition between survival impulses. Indeed, the major historical contests of will, Niebuhr pointed out, are "conflicts of rival lusts and ambitions" rather than mere ventures of self-preservation.[79] The will-to-power places the individual

> more fundamentally in conflict with his fellow-man than democratic liberalism realizes. The fact he cannot realize himself, except in organic relation with his fellows, makes the community more important than bourgeois individualism understands. The fact that the two impulses, though standing in contradiction to each other, are also mixed and compounded with each other on every level of human life, makes the simple distinctions between good and evil, between selfishness and altruism, with which liberal idealism has tried to estimate moral and political facts, invalid. The fact that the will-to-power inevitably justifies itself in terms of the morally more acceptable will to realize man's true nature means that the egoistic corruption of universal ideals is a much more persistent fact in human conduct than any moralistic creed is inclined to admit.[80]

The transmutation of the survival impulse is indicative of the fact that "man is at variance with himself."[81] Niebuhr's recurring approval of the Pauline insight that "the good which I would do, I do not, and the evil which I would not do, that I do" was often cited as the source of a more profound insight into the ambiguities of human virtue than was recognized in the more rationalistic ethical traditions from Plato to Dewey. The "spiritual" character of the self's variance with its neighbor went all the way down, for Niebuhr, affecting the self in its unity and totality. It was not merely a conflict between rationality and vitality or between science and tradition. Moreover, because of the indeterminate freedom of the self, the capacity for good and evil was present on every level of individual and historical development. Consequently, Niebuhr's themes of the permanent ambiguity of history and of history's indeterminate possibilities were, as Langdon Gilkey pointed out, directed primarily against "humanistic groups who counted on man's developing reason, enshrined in cumulative techniques and progressing institutions, to eradicate man's inhumanity to man."[82]

Although the evidence for Dewey's relationship to this excessively optimistic view of history is somewhat mixed, the enthusiastic manner in which he tended to identify scientific and evolutionary attitudes led him to portray historical possibilities in at least quasi-utopian terms— terms that often overwhelmed Dewey's otherwise haunting reservations about the human project. Wilson Carey Williams went so far as to say that "Faith in history, the old creed of progress, was central to all his thought, and it was to validate that faith that Dewey appealed to the metaphor of 'evolution,' the battlecry of reform Darwinism."[83] At minimum Dewey, as R. Alan Lawson noted, "did not forecast Utopianism, but he denied that there were any impassible barriers blocking the way."[84]

As he attempted to rethink democracy in relation to liberal tradition, Niebuhr's central conviction was "that democracy has a more compelling justification and requires a more realistic vindication than it is given by the liberal culture with which it has been associated in modern history."[85] In effect, "it has become important to save what is valuable in democratic life from the destruction of what is false in bourgeois civilization," and that requires distinguishing "what is false in democratic theory from what is true in democratic life."[86] The urgency of this task gave quite a different coloration to Niebuhr's and Dewey's respective agendas with regard to both what was involved in the reconstruction of liberalism and what was to have priority in addressing the nature and prospect of democracy. Because Dewey's and Niebuhr's understanding of human nature differed, their respective democratic accents would differ accordingly. The crisis within democracy as Niebuhr saw it came on the side of its political philosophy and not so much on the side of democracy as an extended "way of life." In fact, on another level, various defective elements within democracy conceived as a "way of life" had become so thoroughly romanticized in the liberal psyche that they had placed the wisdom of democracy as a political philosophy in serious jeopardy. For this very reason Niebuhr's radical critique of liberalism had placed at the center of democratic thought the particular aspect of democracy Dewey had consigned to the sidelines; namely, "political democracy."[87]

The Niebuhrian Critique

To a large extent, Niebuhr argued, "democratic civilization has been built . . . by foolish children of light"[88]—the metaphor *children of light* used paradigmatically to refer to "those who believe that self-interest should be brought under the discipline of a higher law—as opposed to history's "children of darkness" whose moral cynicism knows "no law beyond their will and interest."[89] The foolishness of the "foolish children of light" consisted of their tendency to overestimate the innocence and, therefore, underestimate the perniciousness of self-interest, both in the world around them and, most especially, among themselves. Although the "children of light" can be said to be "good" because of their belief in something more normative than self-interest, they suffered from sentimentality and foolishness. Although judged to be "evil" because they knew no law or norm beyond the law of self-interest, Niebuhr saw the "children of darkness" as nonetheless wiser than the "children of light" for more accurately gauging the power of self-will. The democratic prospect required that the *democratic* "children of light" learn the wisdom of the "children of darkness" without yielding to its dangerous cynicism. In effect, Niebuhr wanted the "children of light" to "know the power of self-interest in human society without giving it moral justification," stating that this wisdom must be theirs "in order that they may beguile, deflect, harness, and restrain self-interest, individual and collective, for the sake of the community."[90]

The "wave of boundless social optimism" that ushered in the modern age conferred on the most divergent forms of modern secular thought the common feature of having rejected the "Christian doctrine of original sin." In the autobiographical section of one of his last books, Niebuhr, looking back on his Gifford Lectures, acknowledged what he described as the "unpardonable pedagogical error" in defining "the persistence and universality of man's self-regard as 'original sin'" because of his own "theological preoccupation."[91] The error, however, was due to the inability of a thoroughly secular age to grasp the "realism" in the religious myth instead of stumbling over the mythic language. The realism so important to properly gauging political life, for Niebuhr, lay in the recognition that injustice was rooted in the destructive force of inordinate self-love that, along with human creativity, stemmed from the self's finite freedom.[92] For all the mythological trappings and for the fact that, however stated, the doctrine "will always be an offense to rationalists,"[93] Niebuhr did not yield in his conviction of the measure of truth in the judgment, as the *London Times Literary Supplement* had once put it, that "the doctrine of original sin is the only empirically verifiable doctrine of the Christian faith."[94]

What might at best be verifiable, of course, was not the doctrinal content or interpretation of "original sin," much less its myriad associations of belief. Rather the character of individual and social existence to which the religious symbol pointed, exclusive of the religious panoply affiliated with the doctrine, was what Niebuhr held to be validated by experience. (This distinction must be made so long as one recognizes that for Niebuhr, the biblical interpretation of such "truths" about life was more profound than alternative interpretations, and the validation of that interpretation within experience was seen by Niebuhr as a "negative" validation of faith itself.) Nonetheless, for Niebuhr in both religious and secular sources "the force and danger of self-interest in human affairs are too obvious to remain long obscure to those who are not blinded by either theory or interest to see the obvious."[95] Earlier on Niebuhr had urged that

> it is necessary to point out that the doctrine makes an important contribution to any adequate social and political theory the lack of which has robbed bourgeois theory of real wisdom; for it emphasizes a fact which every page of human history attests. Through it one may understand that no matter how wide the perspectives which the human mind may reach, how broad the loyalties which the human imagination may conceive, how universal the community which human statecraft may organize, or how pure the aspirations of the saintliest idealists may be, there is no level of human moral or social achievement in which there is not some corruption of inordinate self-love.[96]

According to Niebuhr, Christianity contends "that men are egotists in contradiction to their essential nature. This is the doctrine of original sin stripped of literalistic illusions."[97] Involved here is the view that both love, which is the law of life, and self-love, which is a violation of that law, speak more radically and truly about the heights and depths of existence (the grandeur and misery of man, in the Pascalian terms Niebuhr appreciated so much) than is normally portrayed in secular thought. Whereas Niebuhr saw the vertical dimension of sin between the self and God in terms of idolatry, he identified the horizontal dimension of sin "between man and man," to borrow Martin Buber's phrase, in terms of injustice. Both dimensions were expressions of the self's tendency to center all things in itself.

Like Dewey, Niebuhr held that a generality such as this does not explain, or suffice as an immediate cause of, any specific evil. But, unlike Dewey, he held that this general tendency should be taken seriously to exercise sufficient realism in dealing with specific evils and injustices. It was crucial to comprehend this general tendency lest what we might like to believe about ourselves and our fellows came to govern our assessment of the actual realities of the collective life with which political wisdom must contend.[98]

At the same time, the fact that Niebuhr felt so duty bound by the temper of his times to bring to the foreground of democratic reconstruction arguments in support of political realism ought not to obscure his awareness of the fact that democracy, as such, was a rejection of a too pessimistic view of human nature. He always strove to keep a balance between unjustifiable extremes in this regard, consistent with his usual dialectical approach. "The achievements of democratic societies refuted this pessimism," he wrote,

> and with it the purely negative conception of the relation of government and systems of justice to the ideal of brotherhood. History reveals adjustments of interest without the interposition of superior coercive force to be possible within wide limits. The capacity of communities to synthesize divergent approaches to a common problem and to arrive at a tolerably just solution proves man's capacity to consider interests other than his own. Nevertheless, the fact that a synthesis of conflicting interests and viewpoints is not easy, and may become impossible under certain conditions, is a refutation of a too simple trust in the impartial character of reason. It would be as false to regard rules and principles of justice, slowly elaborated in collective experience, as merely the instruments of the sense of social obligation, as to regard them merely as tools of egoistic interest.[99]

The real value of democracy is its realism, not its idealism. Or to put it in a more accurate way, both its realism and idealism are important, but only insofar as democratic idealism is tempered by its realism. In this sense democratic realism is seen in the context of a highly qualified idealism that overcomes the ever-present tendency of a too consistent realism to embrace cynicism. Niebuhr's strong belief that a realistic correction of democratic liberal idealism was *the* pressing requirement of the times runs through his writings on democracy. And, just as he might not have done justice to Dewey's many insights into democracy as a way of life, Niebuhr perhaps should have articulated more fully than he did his basic agreement with the nexus in Dewey's writings between liberal idealism and democracy. The reason that Niebuhr did not deem it necessary—or even wise—to recount in his own writings the traditional liberal benefits of democracy (which no doubt Dewey, better than all others, had so brilliantly articulated) was that the mood of the time called for a correction of the exaggeration of liberal idealism.

Although Niebuhr emphasized the balance of power as an essential ingredient for the achievement of justice in political life, his notion of "balancing" was far more extensive and complex an activity than sometimes acknowledged. This complexity is evidenced in his oft-quoted aphorism that "man's capacity for justice makes democracy possible; but man's inclination to injustice makes democracy necessary."[100] The balance Niebuhr insisted on, as Gordon Harland pointed out, affirmed that the self's "moral and rational capacities" were every bit as essential to making "a democratic system of government possible" as "the corruptions of interest and passion" were in rendering it necessary for the viability of a just society.[101] Niebuhr argued that the self does, indeed, have a

> capacity for transcendence over self-interest. . . . If there were not, any form of social harmony among men would be impossible; and certainly a democratic version of such harmony would be quite unthinkable. But the same man who displays this capacity also reveals varying degrees of the power of self-interest and of the subservience of the mind to these interests. Sometimes this egotism stands in frank contradiction to the professed ideal or sense of obligation to higher and wider values; and sometimes it uses the ideal as its instrument.[102]

In Niebuhr's extensive discussions of democracy, his emphasis fell more heavily on the side of the aphorism that stated "man's inclination to injustice makes democracy necessary," thus stressing the importance of the structural elements within the democratic process. Dewey, on the other hand, seemed to have emphasized the other side of the Niebuhrian aphorism, that "man's capacity for justice makes democracy possible." That is to say, whereas both Niebuhr and Dewey valued democracy because it allowed human beings to realize their greatest potentialities, Dewey placed overwhelming emphasis on the rational and self-directing aspects made possible and endlessly encouraged by a democratic society. Indeed, for Dewey, the character of human beings had priority in any discussion of democracy precisely because such character is the sine qua non of democracy itself. Niebuhr did not deny this, as he had acknowledged in asserting that "man's capacity for justice makes democracy possible." But because he appreciated, far more than Dewey, "man's inclination to injustice," he placed heavy emphasis on those democratic structures that mitigate the tendencies toward injustice.

Democracy had inestimable value for Niebuhr precisely because it took this life-rending fact of egotism seriously and fashioned ways of controlling its deleterious effects. At the same time, democracy, as Niebuhr saw it, should strike a balance between controlling self-interest and giving as much latitude as possible to the interplay of such interests. On this matter, Niebuhr wrote:

> a free society derives general profit from the interested desires of particular groups, each group leaving a deposit of virtue in the community beyond its intentions and interests. The health and justice of the community is preserved, not so much by the discriminate judgement of the whole community as by the effect of free criticism in moderating the pretensions of every group and by the weight of competing power in balancing power which might become inordinate and oppressive. Democracy in short is not a method which is effective only among virtuous men. It is a method which prevents interested men from following their interests to the detriment of the community. For if groups and individuals merely pursue their interests without a measure of self-restraint, no political restraint, short of a tyrannical and oppressive one, could preserve the unity of the community. Hobbes' proposals for order through despotism are mistaken in assuming a consistency of self-interest which is not apparent in human history. Men do not follow their own interests consistently in defiance of the community. They do however interpret the interests of the community with a reason tainted by considerations of their own interests.[103]

Niebuhr saw the need for a balancing of power as one of the genuine insights of democratic realism. In fact, the measure of realism involved in emphasizing the need for a greater equilibrium of power in society showed that the degree of "our success in establishing justice and issuing domestic tranquility has exceeded the characteristic insights of a bourgeois culture."[104] In his Gifford Lectures Niebuhr wrote that

> all historical forms of justice and injustice are determined to a much larger degree than pure rationalists or idealists realize by the given equilibrium or disproportion within each type of

power and by the balance of various types of power in a given community. It may be taken as axiomatic that great disproportions of power lead to injustice, whatever may be the efforts to mitigate it. Thus the concentration of economic power in modern technical society has made for injustice, while the diffusion of political power has made for justice. The history of modern democratic-capitalistic societies is on the whole determined by the tension between these two forms of power.[105]

Niebuhr was here focusing on the fact that our liberal culture, born out of a struggle with feudal oppression, had come early on to a certain wisdom regarding the need to diffuse and control political power. In effect, our liberal culture has had little problem grasping the relationship between liberty and justice in a democratic society. But the liberal culture, as both Niebuhr and Dewey knew so well, was late in coming to a recognition of the threat to justice posed by excessive concentrations of power in the economic arena. The fact that justice required greater equality in the economic sphere was at the heart of the "social" democracy both Niebuhr and Dewey strenuously urged against the libertarianism of laissez-faire which, for a variety of reasons, consistently failed to bring democratic insights into the heart of economic life.

Niebuhr saw human brotherhood imperiled by the fact that there was an imperial force of will as well as perennial conflicts of interest. Efforts to establish an equilibrium of powers and vitalities in human communities were the most effective ways of controlling the will to dominate by those whose inordinate power always threatened to enslave the weak. Niebuhr's reference to "powers and vitalities" here was necessarily general, as the specific powers and vitalities at issue would change with the fortunes of the times. This is important to recognize in order to understand that "equilibrium," as Niebuhr used it, was not a static or terminal concept in the sense that *an* equilibrium could finally be arrived at. Rather, he understood the situation to be a process and therefore the terms and requirements for a just equilibration of power in democratic society was forever changing. For Niebuhr justice in a democratic society was linked to the constant need to forge an equilibrium of power by a variety of means including the interplay of self-interest as well as by judicial and legislative redress. This was the sine qua non for serious deliberations about the nature and possibility of justice and, therefore, about the special value of democracy itself. He insisted that

Without a tolerable equilibrium no moral or social restraints ever succeed completely in preventing injustice and enslavement. In this sense an equilibrium of vitality is an approximation to brotherhood within the limits of conditions imposed by human selfishness. But an equilibrium of power is not brotherhood. The restraint of the will-to-power of one member of the community by the counter-pressure of power by another member results in a condition of tension. All tension is covert or potential conflict.[106]

Although Niebuhr believed that the excessive optimism of the social liberals had continually underestimated the realities of power and self-interest in the quest for democratic justice, he saw that there were two fundamental limitations to a too consistent emphasis on the balance of power. First of all, while he regarded the equilibration of power to be absolutely essential for any meaningful justice, "justice without love," Niebuhr insisted, "is merely the balance of power."[107] Justice, in Niebuhr's view, "is the approximation to brotherhood under the conditions of sin,"[108] and its relationship to love is a dialectical one in which the ideal of love (agape) is both approximated and contradicted by even the highest attainments of social justice. In Niebuhr's account,

> Love is thus the end term of any system of morals. It is the moral requirement in which all schemes of justice are fulfilled and negated. They are fulfilled because the obligation of life to life is more fully met in love than is possible in an scheme of equity and justice. They are negated because love makes an end of the nicely calculated less and more of structures of justice. It does not carefully arbitrate between the needs of the self and of the other, since it meets the needs of the other without concern for the self.[109]

The normativity of love delineated in the context of a transcendental theology was Niebuhr's "ideal." But because he did not understand love in sentimental terms, his ideal was never articulated idealistically. This is evident in his lifelong struggle with the relationship between love and justice. Niebuhr, as Gordon Harland point out, did "not define justice because it has no independent basis." Justice, for Niebuhr, "is the relative embodiment of *agape* in the structures of society."[110] Although the "ideal" of heedless sacrificial love may find its approximation in extremely rare acts of individual life, it is not directly applicable to the collective life. Much of liberal Christianity's discomfort with the balancing of interests and claims in collective life rested with its recognition that the calculations of interests essential to social justice fell short of the ideal of love. But to sever love from justice, in Niebuhr's account, was to consign love to sentimentality and justice to a mere balance of power. Instead, Niebuhr saw love as representative of the higher possibilities of justice itself, a vantage point from which both the normativity of justice as a calculation of interests can be rejected and the limitations of any historical system of justice can be recognized. All schemes of justice that necessarily assume the presence and power of self-interest are prevented from conceiving self-interest as normative only when it is realized that the highest justice stands under the critical perspective of agape as norm. Love, therefore, fulfills justice in leaving men and women dissatisfied with the finality of any system of justice and in reminding them that the needs of the other are met only in his or her uniqueness and freedom, beyond the boundaries of their best efforts to establish equity. At the same time, a love that seeks relevance to the realities of collective life demands justice. In Niebuhr's view, as Harland put it, "justice is not alien to love, it is love making its way in the world" in the sense that love "prompts us to seek ever wider and more inclusive structures of justice." In essence, as Harland went on the say, for Niebuhr "one simply cannot say that he is concerned that love may be expressed but not concerned with politics, economics, laws, and customs. To be unconcerned for the achievement of more equal justice is to deny the claims of love. Justice is the embodiment of love in complex human relations."[111]

The fact that Niebuhr saw a dialectical relationship between love and justice reveals the extent to which his sociopolitical thought was rooted in his theological reflections. But at the same time, because his theological orientation led him to conclude that self-love had become the operative fact of life, Niebuhr's analysis of the relationship between love and justice was realistic, not idealistic. The problem of power, and not a trust in benevolence, is the central reality for achieving justice in history. Nonetheless, as the transcendent norm, agape stands in critical judgment on all structures of justice.

The second limitation Niebuhr saw in a too consistent doctrine of the balance of power is seen in his views as to the need for government itself. Because of the vast and complex balances of power on the social level, the conflicts and tensions within such balances led Niebuhr to conclude that "a balance of power is in fact a kind of managed anarchy."[112] Therefore, the principle of government as "an organizing center within a given field of social vitalities" was on a "higher plane of moral sanction and social necessity than the balance of power."[113] The social forces of equilibrium were, in themselves, insufficient—revealing the terminus of pure balance of power in conflict and anarchy. Not only was there the obvious fact that the powers and vitalities within society did not automatically achieve an equitable balance, but also that the very centers of vitality were, in the extreme, inimical to the order essential to any society. According to Niebuhr,

Human society therefore requires a conscious control and manipulation of the various equilibria which exist in it. There must be an organizing centre within a given field of social vitalities. This centre must arbitrate conflicts from a more impartial perspective than is available to any party of a given conflict; it must manage and manipulate the processes of mutual support so that the tensions inherent in them will not erupt into conflict; it must coerce submission to the social process by superior power whenever the instruments of arbitrating and composing conflict do not suffice; and finally it must seek to redress the disproportions of power by conscious shifts of the balances whenever they make for injustice.[114]

Niebuhr was not here advocating what he took to be the erroneous features of "rational planning" as social science engineers would have it. Characteristic of the engineering model of "planning" were not just the obvious notions that "organizing" was required in the function of governments, or that "wisdom" should be operative in political life, or that a measure of impartiality can be achieved by the fact of distance from the interested parties. It was, rather, the creed of a scientifically objective and disinterested intelligence that could blueprint long-range goals. As Niebuhr saw it,

Modern culture in its various forms feels certain that, if men could be sufficiently objective or disinterested to recognize the injustice or excessive self-interest, they could also in time transfer the objectivity of their judgments as observers of the human scene to their judgments as actors and agents in human history. This is an absurd notion which every practical statesman or man of affairs knows how to discount because he encounters ambitions and passions in his daily experience, which refute the regnant modern theory of potentially innocent men and nations.[115]

Both Dewey and Niebuhr knew how complex and contextual the issue of justice was. They both polemicized against the libertarian ideology of the business classes and knew that the period of the 1930s demanded a clear emphasis on greater equality as the mark of a just order. Dewey had stressed the fact that liberty was no abstract ideal, but was rather "effective power to do specific things" and, as such, was "always a matter of the *distribution* of powers that exists at [a given] time."[116] Because liberty had only a contextual meaning in relation to others, Dewey argued that the "relativity of liberty to the existing distribution of powers of action . . . means necessarily that wherever there is liberty at one place there is restraint at some other place. *The system of liberties that exist at any time is always the system of restraints or controls that exist at that time.*[117] Given the historical context in which he was then writing, Dewey insisted that, precisely because "liberty is always a *social* question," there was a pressing need "to bring about a changed distribution of power . . . such that there would be a more balanced, a more equal, even, and equitable system of human liberties."[118] Following up on this thesis two months later, Dewey argued that the only reason the combination of "equality and liberty as coordinate ideals" in early modern democracy had recently been judged as fundamentally incompatible was because they were couched in "a highly formal and limited concept of liberty."[119] Dewey concluded:

> The democratic ideal that unites equality and liberty is, on the one hand, a recognition that actual and concrete liberty of opportunity and action is dependent upon equalization of the political and economic conditions under which individuals are alone free *in fact,* not *in some abstract metaphysical way.* The tragic breakdown of democracy is due to the fact that the identification of liberty with the maximum of unrestrained individualistic action in the economic sphere, under the institutions of capitalistic finance, is as fatal to the realization of liberty for all as it is fatal to the realization of equality. It is destructive of liberty for the many precisely because it is destructive of genuine equality of opportunity.[120]

Niebuhr was in basic agreement with Dewey on this particular point, although the way he chose to express the issues revealed at least a different emphasis. Niebuhr came to regard both liberty and equality as essential elements for a proper understanding of democratic justice. He pointed out that, in abstraction, liberty carried to its logical end subverts equality, and conversely, equality taken to its logical extreme subverts liberty. That is to say, if an individual or interest group is free to pursue its ends without restraint, its cunning and power will accentuate the problem of inequality. Thus it was, he pointed out, that "liberty" became the understandable ideology of the "haves" as opposed to the "have nots." Conversely, "equality" was identified with justice among the "have nots" for obvious reasons. However, just as unbridled liberty exacerbates the problem of inequality, so too an attempt to impose full equality must sacrifice liberty in the process. Niebuhr came to the view that just as liberty must be curbed by governmental action for the sake of equality, so also must liberty be preserved for the sake of opposing the tyranny of government. A balance here is the perennial task and problem of justice in a democratic society.

Niebuhr regarded liberty and equality as regulative principles of justice. His view was that "every community is organized through a hierarchy of authority and function, and its forces of cohesion contain such non-voluntary and sub-rational forces as kinship feeling, geographic contiguity, common memories and common fears, and ultimately the police power of the state, the community's chief organ of unity and will." Therefore, it is crucial to understand that "the principle of 'equality' is a relevant criterion of criticism for the social hierarchy, and the principle of 'liberty' serves the same purpose for the community's unity. But neither principle could be wholly nor absolutely applied without destroying the community."[121]

Both Dewey and Niebuhr recognized that, because equality is a crucial dimension of justice, an equilibrium of power between groups (Madison's self-interested factions) is an essential component in the quest for justice in society. (Here, however, it should be remembered that because Niebuhr stressed the intransigence of self-love and Dewey accented the possibilities of rational accord, Niebuhr placed far more emphasis on struggle and conflict in achieving this equilibrium.) Because both men knew that such equilibrium was neither automatic nor permanently assured in history, they were committed to the positive role of government in the endless task of promoting the equilibrium of power.

Niebuhr, however, stressed far more than Dewey the fact that the unifying force of community was part of the problem. In other words, government itself was morally ambiguous. Justice, in Niebuhr's view, required equality because the inordinate inequalities of power and privilege that accrued to the powerful and the privileged were far in excess of the unavoidable inequalities of function. At the same time, justice also required liberty because of the tendency of the necessary sources of unity and stability in human communities to supress dissent as well as resist the presence of independent centers of power in the society at large. Niebuhr, in effect, followed the pluralistic instincts of James Madison, who, although acknowledging the need for a "well constructed Union [to] break and control the violence of faction," nonetheless rejected efforts to cure the "mischiefs of faction" by either "destroying liberty which is essential to its existence [or] by giving to every citizen the same opinions, the same passions, and the same interests."[122] Thus, while emphasizing equity and fairness in an essentially libertarian culture, Niebuhr simultaneously insisted on the connection between liberty and justice over against the tendencies toward both governmental tyranny and totalitarian conformism. Robin Lovin pointed to a dimension in Niebuhr's "conception of the state and its relationship to human dignity" that he called the "paradigm of liberty," a paradigm that Lovin claimed

> begins with the premise that liberty, however it may be defined politically, is not in the first instance a political creation. Liberty begins with the freedom of consciousness to take a distance on the natural limitations that bind it, and on the historical conditions that surround it. Political liberty is grounded in self-transcendence, in the human ability to envision possibilities that differ from present reality and the capacity for goal-oriented patterns of action that do not merely repeat the instincts. The freedom of self-transcendence may be limited by ignorance; it may be stifled by repression, confined by a primitive community, or narcotized by complacency; but it can never fully disappear.[123]

Lovin correctly pointed to this prepolitical sense of self-transcendent freedom. It is also clear that Niebuhr's political application of this freedom in his discussion of liberty and the vitalities of community were not romantically conceived. Fraught with both the creative and destructive possibilities of human life, liberty needs to be constrained. At the same time Niebuhr held fast to the notion that a significant measure of political liberty and its resultant social pluralism were utterly essential to a *just* order. This is precisely why the real genius of democracy is that it deliberately and wisely aims at a balance between liberty and order in its constant quest for justice.

Niebuhr's view of liberty and equality as regulative principles of justice would prohibit him from giving either one a priority abstracted from a specific set of historical conditions. The tendency of excessive liberty to result in anarchy meant, as James Madison knew so well, that democracy must revere governmental power and authority sufficient to the task of maintaining order. But because of the tendency of excessive order to result in tyranny, Madison knew equally well the other side of the democratic coin. He knew that a free society must also establish ways of checking and controlling governmental power because of the temptation of all centralized governing authority toward tyrannical domination.

Niebuhr saw that even more than this was involved in the wisdom of viable democracies. He knew that governments were revered in part because of their function as a source of order over the anarchic vitalities of social life. But precisely because Niebuhr held that social justice was the highest political aim of free societies, he saw that the "majesty" of government resided in its capacity and willingness to establish and maintain justice. As long as the goal of attaining justice was truly a part of government, then he could maintain that in a democracy the government's role in maintaining the cohesiveness of community against the ever-present forces of anarchy was generally acknowledged. Indeed, for Niebuhr, "the majesty of the state is legitimate in so far as it embodies and expresses both the authority and power of the total community over all its members, and the principle of order and justice as such against the peril of anarchy."[124]

At the same time, Niebuhr insisted," there are no historic expressions of the majesty of the state and government without an admixture of illegitimate pretensions of majesty and sanctity."[125] The moral ambiguity of government rests in the fact that those who rule often represent the dominating power of one element or faction of the entire community instead of the community as a whole. But even when this was not the case, Niebuhr contended, "government . . . would, if its pretensions were not checked, generate imperial impulses of its own towards the community."[126] Those who rule, after all, are inclined to see their particular scheme of order as universally valid and are thereby tempted to suppress the diverse and sometimes dissident voices in the community under the pretext of maintaining order. In other words the concentrations of power that governments justifiably possess to overcome anarchy and bring cohesive unity to any given community are themselves subject to "the sin of idolatry and pretension in which all government is potentially involved."[127]

Contrary to holding a stark and narrow view of the balance of power, Niebuhr found that "the whole development of democratic justice in human society has depended upon some comprehension of the moral ambiguities which inhere in both government and the principle of the equilibrium of power."[128] He insisted that

> It is the highest achievement of democratic societies that they embody the principle of resistance to government within the principle of government itself. The citizen is thus armed with "constitutional" power to resist the unjust exactions of government. He can do this without creating anarchy within the community, if government has been so conceived that criticism of the ruler becomes an instrument of better government and not a threat to government itself.[129]

With respect to the grounds Niebuhr laid out for "political democracy," Dewey's rational vision of the democratic "way of life" seemed viscerally offended by the hard realities of politics in spite of Dewey's occasional admissions that "power" politics was sometimes necessary. After all, these admissions were concessions to the intrusion of experience, but in the long run Dewey's political vision was one in which reason was expected increasingly to reign over such dirty business. Consequently, with respect to the balance of power and the hard task of give-and-take involved in partisan conflicts of interest within the democratic process, both *realistically* conceived and seen as perennial features of political life, Dewey, in many instances, seemed downright apolitical.

Dewey, in effect, underestimated the fact that "political life," as Niebuhr stated it in 1969, "is a semirational way of manipulating collective irrationalities."[130] Dewey's persistent failure to seriously acknowledge such facts and incorporate them into his political philosophy underlined liberal naivete and, in Niebuhr's judgment, continued to affect John Dewey's political thought even at its best.

Liberal democracies had been "too Lockean, rationalistic, and voluntaristic to understand that statesmanship must rely primarily on a rational manifestation of the subrational loyalties of men."[131] Fortunately, according to Niebuhr, "in America, the revolution . . . was . . . saved from Lockean principles, which were its original inspiration, not only by many historical factors but also by the thought of such moderate realists as James Madison, Alexander Hamilton, and John Adams."[132] Nonetheless, in its widespread assumption that intelligence could either be understood or practiced in relative isolation from such political realities, rationalistic liberals had disclosed their fundamentally apolitical orientation.[133] Political intelligence had to face what rationalists of all times and places had not wanted to face. It had to accept and accommodate itself to what Niebuhr often called the "organic" aspects of the self (its natural vitalities) and the social substance of human life (those nonrational aspects of communal history such as territory, ethnicity, and linguistic kinship and loyalties that operate as perennial sources of cohesion). In speaking of the difficulties in forging any type of transnational community Niebuhr reminded his readers

> that human communities are never purely artifacts of the human mind and will. Human communities are subject to "organic" growth. This means that they cannot deny their relation to "nature"; for the force of their cohesion is partly drawn from the necessities of nature (kinship, geography, etc.) rather than from the realm of freedom. Even when it is not pure nature but historic tradition and common experience which provides the cement of cohesion, the integrating force is still not in the realm of pure freedom or the fruit of pure volition. . . .
> All these matters are understood intuitively by practical

statesmen who know from experience that the mastery of historical destiny is a tortuous process in which powerful forces may be beguiled, deflected, and transmuted but never simply annulled or defied.[134]

Niebuhr saw the persistent rationalistic component in modern naturalism as a carryover from the excesses of the Enlightenment. Moreover, it even contained some of the assumptions of the classical dualism which, in Dewey's case at least, he had sought so rigorously to overcome. Niebuhr found it supremely ironic that Dewey, the evolutionary thinker so beholden to Darwinianism, should, above all others, have allowed his scientific rationalism to obscure the power of natural "organic" forces in the political life of human beings.

Yet there is a deeper issue in all of this that men such as Louis Hartz and Arthur Schlesinger, Jr., clearly identified—an issue that was taken up later by Wilson Carey Williams and, even more recently, by Christopher Lasch. Hartz pointed to the paradox of liberty and conformity in the American liberal tradition. He saw "the basic ethical problem of a liberal society" to be "the danger of unanimity which has slumbered unconsciously behind" the alleged danger of the majority, a danger de Toqueville called the "tyranny of opinion." He claimed that "at the bottom of the American experience of freedom, not in antagonism to it but as a constituent element of it, there has always lain the inarticulate premise of conformity," concluding that "the ironic flaw in American liberalism lies in the fact that we have never had a real conservative tradition."[135]

In much the same vein Schlesinger pointed out that the "sense of urgency" with which Dewey, in the 1930s, saw the need to subject American corporate life to social direction "led him even to belittle his old faith in individual freedom and political debate." Schlesinger then cited various remarks Dewey made near the end of Part II of *Liberalism and Social Action* to the effect that

> "the idea that the conflict of parties will, by means of public discussion, bring out necessary public truths is a kind of political watered-down version of the Hegelian dialectic, with its synthesis arrived at by the union of antithetical conceptions. The method has *nothing* in common with the procedure of organized cooperative inquiry which has won the triumphs of science in the field of physical nature." Discussion and argument were "weak reeds to depend upon for systematic origination of comprehensive plans, the plans that are required if the problem of social organization is to be met." (Schlesinger's italics.)

Schlesinger then commented somewhat ruefullly, "If such views had grave implications for political freedom Dewey elided this by talking disparagingly of 'the formal concept of liberty' which would be replaced by genuine liberty once the new order had been won."[136]

Ten years earlier, in 1950, Horace Kallen, a man who felt deep admiration for Dewey's vision of democracy, expressed some concern over the issues of conformity and coercion that were later raised by Schlesinger. According to Kallen, Dewey's core religion—"the common faith of freed minds"—embodied the value of intelligence in such a manner as to judge freedom a nuisance in light of the harmony that could best be brought about by "unifying, organizing and controlling" such freedom. Kallen was put off by his judgment that, at bottom, if Dewey's humanism

> calls for a loyalty to our own being it does so conditionally, as a function of the nature in which we live and move and have our being. It assigns to that nature a certain providential harmony with the human creature which is one of its own multitudinous diversifications. It accents intelligence as the art of actualizing and amplifying this harmony in the works and ways of sharing experience and thus of transforming multitude into oneness, discord into peace and thereby mutual obstruction into facilitated liberty . . .[137]

More recently the specter of Dewey's democratic conformism was fronted directly by Wilson Carey Williams, in his massive work *The Idea of Fraternity in America*, published in 1973. Williams took the extreme viewpoint that in spite of his search for a "public" amidst the crisis of its "eclipse" by the forces of the modern industrial age, Dewey's vision of the "Great Community" left him without the very "public" for which he so ardently wished. "A believer in 'democracy,'" Williams claimed, "Dewey was no believer in the public. His confidence in democracy was more open to the 'process of experience' [and] it was *process*, rightly organized, that Dewey trusted, not the substantive decisions of men."[138] Dewey, according to Williams, had a comprehensive and unitive vision of the fraternal brotherhood and sisterhood of human beings such that he had to find a way to overcome the admitted tension between private and public roles. Williams's criticism, based on his reading of Dewey's *The Public and Its Problems*, is so fundamental that it is worthy of extended quotation. According to Williams,

> Dewey's prescription involved a radical change in the idea of constitutional government. Traditional constitutionalism had been based on the separation of an autonomous private

sphere from the area of public control. Dewey proposed what amounted in effect to the abolition of that autonomy. Since society—the sphere of private relations—was inseparably related to the state, Dewey argued for a political order able to construct the kind of private loyalties that would support, or at least not oppose, the advancement of the public good. In other words, the state should provide the individual with group memberships which would give him emotional security but be unable to offer parochial, short-sighted resistance to the course of events. Groups of this character, Dewey argued, would be compatible with order, change, and openness, with history and with the growth of loyalties which would gradually approximate the brotherhood of man. . . . All limited groups lacked, for Dewey, any value in themselves; they were worthy or undesirable insofar as they supported or opposed the course of history. Such groups were little more than a necessary concession to the emotional and intellectual weakness of man.

The control of modern society, the kind of planning which could realize the liberative potential that Dewey saw in modern technology and organization, required the commitment and devotion of a "great community," an "inclusive and fraternally associated public" in which each would feel himself bound to all by reciprocal ties of gratitude and obligation. And Dewey, no less than his liberal predecessors, was confident that such an increasingly broad fraternity was a possible goal. It was a necessary faith, for otherwise Dewey left himself open to the charge that his advocacy of manipulated private loyalties was logically a totalitarianism that would only drive men further into isolation and withdrawal.[139]

The only way to do justice to Dewey's original and oftimes brilliant reflections in *The Public and Its Problems* would be to provide a thorough and fair weighing of the diverse elements in his highly textured position. Such obligation cannot be met in the limited scope of this study. At minimum, however, it must be said that the extent to which Williams's point was a legitimate and worthwhile one, he made it in a highly exaggerated fashion—at least to the extent that he was unduly one-sided in his selection of the conflicting tendencies within Dewey's thought. Certainly his vision of Dewey's totalistic democratic conformism collides sharply with Westbrook's somewhat romantic version of Dewey as the most important participatory democrat of that period in history—a version that, although ignoring Williams altogether, presents us with another perspective.[140]

On balance it seems that there are conflicting tendencies in *The Public and Its Problems* and that Dewey was, on occasion, at cross purposes with himself. The virtue of Williams's analysis is that it points to a definite Rousseauean strain in Dewey's conception of the *Public*. In Dewey this strain lends itself to a conformist view of democracy in which boundaries and limits of government were glossed over, in which the distinction between private and public were obscured (within a legitimate effort to overcome the abstract dichotomy of "individual" and "social"), and in which personal freedom was subsumed under the freedom of the total personality realizable only in that commonly shared social world governed by the public-as-a-state; that is, within the province of those who are responsible for "the extensive and enduring consequences [accompanying "all modes of associated behavior"] which involve others beyond those directly engaged in them."[141] Dewey's vision of the Great Community emphasized the "perfecting of the means and ways of communication of meanings so that genuinely shared interest in the consequences of interdependent activities may inform desire and effort and thereby direct action."[142] The good that is the good for society in Dewey's vision of the "public" was so much a vision of the "common good" that it was embarrassed by all that resisted the shared values of Reason—values that all right-thinking men and women should eventually come to. Independent centers of power vying one with another out of conflicting self-interests, the recalcitrance of "factions" lacking a proper "public" vision, and individuals or groups who would go their own way without too much fervor to participate in the higher good enshrined in Dewey's vision of the public were outside the pale of genuine community. There are echoes here of Rousseau's scorn for the "will of all," which differs from the much desired "general will" insofar as its motivation is merely the coarse interests of diverse pressure groups, rather than in the morally superior and preeminently rational will that is an expression of the desire in each individual that only the common good be served—a desire unsullied by group affiliations.

Whatever the extent of Dewey's flirtation with Rousseauean tendencies toward totalitarian democracy, it is true that Niebuhr, rather than Dewey, insisted upon an understanding of justice inclusive of both liberty and equality. And by liberty Niebuhr meant something more than Dewey's notion of a "secure release and fulfillment of personal potentialities which take place only in a rich and manifold association with others: the power to be an individual self making a distinctive contribution and enjoying in its own way the fruits of association."[143] That is to say, Niebuhr's view of political liberty, although with respect to justice always held in tension with the just requirements of equality, was never expressed in terms of a liberation of the self from self-interest in the higher common good. Instead, Niebuhr's interpretation of the relationship of liberty to justice understood liberty to be a crucial bulwark against the possibilities of both a totalitarian society and a tyrannical government.

Christopher Lasch's recent book recognizes Niebuhr's contribution to this important matter. Lasch's iconoclastic treatise on the ideology of progress in the West entitled *The True and Only Heaven* is, in toto, a wholesale assault on the standardized and conformist vision of society that came, in his view, as the end-product of this ideology of progress. Lasch, who in previous publications had scathingly criticized Niebuhr for having allegedly lost his ability to criticize America because of his bland "cold war" liberalism,[144] now discovers Niebuhr to be a jewel among liberal critics. He discovers within Niebuhr's version of reconstructed liberalism elements that constitute something of a balm and refuge from the benign totalitarian-conformist social vision of state liberalism. Lasch finds in Niebuhr what he calls "the virtue of particularism." In Niebuhr's case a value was discerned in the otherwise dangerous particularism of groups, rooted, in part, in the "organic" aspects of life. This value was that the intractable particularism of human life (which, in the extreme, in Niebuhr's account, also had the downside of manifesting itself in tribal fanaticism such as fascism) was a legitimate resource against the unifying and stultifying conformism that lay at the very heart of the predominant view of progress—a conformism that, in Williams's earlier judgment, led to the paternalistic fraternalism he had attributed to Dewey.[145]

Niebuhr saw that particularism provided a bedrock resistance to the centralizing power of government and (with respect to Williams's and Lasch's concerns) to a conformism that, in the final analysis, abolished liberty. In other words, Niebuhr advocated a type of democratic realism that rejected the temptation to suppress parochialism, outright and unqualifiedly, in the name of some greater good. Niebuhr wanted to properly assess "the indeterminate character of human vitalities, including their most spiritualized forms . . . in its various dimensions," as he once put it.[146] In that assessment Niebuhr certainly acknowledged that the individual's relationship to community was such "that the highest reaches of his individuality are dependent upon the social substance out of which they arise."[147]

At the same time Niebuhr knew that "both individual and collective centers of human vitality may be endlessly elaborated." What was crucial here was Niebuhr's cautionary note that "any premature definition of what the limits of these elaborations ought to be inevitably destroys and suppresses legitimate forms of life and culture," in spite of acknowledging the "destructive capacity of human vitality."[148] The destructive force of the human vitalities required social and government controls. Such a realization, of course, was the measure of superiority Thomas Hobbes's version of the social contract had over that of Rousseau who, in Niebuhr's words, too readily saw "nature as a source of virtue."[149] Nonetheless, Niebuhr insisted,

> A free society is justified by the fact that the indeterminate possibilities of human vitality may be creative. Every definition of the restraints which must be placed upon these vitalities must be tentative; because all such definitions, which are themselves the products of specific historical insights, may prematurely arrest or suppress a legitimate vitality, if they are made absolute and fixed. The community must constantly reexamine the presuppositions upon which it orders its life, because no age can fully anticipate or predict the legitimate and creative vitalities which may arise in subsequent ages.[150]

This matter had other ramifications than those of simply extolling the creative side of freedom. It finally had to do with the heart of political liberty as such. For whereas Niebuhr acknowledged "that the principle of government, or the organization of the whole realm of social vitalities, stands upon a higher plain of moral sanction and social necessity than the principle of the balance of power," he was profoundly aware of the fact "that government is also morally ambiguous."[151] The moral superiority of the principle of government over the principle of the balance of powers was twofold. Not only was justice itself inconceivable without some viable order, but governments represent "a more conscious effort to arrive at justice" than is embodied in the struggle for a balance of power. Yet, just as there is danger in the balance of power degenerating into anarchy, so too there is constant danger in the tendency toward tyranny in governments. In this regard the ceaseless conflict of group interests and the organic particularism of peoples are themselves a bastion against the nullification of liberty by government itself. As troublesome as "factions" are, they are also, as Madison noted, as essential to liberty as air is to fire.

Both Niebuhr's dialectical understanding of the relationship between love and justice and his views as to the moral ambiguity of government set him apart from the voices of political realism. His respect and admiration for George Kennan and Hans Morgenthau, for example, were qualified precisely at the point where Niebuhr believed their respective views on the "national interest" blinded them to broader moral considerations. In Kennan's case Niebuhr claimed that in rightly criticizing the " 'legalistic-moralistic' approach" to international relations Kennan "does not intend to be morally cynical in the advocacy" of returning "to the policy of making the 'national interest' the touchstone of our diplomacy." Nonetheless, Niebuhr insisted, "his solution [to the problem] is wrong" inasmuch as "egotism is not the proper cure for an abstract and pretentious idealism."[152] Morgenthau, whom Niebuhr saw as "the most brilliant and authoritative political realist,"[153] stressed self-interest and the lust for power even in international affairs far too consistently. Niebuhr wrote that "one suspects that in Morgenthau's realistic rigor to isolate the dominant motive of the nations from the pretended higher one, he may have made the mistake of obscuring the important residual creative factor in human rationality."[154]

In referring to the "more circumspect" or "more judicious liberals,"[155] Niebuhr saw liberal reconstruction in the service of democracy consisting in such things as a due appreciation of David Hume's recognition of the difference between the morality of individuals and of nations and, thus, of the need for balancing power against power; of Montesquieu's separation of powers;[156] of Edmund Burke's expounding on the wisdom of historical experience;[157] and, in America, of the special contributions of James Madison and John Adams toward political realism. But, as we have seen, Niebuhr also saw democracy, both in its domestic and international policies, as involving a normative sense of moral responsibility expressed in terms of justice beyond the ken of the realism of realpolitik. According to Christopher Lasch, it is this most important of Niebuhr's contributions that has gotten lost in the historical shuffle, in part due to Niebuhr himself.[158]

Divergent Emphases on Democracy

In the pantheon of America's democratic theorists, Dewey's mind and heart belonged to Jefferson; whereas Niebuhr was most attracted to Madison. At their very best, Dewey and Niebuhr reflected the very best of Jefferson and Madison, respectively. Thus, generally speaking, their own specific democratic accents can best be viewed in that light. "James Madison," Niebuhr claimed, "combined Christian realism in the interpretation of human nature and desires with Jefferson's passion for liberty."[159] Niebuhr's political realism led him to write

James Madison was the only one of the founding fathers who made a realistic analysis of both power and interest from a political and democratic perspective. He was governed by a basic insight of political realism, namely the "intimate relation" between reason and self-love. Unlike the idealists, he knew the need for strong government. Unlike Thomas Hobbes, he feared the dangers of strong government and thought that the "separation of powers" in government itself would prevent tyranny. Madison shared the fear of "factions" with all the Founding Fathers, but gave us the best pre-Marxist analysis of the basis of collective and class interests in the varying "talents" and consequent economic interests of various classes. He did not propose to suppress faction but to manage it, because he wisely realized that the price of liberty was the free play of interests in collective terms. Despite these remarkable insights he did not anticipate that Western democracies would organize their procedures through the very "factions," or parties, which the Founding Fathers so much abhorred.[160]

Dewey's Jeffersonianism rested, in part, on his vision of societal harmony based on a presumption that human ambitions were moderate and conflicts were amenable to rational accommodation. Dewey, who saw Jefferson as "the most universal . . . human being of all his American and perhaps European contemporaries," both appreciated Jefferson for "his faith in scientific advance as a means of popular enlightenment and of social progress," and valued his "belief in the union of theory and experience—or practice."[161] Such Jeffersonian virtues, of course, were surely the virtues Dewey embraced and hoped that his own labors would further advance.

The vital core of Dewey's identification with Jefferson, however, can be found in the Jeffersonian combination of freedom, scientific enlightenment, education, and the practical experiment in self-government on which America was then embarking. Indeed, if one takes "self-government" as meaning "sociocultural" and not merely "political-institutional" democracy, then these core values correspond to the three essential elements of the reconstructed liberal tradition that Dewey identified and strove to advance. Axiomatic here is the fact that one finds Dewey identifying with Jefferson's belief in "the will of the people as the moral basis of government," a trust that Dewey claimed "was temperamental, constitutional with [Jefferson]."[162] Dewey saw "this deep-seated faith in the people and their responsiveness to enlightenment properly presented . . . [as] the cardinal element bequeathed by Jefferson to the American tradition."[163] Dewey not only personified these Jeffersonian dicta, he also viewed his own labors to be, like Jefferson's, representative of "a moral idealism, not a dreamy utopianism,"[164] knowing full-well the resistance of past history to the realization and perpetuation of such ideals.

It must be recognized, however, that there were significant differences between Dewey and Jefferson.[165] Dewey's position in the twentieth century led him to appreciate the role of governmental involvement in the democratic process more fully than Jefferson did,[166] and it is precisely this aspect of Dewey's democratic theorizing that made Dewey, and not Jefferson, the ideological father of post-1929 liberalism. In the hands of laissez-faire capitalism, according to Dewey, "so-called Jeffersonian democracy [had] drifted away from the original ideas and policies of any democracy whatsoever" and had come to define "the liberty of individuals in the terms of the inequality bred by existing economic-legal institutions."[167] Whereas Jefferson held that the government which governs best, governs least, Dewey saw that, in the changed circumstances of the industrialism of the nineteenth and twentieth centuries, the democratic ideal of a just order required greater governmental activity in the economic sphere. Dewey saw no fundamental discrepancy here however, because the differences had more to do with means than with objectives. Dewey's understanding was

> The social philosophy of Thomas Jefferson is regarded as outmoded by many persons because it seems to be based upon the then existing agrarian conditions and to postulate the persistence of the agrarian regime. It is then argued that the rise of industry to a position superior to that of agriculture has destroyed the basis of Jeffersonian democracy. This is a highly superficial view. Jefferson predicted what the effects of (sic) rise of the economics and politics of an industrial regime would be, unless the independence and liberty characteristic of the farmer, under conditions of virtually free land, were conserved. His predictions have been realized. It was not agrarianism per se that he really stood for, but the kind of liberty and equality that the agrarian regime made possible when there was an open frontier.[168]

Jefferson's confidence in the "will of the people as the moral basis of government" also had its counterpart in Niebuhr, who periodically alluded to the "wisdom of common sense." But instead of lauding the capacity of the people for learning and enlightenment, Niebuhr praised "the native shrewdness of the common people who in smaller realms have had something of the same experience with human nature as the statesmen."[169] Acquaintance with self-interest and power in the concrete actualities of their respective corners of life had led them to a wisdom that is wiser than the "wise men" (e.g., social scientists and educators) who believed that "if men could be sufficiently objective or disinterested to recognize the injustice of excessive self-interest, they could also in time transfer the objectivity of their judgments as observers of the human scene to their judgments as actors and agents in human history."[170]

Niebuhr focused on the partial "triumph of experience" over the erroneous "dogma" of liberal tradition, as the best-known chapter of *The Irony of American History* put it.[171] This led him to stress the Madisonian elements in America's democratic experience over against the Jeffersonian elements as the key, within American political thought, to setting democratic philosophy on a more realistic path. Niebuhr found greater wisdom in Madison's more poignant ambivalence toward government. "Madison," Niebuhr contended, "feared the potential tyranny of government as much as Jefferson; but he understood the necessity of government much more. The Constitution [of which Madison was a major inspiration] protects the citizen against abuses of government, not so much by keeping government weak as by introducing the principle of balance of power into government."[172] Of course, Niebuhr, although agreeing with Dewey's seemingly un-Jeffersonian appreciation of the positive role of government in securing justice as well as order, thought that Dewey did not sufficiently appreciate the dangers to liberty posed by government itself. To the degree that Niebuhr sounded the note of liberty against the tyrannical possibilities of government he, paradoxically enough, seemed to be quite Jeffersonian. However, Niebuhr's appreciation of the role of strong government in achieving both order and equal justice, and his fear of the threat of government to those liberties upon which justice also depended, was consistently Madisonian.

For Niebuhr the legacy of Madisonian tradition[173] came to its fullest expression in the wisdom that "the highest achievement of democratic societies" rests in the fact "that they embody the principle of resistance to government within the principle of government itself."[174] Democracy's genius was in acknowledging the need for sufficient power to cajole the anarchic forces of life's vitalities and the inordinate self-interest of individuals and groups while, at the same time, grasping the need to place restraint upon both governmental and social centers of power. Thus the reason democracy "is a perennially valuable form of social organization," according to Niebuhr, is that by its wisdom "freedom and order are made to support, and not to contradict each other."[175] The reality of power and its arbitrary exercise are what rightly captured the attention of democracy's "realists." And, according to Niebuhr, a measure of such realism amidst the rampant idealism of liberal thought was worth infinitely more than reciting the broad humanistic values of the Jeffersonian tradition whose truths were not only commonplace to democratic liberalism but whose sentimental exaggerations had proved irrelevant to the vindication of democracy in its time of crisis.

Niebuhr's Madisonian realism was far more modest in its aims than Dewey's Jeffersonian idealism. It saw democracy, not in terms of a vast liberal vision of rational fraternity, but as a pluralistic, ever-contesting, proximate solving society cajoled into a workable but free community of sometime divisive groups. These groups must not only concern them- selves with balancing power, they must also worry about checking the power of those who impose unity on the society in which they live. This was certainly not as romantic a view of democracy as Dewey's was in- clined to be, but for some it struck a more sober, realistic and much needed note. To that very extent Niebuhr's analysis of the democratic crisis of the 1930s and 1940s, confronted by fascist and communist re- pudiation from without as well as a general malaise from within liberal democratic circles, was every bit as important, and perhaps more timely, than the vision provided by Dewey.

At the same time, to the extent Dewey's Great Community was not excessively conformist or wholly utopian, its vision of public spirited- ness and grass-roots democratic action might well have sounded a much needed note of "realism" at this particular juncture in history. For with the Reagan-Bush administrations, particularly in the wake of the col- lapse of communist collectivism, the nation experienced a resurgence of the free market utopianism of the Right every bit as naive and danger- ous as the utopianisms of the Left. This development, according to Michael Walzer, has both presented an opportunity and charted a viable and realistic course for a much-needed renascent liberalism.[176] On this point, it seems that Dewey and Niebuhr would have been in total agree- ment. Nor is there much doubt that they would both have been deeply in- volved in bringing about the liberal reconstruction.

Of course, many developments both taking shape while Dewey and Niebuhr were still alive and emerging since both men passed from the scene, have posed severe problems for the survival of democracy. Altered circumstances have generated concern and sometimes despair regard- ing the continuing applicability of the balance of power to the "common good."[177] At the very least, certain developments have raised issues that neither Dewey nor Niebuhr addressed. Some of these developments are extremely pressing ones and do not bode at all well for the survival of democracy as we have known it. Lasch and Williams both mention the anachronism that loyalty and participatory democracy *via* local com- munity life have become in light of "a world," as Lasch puts it, "domi- nated by large-scale production and mass communications."[178] Then, too, the problems inherent in traditional corporate liberalism are in- creasingly exacerbated by the vague forms of transnational economic life now taking shape.

None of this gainsays the fact that both Dewey and Niebuhr had im- portant things to say on the subject of democracy and would most likely continue to speak with force and relevance to changed conditions. Given their prestige and influence on democracy in America in the early part of the century, they would have as much relevance to the ongoing democratic dialogue as the Jeffersonian and Madisonian traditions they so ably represented.

Aside from such considerations it seems rather unfortunate that both their differences in age and career and their disagreements on substantive matters prevented Dewey and Niebuhr from leisurely addressing together the nature and prospect of democracy. The fruitfulness of such a dialogue is strictly a matter for that most seductive of sirens—historical speculation on what "might have been." Dewey and Niebuhr would no doubt have failed to reach anything like full accord. But, as their respective accents on democracy can be presumed to have a measure of validity, it seems fair to say that both their age and ours would have benefited from such a conversation. This is all a matter of wishful thinking, of course. Nonetheless, perhaps Dewey's recommendation regarding the controversy between Hamilton and Jefferson should be heeded with respect to the dispute between himself and Niebuhr. "We should do well," Dewey urged, "to declare a truce in party controversy till we have congratulated ourselves upon our great good fortune in having two extraordinarily able men formulate the fundamental principles upon which men divide."[179]

Afterword

There is no small measure of irony in the fact that the differences that set Niebuhr and Dewey at odds also obscured the profound degree to which they were brothers under the skin. Niebuhr's clash with Dewey was indisputably far-reaching, ranging as it did across a landscape populated with divergent emphases on the character and limits of human beings, the interpretation of dominant Western institutions and traditions, the relevant range of scientific method, and finally, the best way to represent the religious dimension of human existence. Nonetheless, there was substantial agreement on such matters as their mutual objections to Platonic and Cartesian dualism, their overall suspicion of the Western metaphysical tradition, their sense of the social relevance of religion and a corresponding rejection of religious fanaticism and escapism, and their insistence on both the social matrix and applied praxis of thought. It is in this set of agreements that one finds evidence of Niebuhr and Dewey's common pragmatic heritage and orientation. And, most important, it is in the interplay between their areas of agreement and disagreement one discovers that, at heart, Niebuhr and Dewey represented divergent views of pragmatism.

The degree to which Dewey and Niebuhr both shared and contested the pragmatic heritage has, with a few notable exceptions, been overlooked until recently by the very fact that Niebuhr's pragmatic affiliations have themselves been largely obscured. Niebuhr's pragmatic affiliations, especially in the heyday of his career, proved to have been a source of embarrassment to both friends and adversaries alike. The embarrassment clearly flowed two ways; for, although theologians sympathetic to Niebuhr generally found themselves disturbed by the very specter of pragmatism: pragmatists friendly to Dewey generally found themselves extremely uncomfortable with Niebuhr's theological identification and interests. The supreme irony here is that a pragmatic Niebuhr was disturbing to both the religious and secular communities, lest, in the first instance, pragmatism taint the purity of religion and, in the second, Niebuhrianism infect the comfortably desacralized world of the pragmatic naturalists.

Early recognition and acknowledgment of the wide-ranging prag-

matic dimension in Niebuhr's thought was left primarily to friendly critics such as Robert Fitch and historian Arthur Schlesinger, Jr., and adversarial philosophers such as Henry Nelson Wieman and Sidney Hook,
among others.[1] Robert Fitch's 1956 observation expressed the matter unequivocally:

> So far as Niebuhr's relation to the general history of philosophy
> is concerned, we may place him squarely in the great American
> tradition of pragmatism. He is the grateful heir of William
> James, and the understandably uncomfortable colleague of
> John Dewey. . . . Nevertheless, for all the differences in sensitiv-
> ity and in insights, these men belong together, in methodology
> and in metaphysics like variations upon a common theme.[2]

As an added dimension to Fitch's observation, Arthur Schlesinger,
Jr., early on, accurately described Niebuhr as a "Christian pragmatist,"
although he did not see the full ramifications of that insight.
Schlesinger had written,

> Niebuhr's Christian radicalism thus constituted a funda-
> mental critique of the liberalism created by the fusion of the So-
> cial Gospel and Dewey. In the political field Niebuhr rejected the
> Sermon on the Mount for pragmatism. . . . But Pragmatism had
> its limits: social redemption was impossible within history; the
> realm of power and sin were eternally under the judgment of the
> absolute; ultimately he rejected pragmatism for the Gospel.[3]

It is certainly the case, as Schlesinger suggested, that Niebuhr
came to reject the limits of pragmatism under the force of a vision of the
gospel. But here one must be extremely careful, for Schlesinger's judgment is, while illuminating, also very misleading. The limits of pragmatism from which Niebuhr dissented were precisely the limits of the
"pragmatic rationalism" of John Dewey, and these were bound up with
what Niebuhr regarded as the errors of the liberal tradition overall. It
would be more helpful to suggest that Niebuhr set a Christian "pragmatic realism" over against liberalism's "pragmatic rationalism." What
was at stake, to a large degree, was a battle over the grounds of pragmatism itself and what kind of pragmatic vision should direct the course
of liberal reconstruction. Niebuhr, from this perspective, was seeking to
disengage pragmatism from its affiliations with the otiose aspects of secular liberal thought. And he did so by reformulating pragmatism within
a theological framework aided, with inestimable pragmatic openness,

by whatever ammunition he could garner from other "realist" resources within Western thought.

At the same time that Niebuhr was attempting to provide a theological pragmatism, he was also seeking to forge a pragmatic theology. This he strove to do at the very center of theological activity; that is, at the level of reconceiving theology pragmatically. Schlesinger was quite correct in pointing out that Niebuhr was setting the gospel over against the limitations of pragmatism in its rationalistic and sentimental liberal associations. Yet it must be recognized that there is simply no such thing as "the gospel" in the sense of a body of truths floating independently free of cultural and historical contexts—as Schlesinger the sophisticated historian would know so well. At a deeper level pragmatic motifs informed the very sense "theology" and "theological relevance" held for Niebuhr. To say that Niebuhr "rejected pragmatism for the gospel" is to gloss over the more complex, constructive and, above all else, crucial relationship between theology and pragmatism in Niebuhr's thought. Schlesinger wrote that Niebuhr "retained both the divine purpose and the pragmatic method which had characterized the liberal amalgam."[4] This is quite true as far as it goes. What is important to realize is the degree to which the "pragmatic method" came to function in Niebuhr's way of interpreting and applying the "divine purpose." Consequently, when Schlesinger added that Niebuhr "sought to save each from the other by affirming the separateness of both," he missed a most interesting dimension of Niebuhr's theology.[5] Pragmatism was a major component making up the filter through which "the Gospel" was received into Niebuhr's world. Niebuhr, it seems to me, was engaged as much in a pragmatic interpretation of "the Gospel" as he was in a theological critique of pragmatism. It was precisely the interrelationship and interdependency of these efforts that characterized Niebuhr's reconstruction of liberalism.

In addition to Roger Shinn's justifiable claim that Niebuhr's pragmatism "was a pragmatism in a theological context,"[6] it should also be recognized that Niebuhr's theology was a theology in a pragmatic context. Niebuhr's *theological* pragmatism is the proper clue to both his lack of interest in establishing himself as a theologian in the usual sense and to his basic dispute with Paul Tillich. Niebuhr's confession of a lack of interest in the fine points of theology understood in the European context and his acknowledgment of de Toqueville's observation of the "strong pragmatic interest of American Christianity" go much more deeply than has been generally recognized.[7] His claim that he was a social ethicist and not a theologian, as well as his self-description as a latter-day Schleiermacherian apologetical gadfly for the Christian faith in a secular age, are, it seems to me, profoundly pragmatic expressions of

America's premier *theological* pragmatist. Similarly, Niebuhr's particular brand of the pragmatic revolt was the source of his rejection of the essentialist metaphysics he found in Tillich's ontology. His dismissal of Tillichian ontology was, therefore, far from a matter of philosophical carelessness or indifference on his part. Niebuhr's rejection of Tillich's approach seems to have been based on preeminently pragmatic instincts on two counts. First of all, Niebuhr saw a violation of experience (the self's historical character) in the kind of epistemological grounding and foundational metaphysics that so appealed to Tillich. Second, Niebuhr's pragmatic theology valued a set of apologetical tasks quite at variance with the concerns of systematic theology rooted in a preoccupation with ontology. Niebuhr's version of the pragmatist's "radical empiricism" took the form of appealing to both the historical-dramatic language of the Hebraic tradition and to the intractable incoherences of all experiences. Out of his own pragmatic approach to theology itself, Niebuhr rejected the fideism of Karl Barth and the metaphysics of Paul Tillich, men whom Niebuhr labeled "the Tertullian of our day" and "the Origen of our period." respectively.[8] Similarly, Niebuhr's pragmatic openness to "truth from whatever quarter" resulted in a theological style the neo-pragmatist Richard Rorty most envies for the philosopher; that is, a style which makes one's role "that of the informed dilettante, the poly-pragmatic, Socratic intermediary between various discourses" in whose "salon, so to speak, hermetic thinkers are charmed out of their self-enclosed practices" and where "disagreements between disciplines and discourses are compromised or transcended in the course of conversation."[9]

Unfortunately, within the scope of the present work this matter of Niebuhr's *theological* pragmatism can only be introduced, but it is an important issue for future investigation. It must be pointed out here, however, that, although Niebuhr indeed shared "distaste for the merely 'pragmatic liberalism' that by World War I, rightly or wrongly, had come to be associated with John Dewey," as Fox points out,[10] that fact has far deeper and more complex roots. Niebuhr's "realism" was set solidly against what might be termed a *pragmatic rationalism*, as long as that term is not taken in the strict mechanistic sense that R. Alan Lawson showed it meant to so many in Dewey's era.[11] Niebuhr inveighed against the excessive rational expectations, social optimism, and sentimental idealism which had found expression in pragmatists such as Dewey. He saw these elements linked to the more broadly based liberal tradition which the political philosophy of the "pragmatic rationalists" had come to reflect—part of the "miles of submerged conviction" that Louis Hartz claimed pragmatism rested on.[12] Realism was the antidote liberalism required and, in Niebuhr's view, a sizable does of realism was necessary for both theology and pragmatism.

In this connection it is illuminating to see that Niebuhr's *liberal realism* drew much of its inspiration and force from a *Christian pragmatism* in which a *pragmatic* reading of Christianity was every bit as important as a *Christian* reading of pragmatism. In effect, the relationship between theology and pragmatism in Niebuhr seems to have been dialectical and not dichotomous. Certainly, *biblical faith* as Niebuhr conceived it transcended and transformed the boundaries of historic pragmatism as Schlesinger had suggested. Conversely, however, pragmatism's radical empiricism, epistemological restraints, and antiessentialism gave form and direction to Niebuhr's understanding of theology. To the extent that the pragmatic tradition not only supplied the basis for Niebuhr's sense of theology as praxis, but also provided direction for his understanding of theology in terms of its limitations, its character, and its apologetical orientation, it is of some importance to Niebuhr studies. The extent to which Niebuhr turned some of the insights of pragmatism back upon what he felt to be the excessive and unpragmatic claims of the pragmatists is also of some importance to American pragmatism. In the final analysis, this suggests that a goodly portion of the overlapping odyssey traveled by Niebuhr and Dewey did indeed involve a contest over pragmatism itself.[13]

Notes

Abbreviations

Reinhold Niebuhr

AC:	*Applied Christianity (ed. D.B. Robertson)*
BT:	*Beyond Tragedy*
CLCD:	*Children of Light and Children of Darkness*
CPP:	*Christianity and Power Politics*
CRPP:	*Christian Realism and Political Problems*
DCNR:	*Does Civilization Need Religion?*
DST:	*Discerning the Signs of the Times*
FH:	*Faith and History*
IAH:	*Irony of American History*
ICE:	*Interpretation of Christian Ethics*
MMIS:	*Moral Man and Immoral Society*
MNHC:	*Man's Nature and His Communities*
NDM-I:	*Nature and Destiny of Man*, vol. 1 (*Human Nature*)
NDM-II:	*Nature and Destiny and Man*, vol. 2 (*Human Destiny*)
PSA:	*Pious and Secular America*
REE:	*Reflections on the End of an Era*
SDH:	*Self and the Dramas of History*
SNE:	*Structure of Nations and Empires*

John Dewey

Dewey's works are cross-referenced wherever possible. Jo Ann Boydston is the editor of the multivolume edition of Dewey's works, a truly monumental project, published by Southern Illinois University Press, which is fast becoming the definitive source in Dewey studies. When my citation has not been solely from this source, I have listed Dewey's major text followed by a cross-reference to the proper volume in the *Early, Middle,* or

Later Works of John Dewey (Carbondale: Southern Illinois University Press, 1967–1991).

EW:	*The Early Work of John Dewey, 1882–1898*, 5 vols.
MW:	*The Middle Works of John Dewey, 1889–1924*, 15 vols.
LW:	*The Later Works of John Dewey, 1925–1953*, 18 vols.
AAE:	*Art as Experience*
CE:	*Characters and Events*
CF:	*Common Faith*
DE:	*Democracy and Education*
EN:	*Experience and Nature*
HNC:	*Human Nature and Conduct*
L:	*Logic: The Theory of Inquiry*
LSA:	*Liberalism and Social Action*
PC:	*Philosophy and Civilization*
POM:	*Problems of Men*
PP:	*Public and Its Problems*
QC:	*Quest for Certainty*
RIP:	*Reconstruction in Philosophy*

Foreword

1. Dewey's Gifford Lectures were delivered in 1929 and published under the title *The Quest for Certainty*. Niebuhr gave his ten years later, and they were published as *The Nature and Destiny of Man*. Americans invited to give these lectures prior to Dewey included Josiah Royce, William James, and William Ernest Hocking.

2. Robert T. Handy, *A History of Union Theological Seminary in New York* (New York: Columbia University Press, 1987), p. 175.

3. Ibid.

4. Bruce A. Jannusch, "Pragmatism: Old and New" (unpublished paper presented at Waseda University in Tokyo, Japan on June 17, 1989), pp. 2–3.

5. Horace L. Friess "Growth in Study of Religion at Columbia University, 1924–1954" *Review of Religion* 19, nos. 1–2 (November, 1954): 17. Schneider's own recollection was "Then in about 1928 or somewhere around there they [Columbia] began wanting to do some work in religion. They had had a religion department run by the chaplain [Knox] which wasn't a teaching department at all and didn't amount to much, and they felt that it was time to get some graduate work done in religion. And there were three or four of us who were interested in this, and I think I was perhaps the leader of that particular group at this time—I

was a little older. But Blau [Joseph] and Edman [Irwin] and well, there were half a dozen. Friess and I took the lead in organizing it. We developed some courses about religion as a subject matter, not religious courses but courses on religion and religion in the plural primarily and related to the culture," in Herbert W. Schneider (with John P. Diggins), Columbia University Oral History Collection, Part 4, pp. 87–88, interviewed by Constance Myers.

6. Ibid., p. 27. For an overall history of the relationship between Columbia University and Union Theological Seminary, see Handy, *History of Union Theological Seminary in New York*, passim.

7. Ibid., p. 28. In the other subfields forming the program, the staff included "(1) *History of Religion* by Professors Arthur Jeffery and Horace Friess at Columbia, Professors John McNeill and recently Wilhelm Pauck at Union Seminary in Church History; (2) *Literature of Religion* by Professors Frederick C. Grant and James Muilenburg at the Seminary, Salo W. Baron and Arthur Jeffery at Columbia; (3) *Philosophy of Religion and Ethics* by Professors Herbert Schneider and Horace Friess at Columbia, David E. Roberts and others at the Seminary" (Ibid.).

8. Roger L. Shinn to the author, April 1, 1991.

9. Herbert W. Schneider (with John P. Diggins) Columbia University Oral History Collection, Part 4, p. 38, interviewed by Constance Myers.

10. Ibid., p. 92.

11. James Gutmann, pp. Columbia University Oral History Collection, Part 5, pp. 12–13, interviewed by Kenneth K. Goldstein. Dewey's writing also came in for its share of commentary. Among the remarks that have become legendary, three are worthy of note. The historian Richard Hofstadter once remarked that Dewey's "style is suggestive of the cannonading of distant armies: one concludes that something portentous is going on at a remote and inaccessible distance but one cannot determine just what it is" (*Anti-Intellectualism in American Life* [New York: Alfred A. Knopf, 1964], p. 361). According to historian Robert B. Westbrook, Edmund Wilson once said of Dewey that he had a propensity for "generalizing in terms of abstractions." Westbrook also cites the classic remark of Oliver Wendell Holmes, who commented that Dewey wrote as "God would have spoken had He been inarticulate but keenly desirous to tell you how it was" (quoted from Robert B. Westbrook, *John Dewey and American Democracy* [Ithaca, N.Y.: Cornell University Press, 1991], p. xiii).

12. James Gutmann to the author (taped interview), January 14, 1988.

13. June Bingham, *Courage to Change: An Introduction to the Life and Thought of Reinhold Niebuhr* (New York: Charles Scribner's Sons, 1961), p. 189.

14. Richard W. Fox, "Reinhold Niebuhr's 'Revolution,'" *Wilson Quarterly* 8, no. 4 (Autumn 1984): 84.

15. Horace M. Kallen, "John Dewey and the Spirit of Pragmatism," in Sidney Hook (ed.), *John Dewey: Philosopher of Science and Freedom: A Symposium* (New York: Barnes and Noble, 1967 [1950]), 28.

16. Arthur Schlesinger, Jr., in an essay published soon after Niebuhr's death, reflected: "No one who knew Reinhold Niebuhr will ever forget him. One remembers in so many conversations through the years the sparkling play of his marvelous human qualities—the trenchancy, the humor, the inexhaustible curiosity, the passion, the generosity, the sweetness, the grandeur, all contained in an energy so overpowering that he seemed never to able to sit still. One remembers him above all restlessly pacing the floor, throwing out ideas, jokes and challenges" ("Prophet for a Secular Age," *New Leader* 55 [January 24, 1972], p. 14).

Coming quite late onto the scene, my contacts with Niebuhr were limited to two occasions. The first involved attending a lecture of his at Union when I was at Drew Theological Seminary in the late 1950s and early 1960s. Later on in my first year as a graduate student I prevailed upon Will Herberg to get me into a seminar Niebuhr was offering in 1961 at Union, even though he had officially retired the year before. This, of course, was almost a decade after Niebuhr had been severely impeded in his ability to speak. I can attest to two things, however. First, Niebuhr still had fire in him when he spoke. Second, he still showed signs of tremendous frustration as his thoughts raced ahead of his ability to translate them into words.

17. Richard W. Fox, *Reinhold Niebuhr: A Biography* (New York: Pantheon Books, 1985), p. viii. As yet no fullfledged biography of John Dewey has appeared. The work that comes closest thus far is George Dykhuizen, *The Life and Mind of John Dewey* (Carbondale: Southern Illinois University Press, 1973). James Gutmann conjectured about this matter of a Dewey biography in a 1966 interview. In response to a question as to when Dewey, who was forever available to people, ever found time to write as much as he had, Gutmann wrote: "In the first place he lived a *long* life. I heard yesterday a statement quoted from George Bernard Shaw, which, it suddenly occurs to me, applies in equal measure to John Dewey. Shaw said . . . that he thought there couldn't be an adequate biography of him, first because he had lived so many years, and second, he had been involved in such a great variety of diverse activities that a biography of George Bernard Shaw would be a history of the western world in the years of his life. It's funny and undoubtedly is was meant to be funny, but it may account for the difficulties that Shaw biographers have encountered and all I mean to say at the moment is that that is quite literally true also of Dewey" (interview with James Gutmann at his home,

New York City, May 19, 1966. Special Collections, Morris Library, Southern Illinois University at Carbondale, pp. 4–5.

18. Roger Shinn, in seeking to correct a mistaken impression given by Niebuhr's biographer Richard Fox, noted that although Niebuhr "did lead a crowded life ... it's amazing that he packed so much into it. [Niebuhr's] regular schedule at Union (prior to his series of strokes) involved five hours per week in the classroom plus a two-hour seminar. He almost always attended the regular chapel services, 8–8:20 a.m., Tuesday through Friday. ... He kept his office hours faithfully. On Sundays he usually preached twice a semester at the seminary services and occasionally elsewhere in New York. He was on the circuit most other weekends and could (but rarely did) leave as early as Friday afternoon and return as late as Monday evening. No one on the faculty, with the possible exception of the two youngest assistant professors ([David] Roberts and [Cyril] Richardson), was more accessible to students or knew more by name. ... He frequently had lunch in the refectory. One night a week he and his wife [Ursula] ate together there" (Roger L. Shinn to the author, April 1, 1991).

19. Schneider, Columbia Oral History Collection, p. 233.

20. Ibid., pp. 241–242.

21. Interview of Herbert W. Schneider, June 29, 1967, taped at the Office of Cooperative Research on Dewey Publications, S.I.U. Special Collections, Morris Library, Southern Illinois University at Carbondale, p. 20, interviewed by Kenneth W. Duckett.

22. Corliss Lamont, *Dialogue on John Dewey* (New York: Horizon Press, 1959), p. 104.

23. John Herman Randall, Jr., "Art and Religion in Education," *Social Frontiers* 11, no. 4 (January 1936): 109.

24. Quoted in June Bingham, *Courage to Change*, p. 316. Recalling his remarks, Dillenberger later commented: "It was true that Niebuhr was getting criticism from many for his impatience with opposition and some of us spoke with him about it, and I think I was asked to be the spokesperson. His reply was that on the public platform, he had no time to be gentle, that he was trying to move things along, that major issues were at stake [and] that academic life was quite different from public and political life" (John Dillenberger to the author, August 3, 1986).

25. Reinhold Niebuhr to Morton White, May 17, 1956. This letter was Niebuhr's initial response to White after White had sent him a copy of his recent article on "Original Sin, Natural Law, and Politics," published that spring in *Partisan Review*. In revised form this article found its way into a new edition of White's book *Social Thought in America: The Revolt Against Formalism* (Boston: Beacon Press, 1957).

In an aside, Morton White's cover letter to Niebuhr read: "I am enclosing a copy of an article which you may have seen in the *Partisan Review*. While we disagree fundamentally I trust that you will realize the great respect in which I hold your work. It would be very helpful to me to be able to exchange ideas with you some day. We have so many mutual friends that I almost feel that we have met" (White to Niebuhr, May 15, 1956). In point of fact White visited Niebuhr in his office at Union Seminary later that same month. Dr. Ursula Niebuhr later wrote to me saying that "when my husband had a Visiting Professorship at Harvard, 1961–62, we had many occasions of meeting him and his wife again, and particularly one wonderful dinner party when he and Morton White were like a couple of old buddies together" (Ursula Niebuhr to the author, April 6, 1986).

26. Patrick Granfield, "An Interview with Reinhold Niebuhr, *Commonweal* (December 16, 1966), p. 316.

27. James Alfred Martin Jr., to the author, March 5, 1992. I am indebted to Steven C. Rockefeller for being made aware of the informal gathering to which Professor Martin refers. In his recent book *John Dewey: Religious Faith and Democratic Humanism* (New York: Columbia University Press, 1991), Professor Rockefeller cites this important incident which was based on his own interview with Professor Martin on November 21, 1988. See Rockefeller, *John Dewey*, p. 464 and p. 620, note 44.

28. James Gutmann to the author, (taped interview), January 14, 1988.

29. Ibid.

30. John Bennett to the author, February 14, 1988.

31. Sidney Hook to the author, August 27, 1986.

32. John Bennett to the author, February 14, 1988. Two years earlier Bennett had written in much the same vein. He "wondered whether, if Niebuhr had gone through the usual graduate program, he would have been free enough from inhibitions to become such an illuminating generalist who combined wide learning with insight that was appreciated by specialists in various fields." Bennett went on to say that while "Niebuhr often claimed that he was neither a scholar nor a theologian . . . few recent thinkers have given scholarly theologians more to write about. He did not have a Ph.D., but few persons in the field of religion have had as many Ph.D. theses written about them" (John C. Bennett, "On Looking into Fox's Niebuhr" *Christianity and Crisis* [February 3, 1986], p. 6).

33. Sidney Hook, "The Moral Vision of Reinhold Niebuhr," in *Pragmatism and the Tragic Sense of Life* (New York: Basic Books, 1974), p. 184.

34. See Fox, *Reinhold Niebuhr*, pp. 135–136.

35. Dr. Ursula Niebuhr shared a letter written to her by Reinhold on November 24, 1931, relating to LIPA activities in which he wrote: "Have

just come back from my political meeting where we conferred with John Dewey, Oswald Villard of the *Nation*, Devere Allen, etc. on the possibilities of a new party next year. We didn't realize how much we were academics and really were unable to bring a new party to birth, but it was interesting" (Ursula Niebuhr to the author, April 6, 1986). This letter has since been included by Dr. Niebuhr in her book *Remembering Reinhold Niebuhr* (San Francisco: Harper San Francisco, 1991), p. 73.

36. Sidney Hook's account of this organization can be found in Chapter 27 of his book, *Out of Step: An Unquiet Life in the 20th Century* (New York: Harper and Row, 1987), pp. 432–460.

37. A glimpse into the history and flavor of the New York Philosophy Club can be found in James Gutmann, Columbia University Oral History Collection, Part 5, pp. 183–188.

38. Certainly that was Sidney Hook's recollection. Hook did tell of a paper Niebuhr first delivered at Hook's invitation at the Conference on Scientific Method in Philosophy held at the New School for Social Research in 1942. Bertrand Russell was in the country at that time and Hook wanted to get Russell and Niebuhr together for a debate over materialistic naturalism. Hook thought Niebuhr would provide a critique of materialism and give a theological defense of some kind. Instead Niebuhr delivered a paper on the naturalism of Frederick J. Woodbridge. With Russell's not knowing who Woodbridge was, there was little or no debate. Hook was plainly disappointed. By dealing with Woodbridge, Niebuhr had not put himself on the line. He not only chose to deal with Woodbridge's thought instead of his own, but in so doing he dealt with the problem of naturalism and not materialism as Hook had hoped he would. Hook always thought Niebuhr was being deliberately evasive. As Hook recalls it, Niebuhr later presented that paper before the New York Philosophy Club. Sidney Hook to the author (taped interview), June 17, 1986.

39. Quoted from George Dykhuizen, *The Life and Mind of John Dewey* (Carbondale: Southern Illinois University Press, 1973), p. 248.

40. Ibid., p. 300.

41. Ibid., p. 297.

42. Gutmann recalled that "Niebuhr and Tillich were active members. Both of them could lay claim to being called philosophers, perhaps fully as eminent as anyone in the rest of the group. They were professional theologians, and contributed a distinctive element." Columbia University Oral History Collection, Part 5, p. 196, interviewed by Kenneth K. Goldstein.

43. Henry Steele Commager, *The American Mind: An Interpretation of American Thought and Character Since the 1880's* (New Haven, Conn.: Yale University Press, 1950), p. 100.

44. Paul Merkley, *Reinhold Niebuhr: A Political Account* (Montreal and London: McGill-Queen's University Press, 1975), p. 23.

Chapter 1. The Early Years

1. Reinhold Niebuhr, "John Dewey," *The World Tomorrow* (November 1929), p. 472.
2. Ibid., p. 473.
3. Ibid., pp. 472–473.
4. Ibid.
5. Arthur Schlesinger, Jr., "Reinhold Niebuhr's Role in American Political Thought and Life," in Charles W. Kegely, (ed.), *Reinhold Niebuhr: His Religious, Social and Political Thought* (New York: Pilgrim Press, 1984), p. 195.
6. Reinhold Niebuhr, *Does Civilization Need Religion?* (New York: Macmillan, 1927), p. 46; henceforth *DCNR*
7. Ibid., pp. 4 and 5.
8. Ibid., p. 238.
9. Ibid., pp. 209–210.
10. Ibid., p. 12.
11. Ibid., p. 220.
12. Richard W. Fox, *Reinhold Niebuhr: A Biography* (New York: Pantheon Books, 1985), p. 100.
13. Ibid., p. 102.
14. Niebuhr, *DCNR*, p. 307.
15. Ibid., pp. 239–240.
16. Ibid., pp. 109–110.
17. Ibid., p. 129.
18. Ibid., p. 144.
19. Ibid., p. 145.
20. Ibid., p. 154.
21. Ibid., p. 57.
22. Ibid., p. 156.
23. Ibid., pp. 139–140.

Chapter 2. Queries: Pragmatic and Social

1. The very title of Niebuhr's address, "The Spirit of Life," assigned to him by President Cody prompted him to relate "a story that Professor William James used to tell of a student who came to him with a topic for his Ph.D. thesis. He said 'I have thought of all kinds of topics

but finally decided to write on the subject, "The Universe and What's in It"'" Reinhold Niebuhr, "The Spirit of Life," *Addresses and Proceedings*, The National Education Association of the United States (New York: NEA, 1930), p. 610, n. 2.

2. Ibid., p. 610

3. Ibid., p. 611.

4. Ibid.

5. Ibid., p. 616.

6. Ibid., pp. 616–617.

7. Ibid., p. 617.

8. Ibid.

9. Reinhold Niebuhr, *Moral Man and Immoral Society: A Study in Ethics and Politics* (New York: Charles Scribner's Sons, 1960 [1932]) p. 81; henceforth, *MMIS*.

10. Niebuhr, "The Spirit of Life," p. 618.

11. Reinhold Niebuhr, "Mechanical Man in a Mechanical Age," *The World Tomorrow* (December 1930), p. 493.

12. Fox, *Reinhold Niebuhr*, p. 131.

13. Ibid., p. 135.

14. "Dewey to Mercedes Randall," May 2, 1932, in John Herman Randall Papers, Rare Book and Manuscript Library, Columbia University Libraries.

15. Reinhold Niebuhr, "Why We Need a New Economic Order," *The World Tomorrow* (October 1928), p. 397.

16. Reinhold Niebuhr, "Property and the Ethical Life," *The World Tomorrow* (January 1931), p. 19.

17. Ibid., p. 21.

18. Reinhold Niebuhr, "Is Peace or Justice the Goal?" *The World Tomorrow* (September 21, 1932), 275.

19. Ibid., p. 276.

20. Ibid.

Chapter 3. The Opening Attack on Liberalism

1. Niebuhr, *MMIS*, p. x.

2. Schlesinger, "Reinhold Niebuhr's Role in American Political Thought and Life," in Kegley, *Reinhold Niebuhr*, p. 198.

3. Fox, *Reinhold Niebuhr*, p. 136.

4. Daniel Day William. "Niebuhr and Liberalism," in Kegley, *Reinhold Niebuhr*, pp. 271–271.

5. Fox, *Reinhold Niebuhr*, p. 136.

6. Niebuhr, *MMIS*, pp. xi–xii.

7. Ibid., p. 215

8. Niebuhr, of course, was setting such partial capacities of individual life over against the collective life of persons with respect to which "all these achievements are more difficult, if not impossible, for human societies and social groups" (ibid.). Nonetheless, years later in his last book Niebuhr would restate his intention by suggesting that his basic point was the "collective self-regard of class, race, and nation is more stubborn and persistent that the egoism of individuals." And in the wake of many years of criticism of his ill-advised title, Niebuhr acknowledged the advice of a young friend who "recently observed that, in the light of all the facts and my more consistent 'realism' in regard to both individual and collective behavior, a better title might have been *The Not So Moral Man and His Less Moral Communities*" (in *Man's Nature and His Communities* [New York: Charles Scribner's Sons, 1965], p. 22.

9. Niebuhr, *MMIS*, p. x.

10. Ibid., p. 212.

11. Ibid., 212–213.

12. Ibid., pp. 213–214.

13. Ibid., p. 214.

14. Ibid., p. xii.

15. Ibid., p. x.

16. Ibid., p. xii.

17. Ibid., p. xiii.

18. Ibid.

19. Ibid., p. xiv.

20. Ibid.

21. Arthur Schlesinger, Jr. to the author, April 22, 1986.

22. Niebuhr, *MMIS*, pp. xiv–xv.

23. Ibid., p. xix.

24. Ibid., p. xxv.

25. Ibid., p. xx.

26. Reinhold Niebuhr to Morton White, May 17, 1956, in Ursula M. Niebuhr, *Remembering Reinhold Niebuhr* (San Francisco: Harper San Francisco, 1991), p. 379

27. Reinhold Niebuhr to Morton White, July 4, 1956, in ibid.

28. Waldo Frank, *Memoirs of Waldo Frank*, ed. Alan Trachtenberg (Amherst: University of Massachusetts Press, 1973), p. 235.

29. Niebuhr, *MMIS*, p. 31.

30. Ibid.

31. Ibid., p. 30.

32. Ibid., p. 35.

33. Ibid.

34. Ibid.
35. Ibid.

Chapter 4. The Dialogue Begins in Earnest

1. Reinhold Niebuhr, "After Capitalism—What?" *The World Tomorrow* (March 1, 1933), p. 203.
2. John Dewey, "Unity and Progress," *The World Tomorrow* (March 8, 1933), p. 232. Reprinted in *The Later Works of John Dewey, 1925–1953* (Carbondale: Southern Illinois University Press), vol. 9, p. 71; henceforth *LW*.
3. Ibid.; *LW*, vol. 9, p. 72. Niebuhr indulged in rather sweeping generalizations and even apocalyptic prognostications in his essay. He predicted the death of capitalism, the futility of liberalism, and the inevitability of fascism in the West. In the context of such dire events, Niebuhr's counsel was for the West to gird itself for the social transformation to come, hesitating only with respect to the degree of brutality that would accompany such radical social upheaval.
4. Ibid.; *LW*, vol. 9; p. 73.
5. Niebuhr, "After Capitalism—What?" p. 205.
6. Dewey, "Unity and Progress," p. 232; *LW*, vol. 9, p. 71.
7. Ibid.; *LW*, vol. 9, p. 72.
8. Niebuhr, "After Capitalism—What?" p. 205.
9. Dewey, "Unity and Progress," p. 233; *LW*, vol. 9, pp. 73–74.
10. John Dewey, *Reconstruction in Philosophy* (Boston: Beacon Press, 1948 [1920]), p. 97, henceforth *RIP*. Reprinted in *The Middle Works of John Dewey, 1899–1924* (Carbondale: Southern Illinois University Press), vol. 12, p. 135; henceforth *MW*.
11. Ibid., pp. 95–96; *MW*, vol. 12, p. 134.
12. Ibid., pp. viii–ix.
13. Niebuhr, "After Capitalism—What?" The language Niebuhr used in regard to the "impulses" changed over the years. The significant parameters for his views on this are to be found in *Moral Man and Immoral Society*, Chapter 11; "The Rational Resources of the Individual for Social Living"; and *The Nature and Destiny of Man*, vol. 1, Chapter 11, "The Problem of Vitality and Form in Human Nature."
14. Dewey, "Unity and Progress," p. 233; *LW*, vol. 9, p. 73.
15. Niebuhr, "After Capitalism—What?" p. 205.
16. Ibid.
17. Ibid., pp. 203–204.
18. John Dewey, "Intelligence and Power," *New Republic* (April 25, 1934), p. 306; *LW*, vol. 9, p. 107.

19. Ibid.; *LW*, vol. 9, p. 107.
20. Ibid., p. 307; *LW*, vol. 9, p. 110.
21. Ibid.; *LW*, vol. 9, p. 109.
22. Ibid.; *LW*, vol. 9, p. 109.
23. Ibid.; *LW*, vol. 9, p. 109.
24. Ibid.; *LW*, vol. 9, p. 109.
25. Reinhold Niebuhr, *The Nature and Destiny of Man*, vol. 2. *Human Destiny* (London: Nisbet and Co., 1943), p. 246 n. 1; henceforth *NDM-II*.
26. Reinhold Niebuhr, *The Children of Light and the Children of Darkness: A Vindicaton of Democracy and a Critique of Its Traditional Defense* (New York: Charles Scribner's Sons, 1944), pp. 16–17; henceforth *CLCD*.
27. Dewey, "Intelligence and Power," p. 307; *LW*, vol. 9, pp. 110–111.
28. Ibid.
29. Fox, *Reinhold Niebuhr*, p. 139. Fox accuses Niebuhr of being "so defensively polemical" and "plainly disingenuous" in his response to Coe. Fox interprets Niebuhr's reply as a "sentimental hope quite at odds with the dominant tone of *Moral Man*" adding that "Niebuhr was scrambling to prove that he really did value intelligence and love" (Fox, ibid., p. 143). Fox's impression is both unfortunate and misleading. Niebuhr was not presenting a cynical and irrational view of reason from which he would later backpedal as Fox suggested. Rather, over against the naive and excessive rationalism of the age, Niebuhr was pointing to the unavoidable irrationality in all rational schemes as well as the element of *rationalism* in all pretentions to rationality.
30. Reinhold Niebuhr, "Two Communications: Coe vs. Niebuhr," *The Christian Century* (March 15, 1933), p. 363.
31. Ibid., p. 364.
32. Reinhold Niebuhr, *Reflections on the End of an Era* (New York: Charles Scribner's Sons, 1934), p. 45; henceforth *REE*.
33. Dewey, "Intelligence and Power," p. 306; *LW*, vol. 9, pp. 107–108.
34. Niebuhr, *MMIS*, p. 81.
35. Ibid., p. 277.
36. In a rejoinder to an assortment of reviews of *MMIS* Niebuhr wrote: "Unfortunately it is difficult to achieve the highest social energy without the illusion that this energy will accomplish more than the facts warrant. That is why I closed my book with the suggestion that it would be well if some of these illusions are not destroyed until they have helped our age to build a new society. That suggestion was probably the greatest mistake in my book. It is true that illusions are serviceable but it is also true that they are dangerous. It would have been better to close on a warning against their danger" ("Optimism and Utopianism," *The World Tomorrow*, 16 no. 8 [February 22, 1933], p. 180).
37. Niebuhr, *MMIS*, p. 277.

38. Reinhold Niebuhr, *An Interpretation of Christian Ethics* (New York: Harper and Brothers, 1935), p. 132; henceforth *ICE*.

39. Dewey, *RIP*, pp. 212–213; *MW*, vol. 12, p. 201.

Chapter 5. A "Common Faith"

1. Horace Friess. "Dewey's Philosophy of Religion," in Jo Ann Boydston, ed., *Guide to the Works of John Dewey* (Carbondale: Southern Illinois University Press, 1972), p. 201.

2. James Gutmann confessed, "when Yale announced that Dewey was giving the lectures which became the book *A Common Faith* I thought, oh goodness, here is Dewey doing what he's always preached against and building up a sustaining ground honesty, but reading the book I came to feel very differently about it." James Gutmann to the author (taped interview), January 14, 1988.

3. John Dewey, "From Absolutism to Experimentalism," in *On Experience, Nature and Freedom*, ed. R. Bernstein (New York: Bobbs-Merrill, 1960 [1930]), p. 11.

4. Published in *Religious Thought at the University of Michigan* (Ann Arbor: Inland Press, 1893).

5. Willard Arnett, "Critique of Dewey's Anticlerical Religious Philosophy," *Journal of Religion* (October 1954), p. 256. While this is correct in the narrow sense Arnett has in mind, Steven C. Rockefeller, in a recent book that seeks "to retrieve for our time the intellectual, moral, and religious traditions associated with the John Dewey story," examines Dewey's "life and work from the perspective of its religious significance." In so doing Rockefeller discerns the religious significance of Dewey's labors in much broader terms and contends that "approaching Dewey's thought from the perspective of its religious meaning and value provides a particularly effective way of entering into an appreciative understanding of the larger unified vision toward which Dewey was working throughout his career." *John Dewey: Religious Faith and Democratic Humanism* (New York: Columbia University Press, 1991), pp. vix and x.

6. Herbert Schneider, interview, June 29, 1967, taped at the Office of Cooperative Research on Dewey Publications, S.I.U. Special Collections, Morris Library, at Southern Illinois University at Carbondale, pp. 18 and 19, interviewed by Kenneth W. Duckett.

7. Horace Friess, interview, October 10, 1966, taped at the Office of the Bush Collection of Religion and Culture, Columbia University. Special Collections, Morris Library, Southern Illinois University at Carbondale, interviewed by Kenneth W. Duckett.

8. Ibid.

9. Schneider, Interview, June 29, 1967, p. 19.

10. John Dewey, *A Common Faith* (New Haven: Yale University Press, 1934), pp. 30 and 52; henceforth *CF*.

11. Ibid., p. 3.

12. Ibid., p. 10.

13. Friess, "Dewey's Philosophy of Religion," p. 202.

14. John Herman Randall, Jr., "The Religion of Shared Experience" in *The Philosopher of the Common Man: Essays in Honor of John Dewey to Celebrate His Eightieth Birthday* (New York: Greenwood Press, 1968 [1940]), p. 114.

15. John Dewey, "Experience, Knowledge and Value: A Rejoinder," in Paul Arthur Schilpp, ed., *The Philosophy of John Dewey* (Evanston, Ill.: Northwestern University Press, 1939), p. 595.

16. Steven C. Rockefeller, in sketching out the contours of the religious situation in 1934, contends that *"A Common Faith* contains Dewey's response to Niebuhr's fresh emphasis on sin as well as to the fundamentalist's rejection of modernity, the liberal's effort to reconcile Christianity and culture, [Joseph Wood] Krutch's despairing atheism, and the debate over religion without God." *John Dewey*, p. 466.

17. Randall, "The Religion of Shared Experience," p. 127.

18. Dewey, *CF*, p. 28.

19. Randall, "The Religion of Shared Experience," p. 132.

20. Dewey, *CF*, p. 11.

21. Ibid., p. 10.

22. Ibid., p. 36.

23. Ibid., pp. 13–14.

24. Ibid., p. 9.

25. Ibid., p. 23.

26. Ibid., p. 18.

27. Ibid., pp. 18–19.

28. Ibid., p. 19.

29. Dewey, "Experience, Knowledge and Value: A Rejoinder," p. 530.

30. Dewey, *CF*, p. 19.

31. Ibid., p. 20.

32. Ibid.

33. Friess, "Dewey's Philosophy of Religion," p. 206.

34. Dewey, *CF*, p. 33.

35. Ibid., p. 20.

36. Steven C. Rockefeller, *John Dewey: Religious Faith and Democratic Humanism* (New York: Columbia University Press, 1991), p. 378. Rockefeller also remarked that "in some ways Dewey is an American Feuerbach. Like the author of *The Essence of Christianity* he left the church in the

name of human community, abandoned the idea of special revelation in the name of truth and morality, and eventually rejected the God of the church theologians in order to overcome humanity's alienation from its own essential goodness and in order to realize the spiritual meaning inherent in ordinary human relations."

Neither Feuerbach nor young Dewey believed that they had rejected the true essence of Christianity—what Feuerbach like to call the true anthropological essence as distinct from the false theological essence. Both of them argue that their new humanism and ethical naturalism preserves the most important values in the Western tradition." Ibid., pp. 216–217.

37. Ibid., pp. 22–23.
38. Ibid., p. 24.
39. Ibid., p. 31.
40. Ibid., p. 32.
41. Ibid., p. 38.
42. Ibid.
43. Ibid., on pp. 38–39.
44. Richard J. Berstein. *John Dewey* (New York: Washington Square Press, 1966), p. 163.
45. Dewey, *CF*, pp. 50–51.
46. Ibid., pp. 24–25.
47. Ibid., p. 56.
48. Ibid., pp. 55–56.
49. Reinhold Niebuhr, *Faith and History* (New York: Charles Scribner's Sons, 1949), pp. 187–188; henceforth *FH*. Niebuhr quotes from Dewey's *Democracy and Eduction* (New York: Macmillan, 1916), pp. 60–62.
50. Ibid., p. 188.
51. Ibid.
52. Niebuhr, *CLCD*, p. 129.
53. Dewey, *CF*, pp. 80–81.
54. Ibid., p. 79.
55. Ibid., p. 26.
56. Ibid., p. 86.
57. Ibid., p. 87.
58. Reinhold Niebuhr, "A Footnote on Religion," *The Nation* (September 26, 1934), p. 358.
59. Berstein, *John Dewey*, p. 161.
60. Hook insisted that "when Dewey participated in the series which I organized on the New Failure of Nerve . . . it was really a sort of out and out declaration. He had written his book on *A Common Faith* in which he used the word God despite my efforts to persuade him not to use it." Sidney Hook to the author (taped phone conversation), June 17,

1986. In the wake of Henry Nelson Wieman's review of Dewey's book, *Christian Century* elected to publish an exchange of views between Edwin Aubrey, Wieman, and Dewey with the title "Is John Dewey a Theist?" On the surface, of course, the question is patently absurd. Dewey's view of religion is clearly in the tradition of Feuerbachian anthropocentrism, or as Willard Arnett put it, Dewey's "hypothesis that God would refer to the active relation between the ideal and the actual" finally "suggests that the only source of the divine is [the] human" (Arnett, "Critique of Dewey's Anticlerical Religious Philosophy," p. 265). Clearly, in the context of "supernaturalistic theism" Dewey is nontheistic, although by his own admission and witness, he is not nonreligious. What Dewey would have liked to see, as he stated in his reply to Wieman, was a recognition of "the need of transferring to intelligence some of the zeal and devotion that in historic religions have been expended upon the supernatural" (Dewey, in Aubry, Wieman, and Dewey, "Is John Dewey a Theist?" *Christian Century* [December 5, 1934], p. 1552).

Of course, Wieman was claiming that Dewey's theism was the pantheistic variety whereas Dewey outrightly denied the charge, rejecting theism in both its supernaturalistic and pantheistic forms. Dewey made it extremely clear that he openly and totally rejected Wieman's attempt to read "his own position into his interpretation of mine," and confessed that the exchange "does not in any way modify my previous complete approval of Mr. Aubrey's statement of my position" (ibid., p. 1551). Aubrey's position was simply that "Dewey is not yet thinking of a God who is a trans-human power or principle of integration, as the review by Mr. Wieman seems to claim, but rather of a divinely creative human intelligence" (ibid., p. 1550). This is to say, for Dewey "God" was neither "other than" the universe in the sense of transcendental theism, nor identified with the universe in any way akin to pantheism. Dewey's *A Common Faith*, according to Aubrey, affirmed "the power of corporate human nature to draw the actual given of nature and the projected ideals of the imagination together in a plan of directed activity," and consequently, "the integrative power binding actual and ideal is still restricted, in Mr. Dewey's thought, to human imaginative intelligence" (ibid.).

The fact that Sidney Hook's early opposition to Dewey's use of the word *God* had some point is evidenced in Dewey's subsequent frustration over the entire dispute and is echoed in his own attempt to set things straight. He writes that "There is a fundamental difference between that to which I said, with some reservations, 'the *name* God might be applied and Mr. Wieman's attribution to me of something that holds the actual and ideal together.' What is said was that the union of ideals with *some* natural forces that generate and sustain them, accomplished in human imagination and to be realized through human choice and action, is that to which the name God might be applied, with of course the understanding that that is just what is meant by the word. I thought the *word* might be used because it seems to me that it is this union which has actually functioned in human experience in its religious dimension" (ibid., p. 1551).

61. Niebuhr, "A Footnote on Religion," p. 358.

62. Ibid. In light of Dewey's own assertion that the title of his book *Experience and Nature* "is intended to signify that the philosophy here presented may be termed either empirical naturalism or naturalistic empiricism, or, taking 'experience' in its usual signification, naturalistic humanism" (Dewey, *Experience and Nature*, p. 1a), Niebuhr was quite content to let Dewey be an expression of the "naturalistic humanism" he claimed to represent.

63. See *New Humanist*, vol. 6, (1933), pp. 1–5. Steven Rockefeller notes that "The 'Manifesto' had been originally drafted by Roy Wood Sellars, a professor of philosophy at the University of Michigan, for the Humanist Fellowship in Chicago. . . . Notable among the signers along with Dewey were ten Unitarian ministers, as well as J.H.C. Fagginger Auer (Professor of Church History and Theology at Harvard Divinity School), E.H. Burtt (Professor of Philosophy at Cornell University), A. Eustace Haydon (Professor of Comparative Religions at the University of Chicago), John Herman Randall, Jr. (Professor of Philosophy at Columbia University), Roy Wood Sellars, Robert Morse Lovett (Editor of the *New Republic*), V.T. Thayer (Educational Director of the Ethical Culture Schools), and Jacob J. Weinstein (a Reformed Jewish Rabbi associated with Columbia University).

"The 'Manifesto' was initially published in the *New Humanist*, the publication of the Chicago Humanist Fellowship, but it also appeared in the *Christian Century* and the *Christian Register* (a Boston publication of the Unitarian Church). The appearance of the 'Manifesto' provoked considerable comment and debate, especially on the subject of the meaning and possibility of religion without God, and it focused public attention on the fact that the philosophy of naturalism and religious humanism had significant support, at least in academic circles and among Unitarians. It also made clear that there were those who identified themselves as humanists but who had nothing in common with the aristocratic and rather negative humanism of Irving Babbitt and Paul Elmer More." (*John Dewey*, pp. 450–451).

64. Dewey, *CF*, p. 51.

65. Robert E. Fitch, "John Dewey—The 'Last Protestant,'" *The Pacific Spectator* (Spring 1953), p. 228.

66. Friess, "Dewey's Philosophy of Religion," p. 202.

67. Niebuhr, "A Footnote on Religion," p. 358.

68. Ibid.

69. Ibid., p. 359. Niebuhr never really moved away from similar pragmatic "reasons" for belief. Interestingly enough, Henry Nelson Wieman makes this a major point in his attack on Niebuhr in 1956—whatever the accuracy or inaccuracy of his representation of Niebuhr's position. See Wieman, "A Religious Naturalist Looks at Reinhold Niebuhr," in Kegley, *Reinhold Niebuhr*, pp. 334–354.

70. Ibid., p. 358.

71. Ibid.

72. Ibid.

73. Niebuhr, *NDM*-II, p. 7.

74. Dewey wrote that "*A Common Faith* was not addressed to those who are content with traditions in which 'metaphysical' is substantially identical with 'supernatural.' It was addressed to those who have abandoned supernaturalism, and who on that account are reproached by traditionalists for having turned their backs on everything religious. The book was an attempt to show such persons that they still have within their experience all the elements which give the religious attitude its value," "Experience, Knowledge and Value," p. 597.

Chapter 6. A Broadening Out of the Issues

1. Niebuhr, *CLCD*, p. 129.

2. John Dewey, *The Quest for Certainty* (New York: G. P. Putnam's Sons, 1960 [1929]), p. 306, henceforth *QC*; *LW*, vol. 4, p. 244.

3. Reinhold Niebuhr, *The Self and the Dramas of History*, (New York: Charles Scribner's Sons, 1955), p. 115; henceforth *SDH*.

4. Niebuhr, *ICE*, p. 234.

5. Reinhold Niebuhr, *Christian Realism and Political Problems* (New York: Charles Scribner's Sons, 1953), pp. 9–10; henceforth *CRPP*.

6. Reinhold Niebuhr, "The Pathos of Liberalism," *The Nation*, (September 11, 1935), p. 303.

7. Ibid.

8. Ibid. In his 1956 essay for the Kegley-Bretall volume on Niebuhr's thought Arthur Schlesinger, Jr., writes the following: In the setting of the late 1930s "Niebuhr and Dewey, despite their differences in presupposition, had no differences in program. For all their professed dislike of doctrine, they were both in this period staunch economic doctrinaires. For all their rejection of closed abstract systems, each saw the contemporary American problem in closed and abstract terms. The passionate champions of experiment, both flatly condemned the most mas-

sive and brilliant period of political and economic experimentation in American history. With a supreme political pragmatist as President, and with the most resourceful and creative economic and legal pragmatists of the time seeking patiently and tirelessly to work out a middle way between *laissez-faire* and collectivism, neither the secular pragmatist nor the Christian pragmatist managed to work up much interest. The pragmatic philosophers, abandoning pragmatism to Franklin D. Roosevelt, retreated precipitately to their own crypto-utopias. In the case of Dewey, it should be said that his disdain for the New Deal and his commitment to socialization proceeded naturally enough from his disregard for power in society and from his faith in human rationality and scientific planning; but for Niebuhr, who was realistic about man and who wanted to equilibrate power in society, the commitment to socialization was both the price of indifference to the achievements of piecemeal reform and a symptom of despair. Where Dewey spurned the New Deal because of his optimism about man and his belief in science, Niebuhr seemed to spurn it because of his pessimism about man and his belief in catastrophe. . . . the New Deal continued to figure in his writings of the period as an image of incoherent and aimless triviality," and "Niebuhr, blinkered by doctrine, scornfully rejected in practice the very pragmatism he called for in theory" (Schlesinger, "Reinhold Niebuhr's Role in American Political Thought and Life," in Kegley, *Reinhold Niebuhr,* pp. 204–206.

9. Ibid.

10. Ibid.

11. Reinhold Niebuhr, *Discerning the Signs of the Times* (New York: Charles Scribner's Sons, 1949), p. 43; henceforth *DST*.

12. Niebuhr, "The Pathos of Liberalism," p. 304.

13. Ibid.

14. Ibid.

15. Ibid.

16. Ibid.

17. Ibid.

18. Ibid.

19. Niebuhr, *NDM*-II, p. 274.

20. Ibid.

21. Reinhold Niebuhr, *The Nature and Destiny of Man*, vol. 1. *Human Nature* (London: Nisbet and Co., 1941), pp. 117–119; henceforth *NDM*-I.

22. Reinhold Niebuhr, "Communications: A Reply to Professor Macintosh," *The Review of Religion* (March 1940): 307.

23. John Dewey, "Review of *Social Religion*," *The Review of Religion* (March 1940): 359; *LW*, vol. 14, p. 288. In 1934 after Dewey's Terry Lectures had been given which would soon be published as *A Common Faith*,

Herbert Schneider, in a letter to the Randalls, made the following remark: "He [Dewey] is working on the Three Lectures on Religion he delivered at Yale last month. . . . Macintosh is reported to have said that he
did not disagree with Dewey as much as he had hoped to." Herbert W.
Schneider to John and Mercedes Randall, March 18, 1934, in John Herman Randall Papers, Rare Book and Manuscript Library, Columbia University Libraries.

24. It is questionable if Dewey read Niebuhr's *Nature and Destiny of
Man*, although he was well aware of it and knew something of its impact.
Dewey was aware of Sidney Hook's review of the initial volume published
in the November 8, 1941, issue of the *New Leader* under the title "Social
Change and Original Sin: Answer to Niebuhr." And he was definitely
familiar with Hook's *Partisan Review* piece on "The New Failure of Nerve,"
published in January–February 1943. Hook is of the opinion that, at
least with respect to the mature theological writings, Dewey's knowledge of what Niebuhr was saying came mostly through others—individuals such as Hook himself and Joseph Ratner, who was busily at work
on a manuscript that was scathingly critical of Niebuhr.

25. John Dewey, "One Current Religious Problem," *The Journal of
Philosophy* (June 4, 1936), pp. 325 and 326; *LW*, vol. 11; p. 116.

26. Ibid., p. 326; *LW*, vol. 11; p. 117.

27. John Dewey, "Religion, Science, and Philosophy," *The Southern
Review* 1 (1936–1937): 53; *LW*, vol. 11, p. 454.

28. Ibid., pp. 53–54; *LW*, vol. 11, p. 454.

29. Ibid., p. 55; *LW*, vol. 11, p. 456.

30. Ibid., p. 56; *LW*, vol. 11, p. 456.

31. Ibid., p. 57; *LW*, vol. 11, p. 458.

32. Ibid., p. 59; *LW*, vol. 11, p. 460.

Chapter 7. Conflict in the Closing Years

1. The Conference on Science, Philosophy and Religion listed as
its "Founding Members" the following individuals: Mortimer J. Adler,
University of Chicago; William F. Albright, Johns Hopkins University;
Edwin E. Aubrey, University of Chicago; Chester I. Barnard; Franz Boas,
Columbia University; Van Wyck Brooks; Lyman Bryson, Teachers Col-
lege, Columbia University; Scott Buchanan, St. John's College; Ludlow
Bull, Metropolitan Museum of Art; George A. Buttrick, Federal Council
of Churches of Christ in America; Robert L. Calhoun, Yale University;
Harry J. Carman, Columbia University; Emmanuel Chapman, Ford-
ham University; Henry S. Coffin, Union Theological Seminary; Stewart
G. Cole, Service Bureau for Intercultural Education; Arthur H. Comp-

ton, University of Chicago; Edwin G. Conklin, Princeton University; John M. Cooper, Catholic University of America; Karl K. Darrow, Bell Telephone Laboratories; Irwin Edman, Columbia University; Albert Einstein, Institute for Advanced Study, Princeton; Harrison S. Elliott, Union Theological Seminary; Hoxie N. Fairchild, Hunter College of the City of New York; Enrico Fermi, Columbia University; Louis Finkelstein, Jewish Theological Seminary of America; Hughell E. W. Fosbroke, General Theological Seminary; Harry E. Fosdick, Riverside Church; Lawrence K. Frank, Josiah Macy, Jr., Foundation; Phillipp Frank, Harvard University; Horace L. Friess, Columbia University; Erwin R. Goodenough, Yale University; Frederick C. Grant, Union Theological Seminary; Theodore M. Greene, Princeton University; Moses Hadas, Columbia University; Hugh Hartshorne, Yale University; C. P. Haskins, Union College; Robert J. Havighurst, General Education Board; Victor F. Hess, Fordham University; William E. Hocking, Harvard University; Robert M. Hutchins, University of Chicago; Raphael Isaacs, University of Michigan; E. Jerome Johanson, Hartford Theological Seminary; F. Ernest Johnson, Teachers College, Columbia University; Edward Kasner, Columbia University; C. J. Keyser, Columbia University; Robert W. King, Bell Telephone Laboratories; Carl H. Kraeling, Yale University; Harold D. Lasswell, Washington School of Psychiatry; Ralph S. Lillie, University of Chicago; Alain Locke, Howard University; Eugene W. Lyman, Union Theological Seminary; Mary E. Lyman, Sweet Briar College; Douglas C. Macintosh, Yale University; Robert M. MacIver, Columbia University; John A. Mackay, Princeton Theological Seminary; William de B. MacNider, University of North Carolina; Jacques Maritain, Institut Catholique, Paris; Alexander Marx, Jewish Theological Seminary of America; Conrad H. Moehlman, Colgate-Rochester Divinity School; Roland S. Morris, American Philosophical Society; Forest Ray Moulton, American Association for the Advancement of Science; A. J. Muste, The Labor Temple; Allan Nevins, Columbia University; Filmer S. C. Northrop, Yale University; Harry A. Overstreet, College of the City of New York; Anton C. Pegis, Fordham University; Gerald B. Phelan, Pontifical Institute of Mediaeval Studies, Toronto; I. I. Rabi, Columbia University; Donald Riddle, Univerity of Chicago; William E. Ritter, University of California; Michael M. Rostovtzeff, Yale University; George Sarton, Carnegie Institution; Herbert W. Schneider, Columbia University; Harlow Shapley, Harvard College Observatory; Harry Schulman, Yale University; George N. Shuster, Hunter College of the City of New York; Yves R. Simon, Notre Dame University; Pitirim A. Sorokin, Harvard University; Hugh S. Taylor, Princeton University; George F. Thomas, Princeton University; Paul Tillich, Union Theological Seminary; Harold C. Urey, Columbia University; Henry P. Van Dusen, Union Theological Semi-

ary; Gerald G. Walsh, S.J., Fordham University; Luther A. Weigle, Yale
University; Paul Weiss, Bryn Mawr College.

   2. Dewey to Overstreet, October 27, 1942. Sidney Hook Collection
of John Dewey, Special Collections, Morris Library, Southern Illinois
University at Carbondale.

   3. Niebuhr's whereabouts during the Conference on Science,
Philosophy and Religion in its formative years is itself something of a
mystery. It is clear that Niebuhr did not participate in those controver-
sial early years, although his name is listed among the more than one-
hundred-seventy names listed as those who "convoked" the Conference
for a few years beginning in 1944. Yet, given Niebuhr's reputation for,
and interest in religion and politics, his absence from the Conference is
as unthinkable as was Dewey's. Certain facts are known. Marjorie Wyler
of the Jewish Theological Seminary informed me that "Reinhold
Niebuhr was invited to submit a paper to Conference sessions in 1940,
'42, '43, '44, '45, '50 and '52. However, he did not submit papers, and the
records do not show whether or not he attended the sessions. He did attend sessions in '46, '47, and '48—mostly executive session or meetings
of the planning committee." (Marjorie Wyler to the author, February 27,
1992). Paul Weiss, who directed me to Ms. Wyler, wrote that although his
own memory was poor, his opinion was that "Niebuhr was such a distinguished figure that I think I would have remembered if he were there; I
do not." (Paul Weiss to the author, February 3, 1992). Mortimer Adler, a
principal at the center of the controversy, specifically recalled, "No,
Niebuhr was not at that first conference and I have no information whatsoever concerning why he was not there." (Mortimer J. Adler to the author, February 11, 1992). Aside from pure speculation as to the possible
motives for Niebuhr's absence, one factor surfaces above all others.
Niebuhr had delivered his Gifford Lecture in Edinburgh the previous
year and was busily reworking them for publication with volume 1 appearing in 1941. In this connection Niebuhr's friend and colleague John
C. Bennett stated that he was "not surprised that Niebuhr did not attend
the Finkelstein conferences [in those early years]. He had to cut back at
the time after his Giffords when he was so much in demand." Bennett
went on to note that "the kind of criticism that Hook must have engaged
in, making him a contributor to religious obscurantism would have an-
noyed [Niebuhr]." (John C. Bennett to the author, March 17, 1992).

   4. Louis Finkelstein to the author, January 17, 1988.

   5. Overstreet to Dewey, November 17, 1942. Sidney Hook Collection of John Dewey, Special Collections, Morris Library, Southern Illinois University at Carbondale.

   6. Weiss to Dewey, May 2, 1941, Sidney Hook Collection of John

Dewey, Special Collections, Morris Library, Southern Illinois University at Carbondale.

7. Dewey to Finkelstein, April 30, 1941, Sidney Hook Collection of John Dewey, Special Collections, Morris Library, Southern Illinois University at Carbondale.

8. Sidney Hook to author (taped telephone conversation), June 17, 1986.

9. James Gutmann to author (taped interview), January 14, 1988.

10. Hook's recollected account of his involvement in this conference appear in his book *Out of Step: An Unquiet Life in the 20th Century* (New York: Harper and Row, 1987), Chapter 22. "God and the Professors," pp. 335–355. To counter the Conference on Science, Religion, and Philosophy, Dewey and others organized the Conference on the Scientific Spirit and Democratic Faith, which convened in New York City on May 29, 1943, with Dewey as its chairman. Of this event Hook writes: "At the height of the Hutchins-Adler crusade against naturalism, Dewey, Kallen, and Jerome Nathanson of the Ethical Culture Society decided to launch another conference and organization. . . . Two well-attended meetings were held, which resulted in the publication of two interesting volumes. For reasons that were never clear to me, the energies behind the organization petered out as the educational and intellectual threat from neo-Thomism dwindled.

"There were two contributing factors. Jacques Maritain, although doctrinally orthodox, shared the same passion for political freedom and opposition to current forms of totalitarianism as we did and was distancing himself from the dogmatic pronouncements of Adler. In the Ethical Culture Society, a faction headed by Algernon Black, a notorious fellow-traveler, was placing obstacles in Nathanson's path" (ibid., p. 347).

11. Overstreet to Dewey, November 17, 1942.

12. Dewey to Farrell, February 18, 1941, John Dewey Papers, Special Collections, Morris Library, Southern Illinois University at Carbondale.

13. Dewey to Overstreet, October 27, 1942. Sidney Hook Collection of John Dewey, Special Collections, Morris Library, Southern Illinois University at Carbondale.

14. Part I of the series appeared in *Partisan Review* 10, no. 1 (January–February 1943) and included the following articles: Sidney Hook, "The New Failure of Nerve"; John Dewey, "Anti-Naturalism in Extremis"; and, Ernest Nagel, "Malicious Philosophies of Science." Part II of the series appeared in the subsequent issue of *Partisan Review* 10, no. 2 (March–April 1943). It contained the following essays: Ruth Benedict, "Human Nature Is Not a Trap"; Richard V. Chase, "The Huxley-Head

Paradise"; and Norbert Guterman, "Kierkegaard and His Faith." In addition Hook added a follow-up essay on "The Failure of the Left," in which he shifted attention to political issues.

15. Niebuhr readily acknowledged the tendency toward obscurantism and fanaticism in religious history and criticized these tendencies far better than many of his adversaries. Indeed, he was sometimes capable of criticizing his own confessional orientation far more adeptly than some of his secular critics were able to criticize their own. Niebuhr could write, for example, that "The Renaissance spirits of our day have vaguely equated what they regard as the cultural and social obscurantism of the Catholic and Protestant church. They have seldom understood how different the strategies of the two forms of Christianity are. If the one is obscurantist it is because it places premature limits and unjustified restraints upon the pursuit of knowledge and development of social institutions. If the other is obscurantist, it is because it is either indifferent towards the problems of thought and life which all men must consider though they are short of the ultimate problem of salvation; or because it interposes a new authority, that of Scripture, in such a way as to make the ultimate meaning of life, as contained in the gospel, a substitute for all subordinate realms of meaning or as obviating the necessity of establishing these subordinate realms. . . . The secularists may be pardoned if, as they watch this curious drama, they cry 'a plague o' both your houses'; and if they come to the conclusion that all ladders to heaven are dangerous. It must be observed, however, that these ladders cannot be disavowed so simply as the secularists imagine. Pride may ascend the ladder which was meant for the descent of grace; but that is a peril which inheres in the whole human cultural enterprise. The secularists end by building ladders of their own; or they wallow in a nihilistic culture which has no vantage point from which 'my' truth can be distinguished from 'the' truth." . . . Secularists in our time find "difficulty in avoiding irresponsibility and scepticism on the one hand and new fanaticism on the other" *NDM*-II, pp. 218, 239, and 245.

16. Hook notes that in Niebuhr's eyes "I was wrong about the historical role of religious movements and that sometimes they had a genuinely social revolutionary outlook despite their theological language. He was right about this. But then he went on to try to make sense of the language." Hook to the author, September 27, 1986.

17. Sidney Hook, "The New Failure of Nerve," *Partisan Review* (January–February 1943), p. 19.

18. Sidney Hook to the author, September 27, 1986.

19. John Dewey, "Anti-Naturalism in Extremis," *Partisan Review* (January–February 1943), p. 35; *LW*, vol. 15, p. 57.

20. Ibid., pp. 26–27; *LW*, vol. 15, p. 49.

21. Ibid., p. 27; *LW*, vol. 15; p. 49.

22. Ibid., p. 32; *LW*, vol. 15, p. 53. The Princeton statement was published in *Science, Philosophy and Religion: Second Symposium* (New York: Conference on Science, Philosophy and Religion in Their Relation to the Democratic Way of Life, Inc., 1942), XIII "The Spiritual Basis of Democracy, Princeton Group," pp. 251–257. Signators included J. Douglas Brown, Department of Economics; Theodore M. Greene, Department of Philosophy; E. H. Harbison, Department of History; Whitney J. Oates, Department of Classics; Henry Norris Russell, Department of Astronomy; Hugh S. Taylor, Department of Chemistry; George F. Thomas, Department of Religious Thought; and, John A. Mackay, President, Princeton Theological Seminary.

After affirming the link between democratic institutions and human beings understood as "spiritual beings," the Princeton Group argued that authentic conceptions of the "spiritual life" derive "primarily from the Greeks and the Hebraic-Christian moral of religious" traditions. After insisting on the superiority of the Hebraic-Christian conception, the salient issue of the statement is broached. The Princeton Group claimed:

"13. Both the contemplative-mystical and the moral-religious conceptions of man as a spiritual being are superior to the modern naturalistic view, which exalts man by himself or as a part of nature. Naturalism denies both man's relation to an order of ultimate values and his dependence upon a cosmic spiritual Power. It thus divorces him from the moral and spiritual order to which he belongs and upon which he depends for strength and direction. It encourages him to determine his ends for himself as a completely autonomous being, without any norm above his own interests and desires, individual and collective. As a result, it leads *inevitably* [italics mine] to pride and egoism. The individual, having nothing higher than himself to worship or serve, worships himself, his reason, his culture, or his race.

"14. Many who hold to this naturalistic view in democratic countries are unaware of the dangers in their position. Influences by the last remnants of philosophical Idealism, romantic Transcendentalism, or religious Theism in our day, they act as if they still believed in the spiritual conception of man which they have intellectually repudiated. They try to maintain their feeling for the dignity of man, while paying homage to an essentially materialistic philosophy according to which man is simply a highly developed animal. They are loyal to their democratic society and culture, but by their theory they deny the spiritual nature of man and his values upon which it has been built. In short, they are living off the spiritual capital which has come down to them from their classical and religious heritage, while at the same time they ignore that heritage itself as antiquated and false." Ibid., pp. 254–255.

The Princeton Group then suggested in the tradition of guilt by association that naturalism leads to totalitarianism. Nowhere in this statement is there any recognition of the complex history of democracy's emergence or any humility shown with respect to the dismal record of those privy to "spiritual" reality in that history.

23. Ibid., p. 32; *LW*, vol. 15, p. 54.

24. Ibid.; *LW*, vol. 15; p. 54.

25. Ibid., p. 33; *LW*, vol. 15, p. 55.

26. Ibid., p. 34; *LW*, vol. 15, p. 56.

27. Ibid., p. 35; *LW*, vol. 15, p. 57.

28. Ibid., p. 37; *LW*, vol. 15, p. 59.

29. Dewey to Hook, March 29, 1943, Sidney Hook Collection of John Dewey, Special Collections, Morris Library, Southern Illinois University at Carbondale.

30. Sidney Hook to the author, September 27, 1986.

31. Sidney Hook to the author (taped phone interview), June 17, 1986.

32. Sidney Hook, "Theological Tom-Tom and Metaphysical Bagpipe," *The Humanist* (Autumn 1942), p. 102.

33. Farrell to Dewey, March 31, 1941, John Dewey Papers, Special Collections, Morris Library, Southern Illinois University at Carbondale.

34. Dewey to Hook, October 28, 1942, Sidney Hook Collection of John Dewey, Special Collections, Morris Library, Southern Illinois University at Carbondale.

35. Sidney Hook, "Social Change and Original Sin: Answer to Niebuhr," *New Leader* (November 8, 1941), p. 7.

36. Niebuhr to Dewey, May 22, 1944, Sidney Hook Collection of John Dewey, Special Collections, Morris Library, Southern Illinois University at Carbondale.

37. Sidney Hook to the author, August 27, 1986.

38. Dewey to Ratner, March 25, 1946, Joseph Ratner Papers, Special Collection, Morris Library, Southern Illinois University at Carbondale.

39. Reinhold Niebuhr, "Will Civilization Survive Technics?" *Commentary* (December 1945), p. 2.

40. Ibid., p. 4.

41. Ibid.

42. Ibid., p. 8.

43. Ibid., pp. 5–6.

44. Ibid., p. 6.

45. John Dewey, "The Crisis in Human History," *Commentary* (March 1946), p. 3; *LW*, vol. 15, p. 212.

46. Ibid., pp. 3–4; *LW*, vol. 15, p. 213.

47. John Dewey, "Letters of John Dewey to Robert V. Daniels, 1946–1950" (November 17, 1947), *Journal of the History of Ideas* (October–December, 1959): 571.

48. Niebuhr, *ICE.*, p. 173.

49. Niebuhr, *NDM*-II, p. 189.

50. Ibid.

51. Ibid., p. 162.

52. The manuscript was given the provisional title, "Reinhold Niebuhr: Dialectical Synthesizer," and it is acerbic to the point of vindictiveness. See Joseph Ratner Papers, Special Collections, Morris Library, Southern Illinois University at Carbondale.

53. Ratner to Dewey, December 8, 1948, Joseph Ratner Papers, Special Collections, Morris Library, Southern Illinois University at Carbondale.

54. Dewey to Ratner, December 9, 1948.

55. Dewey to Ratner, September 6, 1950.

56. John Dewey, contribution to a symposium entitled "Religion and the Intellectuals," *Partisan Review* (February 1950), pp. 129, 132, and 133; *LW*, vol. 16, pp. 390, 393, and 394.

57. James Gutmann, *Columbia University Oral History Collection*, Part 5, p. 149, interviewed by Kenneth K. Goldstein.

Chapter 8. Conflict over Naturalism

1. John Herman Randall, Jr., (et al.), "Human Destiny—Reinhold Niebuhr: A Symposium," *The Union Review* 4, no. 2 (March 1943), p. 22.

2. Sidney Hook to the author (taped telephone conversation), June 17, 1986. Randall developed his notion of Niebuhr's "naturalism" with a chiding humor in his contribution to "Human Destiny—Reinhold Niebuhr, pp. 22–24.

3. Dewey, *EN*, p. 157; *LW*, vol. 1, pp. 125–126.

4. Paul K. Conkin, *Puritans and Pragmatists: Eight Eminent American Thinkers* (New York: Dodd, Mead and Co., 1968), p. 351.

5. Niebuhr, *NDM*-I, p. 78.

6. Niebuhr, ibid., p. 120 Niebuhr went on to say that "Idealism always has the provisional advantage over naturalism that it sees the human spirit in a deeper dimension than a pure naturalism. The proof that this is an advantage is given by the fact that naturalism is always forced to contradict itself to explain the facts of human history. The

human spirit obviously transcends natural process too much to be bound by the harmony of natural necessity. This is proved both by the character of human creativity and by the emergence of a distinctively historical rather than natural chaos and destruction. The rationalist realizes that the human spirit is *nous* and not *physis*. But he immediately sacrifices his provisional advantage by identifying *nous* with *logos*, spirit with rationality. He believes therefore that the human spirit has a certain protection against the perils of its freedom within its own law-giving rationality. The possible evil of human actions is recognized but it is attributed to the body or, more exactly, to the *psyche*, that is, to the vitality of a particular form of existence" (ibid., pp. 121–122).

7. See Bruce Kuklick, *Churchmen and Philosophers: From Jonathan Edwards to John Dewey* (New Haven, Conn.: Yale University Press, 1985), p. 238.

8. John Dewey, "The Metaphysical Assumptions of Materialism," in *The Early Works of John Dewey, 1882–1898* (Carbondale: Southern Illinois University Press), vol. 1, pp. 5 and 8 (henceforth *EW*); first published in the *Journal of Speculative Philosophy*, 14 (April 1882).

9. John Dewey, "Anti-Naturalism in Extremis," pp. 25–26; *LW*, vol. 15, pp. 47–48.

10. Biographical sketches germaine to this development and beyond are to be found in George Dykhuizen's *The Life and Mind of John Dewey* (Carbondale: Southern Illinois University Press, 1973), Chapters 1–5. A more recent interpretation of Dewey's early years is provided in Kuklick, *Churchmen and Philosophers*, Chapter 16, "John Dewey: From Absolutism to Experimental Idealism." The most recent contributions to an understanding of this history can be found in Robert B. Westbrook, *John Dewey and American Democracy* (Ithaca, NY: Cornell University Press, 1991), Chapter 1, "The Hegelian Bacillus," and Steven C. Rockefeller, *John Dewey: Religious Faith and Democratic Humanism* (New York: Columbia University Press, 1991), Chapter 2, "Neo-Hegelian Idealism and the New Psychology."

11. Dewey, *CF,* pp. 23–24; *LW*, vol. 9, p. 17.

12. Dewey, *EN*, p. 158; *LW*, vol. 1, p. 126.

13. Dewey, *QC*, p. 302; *LW*, vol. 4, p. 241.

14. Niebuhr, "The Validity and Certainty of Religious Knowledge," B.D. thesis, Yale University, 1914, pp. 13 and 14.

15. Ibid., p. 21.

16. Ibid., p. 14.

17. Niebuhr, *DCNR* p. 16.

18. Ibid., p. 212.

19. Transcendent absolutes of either the idealistic or theistic type always bothered Dewey for what he deemed their morally reprehensible

determinism above all else. This moral failing is to be understood as having two foci: the undermining of responsibility for both oneself and one's world. Such determinism throttles both ethical conduct and redirection and control of nature, which, after all for Dewey, were inseparable. In 1920, while commenting on the transitional role of idealism, Dewey wrote: "The effect of the objective theological idealism that had developed out of classical metaphysical idealism was to make the mind submissive and acquiescent. The new individualism chafed under the restrictions imposed upon it by the notion of a universal reason of God which had once and for all shaped nature and destiny" (*Reconstruction in Philosophy* [New York: Henry Holt and Co., 1920], p. 50).

20. Kuklick, *Churchmen and Philosophers*, p. 241.

21. Niebuhr, *DCNR* p. 212.

22. Ibid.

23. Conkin, *Puritans and Pragmatists*, p. 345.

24. Richard J. Bernstein, *John Dewey* (New York: Washington Square Press, 1966), pp. 11–12.

25. In a letter to Wendell T. Bush, Dewey confessed that "I learned a good deal from him [Hegel]—especially about the place of conflict in the direction of inquiry—but conflict needs an *empirical* not a dialectical interpretation" (Dewey to Bush, January 6, 1939), Rare Book and Manuscript Library, Columbia University Libraries.

26. Dewey, *CF*, p. 54; *LW*, vol. 9, p. 37.

27. Dewey wrote in 1920 that "The banishing of ends and forms from the universe has seemed to many an ideal and spiritual impoverishment. When nature was regarded as a set of mechanical interactions, it apparently lost all meaning and purpose. Its glory departed. Elimination of differences of quality deprived it of beauty. Denial to nature of all inherent longings and aspiring tendencies toward ideal ends removed nature and natural science from contact with poetry, religion and divine things. There seemed to be left only a harsh, brutal despiritualized exhibition of mechanical forces. As a consequence, it has seemed to many philosophers that one of their chief problems was to reconcile the existence of this purely mechanical world with belief in objective rationality and purpose—to save life from a degrading materialism. . . . But when it is recognized that the mechanical view is determined by the requirements of an experiemental control of natural energies, this problem of reconciliation no longer vexes us" (*RIP*, pp. 69–70; *MW*, vol. 12, p. 119).

28. Ibid., pp. 68–69; *MW*, vol. 12, p. 119.

29. Ibid., p. 72; *MW*, vol. 12, pp.120–121. Dewey also cautioned against the premature euphoria in religious circles with the unraveling of the "classical type of mechanism," arguing that such an attitude

"seems ill-advised from their [the apologists of religion] own point of view. For the change in the modern scientific view of nature simply brings man and nature closer together. We are no longer compelled to choose between explaining away what is distinctive in man through reducing him to another form of a mechanical model and the doctrine that something literally supernatural marks him off from nature. The less mechanical—in the older sense—physical nature is found to be, the closer man is to nature." *CF*, p. 55; *LW*, vol. 9, p. 37.

30. Niebuhr, *FH*, p. 78.

31. Bernstein wrote that "In his *Psychology*, published in 1887, Dewey mixed and juggled Hegelian ideas with experimental data. [G. Stanley] Hall, who reviewed the book, criticized it in the same manner in which Dewey had criticized others. Hall accused Dewey of imposing an alien philosophical dogma upon the facts of experimental science" (*John Dewey*, pp. 14–15).

32. John H. Randall, Jr., "Epilogue: The Nature of Naturalism" in Yeavert H. Kaikorian, ed., *Naturalism and the Human Spirit* (New York: Columbia University Press, 1944), p. 356.

33. John Dewey, "The Influence of Darwinism on Philosophy," in *The Influence of Dawrinism on Philosophy and other Essays in Contemporary Thought* (New York: Henry Holt and Co., 1910), p. 2.

34. Reinhold Niebuhr, "Christianity and Darwin's Revolution," in *A Book That Shook the World: Anniversary Essays on Charles Darwin's "Origin of Species"* (Pittsburgh: University of Pittsburgh Press, 1958), p. 31.

35. Ibid., p. 33.

36. Ibid., pp. 34, 30, and 32.

37. Niebuhr, *SDH*, p. 110.

38. Niebuhr, "Christianity and Darwin's Revolution," pp. 31 and 32.

39. Niebuhr, *NDM*-I, p. 78.

40. Sidney Hook, "The New Failure of Nerve," *Partisan Review* 10, no. 1 (January–February 1943), p. 8. Hook's lament was that precisely because he had such a pervasive impact upon influential figures within American culture, Niebuhr's attacks on scientific naturalism inadvertently aided and abetted those religionists whose "*obscurantism is no longer apologetic*" but "*has now become precious and willful*," having in our day "*donned a top hat and gone high church*" (ibid., p. 3). We are thus beseiged by those who exibit a widespread "loss of confidence in scientific method" and a dangerous proclivity for "varied quests for a 'knowledge' and 'truth' which . . . are uniquely different from those won by the process of scientific inquiry" (ibid., p. 4).

41. Ibid., p. 16.

42. Niebuhr, *NDM*-I, p. 78.

43. Reinhold Niebuhr, "The Reminiscences of Reinhold Niebuhr, *Columbia University Oral History Collection*, Part 1, p. 93, interviewed by Harlan P. Phillips.

44. Niebuhr, *SDH*, pp. 110–111.

45. Alfred N. Whitehead, *Science and Philosophy* (New York: Philosophical Library, 1948), p. 129.

46. Niebuhr, *SDH*, p. 113.

47. Niebuhr, *FH*, p. 53.

48. Dewey, *EN*, p. 37; *LW*, vol. 1, p. 40.

49. Niebuhr, *FH*, p. 53.

50. Dewey, *QC*, p. 220; *LW*, vol. 4, p. 176.

51. Ibid., p. 221; *LW*, vol. 4, p. 176.

52. Ibid., p. 228; *LW*, vol. 4, p. 182.

53. Ibid., p. 220; *LW*, vol. 4, p. 175.

54. Ibid.; *LW*, vol. 4, p. 176.

55. William M. Shea, *The Naturalists and the Supernatural* (Macon, Ga.: Mercer University Press, 1984), pp. 75ff.

56. Richard Rorty, *Philosophy and the Mirror of Nature* (Princeton, N.J.: Princeton University Press, 1979), p. 362.

57. Ibid., in n. 8.

58. Bruce Jannusch, "Pragmatism: Old and New," unpublished paper presented at Waseda University in Tokyo, Japan on June 17, 1989, p. 18.

59. Dewey, *CF*, p. 31; *LW*, vol. 9, pp. 22–23. The obvious should at least be noted here. Certainly, overall, Niebuhr's representation of "scientism" reflected a cliched view of science. But because Dewey seems also to have had at least one foot in that cliche himself, the conflicts between them on the issues of science and scientific method clearly reflected a pre-Kuhnian context.

60. Niebuhr, *SDH*, p. 114.

61. Ibid.

62. Ibid., p. 115.

63. Ibid.

64. Dewey, *EN*, p. 14; *LW*, vol. 1, p. 23.

65. Even so staunch a defender of Niebuhr as Gordon Harland acknowledged that Niebuhr's "method is typological in the sense that he speaks about idealism and naturalism rather than giving detailed analyses of particular idealists and naturalists. This has the result that he is usually something less than just to the special nuances of particular thinkers." Harland tempered his criticism by noting what many others recognized to be Niebuhr's forte; namely, that "few possess his capacity to penetrate to the core of the thought of a movement or tradition" *The Thought of Reinhold Niebuhr* [New York: Oxford Press, 1960], p.

58). Certainly in the case of Dewey it was much more than nuances that Niebuhr overlooked. Although the view that Niebuhr could "penetrate to the core of the thought of a movement or tradition" is one with which this author finds himself in agreement, it is also true that Niebuhr missed most of what Dewey was up to as a critic of the philosophical tradition in the West. Niebuhr certainly failed to see or acknowledge the highly creative and expansive aspects of Dewey's naturalistic anthropology.

66. Dewey, *EN*, p. 2; *LW*, vol. 1, p. 13.

67. Shea, *The Naturalists and the Supernatural*, p. 79. Shea, however, holds the position that "the charge [of materialism] makes sense in this way: the naturalists take sensing as the transcendental condition for human understanding, and also as a consequence take matter as the transcendental condition for existence. The metaphysical position depends upon the cognitional position. If they are correct in their cognitional theory, they may be correct in their metaphysical stand. But in my view they accept the first uncritically" (ibid., pp. 79–80).

68. Dewey, *EN*, 11–12; *LW* vol. 1, pp. 20–21.

69. S. Morris Eames, *Pragmatic Naturalism: An Introduction* (Carbondale: Southern Illinois University Press, 1977), passim, in surveying the pragmatic legacy of James, Dewey and Mead, Eames purposely chose the term "pragmatic naturalism" to distill a common tie between otherwise diverse figures.

70. Reinhold Niebuhr, "Limitations of the Scientific Method: An Answer to Pierre Auger," *Bulletin of the Atomic Scientists* 11, no. 3 (March 1955): 87.

71. Niebuhr, *SDH*, p. 104.

72. Ibid., p. 128.

73. Niebuhr, *FH*, p. 1.

74. A sometimes interesting but exaggerated attempt to make the case that Niebuhr was a nihilist based on a nihilistic reading of pragmatism is offered in Harry J. Ausmus, *The Pragmatic God: On the Nihilism of Reinhold Niebuhr* (New York: Peter Lang, 1990).

75. Jannusch, "Pragmatism: Old and New," p. 18.

76. Although I think that what Niebuhr was all about includes and justifies my point about the point Niebuhr here made, it must also be noted that one of Niebuhr's most trenchant critics, Yale's Julian Hartt, indicts Niebuhr for a barely veiled fideistic apologetic on behalf of the Christian faith. What offends Hartt the most is what he considers to be Niebuhr's misunderstanding or misapplication of dialectic, analysis, and empirical generalization, both in his defense of Christianity and his portrayal and criticism of rival positions. See Hartt's assessment of Niebuhr's *The Nature and Destiny of Man* (along with Austin Farrer's *Finite*

and Infinite) in his "Dialectic, Analysis, and Empirical Generalization in Theology," *Crozer Quarterly* 29, no. 1 (January 1952): 1–17.

Chapter 9. The "Human Studies"

1. Niebuhr, *SDH*, p. 128.

2. Nothing can substitute for original sources, but for a succinct summary of these major themes, see Gordon Harland, *The Thought of Reinhold Niebuhr* (New York: Oxford Press, 1960), particularly Chapter 3, "Love, Justice and the Self," and Chapter 4, "Love, Justice and History."

3. John Dewey, *Problems of Men* (New York: Greenwood Press, 1968; originally published by Philosophical Library, 1946), p. 17, henceforth *POM; LW*, vol. 15, pp. 166–167.

4. Dewey, *RIP*, p. 42; *MW*, vol. 12, p. 103.

5. Dewey, *POM*, pp. 42–43; *LW*, vol. 15, p. 167.

6. Shea, *The Naturalists and the Supernatural*, p. 13.

7. Ibid.

8. John E. Smith, *Reason and God: Encounters of Philosophy with Religion* (New Haven, Conn.: Yale University Press, 1961), p. 114. Smith is of the opinion that "For Dewey the name for the real is Nature, and we are often told by him that no differential meaning should be attached to the term. Nature is all there is and we must not suppose that the concept of nature derives its meaning from the contrast situation in which it stood in the traditional 'great chain of being' where it was bounded by man at one end and by God at the other. But if the term Nature is to have no differential and simply denotes 'whatever is,' then it is gratuitous" (ibid.).

9. Ibid., p. 113.

10. Niebuhr, "Christianity and Darwin's Revolution," p. 32.

11. Niebuhr, *MMIS*, pp. xiv–xv.

12. At one point where Dewey was lauding the role of intelligence in challenging the status quo, he lamented that "one of the greatest obstacles in conducting this combat is the tendency to dispose of social evils in terms of general moral causes. The sinfulness of man, the corruption of his heart, his self-love and love of power, when referred to as causes are precisely of the same nature as was the appeal to abstract powers (which in fact only reduplicated under a general name a multitude of particular effects) that once prevailed in physical 'science,' that operated as a chief obstacle to the generation and growth of the latter. Demons were once appealed to in order to explain bodily disease and no such thing as a strictly natural death was supposed to happen. The importation of general moral causes to explain present *social* phenomena is on the same intellectual level" (*CF*, pp. 77–78; *LW*, vol. 9, pp. 51–52).

13. See Dewey, *RIP*, pp. xxi–xxiii and xxxi. These remarks appear in Dewey's retrospective introduction to the 1948 edition and are not in the original edition published in 1920.

14. Ibid., pp. 75–76; *MW*, vol. 12, p. 123.

15. In the context of discussing "general moral causes" as obstacles in dealing with social evils, Dewey wrote, "Reinforced by the prestige of traditional religions, and backed by the emotional force of beliefs in the supernatural it stifles the growth of that social intelligence by means of which direction of social change could be taken out of the region of accident, as accident has been defined. Accident in this broad sense and the idea of the supernatural are twins. Interest in the supernatural therefore reinforces other vested interests to prolong the social reign of accident" (*CF*, p. 78; *LW*, vol. 9, p. 52).

16. An excellent example of this can be found in Niebuhr's chapter on the "The Debate on Human Destiny in Modern Culture: The Reformation" in *NDM*-II, pp. 191–220.

17. Niebuhr, *NDM*-II, p. 246, n. 1.

18. Niebuhr, *NDM*-I, p. 121. Niebuhr here criticizes Dewey along with Whitehead and cites Dewey's *Philosophy and Civilization* as the locus of Niebuhr's remarks.

19. Randall, "Dewey's Interpretation of the History of Philosophy," in Schilpp, *The Philosophy of John Dewey*, p. 82.

20. Dewey, *EN*, p. 219; *LW*, vol. 1, p. 170.

21. Dewey, "Experience, Knowledge and Value: A Rejoinder," p. 522; *LW*, vol. 14, p. 8.

22. Randall, "Dewey's Interpretation of the History of Philosophy," in Schilpp, *The Philosophy of John Dewey*, pp. 82–83.

23. Ibid., p. 90.

24. John Dewey, *Liberalism and Social Action* (New York: G. Putman's Sons, 1980), pp. 76 and 58, henceforth *LSA*; *LW*, vol. 11, pp. 54 and 42.

25. Niebuhr remarked in his published sermons in 1946 that "This idea of a cultural lag is plausible enough, and partly true. But it does not represent the whole truth about the defect of our will" (*DST*, p. 43). In 1955 he had commented on the issues more fully: "The social conditions of community have shifted so rapidly and the factors to be taken into consideration are so endlessly varied that it would seem that the primary necessity is a development of all the social and political sciences with a particular view of overcoming the 'cultural lag.' This favorite diagnosis for all our ills seems to have acquired new relevance today. Must we not help people to meet the new situations which they confront by measures appropriate to the situation? Must we not establish educational programs to impress upon the new generation the responsibilities and perils of 'one world'? Must we not help Americans, living in a paradise of

luxury in comparison with world standards, to recognize the problems of peoples emerging from a primitive economy and possibly from colonial tutelage? Must we not, as our sensitive spirits insist, make technical instruments and skills available to them to overcome their poverty? Having done that, must we not be wise enough to send cultural anthropologists along with our technicians in recognition of the fact that 'raising living standards' is not a simple procedure? It involves breaking the mold of organic societies and exposing communities to the peril of social disintegration.

"In all these problems a greater perspective upon the total situation is certainly a primary necessity for the kind of statesmanship which will guide the nations toward a political and moral integration.

"But perhaps this is another instance in which the presuppositions, from the standpoint of which we gather the facts, are as important as the diligence and honesty with which we try to ascertain the facts.

"The most diligent elaboration of social and political skills seems not to have challenged the basic presuppositions of our culture in regard to the problem which we confront. That presupposition is that the forces of history are tractable if we only amass sufficient insight and skill to manage them; that even the most complex problems may be solved if we approach them with sufficient knowledge and resolution. In short, we approach them as potential managers of our own and other people's destiny. It has seemingly not dawned upon us that we have only limited competence in deflecting historical destinies in the drama of history in which we are creatures as well as creators and in which we meet competitive creators who have contrasting ideas of our common destiny" (*SDH*, pp. 203–204).

26. Niebuhr, *FH*, pp. 11–12.
27. Niebuhr, *CLCD*, p. 129.
28. Niebuhr, *ICE*, pp. 234–235.
29. Niebuhr, *SDH*, pp. 82–83.
30. Dewey, *LSA*, pp. 82 and 83; *LW*, vol. 11, p. 58.
31. Niebuhr, *NDM*-1, p. 117.
32. Niebuhr, ibid. The quotation Niebuhr cites from Dewey appears in *LSA*, p. 51; *LW*, vol. 11, p. 37.
33. Ibid., pp. 118–119.
34. Ibid., p. 119.
35. John Dewey, "Intelligence and Power," *New Republic* (April 25, 1934), p. 307; *LW*, vol. 9, p. 110.
36. Ibid., p. 306; *LW*, vol. 9, p. 108.
37. Ibid.; *LW*, vol. 9, p. 108.
38. Ibid.; *LW*, vol. 9, p. 108. In a footnote following this remark, Dewey quoted what surely is one of the most perplexing and unfortunate

remarks Niebuhr gave voice to; namely, that "The truest visions of religion are illusions, which may be partially realised [sic.] by being resolutely believed. For what religion believes to be true is not wholly true but ought to be true; and may become true if its truth is not doubted" (*MMIS*, p. 81). Niebuhr was here speaking of the motivating force of what James termed *overbeliefs*. In Niebuhr's words, "Without the ultrarational hopes and passions of religion no society will ever have the courage to conquer despair and attempt the impossible; for the vision of a just society is an impossible one, which can be approximated only by those who do not regard it as impossible" (ibid.).

39. Dewey, "Intelligence and Power," p . 306; *LW*, vol. 9, p. 108.

40. Reinhold Niebuhr, "The Tyranny of Science," *Theology Today* 10, no. 4 (January 1955), p. 469.

41. Alfred N. Whitehead, *Symbolism, Its Meaning and Effect* (New York: Macmillan, 1927), p. 16.

42. Nancy Frankenberry, *Religion and Radical Empiricism* (Albany: State University of New York Press, 1987), p. ix.

43. Langdon Gilkey, "Response to . . . " *Journal of the American Academy of Religion* 51, no. 3 (September 1983): 487.

44. For an example of the discussion of Dewey's theory of experience see Gail Kennedy, "Dewey's Concept of Experience: Determinate, Indeterminate, and Problematic," *Journal of Philosophy* 56, no. 21 (October 8, 1959): 801–814; Richard Rubenstein, "John Dewey's Metaphysics of Experience," *Journal of Philosophy* 58, no. 1 (January 5, 1961): 5–14; and Gail Kennedy's reply to Rubenstein in "Comment on Professor Bernstein's Paper 'John Dewey's Metaphysics of Experience,'" ibid., pp. 14–21.

45. Dewey remarked, "Other criticisms of my theory of experience are connected with the fact that I have called experiences *situations*, my use of the word antedating, I suppose, the introduction of the *field* idea in physical theory, but nevertheless employed, as far as I can see, to meet pretty much the same need—a need imposed by subject-matter not by theory. The need in both cases—though with different subject-matters—is to find a viable alternative to an atomism which logically involves a denial of connections and to an absolutistic block monism which, in behalf of the reality of relations, leaves no place for the discrete, for plurality, and for individuals" ("Experience, Knowledge, and Value," p. 544; *LW*, vol. 14, pp. 28–29).

46. Gail Kennedy, "Dewey's Concept of Experience," p. 802.

47. Dewey, *EN*, p. 8; *LW*, vol. 1, p. 18.

48. Ibid., p. xii; *LW*, vol. 1, p. 6.

49. Ibid., 2; *LW*, vol. 1, p. 13.

50. Smith, *Reason and God*, p. 95.

51. Niebuhr, *SDH*, p. 110.

52. Shea, *The Naturalists and the Supernatural*, p. 18.

53. Niebuhr, *SDH*, p. 110.

54. Dewey, "Experience, Knowledge and Value," p. 530; *LW*, vol. 14, p. 15.

55. Niebuhr, *SDH*, p. 77.

56. Ibid., pp. 75–76.

57. Reinhold Niebuhr, "Reply to Interpretation and Criticism," in Kegley, ed., *Reinhold Niebuhr*, pp. 508–509.

58. Will Herberg, "Christian Apologist to the Secular World," in "Reinhold Niebuhr: A Symposium," *Union Seminary Quarterly Review* 11, no. 4 (May, 1956): 14.

59. Niebuhr, *SDH*, p. 144.

60. Ibid., p. 84.

61. Niebuhr, "Intellectual Autobiography," in Kegley, *Reinhold Niebuhr*, p. 17.

62. Niebuhr, *SDH*, p. 26.

63. Ibid., p. 29.

64. Niebuhr, *FH*, p. 55.

65. Niebuhr, *NDM*-I, p. 1.

66. Ibid., p. 42.

67. Kuklick, *Churchmen and Philosophers*, p. 245.

68. Dewey, *EN*, p. 352; *LW*, vol. 1, p. 264.

69. Eames, *Pragmatic Naturalism*, pp. 54–55.

70. Although Dewey's writings are replete with discussions of these topics, his response to both Henry W. Stuart and William Savery in the Schilpp volume on Dewey will suffice. In his reply to Stuart, Dewey wrote: "Since apparently it is use of the word 'Naturalism' to characterize my general position which has led Stuart off the track, I call attention to the fact that instead of presenting that kind of mechanistic naturalism that is bound to deny the 'reality' of the qualities which are the raw material of the values with which morals is concerned, I have repeatedly insisted that our theory of Nature is to be framed on the basis of giving full credence to these qualities just as they present themselves. No one philosophic theory has a monopoly on the meaning to be given Nature, and it is the meaning given Nature that is decisive as to the kind of Naturalism that is put forward. Naturalism is opposed to idealistic spiritualism, but it is also opposed to super-naturalism and to that mitigated version of the latter that appeals to transcendent *a priori* principles placed in a realm above Nature and beyond experience. That Nature is purely mechanistic is a particular metaphysical doctrine; it is not an idea implied of necessity in the meaning of the word. And in my *Experience and Nature* I tried to make it clear that while I believe Nature *has* a mechanism—for otherwise knowledge could not be an instrument for its

control—I do not accept its *reduction* to a mechanism" ("Experience, Knowledge, and Value," p. 580; *LW*, vol. 14, pp. 63–64).

Later Dewey wrote: "The final 'metaphysical' question upon which I shall touch has to do with a question raised by Savery—Naturalism or Materialism? I am aware that emotional causes often dictate preference for one word over another. It is then quite proper to ask whether dislike for associations with the word *materialism* have dictated my use of *materialism* to describe my philosophic point of view. Since I hold that all the subject-matter of experience is dependent upon physical conditions, it may be asked why did I not come out frankly and use the word *materialism*? In my case, there are two main reasons. One of them is that there is involved in this view a metaphysical theory of *substance* which I do not accept; and I do not see how any view can be called materialism that does not take 'matter' to be a substance and to be the *only* substance—in the traditional metaphysical sense of substance. The other reason is closely connected with this, being perhaps but a specific empirical version of what has just been said. The meaning of materialism and of matter in *philosophy* is determined by opposition to the physical and mental as *spiritual*. When the antithetical position is completely abandoned, I fail to see what meaning 'matter' and 'materialism' have for philosophy" (ibid., p. 604; *LW*, vol. 14, pp. 86–87).

71. John Dewey, *Logic: The Theory of Inquiry* (New York: Holt, Rinehart and Winston, 1938), p. 23, henceforth *L*; *LW*, vol. 12, p. 30.

72. Eames, *Pragmatic Naturalism*, pp. 27–28.

73. Dewey, "Experience, Knowledge and Values," p. 580; *LW*, vol. 14, pp. 63–64.

74. Ibid., p. 581; *LW*, vol. 14, p. 64.

75. Dewey, *L*, p. 35; *LW*, vol. 12, p. 42.

76. Ibid., p. 42; *LW*, vol. 14, p. 48.

77. Ibid., p. 43; *LW*, vol. 14, p. 49.

78. Ibid., pp. 43–44; *LW*, vol. 14, p. 49.

79. Ibid., p. 44; *LW*, vol. 14, pp. 49–50.

80. See Richard Rorty, *Consequences of Pragmatism* (Minneapolis: University of Minnesota Press, 1982), passim, but particularly Chapter 3, "Overcoming the Tradition," and Chapter 5 "Dewey's Metaphysics."

81. Dewey, *L*, p. 45; *LW*, vol. 12, p. 51.

82. Dewey, "Experience, Knowledge and Value," p. 555; *LW*, vol. 14, p. 39.

83. Lewis E. Hahn, "Dewey's Philosophy and Philosophic Method," in Boydston, *Guide to the Works of John Dewey*, p. 30.

84. Dewey, "Experience, Knowledge and Value," p. 542; *LW*, vol. 14, p. 27.

85. Ibid., p. 554; *LW*, vol. 14, p. 38.

86. Ibid., pp. 555–556; *LW,* vol. 14, p. 40.

87. See Martin Buber, *The Knowledge of Man,* ed Maurice Friedman (New York: Harper and Row, 1965), Appendix: "Dialogue Between Martin Buber and Carl R. Rogers," pp. 166–184.

88. Carl R. Rogers, "Reinhold Niebuhr's *The Self and the Dramas of History:* A Criticism," *Pastoral Psychology* 9, no. 85 (June 1958): 15.

89. Niebuhr once wrote that "Efforts to explain the emergence of 'mind', that is of human freedom, in purely sociological terms are self-contradictory, sometimes to an amusing degree. Thus Professor George H. Mead, who elaborates a social behaviourist viewpoint widely held in America, reasons in his *Mind Self and Society*; '[Our view] must be clearly distinguished from the partially social view of mind. According to this view, mind can get expression only within or in terms of an organized social group, yet it is nevertheless in some sense a native endowment, a congenital or hereditary biological attribute of the individual organism. . . . According to this latter view the social process presupposes and in a sense is the product of mind; in direct contrast is our opposite view that mind presupposes and is the product of the social process. The advantage of our view is that it enables us to give a detailed account of, and actually to explain the genesis and development of mind' (p. 224). This viewpoint, which has nothing to commend it but rigorous consistency, sacrifices its consistency when Professor Mead explains in a footnote; 'Hence it is only in human society, only within the peculiarly complex context of social relations and interactions which the human central nervous system makes physiologically possible, that minds arise or can arise; and thus also human beings are evidently the only biological organisms which are or can be self-conscious or possessed of selves.' p. 235" (*NDM*-I, pp. 59–60, n. 2).

90. See Van Meter Ames, "Buber and Mead," *The Antioch Review* 27, no. 2 (Summer 1967): 181–191.

91. Reinhold Niebuhr, "Review of *Man: Real and Ideal,*" *Religion in Life* 13, no. 2 (Spring 1944): 297.

92. Niebuhr, *SDH*, p. 115.

93. Niebuhr, *FH*, p. 55.

94. Ibid., p. 12.

95. Niebuhr, *CLCD*, p. 49.

96. Reinhold Niebuhr, *The Irony of American History* (New York: Charles Scribner's Sons, 1952), p. 83; henceforth *IAH*.

97. Reinhold Niebuhr, "Democracy, Secularism and Christianity," *Christianity and Crisis* 13, no. 3 (March 12, 1953), p. 20.

98. Niebuhr, "The Tyranny of Science," p. 471.

99. Ibid., p. 465.

100. Niebuhr, *FH*, p. 12.

101. Niebuhr, *NDM*-1, pp. 78–79.

102. In writing on Ernst Troeltsch, Pauck wrote that "Both Reinhold and H. Richard Niebuhr have often acknowledged that their ways of handling theological problems were deeply determined by their study of Troeltsch's writings. Reinhold Neibuhr has been a Troeltschian from the time when he published his first book, *Does Civilization Need Religion?* until these latter days when he wrote an addendum to all his studies on man's historical nature and destiny in the little book on *Man's Nature and His Communities*" (Wilhelm Pauck, *Harnack and Troeltsch: Two Historical Theologians* [New York: Oxford University Press, 1968], pp. 43–44).

103. Langdon Gilkey, "Reinhold Niebuhr's Theology of History," *The Journal of Religion* 54, no. 4 (October 1974): 364.

104. Ibid., p. 366, no. 14.

105. Niebuhr, *FH*, p. 116.

106. Niebuhr observed that Collingwood "proves that a philosopher has almost as great difficulty as a pure scientist in interpreting the dramatic essence of history. He is clear that history must be sharply distinguished from nature." But his analysis in *The Idea of History* ends up with Collingwood making "the mistake of defining as 'thought' what is really the dramatic freedom which distinguishes history" (*The Self and the Dramas of History*, pp. 57–58).

107. Niebuhr, *NDM-I*, p. 246, n. 1.

108. Niebuhr, *FH*, p. 116.

109. Ibid., pp. 116–117.

110. Niebuhr, *SDH*, p. 57.

111. Quoted in Randall, "Dewey's Interpretation of the History of Philosophy," in Schillp, *The Philosophy of John Dewey*, p. 92.

112. Dewey, *RIP*, p. 173; *MW*, vol. 12, p. 179.

113. Ibid., p. xxvi.

114. Dewey, *EN*, p. 163; *LW*, vol. 1, p. 129.

115. Ibid., p. 147; *LW*, vol. 1, p. 118.

116. Ibid., p. 162; *LW*, vol. 1, p. 129.

117. Ibid.; *LW*, vol. 1, pp. 129–130.

118. Ibid., pp. 163–164; *LW*, 1, p. 130.

119. For an interesting essay suggesting the radical character of time in Dewey's philosophy, see Garly Calore, "Towards a Naturalistic Metaphysics of Temporality: A Synthesis of John Dewey's Later Thought," *Journal of Speculative Philosophy* 3; no. 1 (1989): 12–25.

120. Richard Rorty, "A Reply to Dreyfus and Taylor," *The Review of Metaphysics* 34, no. 10 (September 1980): 39.

121. Smith, *Reason and God*, p. 102.

122. See Chapter Eight, n. 75.

Chapter 10. Approaches to Religion

1. Dewey spoke on behalf of the rationally enlightened minority, including both those who had outrightly rejected traditional religion and those whose religious sensitivities had thus far prevented them from taking such a radical step. Garry Wills's book *Under God: Religion and American Politics* (New York: Simon and Schuster, 1990) takes to task those whose strictly academic orientation has blinded them to the persistence and pervasiveness of religion in the American body politic. Dewey, along with Sidney Hook, of course, was clearly worried about the resurgence of religion even in its rather sophisticated form among the Niebuhrians of the late 1940s. Wills's point is, nonetheless, well taken— even in Dewey's case. For Dewey, not unlike Sigmund Freud, waivered between the hope that scientific rationality would gradually supplant traditional religious attitudes, thus becoming a "common faith," and the awareness that the irrational gifts of religion were fundamentally congruent with deeply based needs in human beings such that the masses of men and women would never abandon such gifts.

2. W. Richard Comstock, "Dewey and Santayana in Conflict: Religious Dimensions of Naturalism," *Journal of Religion* 45, no. 2 (April 1965): 128.

3. Randall, "The Religion of Shared Experience," p. 118.

4. Shea writes: "The hard naturalist case against traditional religion . . . finds [such religion] intractably opposed to genuine reflection and to freedom. For some naturalists Supernaturalism is not a prescientific way of explicating moral concern in poetic mythic image (as Santayana had it), but a flight from understanding and responsibility" (*The Naturalists and the Supernatural*, pp. 64–65).

5. See Henry Nelson Wieman, "John Dewey's Common Faith," *Christian Century* (November 1934), pp. 1450–1452); *LW*, 9, pp. 426–434; and Edwin E. Abury, Henry Nelson Wieman and John Dewey, "Is John Dewey a Theist?" *Christian Century* (December 5, 1934), pp. 1550–1553; *LW*, 9, pp. 435–437, 438–440, and 294–295, respectively.

6. In a letter written within three years of his death, Dewey remarked: "You are right in thinking that my knowledge of Wieman's position is based upon his earlier writings; I may add, to my own discredit in some measure, that I acquired a prejudice against his way of thinking when we had a little exchange *via* the *Christian Century*. After I had done my best to state my point of view, he said in the course of a published comment that doubtless I later was sorry for something I said which, as I recall, was the nub of my position. Though his article invited reply I dropped the discussion, as his interpretation of what I wrote seemed to

me so gratuitous as to make anything further on my part wholly useless. I may add that I wouldn't have felt so strongly if I hadn't a high opinion of Wieman" (John Dewey to Mr. Jacobson, July 16, 1949. Dewey Papers, Special Collections, Morris Library, Southern Illinois University at Carbondale).

7. Aubrey, "Is John Dewey a Theist?" p. 1550; *LW*, vol. 9, p. 437

8. In a footnote Steven Rockefeller records that "Jerome Nathanson, who became the leader of the New York Society for Ethical Culture, recalls Dewey saying to him some time after 1942 that he would omit the word 'God,' if he were to write another book along the lines of *A Common Faith*. Dewey made this remark in the context of a conversation in which Nathanson told him that John L. Elliott, an early disciple of Felix Adler and a leader in the Ethical Culture Society, had once said: 'I will never forgive John Dewey for using the word God in *A Common Faith.*'" Interview SR and Jerome Nathanson, July 26, 1972, New York City." (Rockefeller, *John Dewey* p. 628, note 89).

9. Dewey first used the term *God* as denoting "the unity of all ideal ends arousing us to desire and action" (*CF*, 42; *LW*, vol. 9, p. 29). He followed by making the supposition that "'God' means the ideal ends that at a given time and place one acknowledges as having authority over his volition and emotion, the values to which one is supremely devoted, as far as these ends, through imagination, take on unity" (ibid.; *LW*, vol. 9, p. 29). He claimed "that 'God' represents a unification of ideal values that is essentially imaginative in origin when the imagination supervenes in conduct . . . [and that this] unity signifies not a single Being, but the unity of loyalty and effort evoked by the fact that many ends are one in the power of their ideal, or imaginative, quality to stir and hold us" (ibid., p. 43; *LW*, vol. 9, p. 30). He wished to make his reader understand that this "God, or, to avoid misleading conceptions, to the idea of the divine [which is an idea] of ideal possibilities unified through imaginative realization and projection . . . is also connected with all the natural forces and conditions—including man and human association—that promote the growth of the ideal and that further its realization" (ibid., p. 50; *LW*, vol. 9, p. 34). Then, finally, Dewey gives his most widely recognized definition: "It is this *active* relation between ideal and actual to which I would give the name 'God,'" and significantly adds that "I would not insist that the name *must* be given" (ibid., p. 51; *LW*, vol. 9, p. 34).

10. Steven Rockefeller's valuable work on John Dewey did not come to my attention until a very late stage in the publishing process of my own book. Although I have been able to benefit from and occasionally refer to Professor Rockefeller's volume, it has not played the part in my own research that it otherwise certainly would have done. The reader will discern that I have downplayed the mystical aspect in Dewey's

thought; whereas Rockefeller has brought that dimension into prominence. In Professor Rockefeller's view Dewey's early period gave rise to two major themes in his mature understanding of the religious life. "First and foremost," Rockefeller writes, "there is the idea of the religious life as involving a unifying moral faith arising out of the experience of being possessed by a supreme spiritual ideal that harmonized the self and self and world. Here the emphasis falls on the will, practical reason, and moral action, and it reflects the influence of Kant, Coleridge, Marsh and Vermont Transcendentalism generally. . . . Second, in his mature thought Dewey also associates religious experience with an attitude of piety toward nature and with mystical intuitions of oneness with the larger whole which is the universe. In this connection one encounters an eduring element of romanticism in his thought, which shows the influence of Wordsworth." While acknowledging that, given Dewey's "scientific bent of mind and concern with moral autonomy and self-realization, Dewey was not attracted to a Neoplatonic mysticism in which discursive reason and the individual are absorbed into an undifferentiated One," Rockefeller nonetheless finds an enduring mystical aspect in Dewey's religious vision. He claims that "the unity he [Dewey] sought is an organic unity, in which the freedom and significance of the individual are preserved, but he maintained in his mature thought an important place for mystical feelings of unity, for emotional intimations of belonging to the larger community of being. In short, a religious moral faith in a unifying ideal and the mystical sense of belonging are from very early major themes in Dewey's religious outlook, and they remained central. There is here for Dewey then, a realm of religious experience which is to be distinguished from intellectural exerience even though it may influence, and be positively influenced by, the latter," (*John Dewey,* pp. 73–74).

Professor Rockefeller finds the mystical element in Dewey's thought most clearly evident in his poetry and in Dewey's somewhat remarkable correspondence "with an eccentric private philosopher, Scudder Klyce, whom he never met" (ibid., p. 313. See Chapter 7, "Poems, Letters, and Lessons," pp. 312–356). Rockefeller develops his understanding of the mystical element in Dewey's mature thought in Chapter 11, "Nature, God and Religious Feeling," where he analyzes the themes "Natural Piety," "Mystical Intuition and the Religious Emotions," "The Idea of God," and "Humanistic Naturalism and Ultimate Meaning." (See pp. 491–540.) In this context Rockefeller turns to Dewey's published writings where he gleans support for his emphasis on the mystical in Dewey's thought from passages out of *Human Nature and Conduct, Experience and Nature,* a somewhat muted expression in *A Common Faith* and, most prominently, in *Art as Experience.*

11. Dewey, CF, p. 50; *LW*, vol. 9, p. 34.

12. Ibid., p. 53; *LW*, vol. 9, p. 36.

13. See Chapter Five, n. 63.

14. Hook's full statement is worth quoting: "I worked closely with him [Dewey] on the manuscript of his *A Common Faith*. It is a thoroughly naturalistic approach to religion. The only thing I disagreed with was his use of the term 'God' for faith in the validity of moral ideals. Dewey's God is not the God of Abraham, Isaac and Jacob; nor of Plato, Aristotle and Aquinas, nor of Spinoza, Kant or Hegel; nor of James or Schiller. Why then use it, I asked. He argued that the term had no unequivocal meaning in the history of thought; that there was no danger of its being misunderstood (in which he was shortly proved wrong); and that there was no reason why its emotive associations of the sacred, profound and ultimate should be surrendered to the supernaturalist, especially since for him not religion but the religious experience is central. All this seemed to me to be legitimate if not sufficient grounds. But then he added something which men like Russell or Cohen would never have dreamed of saying: Besides there are so many people who would feel bewildered if not hurt were they denied the intellectual right to use the term 'God.' They are not in the churches, they believe what I believe, they would feel at a loss if they could not speak of God. Why shouldn't I use the term?" (Sidney Hook, "Some Memories of John Dewey," *Commentary* 14 (1952), p. 253). This memorial essay, coming soon after Dewey's death, was republished as Chapter 6 in Hook's *Pragmatism and the Tragic Sense of Life* (New York: Basic Books, 1974), pp. 101–102, the quotation appearing on p. 114.

15. Dewey, "Is John Dewey a Theist?" p. 1551; *LW*, vol. 9, p. 294.

16. Quoted in Corliss Lamont, "New Light on Dewey's *Common Faith*," *Journal of Philosophy* 58, no. 1 (January 5, 1961): 25. Lamont related that "On July 28 I answered Dewey's note as follows: 'You ask why both myself and the church people gave so much attention to your use of the word "God" in *A Common Faith*. I think it was because this was the unexpected thing in the book, the point that gave it news value, as it were. Everybody knew that you were opposed to supernaturalism and the old-time religion. But your support of "God" at least as a word—that was new and startling.... The parsons ... saw in your definition *their* religion. The discussion in *The Christian Century* showed this, as well as reviews by such intelligent theologians as Reinhold Niebuhr'" (ibid., p. 24).

17. Ibid., p. 25.

18. Horace Kallen, in Corliss Lamont (ed.), *Dialogues on John Dewey* (New York: Horizon Press, 1959), pp. 99–100. Steven Rockefeller refers to a letter Kallen had written to Ames's son Van Meter Ames in 1958 in which Kallen expressed his personal conviction that Edward Scribner

Ames's writings "enabled Dewey to accept and use the word 'God' with a good conscience." (Cited in Rockefeller, *John Dewey*, p. 522 and further discussed on p. 625, note 70). Rockefeller writes that in Ames's major work, *Religion*, appearing in 1929, "he emphasized the social origin and function of religion, and he presented a theory of religious faith and a naturalistic concept of God that in broad outline are close to the position Dewey adopted in the 1930s. Ames applied and experimented with his philosophy of religion at the University Church of Disciples of Christ whre he served as the minister throughout his academic career. His approach to religious and ethical values was summarized in an essay in the *fetschrift* volume prepared in Dewey's honor in 1929. Writing to express his appreciation to Ames, Dewey states: 'I need not say that I am in general sympathy with the position that you have taken in your essay. . . .' Dewey had a copy of *Religion* in his personal library. It is very likely that he was encouraged by Ames' theology to believe that the idea of God can be employed responsibly in a naturalistic and humanistic context, and he probably found Ames' work helpful in the writing of his Terry Lectures." (Ibid., pp. 522–523).

19. Sidney E. Mead, *The Lively Experiment: The Shaping of Christianity in America* (New York: Harper and Row, 1963), p. 152.

20. Dewey, *CF*, p. 50; *LW*, vol. 9, p. 34.

21. Dewey, "Experience, Knowledge and Value," p. 597; *LW*, vol. 14, pp. 79–80.

22. Dewey, *CF*, p. 10; *LW*, vol. 9, pp. 8 and 9.

23. Lamont, "New Light on Dewey's *Common Faith*," p. 24.

24. Reinhold Niebuhr, "Answering the Humanist," *New York Herald Tribune Books* (Sunday, February 4, 1940), p. 12.

25. Reinhold Niebuhr, "A Footnote on Religion," *The Nation* (September 26, 1934), p. 358.

26. Niebuhr, *ICE*, p. 43.

27. Dewey, "Experience, Knowledge and Value," pp. 553–554; *LW*, vol. 14, p. 38.

28. Ibid., p. 596; *LW*. 14, p. 8. It is this side of Dewey's pragmatism that best accounts for his reluctance to make very much of what Steven Rockefeller identifies as Dewey's awareness of "mystical intuitions." It seems to me that all of the reasons why Dewey scorned speculative metaphysics apply tenfold to the murky arena of Western or Eastern mysticism. It was not just Dewey's ethical activism what was emphasized at the expense of such intuitions, nor was it simply Dewey's unease with the disease of dualism. Dewey's resistance to making much importance philosophically out of mystical experiences went all the way down to the deepest level of his pragmatic restraint. Such restraint not only resisted what Dewey called the "superimposed load" (*CF*, p. 12) re-

ligio-cultural traditions placed on the givenness of such experiences, but it also quickly identified and opposed the language-begging obscurantism so characteristic within mystical circles. While Dewey's radical empiricism paid homage to whatever experience offers, his pragmatic *rationalism* equally demanded scientific restraint on what should be made of and said about such experiences.

Professor Rockefeller, of course, is fully aware of these motifs in Dewey's thought and the resistance they give against making a too consistent case for Deweyan mysticism. Moreover, Rockefeller is quite aboveboard in revealing his own hand in seeking to develop "the implications of Dewey's own mystical intuitions" and in pursuing a "reconstruction of Dewey's idea of the divine" along mystical lines. (See *John Dewey,* p. 528 and the closing chapter, "A Gift of Grace"). Nonetheless, my own inclinations as to the character of Dewey's pragmatic naturalism put me in mind of a remark offered by Kurt Vonnegut with which I fully expect Dewey would have been in complete sympathy. Vonnegut commented: "I'm just sick of people saying they can't explain this and they can't explain that. I just say get out of my house if you can't explain anything. If there is no explaining it you know, well, then shut up." ("Kurt Vonnegut: A Self-Interview," National Public Radio broadcast of a talk given at the University of Northern Iowa at Cedar Falls, 1977).

29. John Dewey, Remarks on "Mystical Naturalism and Religious Humanism," *The New Humanist* 8 (April–May 1935): 74. Dewey was resisting Bernard Meland's position that *mystical* naturalism was a necessary factor in religious humanism relative to safeguarding againt "anthroinflaction."

30. See Chapter Five, n. 63.

31. Dewey, *CF,* p. 54; *LW,* vol. 9, p. 36.

32. Smith, *Reason and God,* p. 113.

33. Sources central to the dispute between Santayana and Dewey include George Santayna, "Dewey's Naturalistic Metaphysics"; John Dewey, "Half-Hearted Naturalism," Santayana's original essay with a few alterations reappeared in Schilpp, *The Philosophy of John Dewey,* vol. 1, Library of Living Philosophers. In the same volume Dewey's response to Santayana is found in "Experience, Knowledge and Value," pp. 530–534.

34. George Santayana, "Dewey's Naturalistic Metaphysics," *Journal of Philosophy* 22, no. 25 (December 3, 1925): 680.

35. Santayana charged that Dewey's view of nature-as-experienced was, in effect, equivalent to a theory of immediacy out of which natural reality is composed. This criticism was tenuous at best. Dewey, of course, insisted that his view of experience was not reducible to subjective feelings and personal perspectives. The richness of gross experience is inter-

preted in interactive terms by Dewey, which ought to refute any suggestion that the natural world was constituted by, restricted to, or unavailable to human experience.

36. John Dewey, "Half-Hearted Naturalism," *Journal of Philosophy* 24 (February 3, 1927): 63 and 58; *LW*, vol. 3, pp. 79 and 74.

37. Dewey wrote that "The primary postulate of a naturalistic theory of logic is continuity of the lower (less complex) and the higher (more complex) activities and forms. The idea of continuity is not self-explanatory. But its meaning excludes complete rupture on one side and mere repetition of identities on the other; it precludes reduction of the 'higher' to the 'lower' just as it precludes complete breaks and gaps" (Dewey, p. 23; *LW*, vol. 12, p. 30).

38. Dewey, *CF*, pp. 24, 25, and 26.

39. John Dewey, *Characters and Events*, ed. Joseph Ratner (New York: Henry Holt and Co., 1929), vol. 2, p. 515; henceforth *CE*–II.

40. Sterling P. Lamprecht, "Naturalism and Religion," in Yervant H. Krikorian (ed.), *Naturalism and the Human Spirit* (New York: Columbia University Press, 1944), p. 20.

41. Santayana was among those individuals who were offended either by American culture or by pragmatism and tended to interpret pragmatism in light of their reading of the culture. Santayana wrote: "Pragmatism may be regarded as a synthesis of all these ways of making the foreground dominant: the most closereefed of philosophical craft, most tightly hugging appearance, use, and relevance to practice today and here, least drawn by the failure of speculative distances. Nor would Dewey, I am sure, or any other pragmatist, ever be a naturalist instinctively or on the wings of speculative insight, like the old Ionians or the Stoics or Spinoza, or like those many mystics, Indian, Jewish, or Mohammedan, who heartily despising the foreground, have fallen in love with the greatness of nature and have sunk speechless before the infinite. The pragmatist becomes, or seems to become, a naturalist only by accident, when as in the present age and in America the dominant foreground is monopolized by material activity; because material activity, as we have seen, involves naturalistic assumptions, and has been the teacher and the proof of naturalism since the beginning of time" (Santayana, "Dewey's Naturalistic Metaphysics," p. 679).

42. Comstock, "Dewey and Santayana in Conflict, pp. 129–140. Comstock's article is an excellent summary of the conflict between these two men. I credit Comstock's essay for helping me see an aspect of this conflict that, I believe, has important bearing on Niebuhr's attitude toward Dewey's sense of the "religious."

43. Santayana, "Dewey's Naturalistic Metaphysics," p. 681.

44. Niebuhr, *ICE*, p. 80.

45. Ibid. Niebuhr also discussed the tendency "to annul the meaning of particular selfhood" within the context of Santayana's mystical naturalism in a critique of Santayana's *Platonism and the Spiritual Life*. See Niebuhr, *SDH*, p. 70.

46. Niebuhr, *REE*, p. 132. Niebuhr made these remarks just after a brief comment on the Marxist criticism of Dewey's influence on the then radical Sidney Hook. Niebuhr wrote: "There is enough pure determinism in the thought of Lenin to prompt modern Leninists (as for instance the official communist party of America) to criticize Sidney Hook's interpretation of the Marxian dialectic [in his book *Toward an Understanding of Karl Marx*], as erring on the side of ascribing too much significance to conscious affirmation of a determined historical goal, and to ascribe this defect to Dewey's influence upon Hook" (ibid.).

47. Dewey, *QC*, p. 306; *LW*, vol 4, p. 244.

48. Niebuhr, *REE*, p. 296.

49. Niebuhr underwent several shifts in the way he gave expression to his understanding of religion. In his B.D. dissertation he conceived of religion as a way of grounding personality and the aims of personality in the cosmos. Although this concern passed over into his book, he then saw religion as a manner of "courageous logic which makes the ethical struggle consistent with world facts," and by which men save "themselves from either arrogance or despair" (*DCNR*, pp. 50 and 52). In his momentous work of 1932, Niebuhr was little interested in religion except in terms of what one chapter labels "The Religious Resources of the Individual for Social Living." Nonetheless, he saw religion as "a sense of the absolute" whose authentic form "is imagined in terms of man's own highest ethical aspirations" but from which "a perspective is created from which all moral judgments are judged to be inadequate"—with the everpresent risk of losing all "moral distinctions in the emphasis upon the religious aspect of sin" (*MMIS*, pp. 52 and 67). By the time *An Interpretation of Christian Ethics* appeared in 1936, Niebuhr spoke with strong Tillichian accents. He spoke of the sense of the religious as a "comprehension of depth in life" that is both prior to and the basis of "any experience of bre[adth] in life. Indeed, "the assumption that life is meaningful a[nd its] meaning transcends the observable facts of existence i[s the basis of] achievements of knowledge by which life in its rich[ness and full]iness is apprehended" (*ICE*, pp. 15 and 18). Niebuh[r in]creasingly employed biblical symbols and did so i[n a way that em]phasized what he called *Hebraic* rather than *Hellenic* [thought. In this] manner he pulled away from Tillich and reflected more [the thought of] Martin Buber. What remained was Niebuhr's long-stand[ing conviction] that "transcendence" is tangentially evidenced within the [realm of nature] and history. Now, however, he spoke of the "eternal" as best e[xpressed]

Indee[d]
from ance[stral]
ligious essence[...]
degree in the proc[ess]
and naturalists seems [...]
118).

67. Niebuhr, *NDM-II*, P. [...]
68. Niebuhr, "The Truth in M[yths,"] pp. 118–119[.]
Ibid., pp. 119–120.
69. Ibid. Niebuhr, *Beyond Tragedy* (N[ew York:]
70. Reinhold Niebuhr, "The Truth in Myths," P. 133.
pp. 4–5, henceforth *BT*.
Sons, 1937), pp. 4–5; *LW*, vol. 9, P. 23.
71. Niebuhr, *SDH*, P. 97.
72. Dewey, *CF*, P. 33; *LW*, vol. 9, P. 23.
73. Niebuhr, "The Truth in Myths," P. 28.
Dewey, *CF*, pp. 40–41; *LW*, vol. 9, P. 28.
74. Niebuhr, *CF*, "Reply to Interpretation and Critic[ism]
75. Dewey, in [...]
Reinhold Niebuhr, FH, p. 509.
76. Niebuhr, P. 509.
77. Niebuhr, "Religion and Modern Knowledge,"
Niebuhr, *NDM-I*, pp. 175–176.
78. Niebuhr, *NDM-II*, P. 57.
79. Niebuhr, *NDM-II*, P. 248. Joseph Wood Kru[tch's]
published in 1929. In a review of that b[ook]
80. Niebuhr, *[...]*
Temper was "a man who has lost all faith but is not happ[y]
Krutch as "a man who realizes, at leas[t]
trast to "the flippant intellectuals who bow down everythin[g]
religion out of the universe with an integrity in Krutch's "dismal[...]
worth living" when all superstition and prejudice ha[ve]
us. Niebuhr found an integrity in Krutch's "dismal[...]
much as here we find "a modern who realizes, at leas[t]
ligious ages agonized about the problem of l[ife]
sees that the problem of religion is the glory depart[...]
therefore, "grateful to him for a noble pessimism [which]
gious faith can not be maintained the moderns to shame." ("A Co[...]
pancy of many of the moderns to shame." ("A Co[...]
Christian Century vol. 46, no. 18, May 1, 1929, pp. 586[...]
81. Niebuhr, *FH*, P. 237.

nified labors. They are met by the contemptuous suggestion that they
have been merely insinuating new meanings into ancient phrases, and
that they have gained nothing for their pains but what might have been
secured more simply by a scientific analysis of the known facts of life and
existence. If science has the final word and authority about life, as many
of those theologians who have been most anxious to adjust religion to the
scientific world-view have assumed, this suggestion is plausible enough.
Indeed some of the supposedly abiding truths which have been distilled
from ancient myths by this process of reinterpretation have lost their religious essence so completely, have been flattened and deflated to such a
degree in the process of adaptation, that the charge of the empiricists
and naturalists seems perfectly justified" (in "The Truth in Myths," p.
118).

    67. Niebuhr, *NDM*-II, p. 79.
    68. Niebuhr, "The Truth in Myths," p. 119.
    69. Ibid., pp. 119–120.
    70. Reinhold Niebuhr, *Beyond Tragedy* (New York: Charles Scribner's
Sons, 1937), pp. 4–5, henceforth *BT.*
    71. Niebuhr, "The Truth in Myths," pp. 118–119.
    72. Niebuhr, *SDH*, p. 97.
    73. Dewey, *CF*, p. 33; *LW*, vol. 9, p. 23.
    74. Niebuhr, "The Truth in Myths," p. 133.
    75. Dewey, *CF*, pp. 40–41; *LW*, vol. 9, p. 28.
    76. Niebuhr, in "Reply to Interpretation and Criticism," in Kegley,
Reinhold Neibuhr, p. 509.
    77. Niebuhr, *FH*, p. 57.
    78. Niebuhr, *NDM*-I, pp. 175–176.
    79. Niebuhr, "Religion and Modern Knowledge," p. 127.
    80. Niebuhr, *NDM*-II, p. 248. Joseph Wood Krutch's *The Modern
Temper* was published in 1929. In a review of that book Niebuhr saw
Krutch as "a man who has lost all faith but is not happy about it" in contrast to "the flippant intellectuals who bow everything which smacks of
religion out of the universe with an airy confidence that life will be more
worth living" when all superstition and prejudice have been put behind
us. Niebuhr found an integrity in Krutch's "dismal pessimism" inasmuch as here we find "a modern who realizes, at least, that what the religious ages agonized about was not simply the fancies of children. He
sees that the problem of religion is the problem of life; and that if religious faith can not be maintained the glory departs from life." We are,
therefore, "grateful to him for a noble pessimism which puts the flip-
pancy of many of the moderns to shame." ("A Consistent Pessimist,"
Christian Century vol. 46, no. 18, May 1, 1929, pp. 586 and 587).
    81. Niebuhr, *FH*, p. 237.

the self-transcending dimension of the self's freedom that can be expressed only dialectically.

50. Niebuhr, "A Footnote on Religion," p. 358.

51. Niebuhr, *NDM*-II, p. 39.

52. Niebuhr, *CRPP*, pp. 177–178.

53. Ibid., pp. 178–179.

54. "Letters of John Dewey to Robert V. Daniels, 1946–1950," *Journal of the History of Ideas* 20, no. 4 (October–December, 1959): 571. It should be noted that neither Pascal nor Kierkegaard receive a reference in any of Dewey's major works.

55. Reinhold Niebuhr, "Religion and Modern Knowledge," in Arthur H. Compton et. al., *Man's Destiny in Eternity* (Boston: Beacon Press, 1949), p. 127.

56. Santayana, "Dewey's Naturalistic Metaphysics," p. 688.

57. Reinhold Niebuhr, "The Truth in Myths," in *The Nature of Religious Experience: Essays in Honor of Douglas Clyde Macintosh* (Freeport, N.Y.: Books for Libraries Press, 1937), p. 119.

58. John Dewey, *Art as Experience* (New York: Minton, Balch and Company, 1934), p. 195, henceforth *AAE*; *LW*, vol. 10, p. 199.

59. Steven C. Rockefeller, *John Dewey*, passim. See my discussion under Chapter 10, notes 10 and 28.

60. See Chapter Six, "A Broadening out of the Issues."

61. Niebuhr, *ICE*.

62. Ibid.

63. Niebuhr's sense of the mythic character of religion is found, of course, in his essay "The Truth in Myths," already noted. He also treated the subject in his sermonic essay, "As Deceivers, Yet True" in his book *Beyond Tragedy* (New York: Charles Scribner's Sons, 1937). Niebuhr returned to the problem of myth and symbol in his Gifford Lectures, most particularly in *Nature and Destiny of Man*, vol. 2, *Human Destiny*, Chapter 10, "The End of History."

64. Niebuhr, *FH*, p. 33.

65. Reinhold Niebuhr, "A Reply to Professor Macintosh," *The Review of Religion* 4, no. 3 (March 1940), p. 307.

66. Apropos to this segment of the religious tradition, Niebuhr wrote: "Since mythical elements are irrevocably enshrined in the canons of all religions it had become the fashion of modern religion to defend itself against the criticisms of science by laborious reinterpretations of its central affirmations with the purpose of sloughing off the mythical elements, apologizing for them as inevitable concepts of infantile cultures, and extracting the perennially valid truths from these husks of the past. Unfortunately the protagonists of modern religion usually fail to placate the devotees of the scientific method by these diligent but not too dig-

45. Ibid. Niebuhr also discussed the tendency "to annul the meaning of particular selfhood" within the context of Santayana's mystical naturalism in a critique of Santayana's *Platonism and the Spiritual Life*. See Niebuhr, *SDH*, p. 70.

46. Niebuhr, *REE*, p. 132. Niebuhr made these remarks just after a brief comment on the Marxist criticism of Dewey's influence on the then radical Sidney Hook. Niebuhr wrote: "There is enough pure determinism in the thought of Lenin to prompt modern Leninists (as for instance the official communist party of America) to criticize Sidney Hook's interpretation of the Marxian dialectic [in his book *Toward an Understanding of Karl Marx*], as erring on the side of ascribing too much significance to conscious affirmation of a determined historical goal, and to ascribe this defect to Dewey's influence upon Hook" (ibid.).

47. Dewey, *QC*, p. 306; *LW*, vol 4, p. 244.

48. Niebuhr, *REE*, p. 296.

49. Niebuhr underwent several shifts in the way he gave expression to his understanding of religion. In his B.D. dissertation he conceived of religion as a way of grounding personality and the aims of personality in the cosmos. Although this concern passed over into his book, he then saw religion as a manner of "courageous logic which makes the ethical struggle consistent with world facts," and by which men save "themselves from either arrogance or despair" (*DCNR*, pp. 50 and 52). In his momentous work of 1932, Niebuhr was little interested in religion except in terms of what one chapter labels "The Religious Resources of the Individual for Social Living." Nonetheless, he saw religion as "a sense of the absolute" whose authentic form "is imagined in terms of man's own highest ethical aspirations" but from which "a perspective is created from which all moral judgments are judged to be inadequate"—with the everpresent risk of losing all "moral distinctions in the emphasis upon the religious aspect of sin" (*MMIS*, pp. 52 and 67). By the time *An Interpretation of Christian Ethics* appeared in 1936, Niebuhr spoke with strong Tillichian accents. He spoke of the sense of the religious as a "comprehension of depth in life" that is both prior to and the basis of "any experience of breadth" in life. Indeed, "the assumption that life is meaningful and that its meaning transcends the observable facts of existence is involved in all achievements of knowledge by which life in its richness and contradictoriness is apprehended" (*ICE*, pp. 15 and 18). Niebuhr's later thought increasingly employed biblical symbols and did so in a way that emphasized what he called *Hebraic* rather than *Hellenic* meanings. In this manner he pulled away from Tillich and reflected more the influence of Martin Buber. What remained was Niebuhr's long-standing conviction that "transcendence" is tangentially evidenced within the world of time and history. Now, however, he spoke of the "eternal" as best evidenced in

preted in interactive terms by Dewey, which ought to refute any suggestion that the natural world was constituted by, restricted to, or unavailable to human experience.

36. John Dewey, "Half-Hearted Naturalism," *Journal of Philosophy* 24 (February 3, 1927): 63 and 58; *LW*, vol. 3, pp. 79 and 74.

37. Dewey wrote that "The primary postulate of a naturalistic theory of logic is continuity of the lower (less complex) and the higher (more complex) activities and forms. The idea of continuity is not self-explanatory. But its meaning excludes complete rupture on one side and mere repetition of identities on the other; it precludes reduction of the 'higher' to the 'lower' just as it precludes complete breaks and gaps" (Dewey, p. 23; *LW*, vol. 12, p. 30).

38. Dewey, *CF*, pp. 24, 25, and 26.

39. John Dewey, *Characters and Events*, ed. Joseph Ratner (New York: Henry Holt and Co., 1929), vol. 2, p. 515; henceforth *CE–II*.

40. Sterling P. Lamprecht, "Naturalism and Religion," in Yervant H. Krikorian (ed.), *Naturalism and the Human Spirit* (New York: Columbia University Press, 1944), p. 20.

41. Santayana was among those individuals who were offended either by American culture or by pragmatism and tended to interpret pragmatism in light of their reading of the culture. Santayana wrote: "Pragmatism may be regarded as a synthesis of all these ways of making the foreground dominant: the most closereefed of philosophical craft, most tightly hugging appearance, use, and relevance to practice today and here, least drawn by the failure of speculative distances. Nor would Dewey, I am sure, or any other pragmatist, ever be a naturalist instinctively or on the wings of speculative insight, like the old Ionians or the Stoics or Spinoza, or like those many mystics, Indian, Jewish, or Mohammedan, who heartily despising the foreground, have fallen in love with the greatness of nature and have sunk speechless before the infinite. The pragmatist becomes, or seems to become, a naturalist only by accident, when as in the present age and in America the dominant foreground is monopolized by material activity; because material activity, as we have seen, involves naturalistic assumptions, and has been the teacher and the proof of naturalism since the beginning of time" (Santayana, "Dewey's Naturalistic Metaphysics," p. 679).

42. Comstock, "Dewey and Santayana in Conflict, pp. 129–140. Comstock's article is an excellent summary of the conflict between these two men. I credit Comstock's essay for helping me see an aspect of this conflict that, I believe, has important bearing on Niebuhr's attitude toward Dewey's sense of the "religious."

43. Santayana, "Dewey's Naturalistic Metaphysics," p. 681.

44. Niebuhr, *ICE*, p. 80.

82. Niebuhr, *BT*, p. 7.

83. Ibid., p. 24.

84. Bertrand Russell, "A Free Man's Worship" in *Why I Am Not a Christian and Other Essays on Religion and Related Subjects* (New York: Simon and Schuster, 1957), p. 116.

85. Dewey, *QC*, p. 33; *LW*, vol. 4, p. 27.

86. Ibid., p. 34; *LW*, vol. 4, p. 27.

87. Ibid., p. 35; *LW*, vol. 4, p. 28.

88. James Joyce, *Ulysses* (New York: Modern Library, 1934), p. 35.

89. Dewey, *EN*, pp. 419–421; *LW*, vol. 1, pp. 313–314.

90. Ibid., p. 421; *LW*, vol. 1, p. 314.

91. John Dewey, in *The Poems of John Dewey*, ed. Jo Ann Boydston (Carbondale: Southern Illinois University Press, 1977), p. 49.

92. Among Dewey's many statements on the problem of "mind" one will suffice. He stated that "There is no separate 'mind' gifted in and of itself with a faculty of thought; such a conception of thought ends in postulating the mytery of a power outside of nature and yet able to intervene within it. Thinking is objectively discoverable as that mode of serial responsive behavior to a problematic situation in which transition to the relatively settled and clear is effected" (*QC*, p. 227; *LW*, vol. 4, p. 181).

93. Dewey, *QC*, p. 227; *LW*, vol. 4, p. 181.

94. John E. Smith, for example, wrote that "The only point in Dewey's thought where an attempt is made to transcend the instrumental attitude is in the aesthetic; this is the one aspect of experience that is offered *for itself* and not as a means to something else" (*Reason and God*, p. 108). It is certainly correct to see Dewey's pragmatism as a problem-solving philosophy. However, because the context for the religious view of life, at bottom, is an aesthetic one, as Smith himself acknowledged, life itself was not a problem to be solved for Dewey. What is true, of course, is that Dewey turned away from questions as to life as a whole. Life remained fundamentally hazardous for Dewey, whereas the "problem" or "meaning" of life as such remained unintelligible. Thus Dewey confined himself to areas within life's course about which something could be accomplished.

95. Dewey, *EN*, p. 44; *LW*, vol. 1, p. 45.

96. Ibid., p. 421; *LW*, vol. 1, pp. 314–315.

97. John Dewey, "What I Believe," *Forum* 83 (March 1930), p. 179; *LW*, vol. 5, p. 272.

98. Dewey, *CF*, p. 14; *LW*, vol. 9, p. 11.

99. Ibid., pp. 14–15; *LW*, vol. 9, p. 11

100. Ibid., pp. 24–25; *LW*, vol. 9, p. 18.

101. Dewey, *AAE*, p. 195; *LW*, vol. 10, p. 199.

102. Horace M. Kallen, "John Dewey and the Spirit of Pragmatism," in Sidney Hook, ed., *John Dewey: Philosopher of Science and Freedom: A Symposium* (New York: Barnes and Noble, 1967 [1950]), p. 37.

103. Dewey, *QC*, p. 255; *LW*, vol. 4, p. 204.

104. Dewey, *CF*, p. 13; *LW*, vol. 9, p. 10. He went on to say, for example, that "A fatalist will give one name to it; a Christian Scientist another, and the one who rejects all supernatural being still another. The determining factor in the interpretation of the experience is the particular doctrinal apparatus into which a person has been inducted. The emotional deposit connected with prior teaching floods the whole situation" (ibid.; *LW*, vol. 9, p. 10).

105. John Dewey, "Individualism, Old and New: II The Lost Individual," *New Republic* 61 (February 5, 1930), pp. 295–296.

106. Charles S. Peirce, "The Fixation of Belief," in Philip P. Wiener (ed.) *Charles Peirce: Selected Writings* (New York: Dover, 1966), pp. 91–112. Peirce's essay originally appeared in *Popular Science Monthly* 12 (November, 1877), pp. 1–15.

107. William A. Clebsch, *American Religious Thought: A History* (Chicago: University of Chicago Press, 1973), pp. 176–177. Clebsch went on to say that "In these relations and realities, to be sure, evil stubbornly persisted. But for Dewey religious value attached to the active, imaginative, intense, social, cooperative promotion of certain concrete and experimental goods. . . . These goods latently awaited the exercise of mankind's common faith to actualize them. Being at home in the universe meant accepting certain liberal goals—liberal in the sense that they would set men and women free from traditional restraints. Dewey wanted to build social institutions that would serve individual freedom. Devotion to building them was his religion" (ibid., p. 177).

108. Dewey, *CF*, p. 26; *LW*, vol. 9, p. 19.

109. See Randall, "The Religion of Shared Experience," pp. 106–145.

110. Dewey, *RIP*, p. 209; *MW*, vol. 12, p. 199.

111. The standard approach seems to be to hold that "science" and "democracy" together *were* Dewey's religion. Randall, for example, makes the case that because Dewey was convinced that "democratic community . . . most fully realizes the possibilities inherent in man's fundamentally social nature. . . . The democratic life, pursued in a conscious unity of interaction with one's fellows, is the religious life. Democratic experience is thus for Dewey not only . . . a *common* experience in which the common man can take part: it is literally a religious *communion* in which men find themselves at one and in unity with their fellow men and with the natural conditions of human achievement" (Randall, "The Religion of Shared Experience," pp. 110–111).

112. Dewey, *RIP*, p. 210; *MW*, vol. 12, p. 200.

113. Niebuhr sharply disagreed with any notion of "democracy as religion." To the extent that Dewey valued democracy and the freedom of intellect as crucial to the well-being of human life, Niebuhr would find much with which to agree. He did, however, radically oppose the idea conceiving democracy as the substance of religion. In a 1947 article entitled "Democracy as a Religion," for example, for all his appreciation of democratic life, Niebuhr cautioned against those who "know no other dimension of existence except the social one" and whose loyalty to democracy might dull the critical edge with which they approach their own institutions" (*Christianity and Crisis* 7; no. 14 [August 4, 1947], pp. 1–2). Niebuhr agonized over his friend Felix Frankfurter's apparent willingness to take a judicial position in *McCollum v. Board of Education*, which seemed to embrace democracy as the nation's religion. See my "Correspondence Essay—Felix Frankfurter and Reinhold Niebuhr: 1940–1964," *The Journal of Law and Religion* 1, no. 2 (1983): 340–348.

114. Dewey, "Religion and Our Schools," in *CE*-II, p. 516. This article was originally published in *The Hibbert Journal* (July 1908).

115. Dewey, *CF*, p. 16; *LW*, vol. 9, p. 2.

116. Dewey wrote: "That in fortunate moments objects of complete and approved enjoyment are had is evidence that nature is capable of giving birth to objects that stay with us as ideal. Nature thus supplies potential material for embodiment of ideals. Nature, if I may use the locution, is idealizable. It lends itself to operations by which it is perfected. The process is not a passive one. Rather nature gives, not always freely but in response to search, means and material by which the values we judge to have supreme quality may be embodied in existence. It depends upon the choice of man whether he employs what nature provides and for what ends he uses it" (*QC*, p. 302; *LW*, vol. 4, p. 241).

117. Dewey, *CF*, p. 16; *LW*, vol. 9, pp. 12–13.

118. Ibid., pp. 17 and 16; *LW*, vol. 9, p. 13.

119. John Dewey, "Matthew Arnold and Robert Browning," in *Characters and Events* Volume 1 (New York: Henry Holt and Co., 1929), p. 5; henceforth, *CE*-I. This essay first appeared in *The Andover Review* (August 1891) and was published under the title "Poetry and Philosophy."

120. Dewey, *RIP*, pp. 212–213; *MW*, vol. 12, p. 201.

121. Dewey, *CF*, p. 17; *LW*, vol. 9, p. 13.

122. Ibid., p. 18; *LW*, vol. 9, pp. 13–14.

123. Niebuhr, "A Footnote on Religion," p. 358.

124. James A. Martin, Jr., "The Esthetic, the Religious, and the Natural" in Maurice Wohlgelernter, (ed.), *History, Religion, and Spiritual Democracy: Essays in Honor of Joseph L. Blau* (New York: Columbia University Press, 1980), p. 89.

125. Dewey, *CF*, p. 43; *LW*, vol. 9, p. 30.

126. Meyer argues that "The religious humanists possessed, or tried to cultivate, an attitude of cosmic piety. They yearned for what may be called secular transcendence. . . . Transcendence implies a reaching out beyond the self, a sense of wonder and awe in contemplating the universe and one's place in it, a surrender to the noblest urges, and the inspiration that leads people to aspire beyond their present level of aspiration. Without postulating the existence of a realm beyond the natural, the humanists determined to provide a new basis for religious integration and transcendence—peace and comfort, inspiration and encouragement" "Secular Transcendence: The American Religious Humanists," *American Quarterly* 34 [Winter 1982] pp. 534–535.

127. Dewey, *CF*, p. 49; *LW*, vol. 9, p. 33.

128. Roy Wood Sellars, "Humanism as a Religion," *The Humanist* (Spring 1941), p. 8. I owe the discovery of this quotation from Sellars to Raymond F. Bulman, " 'The God of Our Children': The Humanist Reconstruction of God," in Wohlgelernter, *History, Religion, and Spiritual Democracy*, p. 40. Niebuhr commented on Sellars, whom he saw in one context as an example of one who manages "to obscure the fixed limits of man's creaturely finiteness even while [pretending] to understand human life in term of its relation to the system of nature." In a footnote to this comment, Niebuhr wrote: "Thus Roy Wood Sellars in one of the most consistently naturalistic interpretations of human life, *Evolutionary Naturalism*, closes his analysis of the human situation with this extravagent estimate of human possiblities: 'Let a man place his hope in those powers which raise him above the ordinary causal nexus. It is in himself that he must trust. If his foolishness and his passions exceed his sanity and intelligence, he will make shipwreck of his opportunity. . . . Evolutionary naturalism does not sink man back into nature. It acknowledges all that is unique in him and vibrates as sensitively as idealism to his aspirations and passions' (p. 343)." Niebuhr concluded: "One of the many mistakes of modern naturalism is that 'it vibrates as sensitively as idealism' to the foolish idea that natural evolution changes the essential human situation and finally places man in a position of freedom and power in which he can negate the conditions of his creaturehood" (*FH*, pp. 74–75).

129. Dewey, *CF*, p. 53; *LW*, vol. 9, p. 36.

130. Ibid., p. 19; *LW*, vol. 9, p. 14.

131. Ibid.; *LW*, vol. 9, p. 14.

132. Ibid., pp. 20–21; *LW*, vol. 9, p. 15. Randall found this intensely convictional language as well as Dewey's emphasis on the "complete unification of the whole by ends so inclusive that they are acknowledged as supreme over conduct" to be very un-Dewey-like. By this he meant that talk

about *the* quality of religious experience clearly departs from Dewey's sense of the religious as "any activity pursued in behalf of an ideal end," conceived in essentially social terms within the context of nature's possibilities. Randall also worried about the theme of religion-as-passionate-intensity that seemed to have Dewey in its grip. He cited the fact that earlier Dewey was "impressed by the 'moving religious quality' of Communism in Russia, and its 'living religious faith in human possibilities.'" And although he pointed out Dewey's declining appreciation for that "particular inclusive ideal," Randall claimed that it is "hard to see how any total faith could fail to be divisive and sectarian in effect, or how any ideal end erected into supremacy over conduct could avoid conflict with the religion of common-ness and shared experience" that Dewey so ardently desires ("The Religion of Shared Experience," p. 143). Randall's overall judgment on this matter is worth quoting at length as it is reminiscent of Dewey's charge against Niebuhr. Randall noted that "One does not usually think of Dewey as a philosopher of faith. . . . The sudden appearance in his argument of a single faith, in ideal ends so all-inclusive that they effect a generic and enduring change of the 'organic plenitude of our being' and vanquish our active nature, without our conscious deliberation and purpose, in subjection to something so supreme over conduct that it completely unifies the self in a way that neither thought nor practical activity can attain—such a faith is hardly what we might have expected from Mr. Dewey. Nor is it evident, as we survey the present scene, that the chief need of the world is for a passionately unifying faith. Such faiths, alas, it has found in plenty, though scarcely the faith in intelligence Dewey would like to see common. On wonders whether in the desire to rid faith of all theological content he has not taken refuge a little too uncritically in a supreme and inclusive moral conviction" (ibid., pp. 142–143).

133. Niebuhr, *FH*, p. 57.
134. Niebuhr, *ICE*, p. 16.
135. Niebuhr, "The Truth in Myths," p. 124.
136. Niebuhr, *FH*, p. 67.
137. Niebuhr, "The Truth in Myths," pp. 122–123.
138. In commenting on this aspect of Dewey's thought in a footnote, Niebuhr saw the play of irony at work. He wrote: "A typical modern statement of this belief and hope [that "the *logos* in history is not emancipated from finiteness and history but gradually prevails within history"] is to be found in Professor Dewey's *A Common Faith*. According to Dewey the divisive elements in human culture are vestigial remnants of outmoded religious prejudices which will yield to the universal perspectives which modern education will inculcate. This education will create practical unanimity among men of good will. Modern culture was generating new

and fierce ideological conflicts, not remotely connected with traditional religious concepts, while Professor Dewey was writing his book" (*NDM-II*, p. 246, n. 1).

139. John Dewey, *Human Nature and Conduct* (New York: The Modern Library, 1922), pp. 331–332, henceforth *HNC*; *MW*, vol. 14, p. 227.

140. Niebuhr, *FH*, p. 156.

141. Dewey, *HNC*, p. 332; *MW*, vol. 14, p. 227.

142. Niebuhr, *FH*, p. 53.

Chapter 11. The Liberal Tradition

1. Arthur M. Schlesinger, Jr., *The Age of Roosevelt*, vol. 1, *The Crisis of the Old Order: 1919–1933* (Boston: Houghton Mifflin Co., 1957), p. 130.

2. See Morton White, *Social Thought in America: The Revolt Against Formalism* (Boston: Beacon Press, 1957 [1947]).

3. Cornel West, *The American Evasion of Philosophy: A Genealogy of Pragmatism* (Madison: University of Wisconsin Press, 1989), p. 86. More recently historian Robert B. Westbrook, following the contention of James Gouinlock that Dewey's moral philosophy "possesses its distinctive character precisely because it is an integral part of a far more inclusive philosophy," develops the thesis that Dewey's democratic theory is, in fact, inseparable from the reconstructed metaphysics of his philosophy. See Robert B. Westbrook, *John Dewey and American Philosophy* (Ithaca, N.Y.: Cornell University Press, 1991), Chapter 10, "Philosophy and Democracy," especially the subsection entitled "A Metaphysics of Democratic Community," pp. 361–366. The quotation from Gouinlock appears on page 362 and comes from James Gouinlock, *Dewey's Philosophy of Value* (New York: Humanities Press, 1972), p. iii.

4. Wayne A. R. Leys observed that "Dewey's major contributions to political, legal, and social philosophy were made during the 1920s and 1930s. It was during that period that he diagnosed the tensions and wastes of modern institutions. It was then that he became well known as an advocate of 'scientific method' in the *reconstruction of society*. This was the period in which his objections to moral and theological 'absolutes' were most explicit in relation to *social policy*" (Wayne A. R. Leys, "Dewey's Social, Political, and Legal Philosophy," in Boydston, *Guide to the Works of John Dewey*, p. 131). Leys also argued that it was only during the 1920s and 1930s that Dewey's "social philosophy . . . was moving . . . to a point of view which he finally called 'transactional'" (ibid., p. 134).

5. John Dewey, "Justice Holmes and the Liberal Mind," *New Republic*, 53 (1928), p. 212; *LW*, vol. 3, p. 183.

6. Paul Krutz, "Introduction," in *John Dewey: The Later Works, 1925–*

1953, ed. Jo Ann Boydston, vol. 5. 1929–1930 (Carbondale and Edwardsville: Southern Illinois University Press, 1984), pp. xvi and xvii.

7. John Dewey, "The Future of Liberalism," *Journal of Philosophy* 32, no. 9 (April 25, 1935): 226; *LW*, vol. 11, p. 290.

8. Niebuhr, *CRPP*, p. 55.

9. Dewey, "The Future of Liberalism," p. 226; *LW*, vol. 11, p. 290.

10. Ibid., pp. 226–227; *LW*, vol. 11, p. 291.

11. Niebuhr, *CRPP*, p. 55. Niebuhr elsewhere wrote that "in every modern industrial nation the world 'liberalism' achieved two contradictory definitions. It was on the one hand the philosophy which insisted that economic life was to be free of any restraint. In this form it was identical with the only conservatism which nations, such as our own, who had no feudal past, could understand. It was the philosophy of the more successful middle classes who possessed enough personal skill, property or power to be able to prefer liberty to security. On the other hand the word was also used to describe the political strategy of those classes which preferred security to absolute liberty and which sought to bring economic enterprise under political control for the sake of establishing minimal standards of security and welfare" (Reinhold Niebuhr, "Liberalism: Illusions and Realities," *New Republic* 133, no. 27 [July 4, 1955]. p. 11).

12. George R. Geiger, *John Dewey in Perspective* (New York: Oxford University Press, 1958), p. 170.

13. John Dewey, "The Future of Liberalism," p. 226; *LW*, vol. 11, p. 290.

14. Ibid., p. 225; *LW*, vol. 11, pp. 289–290.

15. See Richard Hofstadter, *Social Darwinism in American Thought* (Boston: Beacon Press, 1955 [1944]), Chapter 7, "The Current of Pragmatism," pp. 123–142.

16. John Dewey,. "The Meaning of Liberalism," *Social Frontier* (December 1935), p. 74; *LW*, vol. 11, pp. 364–365.

17. Reinhold Niebuhr, "Liberalism: Illusions and Realities," *New Republic* 133, no. 27 (July 4, 1955), p. 11.

18. Ibid.

19. Niebuhr, *IAH*, p. 93.

20. Reinhold Niebuhr, "The Sickness of American Culture," *The Nation* 166 (March 6, 1948), p. 267.

21. Reinhold Niebuhr, "A Faith for History's Greatest Crisis," *Fortune* 26 (July, 1942), p. 125.

22. See his "Liberty and Equality," in *Pious and Secular America* (New York: Charles Scribner's Sons, 1958), Chapter 5, pp. 61–77.

23. Reinhold Niebuhr, "Liberalism: Illusions and Realities," *New Republic* 133, no. 27 (July 4, 1955), p. 11. Niebuhr came eventually to appreciate not only the piecemeal approach of Roosevelt's pragmatic re-

forms, but also—in a qualified way—the vitalities and social dissemination of power represented in a market economy. By 1952, when writing a chapter on "The Triumph of Experience Over Dogma" in *The Irony of American History,* Niebuhr claimed that "There are elements of truth in [the] discovery of classical economics which remain a permanent treasure of a free society, since some forms of a 'free-market' are essential to democracy. The alternative is the regulation of economic process through bureaucratic-political decisions. Such regulation, too consistently applied, involves the final peril of combining political and economic power" (*IAH*, p. 93).

24. Garry Bullert, *The Politics of John Dewey* (Buffalo, New York: Prometheus Books, 1983), Chapter 5, p. 69.

25. Schlesinger, *The Age of Roosevelt,* vol. 1, p. 145.

26. Both Lewis Mumford and Waldo Frank were harsh critics of liberalism in general and Dewey in particular. Because of that fact, in some significant measure, Niebuhr marginally allied himself with both, although more with Mumford than Frank. Although Niebuhr identified with their emphasis upon the "organic" in life over against what Mumford saw as the mechanistic rationalism of "pragmatic liberalism," he rejected both the romanticizing of the organic, especially in Frank's religious version, and the historical nostalgia that the organic represented for both. Niebuhr utilized the "organic" motif both as a resource for discussing the vitalities of life in their complex dialectical relationship to rational forces in human existence and as a way of gaining a deepening appreciation of the weight of tradition in experience, especially via Edmund Burke.

27. John Dewey, "Liberalism in a Vacuum," *Common Sense* 6 (December 1937), p. 9; *LW*, vol. 11, p. 489.

28. Arthur M. Schlesinger, Jr., *The Age of Roosevelt,* vol. 3, *The Politics of Upheaval* (Boston: Houghton Mifflin Co., 1960), pp. 162–163.

29. Reinhold Niebuhr, "Ten Years That Shook My World," *Christian Century* 56 (April 26, 1939), p. 543.

30. Niebuhr, *REE*, p. 80.

31. John Dewey, "Review of *Forward from Liberalism* by Stephen Spender," *Common Sense* 6 (May, 1937), p. 26; *LW*, vol. 11, p. 498.

32. John Herman Randall, Jr., "Liberalism as Faith in Intelligence," *Journal of Philosophy* 32 (May 9, 1935): 255. Symposium participants along with Dewey included William E. Hocking and William P. Montague as principal speakers and Morris R. Cohen, C. M. Bakewill, and Sidney Hook as discussants. Dewey's essay was published as "The Future of Liberalism," *Journal of Philosophy* 32 (April 1935): 225–230.

33. Many of Dewey's essays were published in *Social Frontier,* whose "John Dewey's Page" pleaded his case for radical democracy before an audience that was often far more radical than he. The names of some of these essays convey Dewey's preoccupation at the time: "The Crucial Role of In-

telligence," *SF*-I (February 1935), pp. 9–10; "Liberalism and Social Control," *SF*-II (November 1935), pp. 41–42; "The Meaning of Liberalism," *SF*-II (December 1935), pp. 74–75; and "Liberalism and Equality," *SF*-II (January 1936), pp. 105–106. See *LW*, vol. 11.

34. R. Alan Lawson, *The Failure of Independent Liberalism, 1930–1941* (New York: G. P. Putnam's Sons, 1971), p. 101.

35. Henry Steele Commager, *The American Mind: An Interpretation of American Thought and Character Since the 1880s* (New Haven, Conn.: Yale University Press, 1950), p. 99.

36. Niebuhr, *MMIS*, pp. xii–xiv.

37. See Chapters Three, "The Opening Attack on Liberalism," and Four, "The Dialogue Begins in Earnest."

38. Dewey, "Liberalism in a Vacuum," p. 9; *LW*, 11, p. 489.

39. Niebuhr, *MMIS* (1960), p. ix.

40. Ibid., p. xii.

41. Reinhold Niebuhr, "Optimism and Utopianism," *World Tomorrow* 16, no. 8 (February 22, 1933), p. 180.

42. Ibid., p. 179.

43. The form of Niebuhr's attack was unmistakably iconoclastic, as is evident in his forceful effort to assail liberalism wholesale. The very manner and tone of his polemic generated such sharp reaction that, as British theologian Alan Richardson recalled almost twenty-five years after its appearance, "*Moral Man and Immoral Society* . . . seemed to many to be the outpouring of a cynical and perverse spirit, very far removed from the benevolent and sanguine serenity which was held to be the hallmark of a truly Christian mind" ("Reinhold Niebuhr as Apologist," in Kegley, *Reinhold Niebuhr*, p. 294). Richard Fox gives an account of the reaction to *Moral Man and Immoral Society*, including the response of H. Richard Niebuhr, Reinhold's younger brother, in his *Reinhold Niebuhr*, pp. 136–147.

44. Arthur Schlesinger, Jr., "Reinhold Niebuhr's Role in Political Thought and Life," in Kegley, *Reinhold Niebuhr*, p. 198.

45. Niebuhr, *MMIS*, p. 78.

46. Ibid., p. 72.

47. Ibid., p. 74. Niebuhr wrote, "If nations and other social groups find it difficult to approximate the principles of justice, as we have previously noted, they are naturally even less capable of achieving the principle of love, which demands more than justice. The demand of religious moralists that nations subject themselves to 'the law of Christ' is an unrealistic demand, and the hope that they will do so is a sentimental one. Even a nation composed of individuals who possessed the highest degree of religious goodwill would be less than loving in its relation to other nations. It would fail, if for no other reason because the individuals could not possibly think themselves into the position of the individuals of another

nation in a degree sufficient to insure pure benevolence. Furthermore such goodwill as they did possess would be sluiced into loyalty to their own nation and tend to increase that nation's selfishness" (ibid., pp. 74–75).

48. Reinhold Niebuhr, "We Are Men and Not God" (1948), republished in D. B. Robertson (ed.), *Essays in Applied Christianity—by Reinhold Niebuhr* (New York: Meridian Books, 1959), p. 175; henceforth *AC*.

Richard Fox is quite correct in highlighting H. Richard Niebuhr's contention that Reinhold Niebuhr was indeed a "liberal" at precisely this juncture. It is no doubt true that Niebuhr's *theology* was still undeveloped and uncritically related to his burgeoning sociopolitical realism. Yet Fox ought also to have pointed out that, however much Niebuhr would develop a more relevant theology, he could never sever the knot between theology and social action in the way his brother was inclinded to do without abandoning a politically responsive and responsible theology. Reinhold Niebuhr could never, even in his darkest days, yield to either the mysticism or the monasticism that in his mind spelled the denigration of this world. In this most obvious, almost banal, sense, Fox's point makes sense; i.e., Niebuhr remained a liberal. What is of equal interest, although of little importance in the present context, is the particular theological motives and mixture that led H. Richard Niebuhr in the direction of refusing the political relevance of theology. Fox first discussed H. Richard Niebuhr's influence on Reinhold in *Reinhold Niebuhr*, pp. 143–147. He later returned to the subject in a more detailed manner in "The Niebuhr Brothers and the liberal Protestant heritage" [sic], in Michael J. Lacey (ed.), *Religion and twentieth-century american intellectual life* [sic] (New York: Woodrow Wilson International Center for Scholars and Cambridge University Press, 1989), pp. 94–115.

49. Reinhold Niebuhr, "Would Jesus Be a Modernist Today?" *World Tomorrow* 12, no. 3 (March 1929), p. 123.

50. Niebuhr, "Ten Years that Shook My World," p. 542.

51. Reinhold Niebuhr, "Faith and the Intellect," *Review* of Etienne Gilson's *Christianity and Philosophy* in the *New York Herald Tribune* (December 3, 1939), p. 26.

52. Reinhold Neibuhr, "Barthianism and Political Reaction" (1934), in *AC*, pp. 153–154.

53. Ibid., p. 156.

54. Reinhold Niebuhr, "The Blindness of Liberalism," *Radical Religion* 1, no. 4 (Autumn, 1936), p. 4.

55. Ibid., p. 45.

56. Niebuhr, "Ten Years That Shook My World," p. 543.

57. J. David Hoeveler, Jr., *The New Humanism: A Critique of Modern America: 1900–1940* (Charlottesville: University of Virginia Press, 1977), p. 185.

58. Reinhold Niebuhr, "Intellectual Autobiography," in Kegley, *Reinhold Niebuhr*, p. 15.

59. It is Richard Fox's contention that "Niebuhr's version of liberalism was a caricature of the position of a thinker like Dewey" although he admits that "there were romantic liberals of the sort that Niebuhr condemned" ("Reinhold Niebuhr: Self-Made Intellectual," *Library of Congress Quarterly Journal* 40 [Winter 1983]: 49). Others have specifically accused Niebuhr of portraying both Dewey as the preeminent secular liberal, and Walter Rauschenbush as the preeminent Social Gospel liberal, in ways that did not fit them. (See Cornel West, *The Amerian Evasion of Philosophy: A Geneology of Pragmatism* [Madison: University of Wisconsin Press, 1989], p. 155; and Christopher Lasch, "Religious Contributions to Social Movements: Walter Rauschenbusch, The Social Gospel and Its Critics," *Journal of Religious Ethics*, 18 (Spring 1990), pp. 7–25.

Niebuhr's polemical interests had the tendency to isolate and even exaggerate aspects of another's thought as, indeed, Dewey's polemical stance was quite capable of doing. Nonetheless he had an uncanny ability to get beyond the qualifiers to the heart of a problem or a tendency. Niebuhr's own retrospective assessment of Rauschenbusch is readily available (see his "Walter Rauschenbusch in Historical Perspective," *Religion in Life* 27, no. 2 [Autumn 1958], pp. 527–536). The question in the present context is whether Niebuhr had his finger on the pulse of Dewey's liberalism sufficiently to justify his general polemic against it. The controversy over this point is ongoing. My opinion, of course, is that with the unfortunate exaggeration of the polemicist, Niebuhr was able to discern oversimplifications in Dewey's social thought that led to questionable judgments and serious omissions at critical junctures in his political philosophy. To the extent Niebuhr identified some of these general weaknesses—the persistent residuals in even Dewey's reconstructed liberalism, if you will—then, regardless of the qualifications that should be made, the fact remains that Dewey did give shape to his times and direction to his followers in some unfortunate as well as fortunate ways. As Bruce Kuklick noted, many thinkers could be easily linked "to a Deweyite climate of opinion in the 1930s." Moreover, in wideranging areas of thought "as a high priest, Dewey provided the grammar for a common faith [and while] it is certainly arguable that what many intellectuals took from Dewey was a distortion . . . it is still true that Dewey's words and approximations of his ideas were commonly used in the discourse of the era." (See Kucklick's "John Dewey, American Theology, and scientific politics" [sic], in Lacey, *Religion and twentieth-century American intellectual life* [sic], pp. 86 and 91–92).

60. Niebuhr, *ICE*, p. 218.

61. Niebuhr, *NDM*-I, p. 121. George Geiger insisted that "Disillu-

sion with the rationalism of an Age of Reason cannot legitimately apply to the more modest position which simply sees no generally acceptable alternative to free intelligence as the solver of human problems, an intelligence, moreover, which fits into the pattern of an entire human personality and is not exclusively 'intellectualistic' in some now suspect sense" (in George R. Geiger, *John Dewey in Perspective* [New York: Oxford University Press, 1958], pp. 176–177).

Perhaps this way of stating the obvious has some point, but it missed the point critics like Niebuhr were making. Niebuhr was not denigrating the rational life, as many seem to think. He was critical of those whose rendition of the rational life he believed to be naive and exaggerated. Dewey, in Niebuhr's account, bore the imprint of the naivete so consistent in modern thought since at least the Enlightenment, regardless of the improvements and unique features shown in his views on reason.

62. Lawson, *The Failure of Independent Liberalism*, p. 100.

63. Bruce Kuklick has argued the case that "the emergence of the idea of a scientific politics" with the "social scientific mandarinism" and managerial elitism that came to flower in the "Rooseveltian political revolution" of the mid-1930s, was definitive of "pragmatic liberalism in politics" and was an essential part of the Dewey legacy. See "John Dewey, American theology and scientific politics," pp. 87–91.

64. George H. Nash, *The Conservative Intellectual Movement in America Since 1945* (New York: Basic Books, 1976), p. 42. The only real issue, according to Nash, was whether such a moral basis would be supplied "by secular, pragmatic, scientific intelligence (personified by John Dewey), or by religious faith and the 'Great Tradition' of Western Philosophy" (ibid.).

65. John Dewey, "Science and Society" (1931), in *Philosophy and Civilization* (New York: Capricorn Books, 1963), p. 330, henceforth *PC*; *LW*, vol. 6, p. 63.

66. Niebuhr, MMIS, p. xiii.

67. Ibid., p. xiv.

68. Ibid., pp. 212 and 213–214.

69. John Dewey, "Unity and Progress," *The World Tomorrow* (March 8, 1933), p. 232; *LW*, vol. 9, p. 71.

70. Ibid., p. 233; *LW*, vol. 9, pp. 73–74.

71. Niebuhr, "After Capitalism—What?" pp. 203 and 205.

72. John Dewey, "Intelligence and Power," *New Republic* 78 (April 25, 1934), p. 307; *LW*, vol. 9, p. 109).

73. Ibid.; *LW*, vol. 9, p. 110.

74. Ibid.; *LW*, vol. 9, pp. 108–109.

75. Ibid.; *LW*, vol. 9, p. 109.

76. Ibid.; *LW*, vol. 9, p. 109. In his classic work on liberalism in the

mid-1930s Dewey wrote: "It is frequently asserted that the method of experimental intelligence can be applied to physical facts because physical nature does not present conflicts of class interests, while it is inapplicable to society because the latter is so deeply marked by incompatible interests. It is then assumed that the 'experimentalist' is one who has chosen to ignore the uncomfortable fact of conflicting interests. Of course, there *are* conflicting interests; otherwise there would be no social problems. The problem under discussion is precisely *how* conflicting claims are to be settled in the interests of all—or at least of the great majority. The method of democracy—inasmuch as it is that of organized intelligence—is to bring these conflicts out into the open where their special claims can be seen and appraised, where they can be discussed and judged in the light of more inclusive interests than are represented by either of them separately" (*LSA*, p. 79; *LW*, vol. 11, pp. 55–56).

77. Morton White's brilliant work on *Social Thought in American: The Revolt Againt Formalism*, first published in 1947, was the product of a staunch, but mildly critical, Deweyite. However, in his "Epilogue," published in the 1957 paperback volume of the work, White, although sharply critical of Niebuhr, nonetheless had this to say about Dewey: "It must be said in Niebuhr's behalf that there is an awful lot in Dewey's writings which *might* be construed as meaning that Dewey holds that the way to a better, if not a perfect, society *is* easy. I have in mind what may be called Dewey's 'methodolatry,' that is to say, his tendency to say that if only man would agree to use scientific method in his approach to social problems, the major social and political problems of our time would automatically be solved. I have already dealt with this question in this book, but I do want to say here that I can sympathize with anyone's being impatient with the endless amount of scientific cheer-leading that goes on in Dewey's pages. One becomes somewhat fatigued with hearing that one should use scientific intelligence and impatiently eager to know just what specific intelligently arrived-at scientific conclusions will tell us how to solve our problems. And so I can sympathize with Niebuhr's impatience with Dewey on this score. I can also understand anyone who feels that Dewey has been ambiguous about the relation between scientific intelligence and force. Wherever Dewey suggests that intelligent action is always peaceful action, he *might* be taken to imply that the way to a better world is easier than it appears to be" (Morton White, "Epilogue for 1957: Original Sin, Natural Law, and Politics," in *Social Thought in America*, p. 253).

78. Dewey, *LSA*, p. 49; *LW*, vol. 11, p. 36.

79. Ibid., p. 50; *LW*, vol. 11, p. 37.

80. Niebuhr, *CRPP*, pp. 70–71.

81. Dewey, *CE*-I, p. 101; *LW*, vol. 3, p. 178.

82. Niebuhr, *IAH*, p. 12.
83. Niebuhr, *REE*, p. 45.
84. Reinhold Niebuhr to Morton White, May 17, 1956. This letter has been recently published in Ursula M. Niebuhr (ed.), *Remembering Reinhold Niebuhr* (San Francisco: Harper, 1991), pp. 378–380.
85. Niebuhr wrote that, although "an examination of the whole nature of man's historical freedom led me to an espousal of more of the Christian faith than I possessed in the beginning," in more recent times (he was writing White in 1956) "I have been so shocked by religious obscurantism on the one hand, and religious self-righteousness on the other hand, that I would like to be as polemical against various religious manifestations as I have been against the complacency of the rationalist in the past decades" (Reinhold Niebuhr to Morton White, May 17, 1956, in ibid., p. 380).
86. Reinhold Niebuhr to Morton White, July 4, 1956. Letter provided to the author by Morton White and permission to quote given by Ursula Niebuhr.
87. Ibid.
88. Hook, *Out of Step*, pp. 65–66.
89. Niebuhr, "Two Communications," p. 393.
90. His epigrammatic and oft-quoted statement is that "Man's capacity for justice makes democracy possible; but man's inclination to injustice makes democracy necessary" (*CLCD*, p. xiii).
91. Fox, *Reinhold Niebuhr*, p. 139.
92. Ibid., p. 143.
93. Niebuhr, *CLCD*, p. 72.
94. Dewey, *LSA*, pp. 26–27; *LW*, vol. 11, p. 21.
95. Ibid., p. 27; *LW*, vol. 11, p. 22.
96. Ibid., p. 32; *LW*, vol. 11, p. 25.
97. Ibid., p. 28; *LW*, vol. 11, p. 23.
98. Ibid., p. 54; *LW*, vol. 11, pp. 39–40.
99. Ibid., p. 56; *LW*, vol. 11, p. 41.
100. Niebuhr, "The Pathos of Liberalism," p. 303.
101. Ibid.
102. Ibid.
103. Dewey, *LSA*, pp. 62–63; *LW*, vol. 11, p. 45.
104. Ibid., p. 64; *LW*, vol. 11, p. 46.
105. Niebuhr, "The Pathos of Liberalism," p. 304.
106. Dewey, *LSA*, p. 67; *LW*, vol. 11, p. 48.
107. Niebuhr, "The Pathos of Liberalism," p. 304. The Liberty League was often the brunt of both Niebuhr's and Dewey's jibes. Founded in August 1934, the Liberty League condemned the New Deal as anticonstitutional and opposed a variety of New Deal legislation. Its mem-

bers included financiers, industrialists, corporate lawyers, and sundry conservatives, who obviously formed the organization in the service of antiliberal causes.

108. Ibid.

109. Ibid.

110. James A. Wechsler, *The Age of Superstition* (New York: Random House, 1953), p. 211.

111. Will Herberg, "Reinhold Niebuhr: Burkean Conservative," *National Review* (December 2, 1961), pp. 379 and 394. In a letter to his early biographer, June Bingham, Niebuhr wrote: "I am sorry that Will Herberg persists in linking me with conservatism. I have just written an article for the *New Republic* showing the error of equating realism with conservatism just because the thought of the French Enlightenment was both liberal and illusory. I hope to clarify some concepts in that article." [The article referred to was "Liberalism: Illusions and Realities," *New Rupublic* 133, no. 27 (July 4, 1955), pp. 11–13]. Reinhold Niebuhr to June Bingham, April 19, 1955, in Reinhold Niebuhr Papers, Library of Congress.

112. Reinhold Niebuhr, "Liberalism: Illusions and Realities," *New Republic* 133 (July 4, 1955), p. 11. In a letter responding to David Riesman, Niebuhr had observed that because "realistic views of human nature easily degenerate into cynicism and indifferentism . . . most of the values of our democracy were established by what you call 'utopian and trusting liberals.' As a matter of fact, I spend a good deal of time in politics and most of it in cooperation with these trusting liberals, because I agree with their immediate political objectives." Reinhold Niebuhr to David Riesman, July 2, 1951, in the Reinhold Niebuhr Papers, Library of Congress.

113. Robin W. Lovin, "The Constitution as Covenant: The Moral Foundations of Democracy and the Practice of Desgregration," (Ph.D. thesis, Harvard University, 1978), p. 83.

114. Reinhold Niebuhr, *Man's Nature and His Communities* (New York: Charles Scribner's Sons, 1965), pp. 24–25, henceforth *MNHC*.

115. Michael Walzer, "The Idea of Civil Society," *Dissent* (Spring 1991), p. 298.

116. Ibid., pp. 294, 303, and 293.

117. William Lee Miller, "The Irony of Reinhold Niebuhr," *Reporter* 12, no. 1 (January 13, 1955), p. 12. Miller remarked much more recently that "The problem is not exactly the conservative and neo-conservative appropriations of Niebuhr, although these appropriations do appear to many of us to be a major problem at the moment. (Some chop off that 'conservative' half of Niebuhr, which was instrumental and subordinate, and make it the whole story. Imagine folk who claim to have been influenced by Niebuhr giving their support to an administration that represents

the quintessential effort by the Amerian bourgeoisie to overturn every-thing that was accomplished, everything he fought for, in his lifetime! Fox tells the story of a moment in the Nixon years when Niebuhr, bedrid-den and reduced to silent viewing by his stroke, roused himself after one of Nixon's egregious performances on the TV set to comment: "That *bas-tard!*" Not very dialectical, to be sure, and not what everyone would ex-pect from a Christian preacher, but under the circumstances heartwarm-ing to some of us and not without a certain continuing relevance.)" See Miller, "Some Customer," *Christianity and Crisis* 46, no. 1 (February 3, 1986), p. 20.

118. Ibid., p. 20.

119. Roger Shinn, "Christian Realism: Retrospect and Prospect," *Christianity and Crisis* 28, no. 14 (August 5, 1968), p. 180. Arthur Schles-inger, Jr., chose to address himself to all of these developments in 1982. In my estimation, Schlesinger's efforts, although not comprehensive by any means, are commendable. See "Afterward: 1982," in Kegley, *Reinhold Niebuhr*, pp. 215–222.

120. Stone, *Reinhold Niebuhr*, p. 151.

121. Richard W. Fox, "Reinhold Niebuhr and the Emergence of the Liberal Realist Faith: 1930–1945," *Review of Politics* 38 (April 1976): 246.

122. Arthur Schlesinger, Jr., "Reinhold Niebuhr's Role in Ameri-can Political Thought and Life," in Kegley, *Reinhold Niebuhr*, p. 214. Richard Fox's sharpest criticism of Schlesinger is that "Schlesinger, deeply committed in his essay to an apotheosized New Deal, is primarily concerned to appropriate Niebuhr as a (very belated) New Deal theorist. He tends to see Niebuhr's development in the thirties and forties as a case of progressive, even necessary, evolution away from a flirtation with Marxist 'illusions' towards Roosevelt's hardheaded 'gradualism and mixed economy.' This 'Dark Ages' to 'Enlightenment' model of develop-ment seriously distorts Niebuhr's career." Schlesinger's essay, in Fox's account, fails "to follow out Schlesinger's main insight: that Niebuhr's thinking during the thirties was not only continuous with, but also a gradual elaboration of, his liberal realism of the forties." See "Reinhold Niebuhr and the Emergence of the Liberal Realist Faith, 1930–1945," p. 247, n. 5.

123. Merkley, *Reinhold Niebuhr*, p. 23.

Chapter 12. Democracy

1. Van A. Harvey, "On the Intellectual marginality of American theology" [sic], in Lacey, *Religion and twentieth-century American intellectual life* [sic], p. 172.

2. Morton White, "Epilogue for 1957: Original Sin, Natural Law and Politics," in his *Social Thought in America*, p. 264.

3. Morton White, "Religion, Politics, and the Higher Learning." *Confluence*, 3 (1954), p. 404.

4. In a review of Niebuhr's *Pious and Secular America*, Perry Miller wrote that "we must fully acknowledge the immense stimulation [Niebuhr] has given to the life of the mind in modern America," and counted himself among those who "have copiously availed themselves of Niebuhr's conclusions without pretending to share his basic, and to him, indispensable premise" ("The Influence of Reinhold Niebuhr," *The Reporter* 18, no. 9 [May 1, 1958], pp. 39 and 40).

C. Vann Woodward, while praising Niebuhr's "astute analysis of national character and destiny," confessed that "I realize that Niebuhr's view of human strivings is based on theology, a subject definitely beyond my province. Whatever its theological implications—and I have frankly never explored them—the view has a validity apart from them that appeals to the historian" (*The Burden of Southern History* [New York: Vintage Books, 1960], pp. 171 and 173).

5. Hans Morgenthau. "The Influence of Reinhold Niebuhr in American Political Life and Thought," in Harold R. Landon (ed.), *Reinhold Niebuhr: A Prophetic Voice in Our Time* (Cambridge: Seabury Press, 1962), p. 109. See also Kenneth Thompson's essays "Beyond National Interest: A Critical Evaluation of Reinhold Niebuhr's Theory of International Politics," *Review of Politics* 17, no. 2 (April 1955) and "The Political Philosophy of Reinhold Niebuhr," in Kegley, *Reinhold Niebuhr*, pp. 223–251. Commenting to June Bingham on Morganthau's compliment, Niebuhr wrote: "I was embarressed by Morganthau's comparison with Calhoun, the Apostle of slavery and with his rather amoral conception of politics instead of my conviction of the moral ambiguity of the political order." Reinhold Neibuhr to June Bingham, October 29, 1961, in the Reinhold Niebuhr Papers, Library of Congress.

6. Langdon Gilkey, "Reinhold Niebuhr as Political Theologian," in Richard Harries (ed.), *Reinhold Niebuhr and the Issues of Our Time* (Grand Rapids, Mich.: William B. Eerdman, 1986), pp. 157–182.

7. Schlesinger, "Reinhold Niebuhr's Role in American Political Thought and Life," in Kegley, *Reinhold Niebuhr, p. 214*.

8. Schlesinger *The Age of Roosevelt*, vol. 3, *The Politics of Upheaval*, p. 157. Schlesinger also wrote a memorial essay on Niebuhr shortly after Niebuhr's death in 1971. See "Prophet for a Secular Age," *New Leader* 55 (January 24, 1972), pp. 11–14.

9. Niebuhr, "Ten Years That Shook My World," p. 545.

10. Reinhold Niebuhr, "The Sickness of American Culture," *The Nation* 166 (March 6, 1948), p. 267.

11. Robert B. Westbrook, *John Dewey and American Democracy* (Ithaca, N.Y.: Cornell University Press, 1991), p. x.

12. Ibid., p. xv.

13. Ibid.

14. See, for example, Dewey's exchange with Hans Reichenbach in Paul A. Schilpp, *Philosophy of John Dewey.* Reichenbach's essay was entitled "Dewey's Theory of Science," pp. 157–192. Dewey's reply appears in the same volume on pp. 534–543.

15. It is important here to remember that Dewey's model both for an understanding of democracy and for personal emulation was Thomas Jefferson. In his discussion of Jefferson Dewey took note of the "essentially moral nature of Jefferson's political philosophy." Dewey pointed out that the views of God, nature, and moral purpose in the world that informed Jefferson's views of his notion of "self-evident truths" of human equality and inalienable rights "were not rhetorical flourishes," but provided Jefferson with a fundamentally ethical view of the universe. The modern dilemma, of course, is that the belief system of Jefferson's words are not available to us. "Other days bring other words and other opinions behind words that are used. The terms in which Jefferson expressed his belief in the moral criterion for judging all political arrangements and his belief that republican institutions are the only ones that are morally legitimate are not now current. It is doubtful, however, whether defense of democracy against the attacks to which it is subjected does not depend upon taking once more the position Jefferson took about its moral basis and purpose, even though we have to find another set of words in which to formulate the moral ideal served by democracy. A renewal of faith in common human nature, in its potentialities in general and in its power in particular to respond to reason and truth, is a surer bulwark against totalitarianism than is demonstration of material success or devout worship of special legal and political forms" (John Dewey, "Presenting Thomas Jefferson," *LW,* vol. 14, pp. 218 and 219–220).

16. Dewey, *LSA,* p. 32; *LW,* vol. 11, p. 25.

17. Westbrook, *John Dewey and American Democracy,* p. 365.

18. John Dewey, *The Public and Its Problems,* (Denver: Alan Swallow, 1954 [1927]), p. 148; henceforth *PP.* George Geiger recognized that for Dewey "it may almost be said that democracy is not even one of the political options, since it is implicit in the very meaning of association and free communication" (*John Dewey in Perspective,* p. 185).

19. Neither Dewey nor Niebuhr adhered to a fixed view of "human nature" from which positive principles could be inferred that somehow transcended social, economic, and cultural conditions. In any sense other than minimal biological structures, Niebuhr used the term *human nature* only in the open and indeterminate sense of "finite freedom." The

thought behind Dewey's notion of freedom, development, and democracy here seems to have a certain similarity to Niebuhr.

20. Horace L. Friess, "Social Inquiry and Social Doctrine," in Hook, *John Dewey,* p. 110. Robert Westbrook, writing on this very point, states that "If we read *Experience and Nature* and *The Quest for Certainty* as an effort to fulfill the program laid out in 'Philosophy and Democracy,' then we have at least a partial explanation for why Dewey's metaphysics was so anthropomorphic. For if he was most interested in a metaphysics of democratic community, there was no need to dwell on Santayana's 'background' except insofar as it had some bearing on the fate of democracy, and he dwelt most on those traits of the background—contingency and quality—he had previously identified as most pertinent to a metaphysical support of democracy. Dewey, I must admit, covered his tracks. He gave no explicit indication that he was not construing and interpreting nature in order to sustain a reasonable argument that democracy was not contradicted by the structure of the world. To have done so would perhaps have come too close to the sort of special pleading of which he accused other metaphysicians, and, indeed, some have detected in *Experience and Nature* a whiff of this sort of bad faith. But it must be said in Dewey's defense that he never tried as a metaphysician to secure his most cherished values as 'fixed traits of real Being.' His attempt to establish that democracy was a reasonable regulative ideal in a hazardous world in which such ideals often came to grief was a far cry from the efforts of others to forge for their ideals a false passport of certainty" (*John Dewey and American Democracy,* p. 366).

21. Dewey let it be known that he was not really up to the festivities planned in New York City, and instead had planned to be with the daughter's family in Green Castle, Missouri. See Dykhuizen, *The Life and Mind of John Dewey,* p.298.

22. John Dewey, "Creative Democracy—The Task Before Us," *LW,* vol. 14, p. 225.

23. Ibid.

24. Ibid.

25. Ibid., p. 226.

26. Dewey, *PP,* p. 82; *LW,* vol. 2, p. 286.

27. Ibid., pp. 103 and 104; *LW,* vol. 2, p. 299.

28. Ibid., p. 84; *LW,* vol. 2, pp. 287–288.

29. Ibid., p. 146; *LW,* vol. 2, p. 327.

30. Ibid.; *LW,* vol. 2, p. 327.

31. Ibid.; *LW,* vol. 2, p. 327. A couple of pages earlier Dewey had written: "The old saying that the cure for the ills of democracy is more democracy is not apt if it means that the evils may be remedied by introducing more machinery of the same kind as that which already exists, or by re-

fining and perfecting that machinery. But the phrase may also indicate the need of returning to the idea itself, and of employing our sense of its meaning to criticize and re-make its political manifestations" (ibid., p. 144).

32. Ibid., pp. 146–147; *LW*, vol. 2, p. 327.

33. Ibid., Chapter 5; *LW*, vol. 2, pp. 325–350.

34. Ibid., p. 98; *LW*, vol. 2, p. 296. The term is taken from Graham Wallas's book, *The Great Society*. As Dewey used the term, it applied to a radically altered set of circumstances in which impersonal concerns and organizations had both rendered the individualistic philosophy of a previous age passe and, in the process, undermined the face-to-face associations of a less complex democracy. See *PP*, pp. 96–98; *LW*, vol. 2, pp. 295–296.

35. See Westbrook, *John Dewey and American Democracy*, pp. 306–318.

36. Dewey, *LSA*, p. 31; *LW*, vol. 11, p. 25.

37. John Dewey, "Individualism Old and New: The Crisis in Culture," *New Republic* 62 (March 19, 1930). p. 126; *LW*, vol. 5, p. 108.

38. Ibid., p. 123; *LW*, vol. 5, p. 99.

39. Ibid.; *LW*, vol. 5, p. 100.

40. Ibid.; *LW*, vol. 5, p. 100.

41. John Dewey, "Creative Democracy—The Task Before Us"; *LW*, vol. 14, p. 22.

42. John Dewey, *Democracy and Education* (New York: Macmillan, 1916), p. 59, henceforth *DE*; *MW*, vol. 9, p. 54.

43. Ibid., p. 63; *MW*, vol. 9, p. 59.

44. Dewey, *RIP*, p. 177; *MW*, vol. 12, p. 181.

45. John Dewey, "John Dewey Responds," in Harry W. Laidler (ed.), *John Dewey at Ninety* (New York: League for Industrial Democracy, 1950), p. 34.

46. For a recent critical summation of Dewey's position on fact and value, see Kuklick, "John Dewey, American theology, and scientific politics" [sic], pp. 84–87.

47. In spite of his infernal wish to produce values out of facts, Dewey was a cultural realist insofar as he actually knew values to be tradition specific. Instead of pleading his case on those grounds, he wanted to insist that somehow democracy and its values were metaphysically supportable. Whereas he could not purchase the traditional notion that values could be—indeed must be—validated nonempirically, neither could Dewey allow himself to even brush up against the nihilistic conclusion that the good for democrats was good only for democrats and the good for totalitarians was good only for totalitarians. For recent musings on this ongoing problem in Dewey studies, see Richard Rorty, "The Priority of Democracy to Philosophy," in Merril D. Peterson and

Robert C. Vaughan (eds.) *The Virginia Statute for Religious Freedom* (New York: Cambridge University Press, 1968) and Robert Westbrook's response to Rorty in *John Dewey and American Democracy,* pp. 366–367, n. 37. Examples of others wrestling with the same issue: see Cheryl Noble, "A Common Misunderstanding of Dewey on the Nature of Value Judgments," *Journal of Value Inquiry* 12 (1978): 53–63; and Marion Smiley, "Pragmatic Inquiry and Social Conflict: A Critical Reconstruction of Dewey's Model of Democracy," *Praxis International* 9, no. 4 (January 1990): 365–380.

48. Niebuhr, *FH,* pp. 187–188.

49. Dewey, *CF,* p. 85; *LW,* vol. 9, p. 56.

50. John Dewey, "What I Believe," *Forum* 83 (March, 1930), p. 180; *LW,* vol. 5, pp. 273–274.

51. Dewey, *CF,* p. 87; *LW,* vol. 9, p. 58.

52. Dewey, *LSA,* p. 93; *LW,* vol. 11, p. 65.

53. Geiger, *John Dewey in Perspective,* pp. 71 and 72.

54. Reinhold Niebuhr, "Democracy as a Religion," *Christianity and Crisis* 7 (August 4, 1947), p. 1.

55. Reinhold Niebuhr, "Democracy, Secularism, and Christianity, *Christianity and Crisis* 13, no. 3 (March 2, 1953), p. 19. Niebuhr did believe, however, that the "Biblical faith (from which Judaism and Christianity are derived) is unique in offering three insights into the human situation which are indispensable to democracy." Of these three insights "the one is that it assumes a source of authority from the standpoint of which the individual may defy the authorities of this world ('We must obey God rather than man.') The second is an appreciation of the unique worth of the individual which makes it wrong to fit him into any political program as a mere instrument. . . . The third insight is the Biblical insistence that the same radical freedom which makes man creative also makes him potentially destructive and dangerous, that the dignity and the misery of man therefore have the same root. This insight is the basis of all political realism [and] justifies the institutions of democracy more surely than any sentimentality about man, whether liberal or radical" (ibid., p. 20).

56. Niebuhr, *IAH,* p. 120.

57. Harland, *The Thought of Reinhold Niebuhr,* p. 165.

58. Westbrook, *John Dewey and American Democracy,* p. 531.

59. Christopher Lasch, in writing of the value of particularism in Niebuhr's thought, has written: "Most of those who came to regard Niebuhr as a political mentor . . . shared his disbelief in the political efficacy of moral suasion and 'intelligence,' priding themselves on their political realism." They therefore "concluded that politics would always remain a matter of 'checks and balances and countervailing forces,' in

the words of Michael Novak. Novak quotes *Moral Man and Immoral Society* on the 'power of self-interest and collective egoism in all inter-group relations,' which makes 'social conflict an inevitability in human history.' But this was only the beginning of Niebuhr's argument: one of its premises, not its conclusion. Novak wants to use Niebuhr's thought to justify familiar ideas about the importance of 'institutions, habits and associations that will provide checks and balances against the ineradicable evils of the human heart.' For Niebuhr, however, the irreducible need for coercion in politics defined the problem, not its solution. If politics consisted of nothing more than 'checks and balances,' the struggle of force against counterforce, it could never have anything to do with morality" (*The True and Only Heaven: Progress and Its Critics* [New York: W. W. Norton and Co., 1991], pp. 376–377). Because the moral dimension of Niebuhr's political theology in general, and its application to the matter of the equilibrium of power in particular, are so widely known, it is hard to see how this dimension of Niebuhr's political thought was passed over by Westbrook.

60. In *Moral Man and Immoral Society* Niebuhr wrote, "From the perspective of society the highest moral ideal is justice. From the perspective of the individual the highest ideal is unselfishness....These two moral perspectives are not mutually exclusive and the contradiction between them is not absolute. But neither are they easily harmonized.... The most perfect justice cannot be established if the moral imagination of the individual does not seek to comprehend the needs and interests of his fellow. Nor can any non-rational instrument of justice be used without great peril to society, if it is not brought under the control of moral goodwill. Any justice which is only justice soon degenerates into something less than justice. It must be saved by something which is more than justice" (*MMIS*, pp. 257–258).

61. Niebuhr, *IAH*, p. 11.

62. Niebuhr, *CLCD*, p. 118

63. Niebuhr, "Education and the World Scene," *Daedalus* 88:1 (Winter 1959), p. 116.

64. Schlesinger, "Reinhold Niebuhr's Role in American Political Thought and Life," in Kegley, *Reinhold Niebuhr*, p. 214. Schlesinger also pointed out that "It was as much his personality as his writing which thus helped accomplish in a single generation a revolution in the bases of American liberal political thought" that save many democratic liberals from overwhelming "defeatism and despair" (ibid., pp. 213–214).

65. Niebuhr, *IAH*, pp. 123–124.

66. Niebuhr, *CLCD*, p. 3.

67. Ibid., p. 49.

68. Ibid., p. 121.

69. Ibid.

70. Ibid., p. 49.

71. Ibid., pp. 121 and 123.

72. Niebuhr, *NDM*-II, p. 268; see also *MMIS*, p. 21.

73. Niebuhr, *CLCD*, p. 30.

74. Ibid., p. 15.

75. Niebuhr, *IAH*, p. 128.

76. Niebuhr, *CPP*, p. 85.

77. Niebuhr, *CLCD*, pp. 18–19.

78. Ibid., p. 19. Niebuhr wrote, "When this desire for self-realization is fully explored it becomes apparent that it is subject to the paradox that the highest form of self-realization is the consequence of self-giving, but that it cannot be the intended consequence without being prematurely limited. Thus the will to live is finally transmuted into its opposite in the sense that only in self-giving can the self be fulfilled, for 'He that findeth his life shall lose it: and he that loseth his life for my sake shall find it,'" (ibid.). Niebuhr returned to this theme when, in 1965, he wrote a major section of a book on the topic "Man's Selfhood and Its Self-seeking and Self-giving," *Man's Nature and His Communities* (New York: Charles Scribner's Sons, 1965), pp. 106–125. This later work shows a marked appreciation of current psychological thinking on the subject, particularly that of Erik Erikson.

79. Ibid., p. 28.

80. Ibid., pp. 21–22.

81. Ibid., p. 21.

82. Langdon Gilkey, "Reinhold Niebuhr's Theology of History," *Journal of Religion* 54, no. 4 (October 1974), p. 371.

83. Wilson Carey Williams, *The Idea of Fraternity in America* (Berkeley: University of California Press, 1973), p. 528.

84. Lawson, *The Failure of Independent Liberalism*, p. 99.

85. Niebuhr, *CLCD*, p. xii.

86. Ibid., p. 40.

87. Charles Frankel, who had sharply attacked Niebuhr for his use (or misuse) of sin in his political analysis (see "The Rediscovery of Sin," in *The Case for Modern Man* [New York: Harper and Brothers, 1955], Chapter 6, pp. 85–116), nonetheless, saw the downside of Dewey's view of democracy as a way of life. Frankel went so far as to suggest that "Dewey's sense of democracy as a culture, though it brought a powerfully expanded perspective to the understanding of democracy, did have a cost. Usually he paid comparatively little attention to the forms of political democracy; his attention was on democracy as a style of education, a moral tendency. He may therefore have helped to encourage a fallacy, also encouraged by Marxism, which has caused much harm. It is the fal-

lacy of dismissing the legal and institutional apparatus of democracy as 'mere forms,' as only means, not ends, and saying that what counts about a country is its purposes and ideals" (Charles Frankel, "John Dewey's Social Philosophy," in *New Studies in the Philosophy of John Dewey* [Hanover, N.H.: The University Press of New England for the University of Vermont, 1977], p. 25).

88. Ibid., p. 10.

89. Niebuhr, *CLCD*, p. 9. Niebuhr utilized these biblical images in a paradigmatic way, not unlike Augustine's paradigmatic use of the "city of God" and the "city of this world." Except that in Niebuhr's case the division spoke only to the particular instance of a typology ranging between cynic and idealist in this world with specific reference to questions of self-interest and power and not to the prior and overarching problem of the orientation of the self to God or other selves. Niebuhr here assumed self-love and set up paradigms to indicate oppositions as to how self-interest is viewed in abstract extremes. Some have misread him by thinking he was making oversimplified literal historical contrasts.

90. Ibid., p. 41.

91. Niebuhr, *MNHC*, p. 23.

92. The most extensive discussion of the history and meaning of original sin, for Niebuhr, is found in *NDM*-I, Chapter 9, "Original Sin and Man's Responsibilities." For a sense of Niebuhr's dialectical view of the self, this should be read in conjunction with Chapter 10 of the same volume on "Justitia Originalis."

93. Niebuhr, *FH*, p. 122.

94. Niebuhr, *MNHC*, p. 24.

95. Niebuhr, *IAH*, p. 35.

96. Niebuhr, *CLCD*, pp. 16–17.

97. Reinhold Niebuhr, *Discerning the Signs of the Times* (New York: Charles Scribner's Sons, 1949), p. 38, henceforth *DST*.

98. Dewey argued that, "even if the principle of self-love actuated behavior, it would still be true that the *objects* on which men find their love to be manifested, the objects which they take as constituting their peculiar interests, are set by habits reflecting social customs" (*The Public and Its Problems*, pp. 160–161). Niebuhr could have agreed in the same sense one would have to agree with Freud; namely, that though conscience is universal, the contents of conscience are culturally determined and therefore quite relative. Obviously, Dewey is saying much more than this. Niebuhr's objection to Dewey here would rest with the fact that if Dewey saw the matter of changing habits as somehow the solution for the universality of self-love, he would be mistaken. In this regard Niebuhr once spoke of "Professor Dewey's various efforts to explain the persistence of self-interest in human affairs as due to some easily corrected defect in culture

which has prevented as rigorous an application of the scientific method
to human affairs as to the problems of natural science" (*FH*, p. 83).

99. Niebuhr, *NDM*-II, pp. 258–259.

100. Niebuhr, *CLCD*, p. xiii.

101. Harland, *The Thought of Reinhold Niebuhr*, p. 165.

102. Niebuhr, *CLCD*, pp. 39–40.

103. Niebuhr, *SDH*, p. 198.

104. Niebuhr, *IAH*, p. 89.

105. Niebuhr, *NDM*-II, p. 272.

106. Ibid., p. 275.

107. Reinhold Niebuhr, "Moralists and Politics," *The Christian Century*, (July 6, 1932), p. 858

108. Niebuhr, *NDM*-II, p. 264.

109. Niebuhr, *NDM*-I, p. 313.

110. Harland, *The Thought of Reinhold Niebuhr*, p. 23. My limited summation of these issues in the present context is indebted to Harland's treatment in Chapter 2, "Love and Justice."

111. Ibid., p. 24.

112. Niebuhr, *CLCD*, p. 174.

113. Niebuhr, *NDM*-II, p. 276.

114. Ibid.

115. Niebuhr, *IAH*, p. 17. At a later point in this work Niebuhr continued his relfections: "The triumph of the wisdom of common sense over [those who want to plan and those who want to remove as many restraints as possible from human activities] is, therefore, primarily the wisdom of democracy itself, which prevents either strategy from being carried out to its logical conclusion. There is an element of truth in each position which becomes falsehood, precisely when it is carried through too consistently. The element of truth in each creed is required to do full justice to man's real situation. For man transcends the social and historical process sufficiently to make it possible and necessary deliberately to contrive common ends of life, particularly the end of justice. He cannot count on inadvertence and the coincidence of private desires alone to achieve common ends. On the other hand, man is too immersed in the welter of interest and passion in history and his survey over the total process is too short-range and limited to justify the endowment of any group or institution of 'planners' with complete power. The 'purity' of their idealism and the pretensions of their science must always be suspect. Man simply does not have a 'pure' reason in human affairs; and if such reason as he has is given complete power to attain its ends, the taint will become the more noxious" (ibid., pp. 107–108).

116. John Dewey, "Liberty and Social Control," *Social Frontier* 2 (November 1935), p. 41; *LW*, vol. 11, pp. 360 and 361.

117. Ibid.; *LW*, vol. 11, p. 361.

118. Ibid.; *LW*, vol. 11, p. 362.

119. John Dewey, "Liberty and Equality," *Social Frontier* 2 (January 1936), p. 105; *LW*, vol. 11, pp. 368 and 370.

120. Ibid., pp. 105–106; *LW*, vol. 11, p. 370.

121. Reinhold Niebuhr, *Pious and Secular America* (New York: Charles Scribner's Sons, 1958), p. 62; henceforth *PSA*.

122. James Madison, "Federalist No. 10," in *The Federalist: A Commentary on the Constitution of the United States* (New York: Random House-Modern Library, nd), pp. 53 and 54–55.

123. Robin W. Lovin, "The Constitution as Covenant: The Moral Foundations of Democracy and the Practice of Desegregation" (Ph.D. thesis, Harvard University, 1978), pp. 89–90.

124. Niebuhr, *NDM*-11, p. 277.

125. Ibid., p. 278.

126. Ibid., p. 277.

127. Ibid.

128. Ibid., p. 278.

129. Ibid.

130. Reinhold Niebuhr and Paul E. Sigmund, *The Democratic Experience: Past and Prospects* (New York: Frederick A. Praeger, 1969), p. 6. A collaborative effort undertaken near the end of Niebuhr's life and based on lectures given at Harvard in a class taught jointly by both men, the contribution belonging solely to Niebuhr consists of Part I: "Democratic Experience in Western History," pp. 3–87.

131. Ibid., p. 19.

132. Niebuhr, *MNHC*, pp. 61–62.

133. Hans Morgenthau, one of the more consistent masters of realpolitik, gave eloquent voice to the limits of scientific rationality when he wrote that its failure "to explain the social and, more particularly, political problems of this age and to give guidance for successful action calls for the re-examination of these problems in light of the prerationalist Western tradition. This re-examination must start with the assumption that power politics, rooted in the lust for power which is common to all men, is for this reason inseparable from social life itself. In order to eliminate from the political sphere not power politics—which is beyond the ability of any political philosophy or system—but the destructiveness of power politics, rational faculties are needed which are different from, and superior to, the reason of the scientific age.

"Politics must be understood through reason, yet it is not in reason that it finds its model. The principles of scientific reason are always simple, consistent, and abstract; the social world is always complicated, incongruous, and concrete. To apply the former to the latter is either futile,

in that the social world remains impervious to the attack of that 'one-eyed reason, deficient in its vision of depth'; or it is fatal, in that it will bring about results destructive of the intended purpose. Politics is an art and not a science, and what is required for its mastery is not the rationality of the engineer but the wisdom and the moral strength of the statesman. The social world, deaf to the appeal to pure reason and simple, yields only to that intricate combination of moral and material pressures which the art of the statesman creates and maintains" (Hans J. Morgenthau, *Scientific Man vs. Power Politics* [Chicago: University of Chicago Press, 1946], p. 10).

134. Niebuhr, *IAH*, pp. 142 and 143.

135. Louis Hartz, *The Liberal Tradition in America* (New York: Harcourt, Brace and Co., 1955), pp. 11 and 57.

136. Schlesinger, *The Age of Roosevelt*, vol. 3, *The Politics of Upheaval*, p. 156.

137. Horace M. Kallen, "John Dewey and the Spirit of Pragmatism," in Hook, *John Dewey*, pp. 36 and 37. In siding with William James on the matter of "Freedom" versus "Reason" (dispositions that he saw as the ambivalent center of the very "spirit of Pragmatism"), Kallen thus pointed to something almost paradoxical in Dewey's "ultimate religion" of "the common faith of freed minds"—a paradox between freedom and control that raises the specter of an expansive and coerced conformity. Dewey "once called that freedom [which received primacy with William James] a nuisance and stated that the task of intelligence is to emancipate the thinker alike from this nuisance and from fatality by working out a desired path through change and chance and necessity" (ibid., p. 39).

138. Williams, *The Idea of Fraternity in America*, pp. 530–531.

139. Ibid., pp. 532–533.

140. Westbrook does not refer to Williams's position but he does venture the opinion that "Although Dewey spoke of the need for 'social control,' he, like many progressives, meant by the term only a generic 'capacity' of a society to regulate itelf according to desired principles and values' and he distinguished democratic social control from other forms of control" (*John Dewey and American Democracy*, p. 188). Westbrook provides a concentrated discussion of Dewey's The *Public and Its Problems* on pages 300–318 of the same work.

141. Dewey, *PP*, p. 27.

142. Ibid., p. 155.

143. Ibid., p. 150.

144. Christopher Lasch, *The New Radicalism in America, 1889–1963* (New York: Alfred A. Knopf, 1965), pp. 299–306.

145. Lasch's newfound appreciation of Niebuhr, as well as the re-

vised form of criticism he levels against him, is to be found in Christopher Lasch, *The True and Only Heaven*, pp. 369–388.

146. Niebuhr, *CLCD*, p. 48.

147. Ibid.

148. Ibid.

149. The title given to a section in his writing in which, among others, Niebuhr discussed Rousseau; see *NDM*-I, pp. 111ff. Niebuhr elsewhere noted that "Rousseau's and Hobbes' social contract theories of government have such contradictory estimates of the 'state of nature' because both fail to undertand the ambiguous character of social equilibrium without the interference of government. Rousseau sees only the elements of harmony within it, and Hobbes only the elements of conflict and anarchy. Rousseau on the other hand sees only the principle of domination in government and Hobbes only the principle of order" (*NDM*-II, p. 276, n. 2).

150. Niebuhr, *CLCD*, pp. 63–64.

151. Niebuhr, *NDM*-II, p. 276.

152. Niebuhr, *IAH*, pp. 147–148.

153. Niebuhr, *MNHC*, p. 71.

154. Ibid., p. 75. An excellent discussion of Niebuhr's relationship to the political realists can be found in Robert C. Good, "National Interest and Moral Theory: The 'Debate' Among Contemporary Political Realists," in Roger Hilsman and Robert C. Good (eds.), *Foreign Policy in the Sixties: The Issues and Instruments* (Baltimore: Johns Hopkins Press, 1965), Chapter 15, pp. 271–292.

155. Reinhold Niebuhr, *The Structure of Nations and Empires* (New York: Charles Scribner's Sons, 1959), henceforth *SNE*.

156. Ibid., p. 61.

157. Niebuhr, *IAH*, p. 89.

158. In particular see Lasch's subsections of Chapter 9 on "The 'Endless Cycle of Social Conflict' and How to Break It," "Niebuhr's Challenge to Liberalism Denatured and Deflected," and "Liberal Realism after Niebuhr: The Critique of Tribalism," in *The True and Only Heaven*.

159. Ibid., p. 96.

160. Niebuhr, *MNHC*, pp. 66–67.

161. John Dewey, "Presenting Thomas Jefferson," *LW*, vol. 14, pp. 204 and 205.

162. Ibid., pp. 214 and 216.

163. Ibid., p. 214.

164. Ibid., p. 215.

165. I owe great deal to my colleague Karl Andresen for providing numerous insights throughout the writing of this chapter, including this

emphasis on what I take to be a somewhat paradoxical relationship between Dewey and Jefferson.

166. On this subject Niebuhr once wrote that "The ironic contrast between Jeffersonian hopes and fears for America and the actual realities is increased by the exchange of ideological weapons between the early and the later Jeffersonians. The early Jeffersonians sought to keep political power weak, discouraging both the growth of federal power in relation to the States and confining political control over economic life to the States. They feared that such power would be compounded with the economic power of the privileged and used against the less favored. Subsequently the wielders of great economic power adopted the Jeffersonian maxim that the best government is the least possible government. The American democracy, as every other healthy democracy, had learned to use the more equal distribution of political power, inherent in universal suffrage, as leverage against the tendency toward concentration of power in economic life. Culminating in the 'New Deal,' national governments, based upon an alliance of farmers, workers and middle classes, have used the power of the state to establish minimal standards of 'welfare' in housing, social security, health services, etc. Naturally, the higher income groups benefited less from these minimal standards of justice, and paid a proportionately higher cost for them than the proponents of the measures of a 'welfare state.'

"The former, therefore, used the ideology of Jeffersonianism to counter these tendencies; while the classes in society which had Jefferson's original interest in equality discarded his ideology because they were less certain than he that complete freedom in economic relations would inevitably make for equality.

"In this development the less privileged classes developed a realistic appreciation of the factor of power in social life, while the privileged classes tried to preserve the illusion of classical liberalism that power is not an important element in man's social life. They recognize the force of interest; but they continue to assume that the competition of interests will make for justice without political or moral regulation. This would be possible only if the various powers which support interest were fairly equally divided, which they never are" (*IAH*, pp. 32–33).

167. John Dewey, "Liberalism and Equality," *Social Frontier* 2 (January 1936), p. 106; *LW*, vol. 11, p. 371.

168. Ibid.; *LW*, vol. 11, p. 370.

169. Niebuhr, *IAH*, p. 18.

170. Ibid., p. 17.

171. Ibid., Chapter 5, "The Trumph of Experience over Dogma," pp. 89–108. Niebuhr also claimed that America's achievements over its dog-

matic creed were subject to two reservations: (1) the debate over property, and (2) a tardiness in dealing with economic instability due to the endless lip-service paid to the principles of laissez-faire. See *IAH*, pp. 103–105.

172. Ibid., p. 97.

173. For reasons of close friendship and a shared passion for liberty, Madison and Jefferson resisted openly confronting the differences between them. This task, Niebuhr pointed out, fell to John Adams. In a letter to Jefferson that Niebuhr cited, Adams wrote that "Our passions, ambitions, avarice, love and resentment, etc., possess so much metaphysical subtlety and so much overpowering eloquence that they insinuate themselves into the understanding and the conscience and convert both to their party" (quoted in *IAH*, p. 21).

174. Niebuhr, *NDM*-II, p. 278.

175. Niebuhr, *CLCD*, p. 1.

176. Walzer, "The Idea of Civil Society," passim.

177. Karl Andresen points out how groups such as Comon Cause, Consumer Protection, and various environmentalists have concluded that you have to start with willing (what they perceive to be) the common good and pursuing it vigorously through the political process to ensure that public policy will indeed be behind that *common* good (akin to Rousseau's "general will"?). Andresen suggests that, although these groups have more in common with Dewey's thinking in the reason for organizing, they have more in common with Niebuhr, perhaps, in their willingness to see the political process in terms of power and thereby turn themselves into particular interest groups.

178. Lasch, *The True and Only Heaven*, p. 368. Williams put essentially the same problem in somewhat more poignant and even heartrending terms. He said Dewey knew very well that the functional loyalties of modern life could not suffice to create the fraternity of genuine community, because community depends on face-to-face relations. In the modern world the vast and impersonal forces have rendered fraternal association—upon which democracy so much depends—a mockery. The solution to the dilemma (of which Dewey was certainly aware) "lay in the prospect of a new kind of communication that would make possible a new community. . . . Communication, Dewey noted 'can alone create a great community,' and fortunately technology 'facilitates the rapid and easy circulation of opinion and information,' vastly improving the 'methods and conditions' of debate and creating a 'constant and intricate interaction far beyond the limits of face-to-face communities.' . . .

"But in this case, there was a note of doubt. Dewey spoke of the need for an art of communication, 'subtle, delicate, vivid, and responsive,' which would 'breathe life' into the mass media, and for an artist who could 'kindle emotion' and create involvement across the seemingly impersonal lines of the media. The terms are revealing. Dewey, the declared apostle of science and reason, was forced at this essential point to rely on art to close the gap between local man and the national and international order. And in this, Dewey seems to play John the Baptist to Marshall McLuhan's Messiah. . . . Optimistic as he was, Dewey was also a desperate man, one who saw the social bases of a life he valued slipping away, and who struggled amid that decay to cling to the inherited liberal creed of historical progress and fraternal destiny. He spoke movingly to all those who shared his desperation" (Williams, *The Idea of Fraternity in America*, pp. 535–536).

179. Dewey, "Presenting Thomas Jefferson," *LW*, vol. 14, p. 203.

Afterword

1. Fitch's, Wieman's and Schlesinger's early discernment of Niebuhrian pragmatism are to be found in their respective contributions to the 1956 Kegley and Bretall volume devoted to Niebuhr, a volume by Charles Kegley reissued through Pilgrim Press in 1984, a source frequently cited in this book. Hook's awareness of Niebuhr's pragmatic orientations are evident in virtually all of his writings on Niebuhr from the period of the early 1940s, although it is made explicit in his inclusion of Niebuhr in his *Pragmatism and the Tragic Sense of Life*, published in 1974.

2. Robert E. Fitch, "Reinhold Niebuhr's Philosophy of History," in Kegley, *Reinhold Niebuhr*, pp. 384–385.

3. Schlesinger, "Reinhold Niebuhr's Role in American Political Thought and Life," pp. 199–200.

4. Ibid., p. 200.

5. Ibid. Schlesinger, whose interests were focused on Niebuhr's role in American political thought, nonetheless *almost* caught the importance of what I am suggesting here. In a letter to June Bingham he wrote that "the most important thing about him [Niebuhr] is that he believes in God, and everything follows from that. Obviously, his whole life would make no sense if he were relativistic on this subject. His intellectual triumph has been to absorb the insights of pragmatism and relativism in an explicit form into the Christian tradition. Because man's perception of the absolute is bound to be fragmentary and fallible, then 'either/or propositions' become untenable. But this does not mean that the absolute does not exist." Arthur Schlesinger, Jr., to June Bingham, January 7, 1954, in the Reinhold Niebuhr Papers, Library of Congress.

6. Roger L. Shinn, "Realism, Radicalism, and Eschatology in Reinhold Niebuhr: A Reassessment," *Journal of Religion* 54, no. 4 (October 1974): 415.

7. Although Niebuhr's opening paragraph to his autobiographical fragment was well known in theological circles, it bears repeating to a wider audience of a later time. Niebuhr commented that "It is somewhat embarrassing to be made the subject of a study which assumes theology as the primary interest. I cannot and do not claim to be theologian. I have taught Christian Social Ethics for a quarter of a century and have also dealt in the ancillary field of 'apologetics.' My avocational interest as a kind of circuit rider in the colleges and universities has prompted an interest in the defense and justification of the Christian faith in a secular age, particularly among what Schleiermacher called Christianity's 'intellectual despisers.' I have never been very competent in the nice points of pure theology; and I must confess that I have not been sufficiently interested heretofore to acquire the competence. De Tocqueville long since observed the strong pragmatic interest of American Christianity in comparison with European Christianity; and that distinction is still valid. I have been frequently challenged by the stricter sects of theologians in Europe to prove that my interests were theological rather than practical or 'apologetic,' but I have always refused to enter a defense, partly because I thought the point was well taken and partly because the distinction did not interest me" (in Kegley, *Reinhold Niebuhr*, p. 3).

8. Reinhold Niebuhr, in Charles W. Kegley and Robert W. Bretall (eds.) *The Theology of Paul Tillich* (New York: Macmillan 1959), pp. 217 and 226–227. Niebuhr's dispute with Tillich is to be found in their respective essays and responses in the Kegley and Bretall volumes devoted to both men.

9. Richard Rorty, *Philosophy and the Mirror of Nature* (Princeton, N.J.: Princeton University Press, 1979), p. 317.

10. Richard W. Fox, "Reinhold Niebuhr and the Emergence of the Liberal Realist Faith, 1930–1940," *Review of Politics* 38 (April 1976): 248.

11. Lawson, *The Failure of Independent Liberalism*, Part 2, Chapter 1, "Dewey's Philosophy of Democracy," pp. 99–109 passim.

12. Hartz, *The Liberal Tradition in America*, p. 59.

13. A worthwhile and provocative article by John Patrick Diggins came to my attention too late for consideration in this book. Titled "Power and Suspicion: The Perspectives of Reinhold Niebuhr," Diggins's article appears in *Ethics and International Affairs* Vol. 6 (1992), pp. 141–162. In this essay Diggins seeks to bring Niebuhr into dialogue with poststructuralism and, in the process, compares and contrasts Niebuhr with Dewey at numerous points. One additional source that the reader should be made aware of which also appeared after my own book was in produc-

tion is Charles C. Brown's intellectual biography *Niebuhr and His Age: Reinhold Niebuhr's Prophetic Role in the Twentieth Century,* (Philadelphia: Trinity Press International, 1992). Brown's approach places Niebuhr in a somewhat different light than Richard Fox's book on Niebuhr and highlights recent criticisms of Fox's 1985 biography.

Index